DESTINY
PART TWO

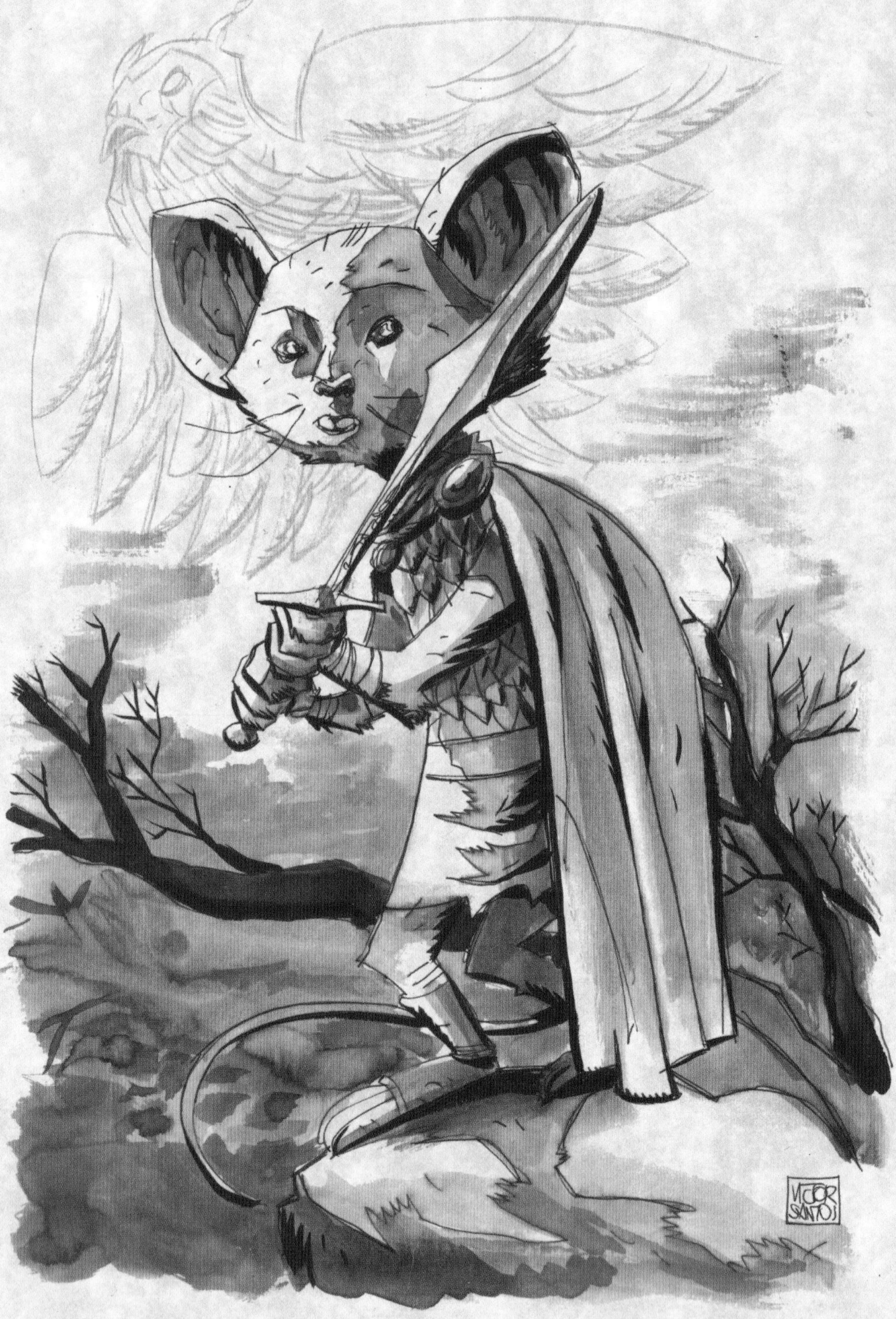
VICTOR SANTOS

VOLUME TWO

DESTINY
PART TWO

CREATED BY
BRYAN J.L. GLASS &
MICHAEL AVON OEMING

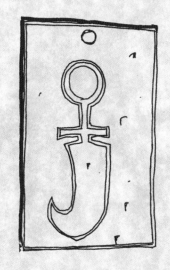

STORY BY
Glass & Oeming
WRITTEN BY
Bryan J.L. Glass
ART BY
Michael Avon Oeming
& Victor Santos
COLORS BY
Veronica Gandini
LETTERING BY
James H. Glass

EDITING BY
Judy Glass

INTERIOR PRODUCTION BY
Harry Lee

BOOK DESIGN BY
James H. Glass

PHOTOSHOP FX BY
James H. Glass

COVER PAINTED BY
Michael Avon Oeming

LOGO BY
Oeming, Kristyn Ferretti,
Tim Daniel & James H. Glass

image®

IMAGE COMICS, INC.

Robert Kirkman - Chief Operating Officer • Erik Larsen - Chief Financial Officer • Todd McFarlane - President
Marc Silvestri - Chief Executive Officer • Jim Valentino - Vice President

Eric Stephenson - Publisher • Todd Martinez - Sales & Licensing Coordinator • Betsy Gomez - PR & Marketing Coordinator
Branwyn Bigglestone - Accounts Manager • Sarah deLaine - Administrative Assistant • Tyler Shainline - Production Manager
Drew Gill - Art Director • Jonathan Chan, Monica Howard, Vincent Kukua, Kevin Yuen - Production Artists

International Rights Representative: Christine Jensen (christine@gfloystudio.com)

THE MICE TEMPLAR, VOL. 2: DESTINY PART TWO
ISBN: 978-1-60706-313-1
First Printing

For Joy Converse
Sister and friend.
—Bryan

For Ethan Alexander Oeming
Love, Dad

To the *Bulldamn* crew
—Victor

To Josh, Chris and Lauren,
who helped me and my career so much.
Thanks for being such amazing people.
—Veronica

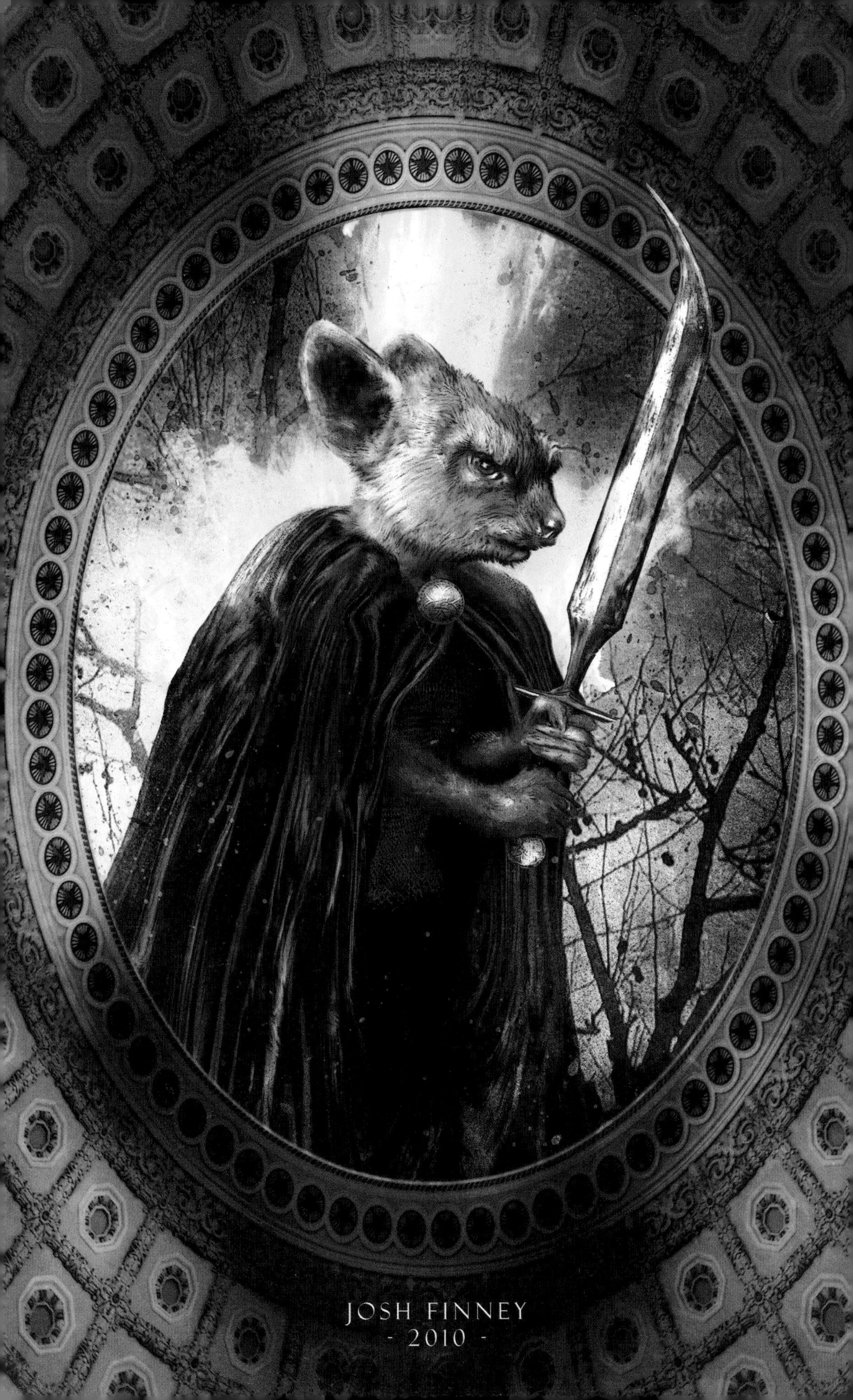
JOSH FINNEY
- 2010 -

Foreword by Ed Brubaker

Subversion of Cliché

I'm not the world's biggest fan of fantasy, but a great story will always grab me no matter what the genre. And a fully-realized world around that story just adds to the pleasure.

That's what I recall most about Tolkien when I think of *The Lord of the Rings*. The maps, the appendices, the history... how he knew every little detail of that world and its creatures and inhabitants. That's one of the things I loved about *Bone*; hell, it's one of my favorite things about a lot of comics, from *Pogo* to *Love and Rockets*, actually. It seems that outside giant fantasy sagas, comics might be the best place to create these unique and intricate worlds, I guess. Because there you can really show them off.

With *The Mice Templar*, Bryan Glass and Michael Oeming have given us their own world, in lushly illustrated comics that thrill and illuminate the various dark corners of this intriguing little place they've made up (and I say "little" only because of the size of the characters, not the size of the imaginations at work).

I remember years ago when Oeming first told me about *Mice Templar* and started putting ads for it in the back of *Powers* – COMING SOON! they said (which really stretched the definition of "soon"). And I remember talking to him about *The Secret of NIMH*, because I think that was when I first discovered the joy of watching a big adventure story with mice and rats with swords and strange underground kingdoms. I think that miniature aspect is part of what makes me dig *Mice Templar* so much. I remember telling Mike after the first issue how cool it was to see a modern human house in the background of one of his panels. I loved the idea that this mystical fantasy epic was going on in the trees and squirrel tunnels just over the fence, out of sight. It gives me a similar feeling to reading *Watership Down* or *Wind in the Willows*... but with a big hero quest in the middle of it all, too.

And that quest is what we're following through this world, but in a nice subversion from the clichés of such a fantasy trope: Glass and Oeming give us a story where we really never know what the hell is coming next. When it started, it seemed Karic was a prophesized "hero" on a quest, but that soon turned out to be a hoax, a manipulation that led the story into a much darker and twisted place... a grand scheme of political machinations, which again served to lead us, as readers, all around the secret hidden world these guys have spent years building.

That's what a great fantasy story does, at least in my opinion... gives you a compelling lead character, thrusts him out into a world he isn't prepared for, and slowly peels back the layers of that world so we get to explore it with him as he struggles on his way. And a more beautifully illustrated world than *Mice Templar* you'd be hard-pressed to find. I spent hours and hours just flipping through the issues, looking at the sets that Oeming and then his successor Victor Santos created and designed, amazed at their talent for this stuff. Wishing I could see 3D versions in theaters.

So, welcome to the world of *The Mice Templar*...I'm glad I don't live there, because there is way too much sword-fighting and rats, but it's sure a great place to visit once in a while. ✑

Ed Brubaker
May 2010

Ed Brubaker is the multiple Eisner and Harvey Award-Winning Writer
of *Criminal*, *Incognito*, *Captain America* and *Sleeper*, among many others.

Author, artist, and full-time obsessive-compulsive, Josh Finney has been working as a comics professional since 2004. His writing and art has graced the pages of *Batman*, *Catwoman*, and *Jetta*, as well as his own book, *Titanium Rain* from Archaia Entertainment.

CONTENTS

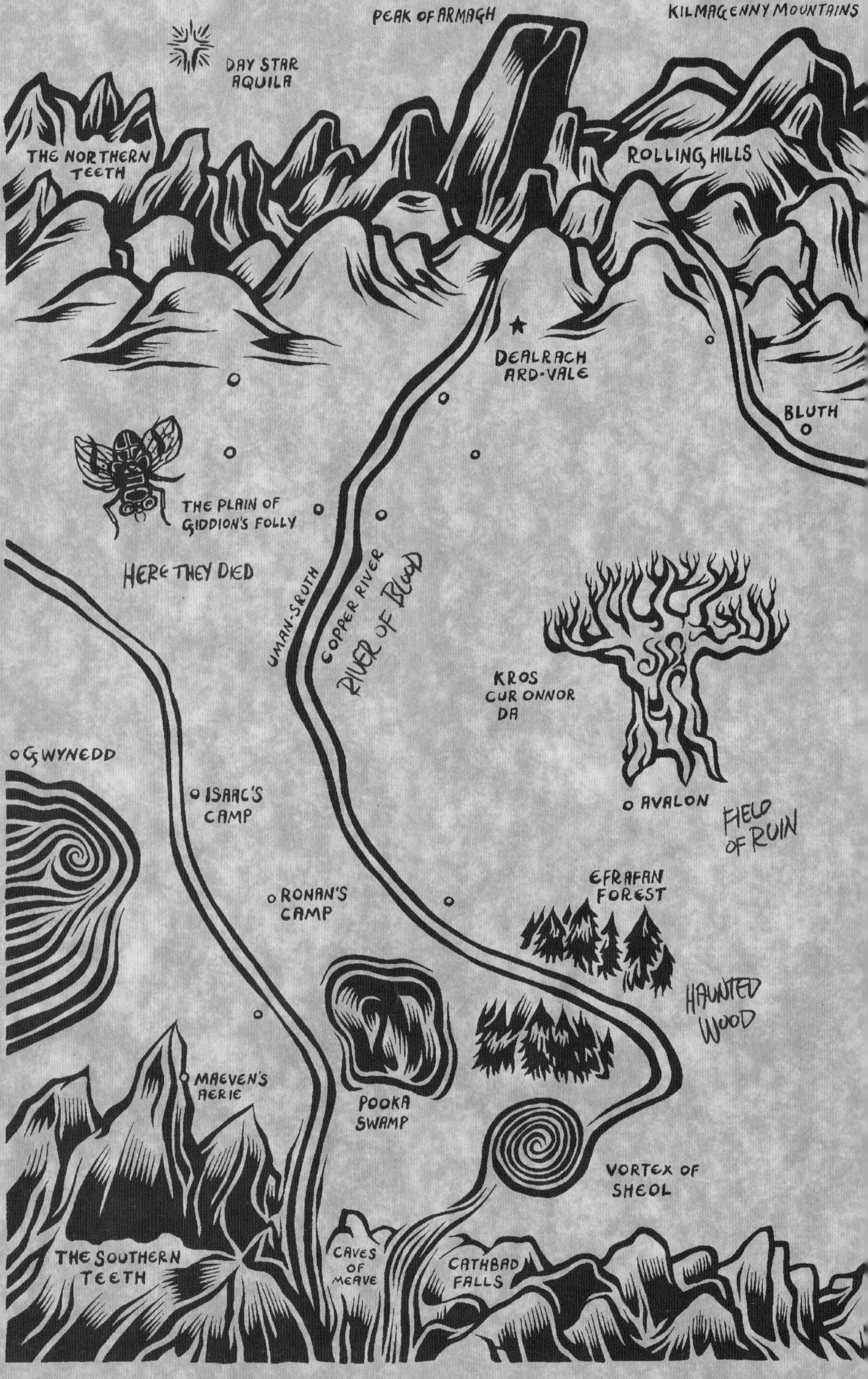

PEAK OF ARMAGH
KILMAGENNY MOUNTAINS
DAY STAR AQUILA
THE NORTHERN TEETH
ROLLING HILLS
DEALRACH ARD-VALE
BLUTH
THE PLAIN OF GIDDION'S FOLLY
HERE THEY DIED
UMAN-SRUTH
COPPER RIVER
RIVER OF BLOOD
KROS CUR ONNOR DA
GWYNEDD
ISAAC'S CAMP
AVALON
FIELD OF RUIN
EFRAFAN FOREST
RONAN'S CAMP
HAUNTED WOOD
MAEVEN'S AERIE
POOKA SWAMP
VORTEX OF SHEOL
THE SOUTHERN TEETH
CAVES OF MEAVE
CATHBAD FALLS

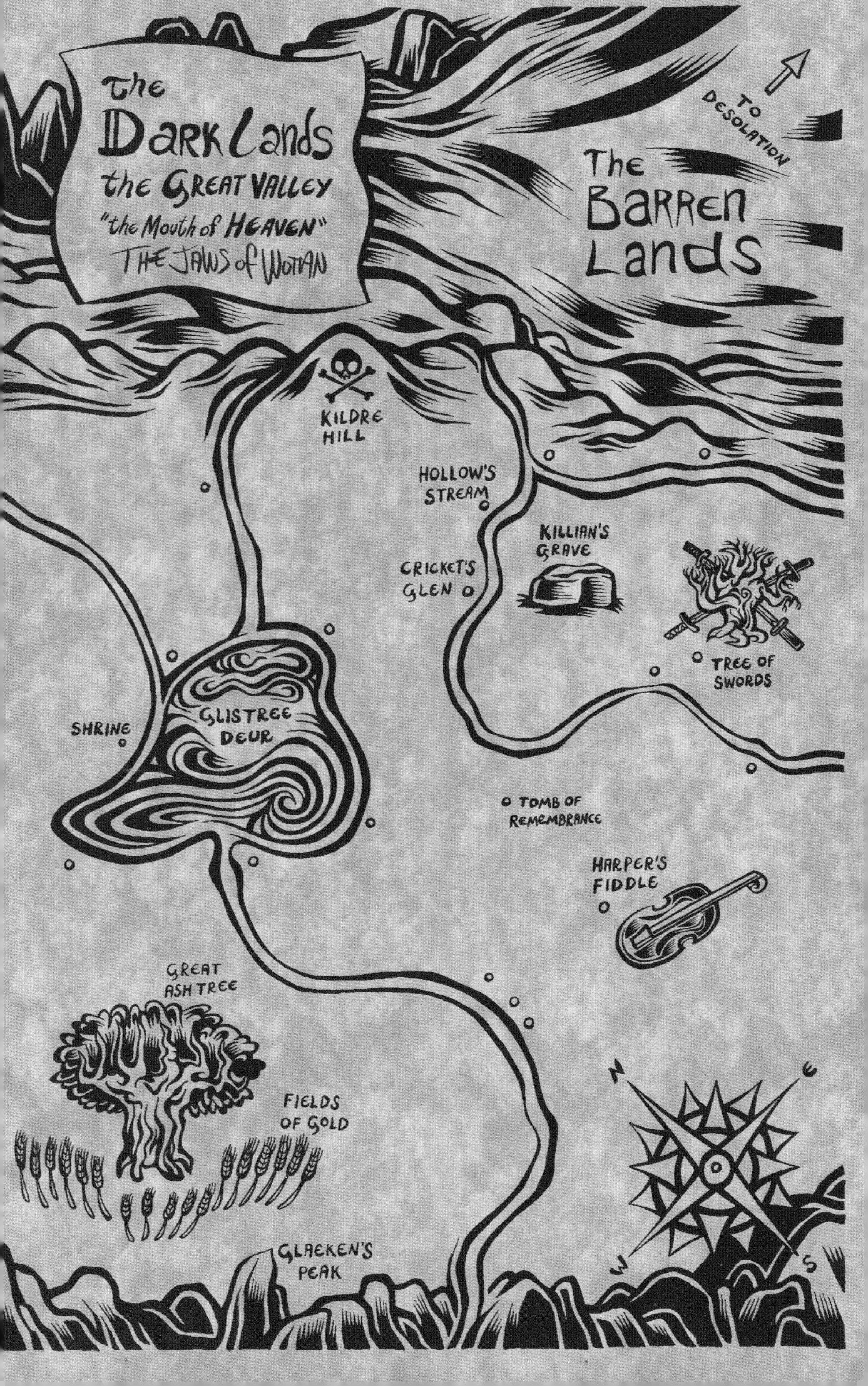
The Dark Lands
the Great Valley
"the Mouth of Heaven"
The Jaws of Wotan
To Desolation
The Barren Lands
Kildre Hill
Hollow's Stream
Killian's Grave
Cricket's Glen
Tree of Swords
Glistree Deur
Shrine
Tomb of Remembrance
Harper's Fiddle
Great Ash Tree
Fields of Gold
Glaeken's Peak
N
E
W
S

PROLOGUE

CHRONICLES OF THE TEMPLAR

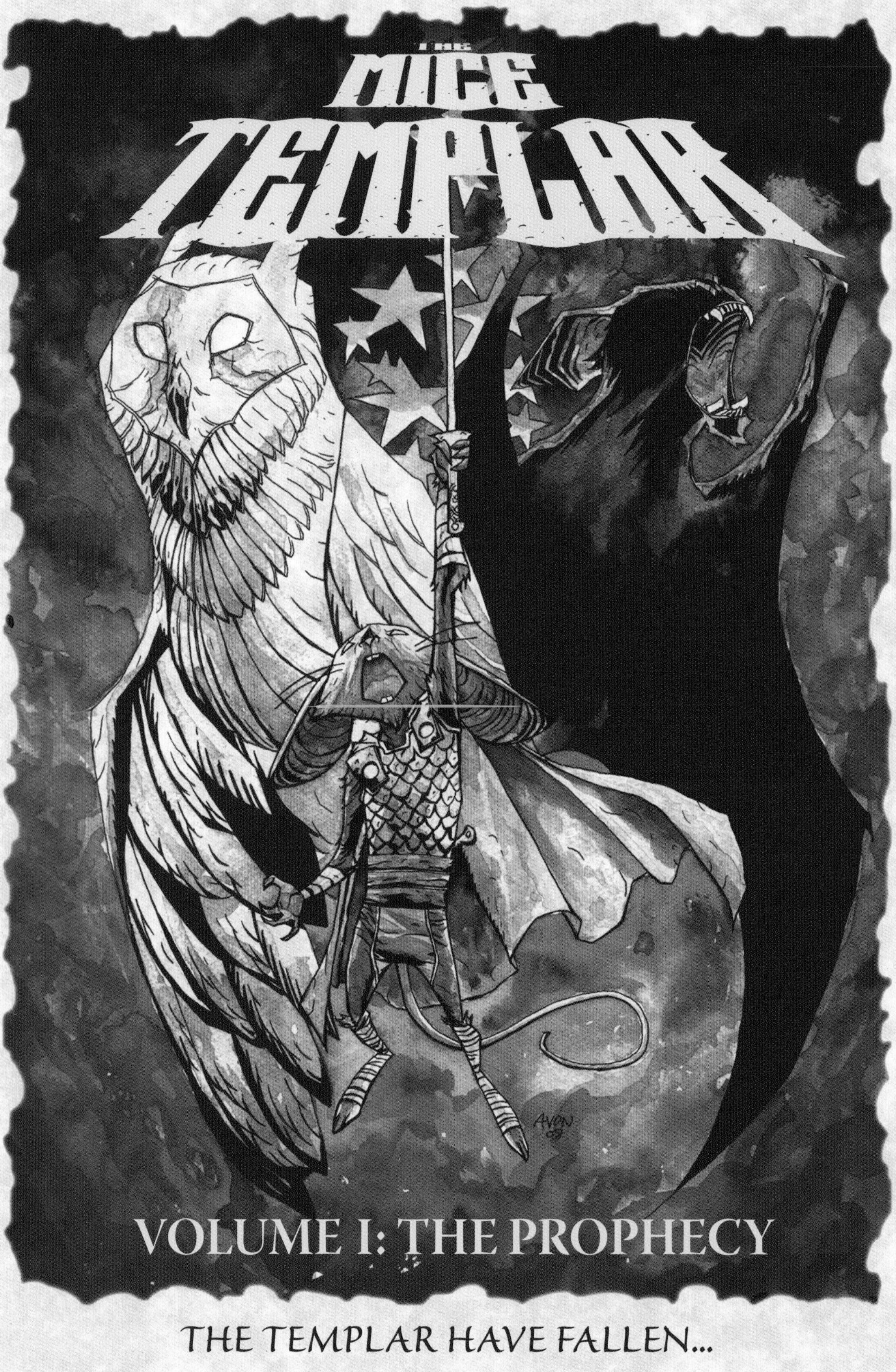
THE
MICE
TEMPLAR
VOLUME I: THE PROPHECY

THE TEMPLAR HAVE FALLEN...

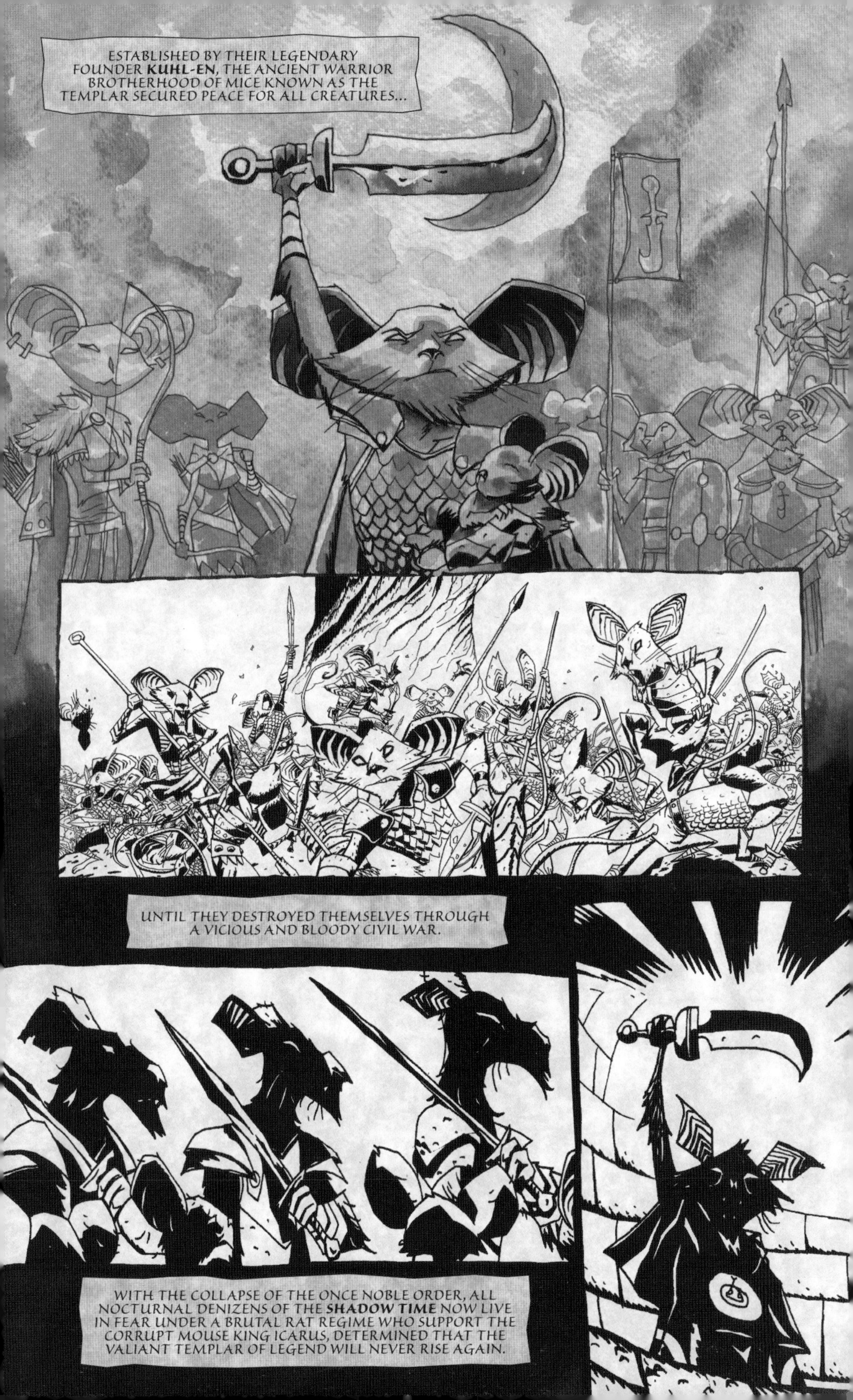
ESTABLISHED BY THEIR LEGENDARY FOUNDER KUHL-EN, THE ANCIENT WARRIOR BROTHERHOOD OF MICE KNOWN AS THE TEMPLAR SECURED PEACE FOR ALL CREATURES...
UNTIL THEY DESTROYED THEMSELVES THROUGH A VICIOUS AND BLOODY CIVIL WAR.
WITH THE COLLAPSE OF THE ONCE NOBLE ORDER, ALL NOCTURNAL DENIZENS OF THE SHADOW TIME NOW LIVE IN FEAR UNDER A BRUTAL RAT REGIME WHO SUPPORT THE CORRUPT MOUSE KING ICARUS, DETERMINED THAT THE VALIANT TEMPLAR OF LEGEND WILL NEVER RISE AGAIN.

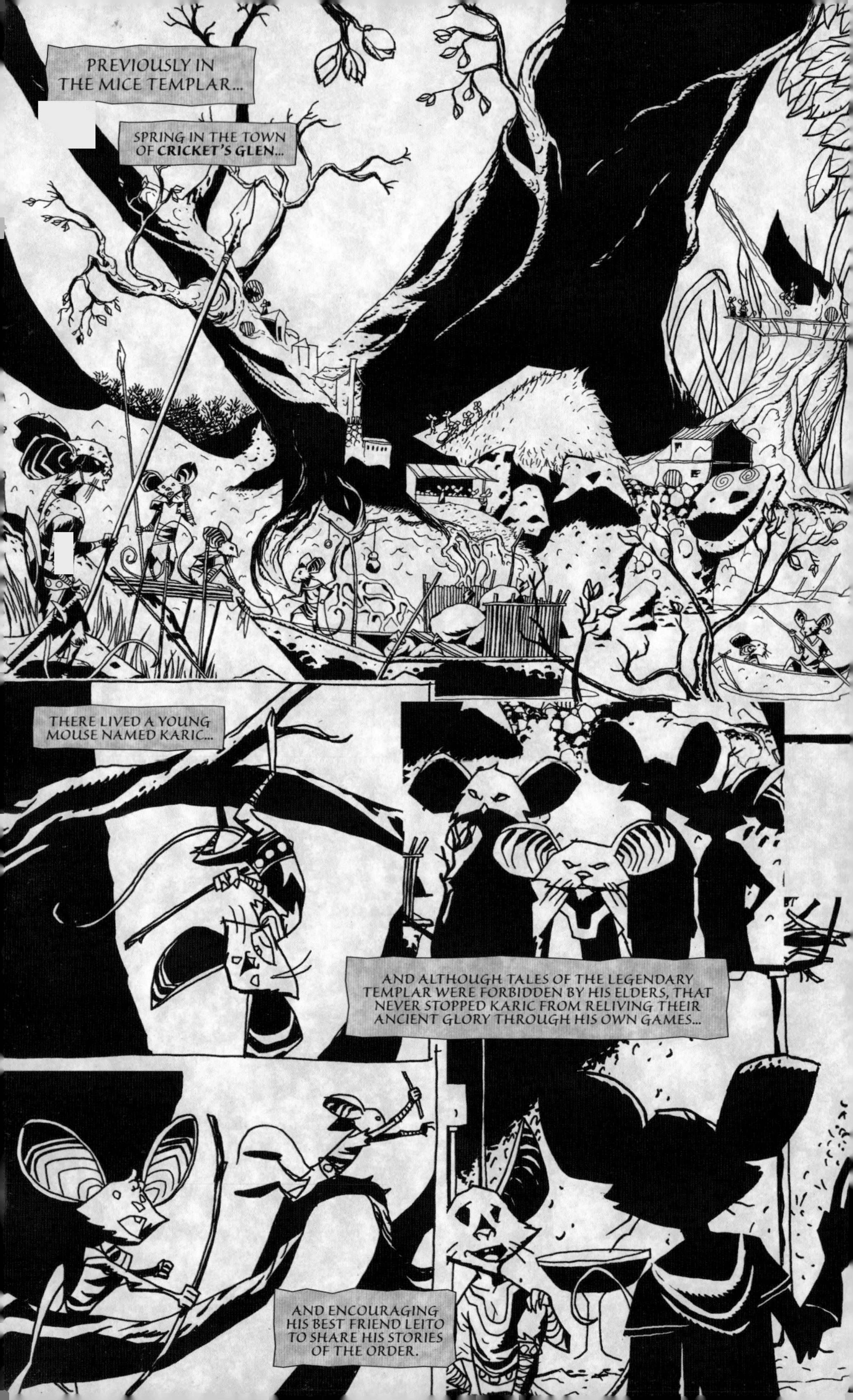
PREVIOUSLY IN THE MICE TEMPLAR...
SPRING IN THE TOWN OF CRICKET'S GLEN...
THERE LIVED A YOUNG MOUSE NAMED KARIC...
AND ALTHOUGH TALES OF THE LEGENDARY TEMPLAR WERE FORBIDDEN BY HIS ELDERS, THAT NEVER STOPPED KARIC FROM RELIVING THEIR ANCIENT GLORY THROUGH HIS OWN GAMES...
AND ENCOURAGING HIS BEST FRIEND LEITO TO SHARE HIS STORIES OF THE ORDER.

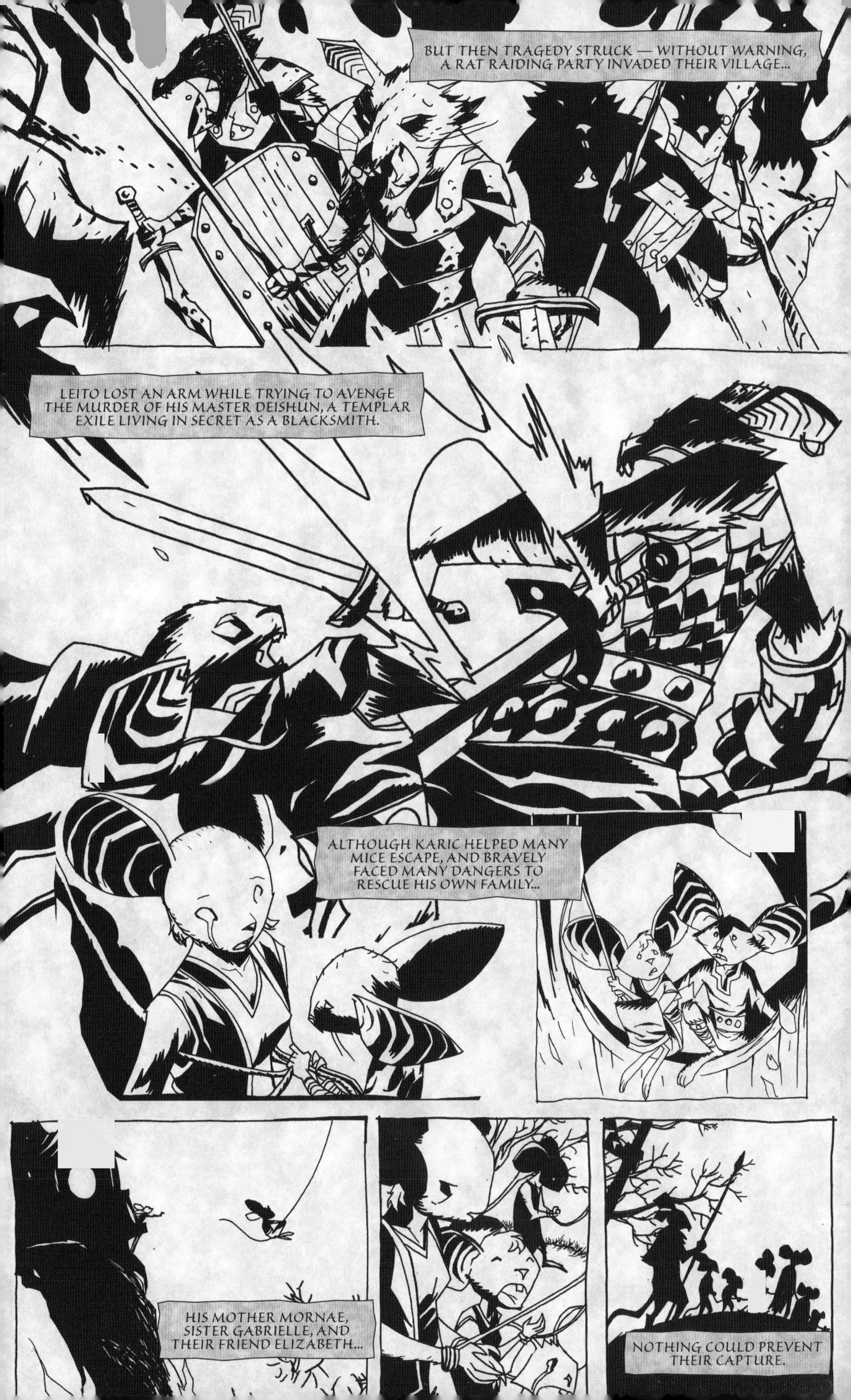
BUT THEN TRAGEDY STRUCK — WITHOUT WARNING, A RAT RAIDING PARTY INVADED THEIR VILLAGE...
LEITO LOST AN ARM WHILE TRYING TO AVENGE THE MURDER OF HIS MASTER DEISHUN, A TEMPLAR EXILE LIVING IN SECRET AS A BLACKSMITH.
ALTHOUGH KARIC HELPED MANY MICE ESCAPE, AND BRAVELY FACED MANY DANGERS TO RESCUE HIS OWN FAMILY...
HIS MOTHER MORNAE, SISTER GABRIELLE, AND THEIR FRIEND ELIZABETH...
NOTHING COULD PREVENT THEIR CAPTURE.

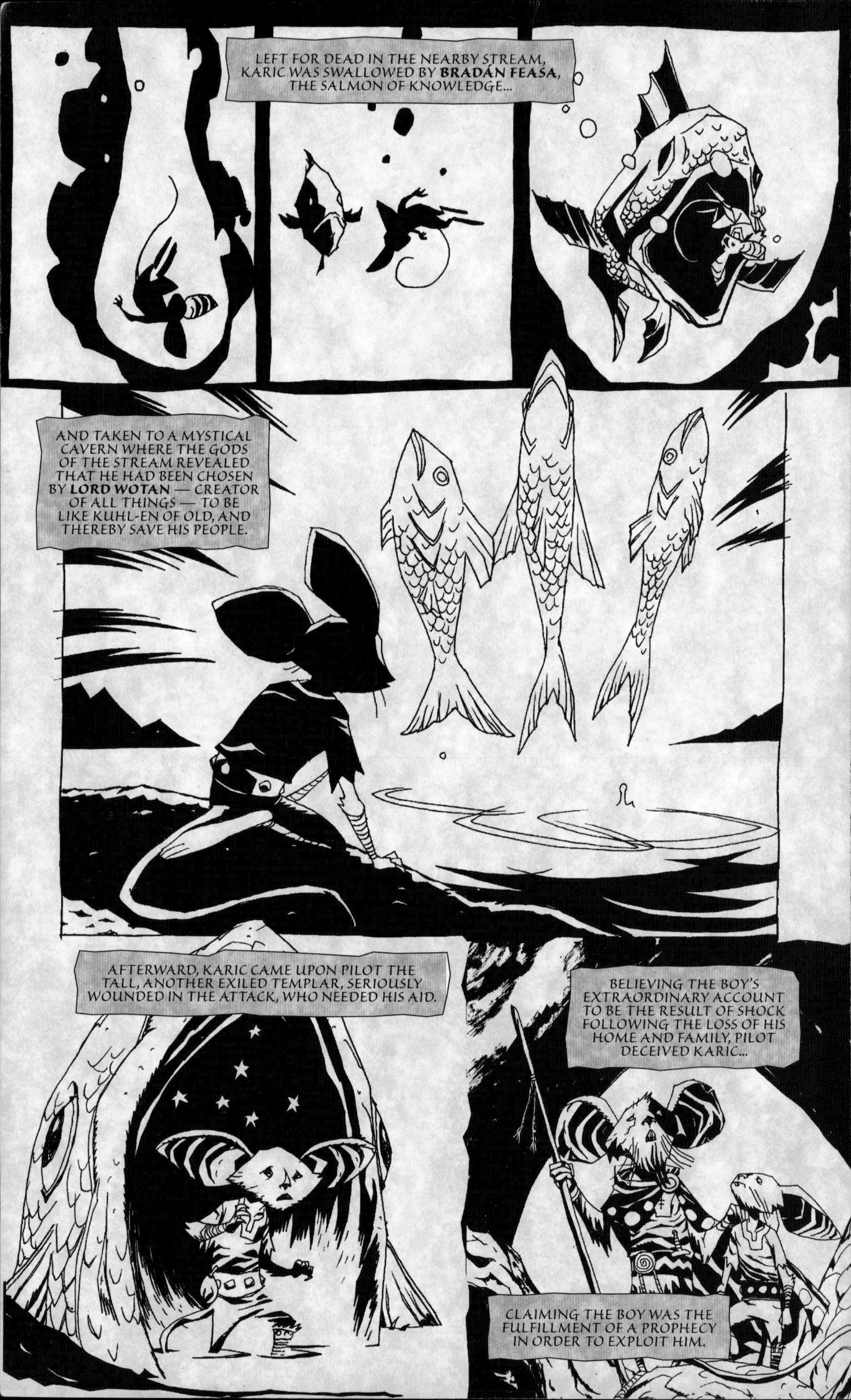
LEFT FOR DEAD IN THE NEARBY STREAM, KARIC WAS SWALLOWED BY **BRADÁN FEASA**, THE SALMON OF KNOWLEDGE...
AND TAKEN TO A MYSTICAL CAVERN WHERE THE GODS OF THE STREAM REVEALED THAT HE HAD BEEN CHOSEN BY **LORD WOTAN** — CREATOR OF ALL THINGS — TO BE LIKE KUHL-EN OF OLD, AND THEREBY SAVE HIS PEOPLE.
AFTERWARD, KARIC CAME UPON PILOT THE TALL, ANOTHER EXILED TEMPLAR, SERIOUSLY WOUNDED IN THE ATTACK, WHO NEEDED HIS AID.
BELIEVING THE BOY'S EXTRAORDINARY ACCOUNT TO BE THE RESULT OF SHOCK FOLLOWING THE LOSS OF HIS HOME AND FAMILY, PILOT DECEIVED KARIC...
CLAIMING THE BOY WAS THE FULFILLMENT OF A PROPHECY IN ORDER TO EXPLOIT HIM.

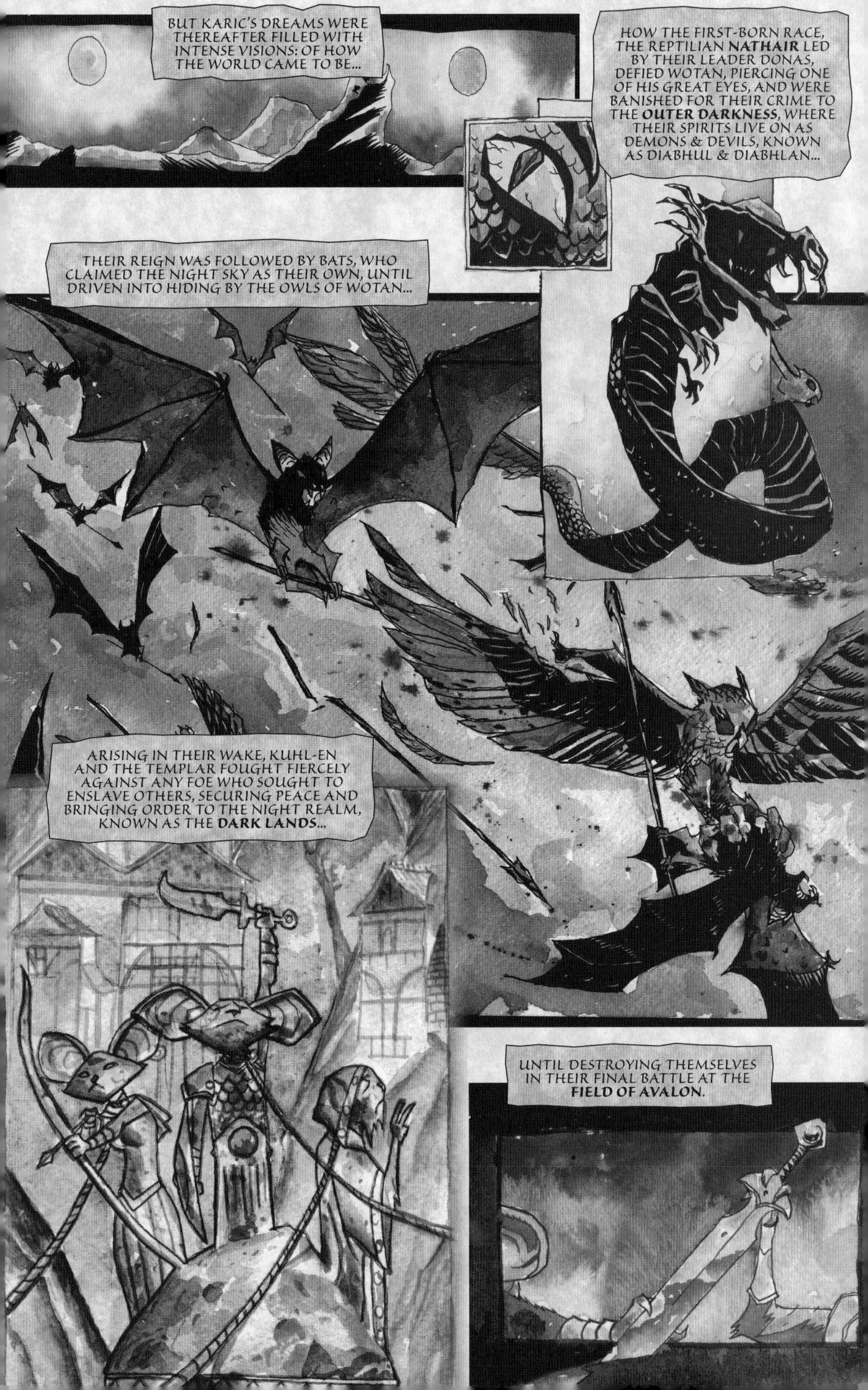
BUT KARIC'S DREAMS WERE THEREAFTER FILLED WITH INTENSE VISIONS: OF HOW THE WORLD CAME TO BE...
HOW THE FIRST-BORN RACE, THE REPTILIAN NATHAIR LED BY THEIR LEADER DONAS, DEFIED WOTAN, PIERCING ONE OF HIS GREAT EYES, AND WERE BANISHED FOR THEIR CRIME TO THE OUTER DARKNESS, WHERE THEIR SPIRITS LIVE ON AS DEMONS & DEVILS, KNOWN AS DIABHUL & DIABHLAN...
THEIR REIGN WAS FOLLOWED BY BATS, WHO CLAIMED THE NIGHT SKY AS THEIR OWN, UNTIL DRIVEN INTO HIDING BY THE OWLS OF WOTAN...
ARISING IN THEIR WAKE, KUHL-EN AND THE TEMPLAR FOUGHT FIERCELY AGAINST ANY FOE WHO SOUGHT TO ENSLAVE OTHERS, SECURING PEACE AND BRINGING ORDER TO THE NIGHT REALM, KNOWN AS THE DARK LANDS...
UNTIL DESTROYING THEMSELVES IN THEIR FINAL BATTLE AT THE FIELD OF AVALON.

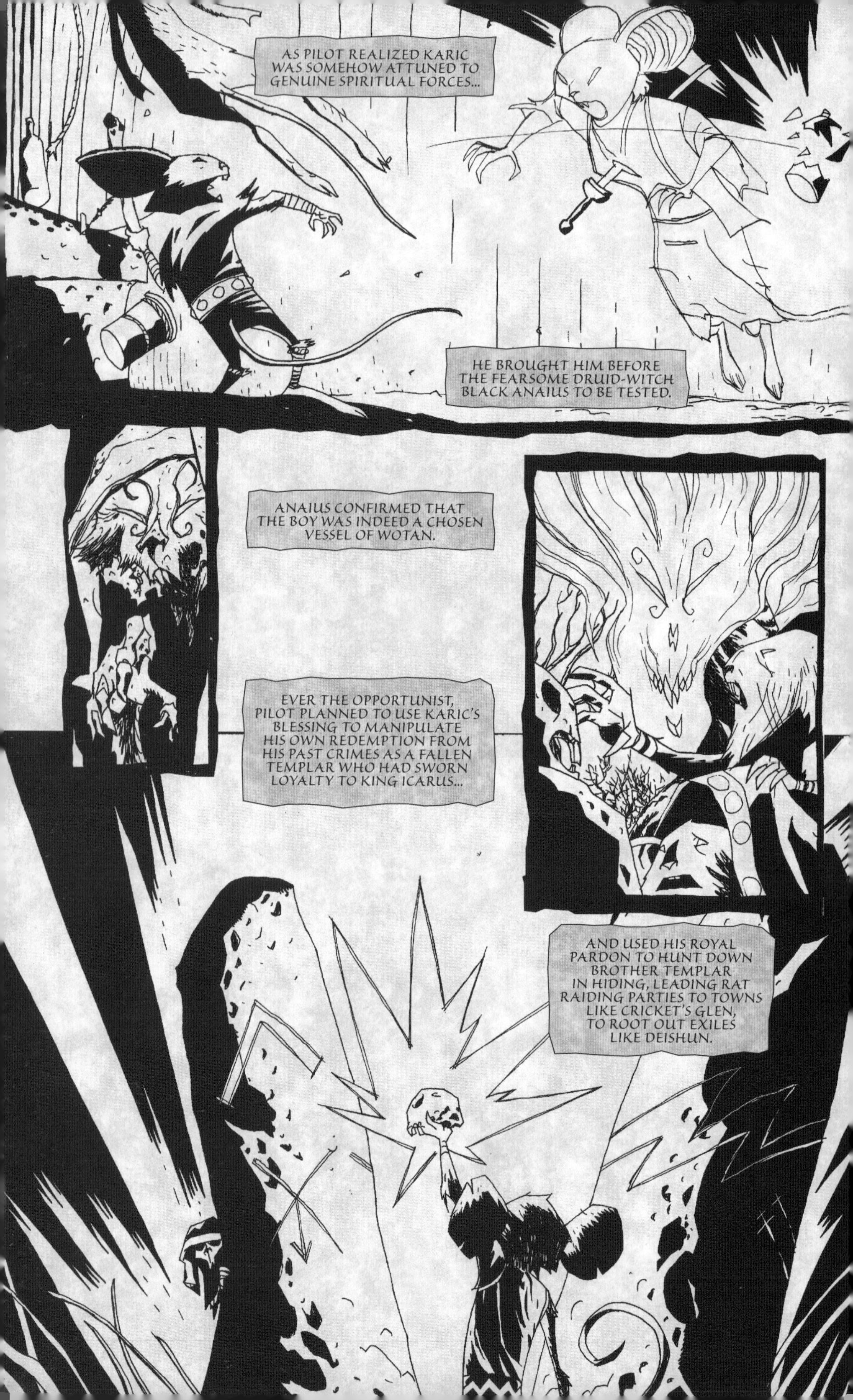
AS PILOT REALIZED KARIC WAS SOMEHOW ATTUNED TO GENUINE SPIRITUAL FORCES...
HE BROUGHT HIM BEFORE THE FEARSOME DRUID-WITCH BLACK ANAIUS TO BE TESTED.
ANAIUS CONFIRMED THAT THE BOY WAS INDEED A CHOSEN VESSEL OF WOTAN.
EVER THE OPPORTUNIST, PILOT PLANNED TO USE KARIC'S BLESSING TO MANIPULATE HIS OWN REDEMPTION FROM HIS PAST CRIMES AS A FALLEN TEMPLAR WHO HAD SWORN LOYALTY TO KING ICARUS...
AND USED HIS ROYAL PARDON TO HUNT DOWN BROTHER TEMPLAR IN HIDING, LEADING RAT RAIDING PARTIES TO TOWNS LIKE CRICKET'S GLEN, TO ROOT OUT EXILES LIKE DEISHUN.

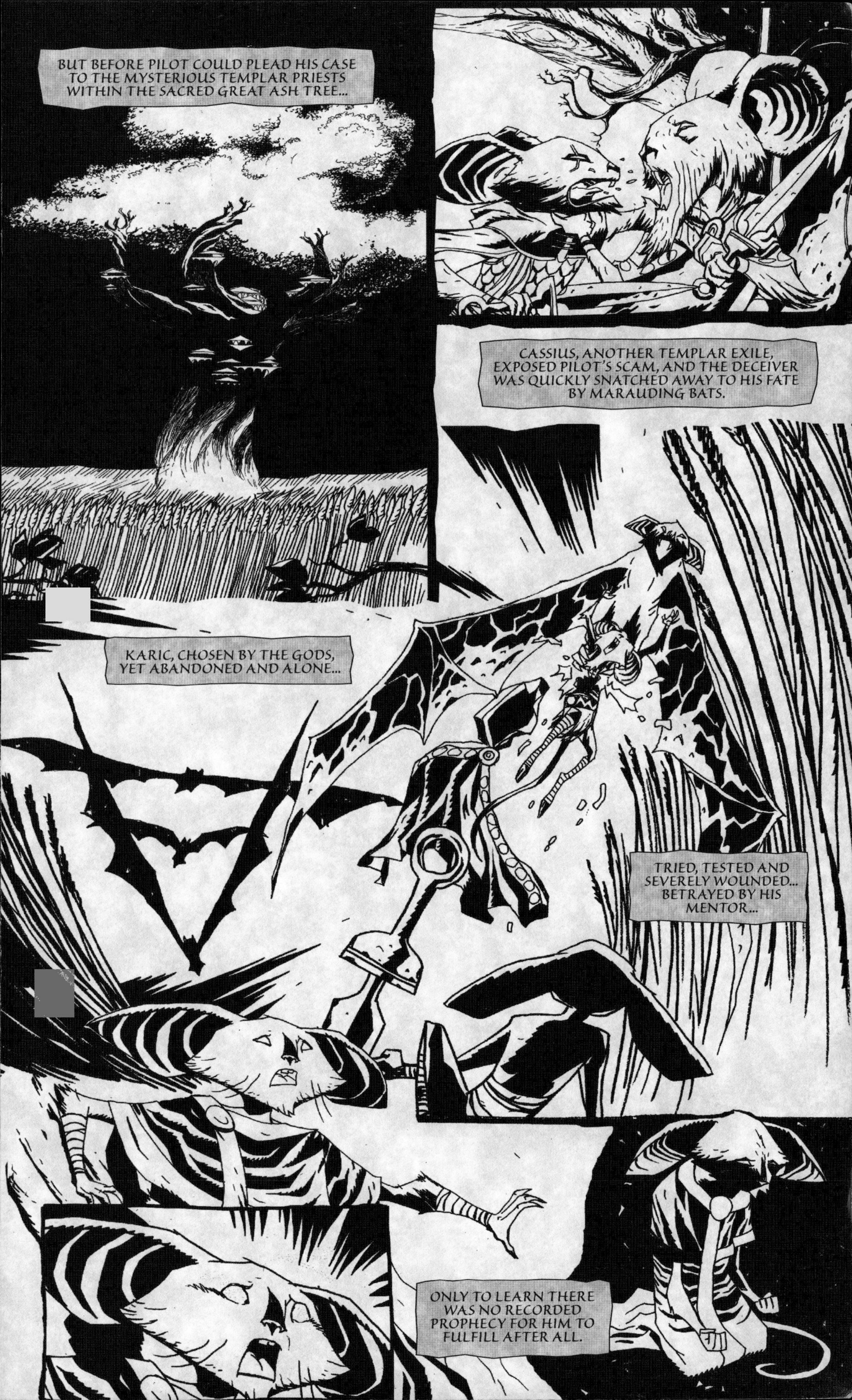
BUT BEFORE PILOT COULD PLEAD HIS CASE TO THE MYSTERIOUS TEMPLAR PRIESTS WITHIN THE SACRED GREAT ASH TREE...
CASSIUS, ANOTHER TEMPLAR EXILE, EXPOSED PILOT'S SCAM, AND THE DECEIVER WAS QUICKLY SNATCHED AWAY TO HIS FATE BY MARAUDING BATS.
KARIC, CHOSEN BY THE GODS, YET ABANDONED AND ALONE...
TRIED, TESTED AND SEVERELY WOUNDED... BETRAYED BY HIS MENTOR...
ONLY TO LEARN THERE WAS NO RECORDED PROPHECY FOR HIM TO FULFILL AFTER ALL.

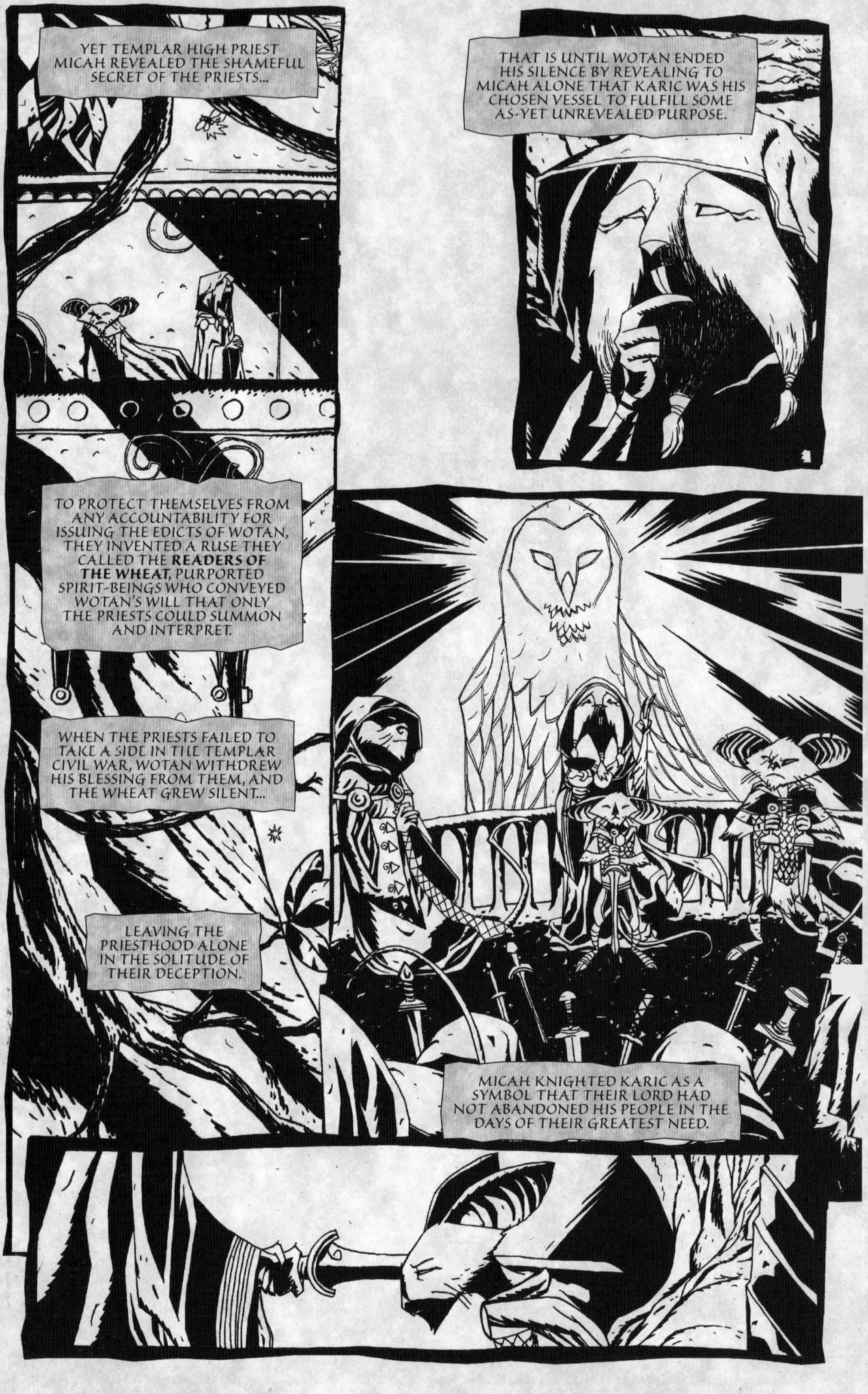
YET TEMPLAR HIGH PRIEST MICAH REVEALED THE SHAMEFUL SECRET OF THE PRIESTS...
TO PROTECT THEMSELVES FROM ANY ACCOUNTABILITY FOR ISSUING THE EDICTS OF WOTAN, THEY INVENTED A RUSE THEY CALLED THE **READERS OF THE WHEAT**, PURPORTED SPIRIT-BEINGS WHO CONVEYED WOTAN'S WILL THAT ONLY THE PRIESTS COULD SUMMON AND INTERPRET.
WHEN THE PRIESTS FAILED TO TAKE A SIDE IN THE TEMPLAR CIVIL WAR, WOTAN WITHDREW HIS BLESSING FROM THEM, AND THE WHEAT GREW SILENT...
LEAVING THE PRIESTHOOD ALONE IN THE SOLITUDE OF THEIR DECEPTION.
THAT IS UNTIL WOTAN ENDED HIS SILENCE BY REVEALING TO MICAH ALONE THAT KARIC WAS HIS CHOSEN VESSEL TO FULFILL SOME AS-YET UNREVEALED PURPOSE.
MICAH KNIGHTED KARIC AS A SYMBOL THAT THEIR LORD HAD NOT ABANDONED HIS PEOPLE IN THE DAYS OF THEIR GREATEST NEED.

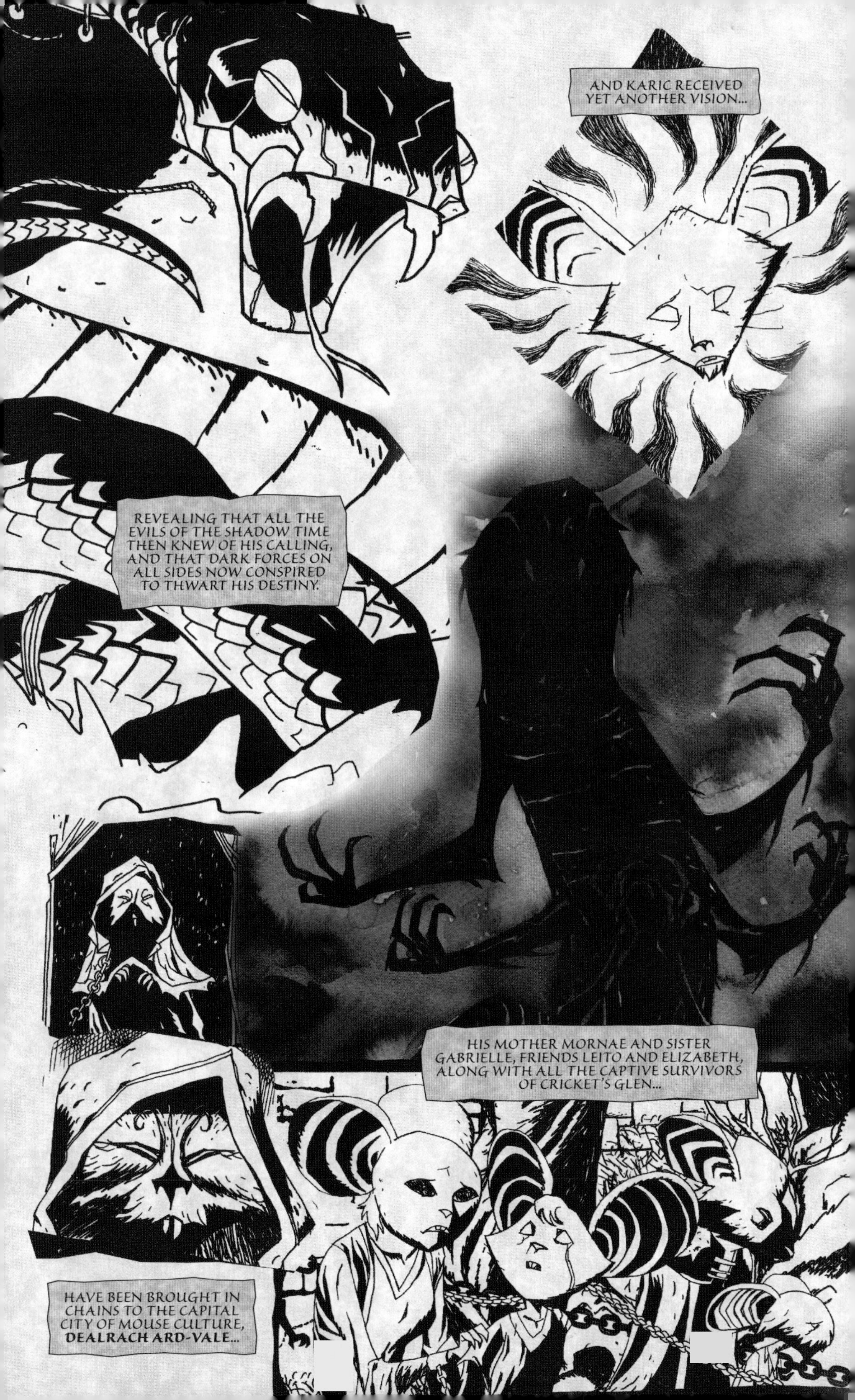
AND KARIC RECEIVED YET ANOTHER VISION...
REVEALING THAT ALL THE EVILS OF THE SHADOW TIME THEN KNEW OF HIS CALLING, AND THAT DARK FORCES ON ALL SIDES NOW CONSPIRED TO THWART HIS DESTINY.
HIS MOTHER MORNAE AND SISTER GABRIELLE, FRIENDS LEITO AND ELIZABETH, ALONG WITH ALL THE CAPTIVE SURVIVORS OF CRICKET'S GLEN...
HAVE BEEN BROUGHT IN CHAINS TO THE CAPITAL CITY OF MOUSE CULTURE, **DEALRACH ARD-VALE**...

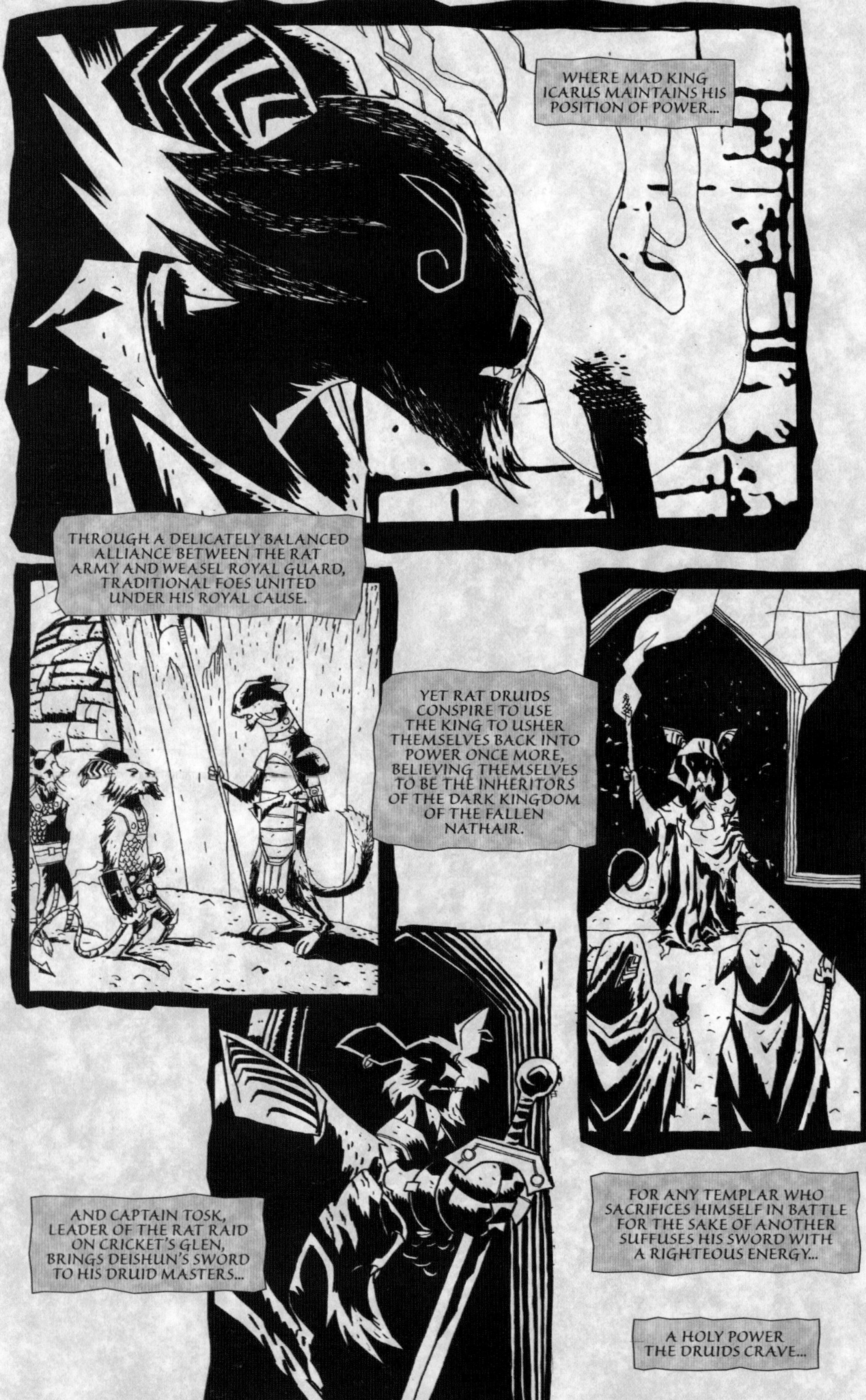
WHERE MAD KING ICARUS MAINTAINS HIS POSITION OF POWER...
THROUGH A DELICATELY BALANCED ALLIANCE BETWEEN THE RAT ARMY AND WEASEL ROYAL GUARD, TRADITIONAL FOES UNITED UNDER HIS ROYAL CAUSE.
YET RAT DRUIDS CONSPIRE TO USE THE KING TO USHER THEMSELVES BACK INTO POWER ONCE MORE, BELIEVING THEMSELVES TO BE THE INHERITORS OF THE DARK KINGDOM OF THE FALLEN NATHAIR.
AND CAPTAIN TOSK, LEADER OF THE RAT RAID ON CRICKET'S GLEN, BRINGS DEISHUN'S SWORD TO HIS DRUID MASTERS...
FOR ANY TEMPLAR WHO SACRIFICES HIMSELF IN BATTLE FOR THE SAKE OF ANOTHER SUFFUSES HIS SWORD WITH A RIGHTEOUS ENERGY...
A HOLY POWER THE DRUIDS CRAVE...

AND THE SAGA CONTINUED...

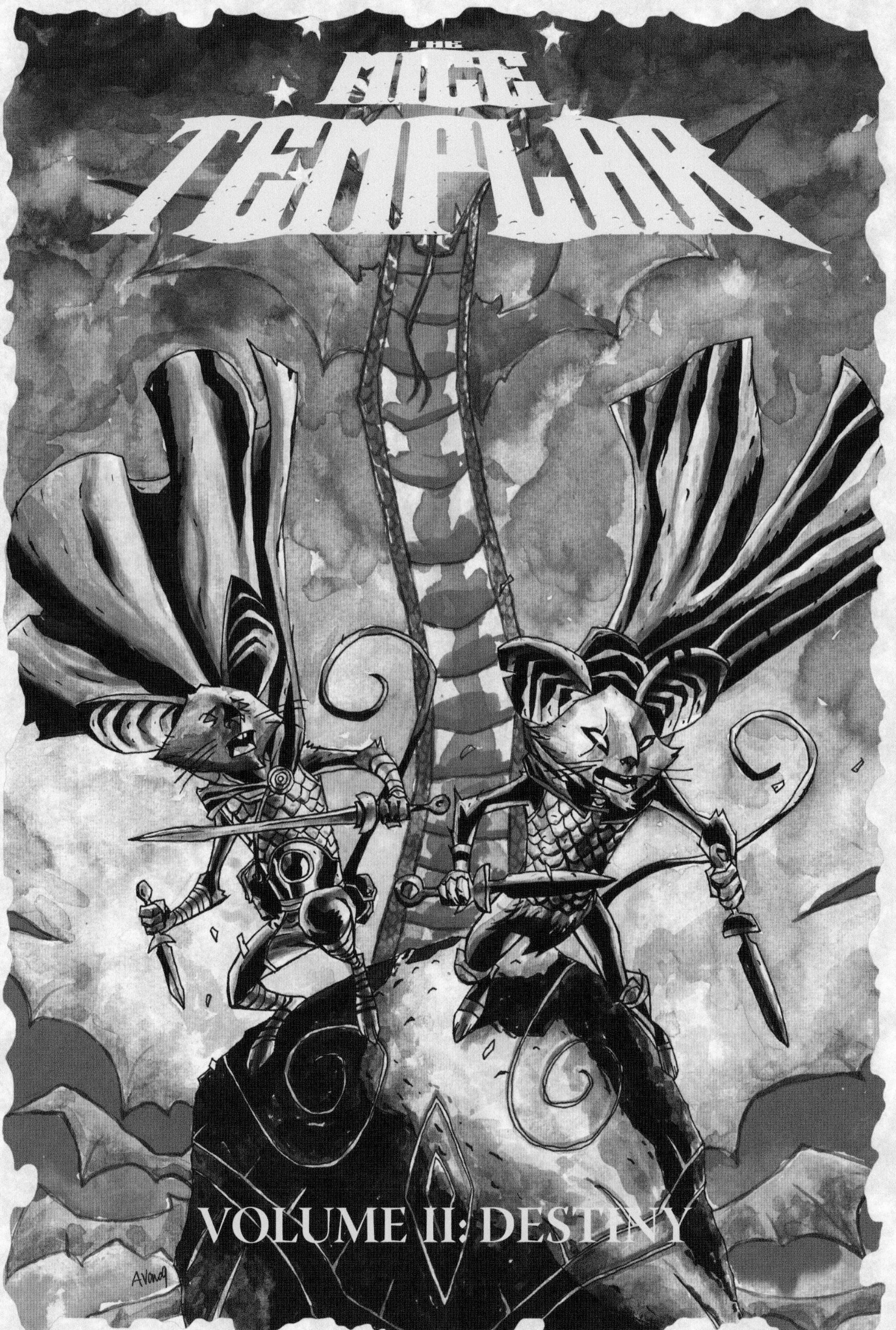
THE
MICE
TEMPLAR
VOLUME II: DESTINY
AVon09

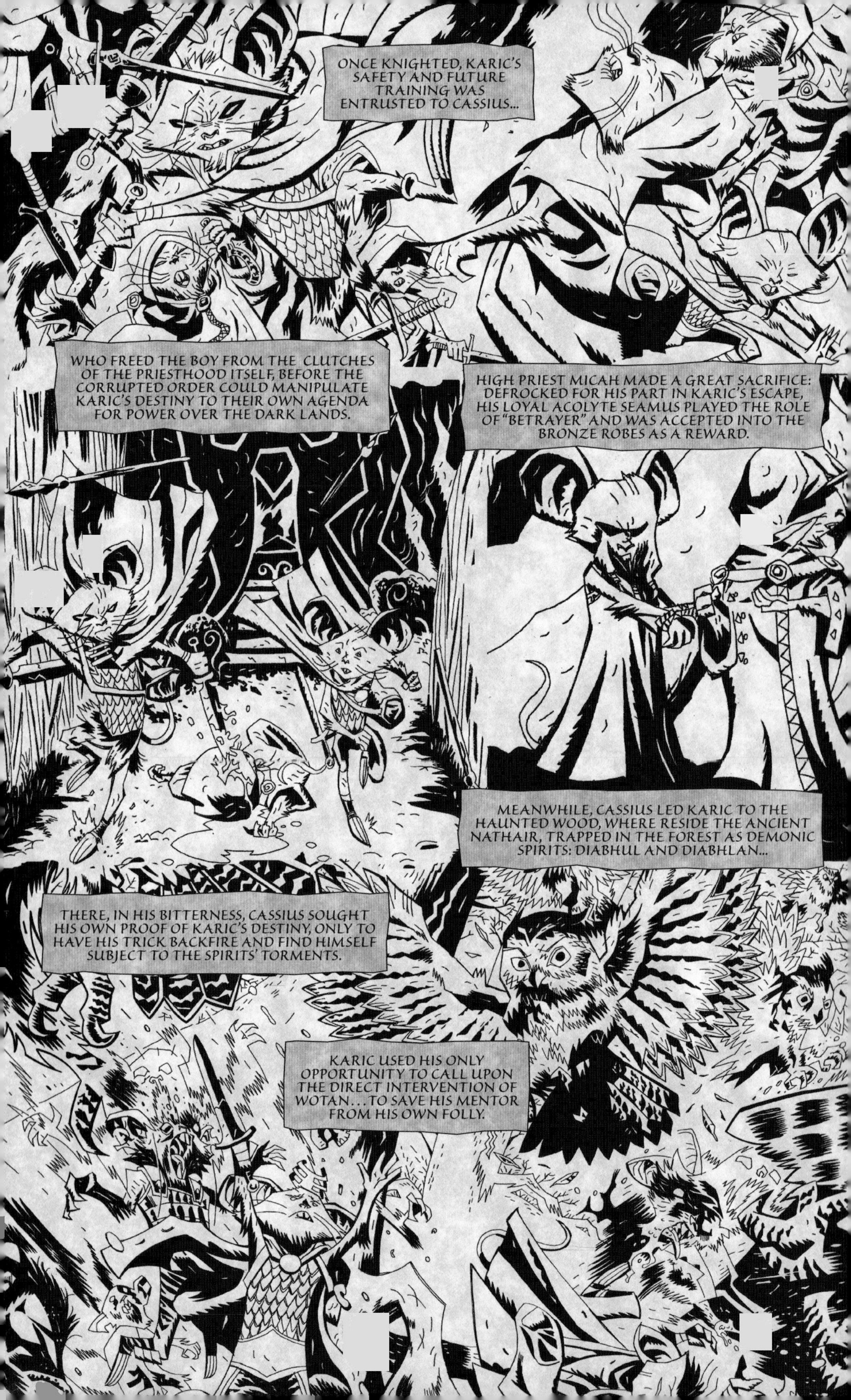
ONCE KNIGHTED, KARIC'S SAFETY AND FUTURE TRAINING WAS ENTRUSTED TO CASSIUS...
WHO FREED THE BOY FROM THE CLUTCHES OF THE PRIESTHOOD ITSELF, BEFORE THE CORRUPTED ORDER COULD MANIPULATE KARIC'S DESTINY TO THEIR OWN AGENDA FOR POWER OVER THE DARK LANDS.
HIGH PRIEST MICAH MADE A GREAT SACRIFICE: DEFROCKED FOR HIS PART IN KARIC'S ESCAPE, HIS LOYAL ACOLYTE SEAMUS PLAYED THE ROLE OF "BETRAYER" AND WAS ACCEPTED INTO THE BRONZE ROBES AS A REWARD.
MEANWHILE, CASSIUS LED KARIC TO THE HAUNTED WOOD, WHERE RESIDE THE ANCIENT NATHAIR, TRAPPED IN THE FOREST AS DEMONIC SPIRITS: DIABHUL AND DIABHLAN...
THERE, IN HIS BITTERNESS, CASSIUS SOUGHT HIS OWN PROOF OF KARIC'S DESTINY, ONLY TO HAVE HIS TRICK BACKFIRE AND FIND HIMSELF SUBJECT TO THE SPIRITS' TORMENTS.
KARIC USED HIS ONLY OPPORTUNITY TO CALL UPON THE DIRECT INTERVENTION OF WOTAN...TO SAVE HIS MENTOR FROM HIS OWN FOLLY.

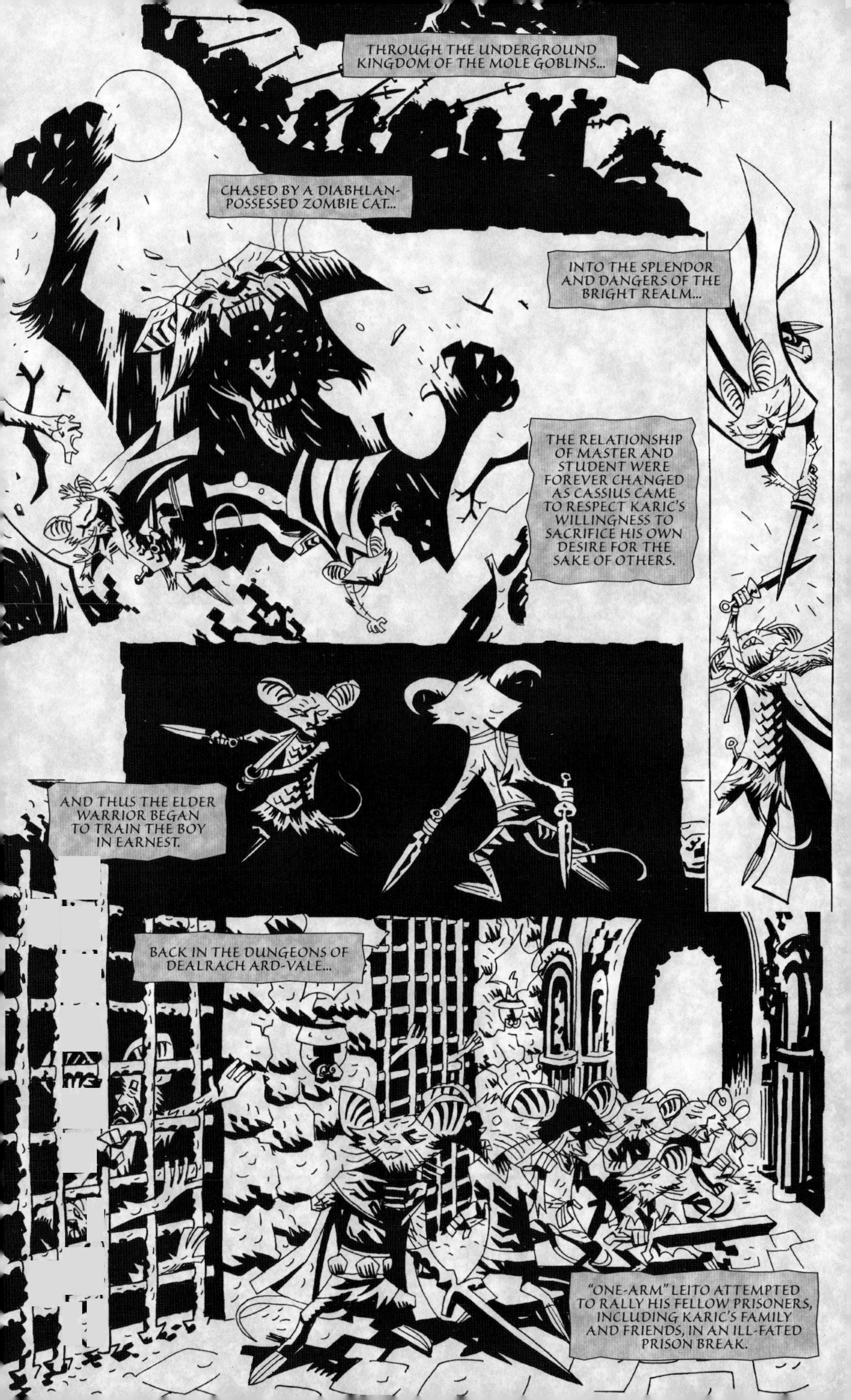
THROUGH THE UNDERGROUND KINGDOM OF THE MOLE GOBLINS...
CHASED BY A DIABHLAN-POSSESSED ZOMBIE CAT...
INTO THE SPLENDOR AND DANGERS OF THE BRIGHT REALM...
THE RELATIONSHIP OF MASTER AND STUDENT WERE FOREVER CHANGED AS CASSIUS CAME TO RESPECT KARIC'S WILLINGNESS TO SACRIFICE HIS OWN DESIRE FOR THE SAKE OF OTHERS.
AND THUS THE ELDER WARRIOR BEGAN TO TRAIN THE BOY IN EARNEST.
BACK IN THE DUNGEONS OF DEALRACH ARD-VALE...
"ONE-ARM" LEITO ATTEMPTED TO RALLY HIS FELLOW PRISONERS, INCLUDING KARIC'S FAMILY AND FRIENDS, IN AN ILL-FATED PRISON BREAK.

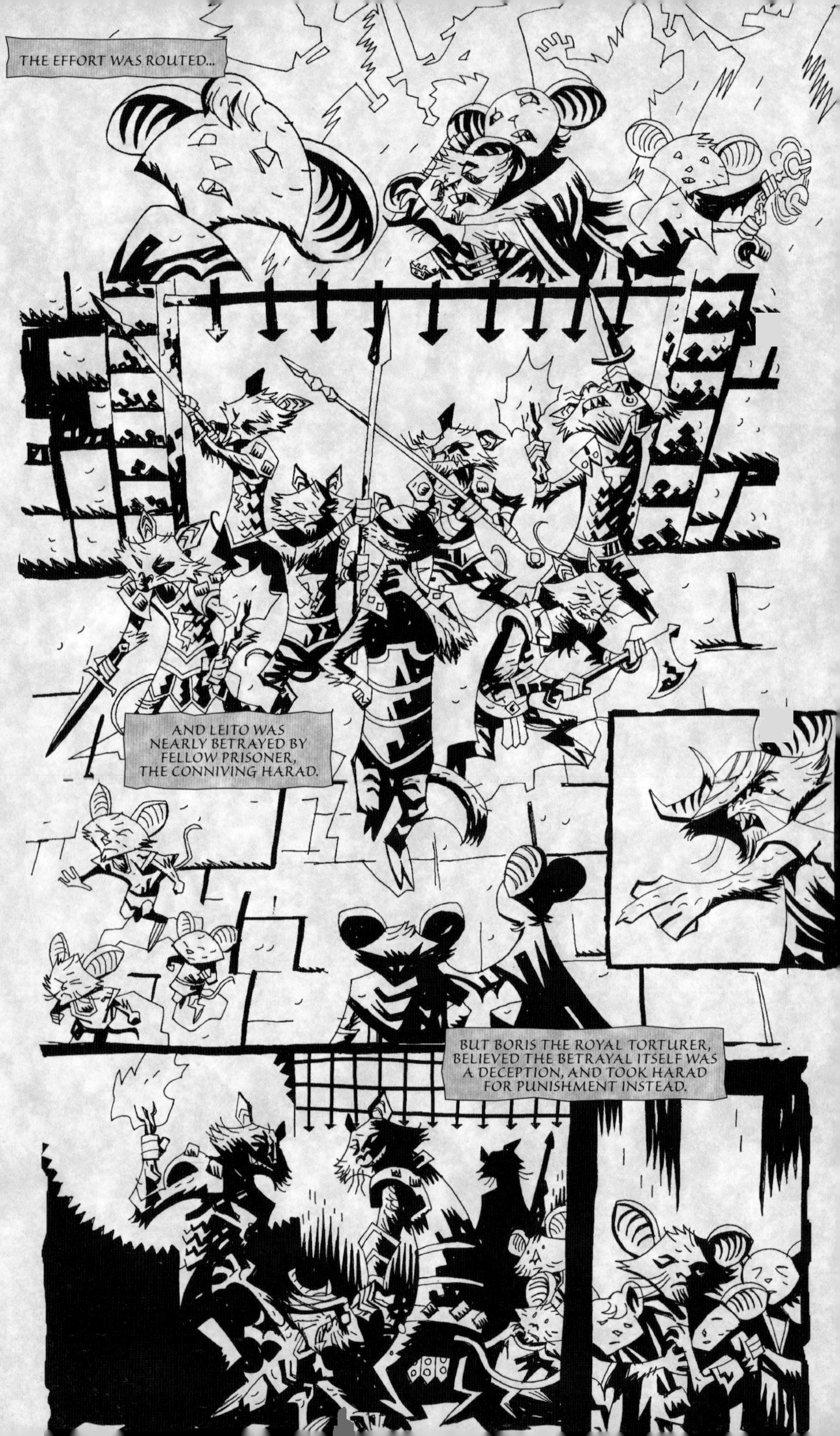
THE EFFORT WAS ROUTED...
AND LEITO WAS NEARLY BETRAYED BY FELLOW PRISONER, THE CONNIVING HARAD.
BUT BORIS THE ROYAL TORTURER, BELIEVED THE BETRAYAL ITSELF WAS A DECEPTION, AND TOOK HARAD FOR PUNISHMENT INSTEAD.

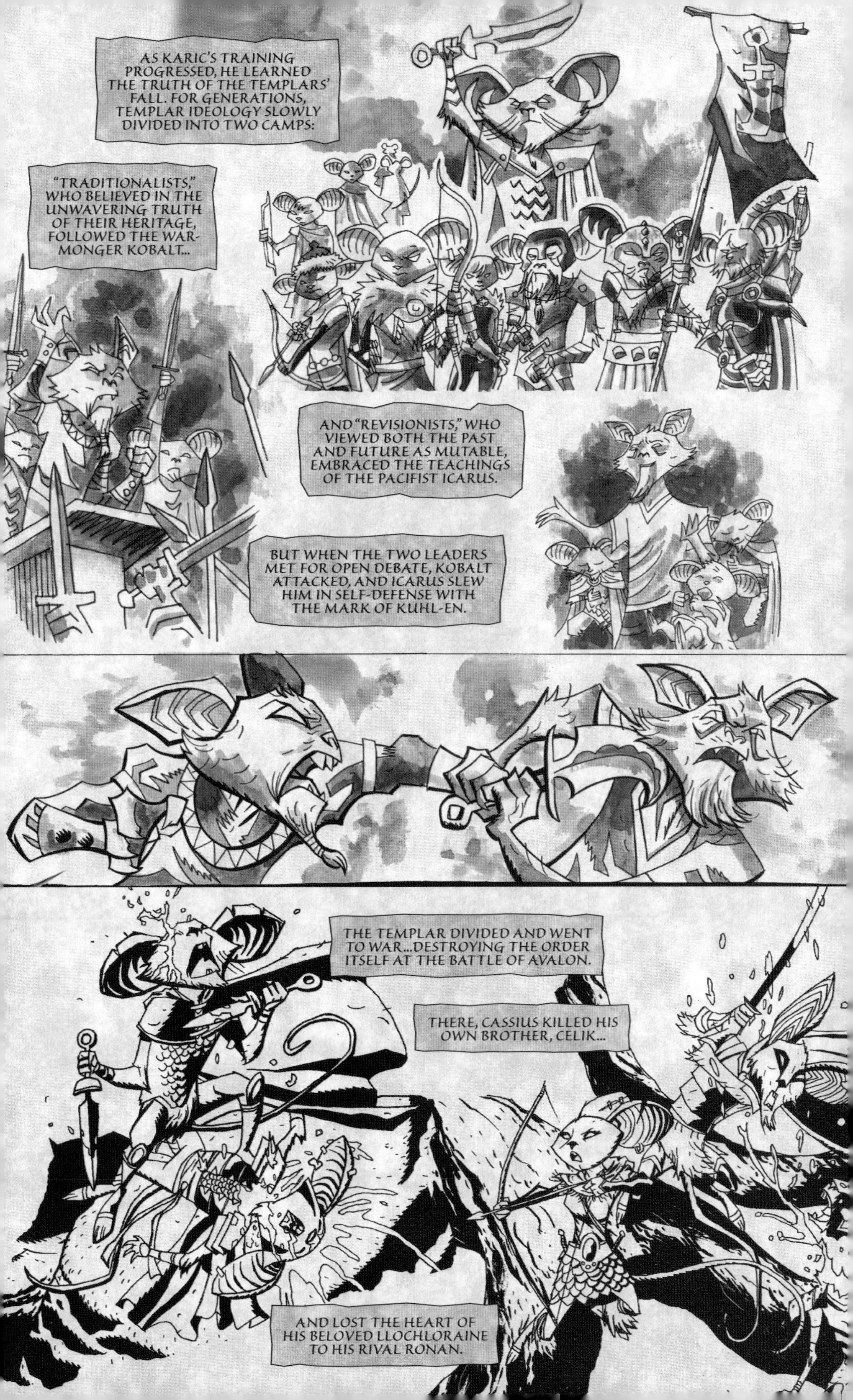
AS KARIC'S TRAINING PROGRESSED, HE LEARNED THE TRUTH OF THE TEMPLARS' FALL. FOR GENERATIONS, TEMPLAR IDEOLOGY SLOWLY DIVIDED INTO TWO CAMPS:
"TRADITIONALISTS," WHO BELIEVED IN THE UNWAVERING TRUTH OF THEIR HERITAGE, FOLLOWED THE WAR-MONGER KOBALT...
AND "REVISIONISTS," WHO VIEWED BOTH THE PAST AND FUTURE AS MUTABLE, EMBRACED THE TEACHINGS OF THE PACIFIST ICARUS.
BUT WHEN THE TWO LEADERS MET FOR OPEN DEBATE, KOBALT ATTACKED, AND ICARUS SLEW HIM IN SELF-DEFENSE WITH THE MARK OF KUHL-EN.
THE TEMPLAR DIVIDED AND WENT TO WAR...DESTROYING THE ORDER ITSELF AT THE BATTLE OF AVALON.
THERE, CASSIUS KILLED HIS OWN BROTHER, CELIK...
AND LOST THE HEART OF HIS BELOVED LLOCHLORAINE TO HIS RIVAL RONAN.

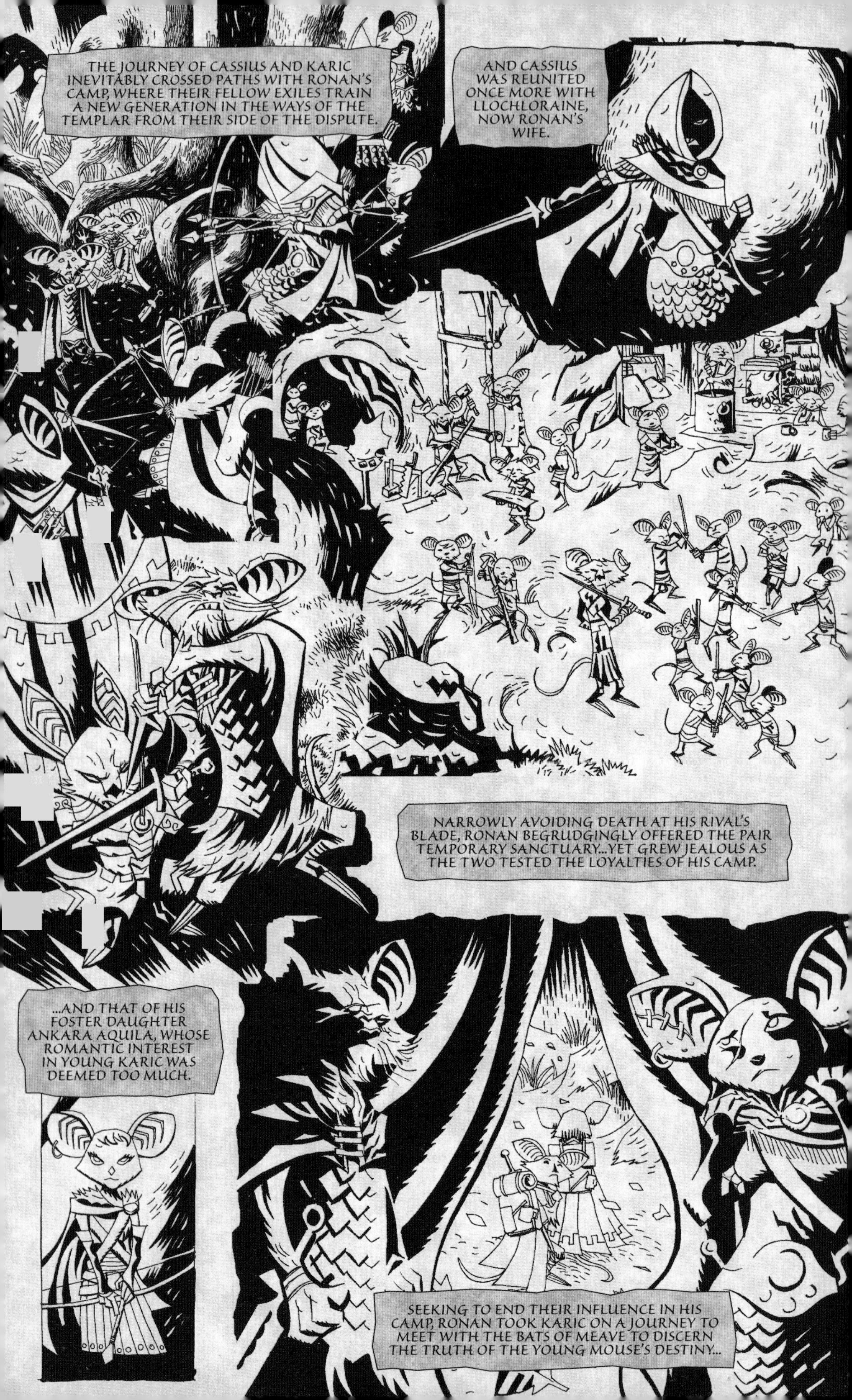
THE JOURNEY OF CASSIUS AND KARIC INEVITABLY CROSSED PATHS WITH RONAN'S CAMP, WHERE THEIR FELLOW EXILES TRAIN A NEW GENERATION IN THE WAYS OF THE TEMPLAR FROM THEIR SIDE OF THE DISPUTE.
AND CASSIUS WAS REUNITED ONCE MORE WITH LLOCHLORAINE, NOW RONAN'S WIFE.
NARROWLY AVOIDING DEATH AT HIS RIVAL'S BLADE, RONAN BEGRUDGINGLY OFFERED THE PAIR TEMPORARY SANCTUARY...YET GREW JEALOUS AS THE TWO TESTED THE LOYALTIES OF HIS CAMP.
...AND THAT OF HIS FOSTER DAUGHTER ANKARA AQUILA, WHOSE ROMANTIC INTEREST IN YOUNG KARIC WAS DEEMED TOO MUCH.
SEEKING TO END THEIR INFLUENCE IN HIS CAMP, RONAN TOOK KARIC ON A JOURNEY TO MEET WITH THE BATS OF MEAVE TO DISCERN THE TRUTH OF THE YOUNG MOUSE'S DESTINY...

CHAPTER SIX
THE BATS OF MEAVE

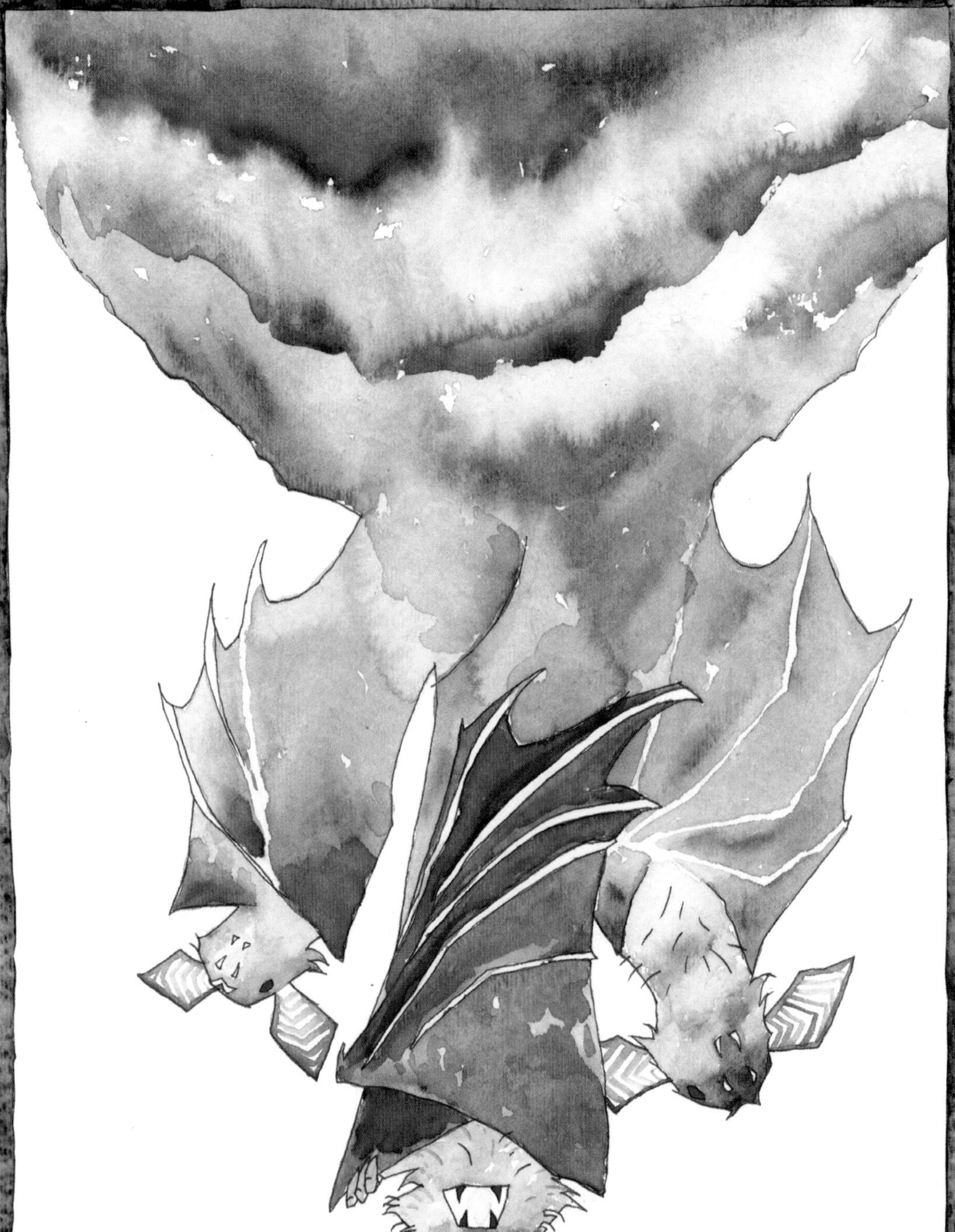

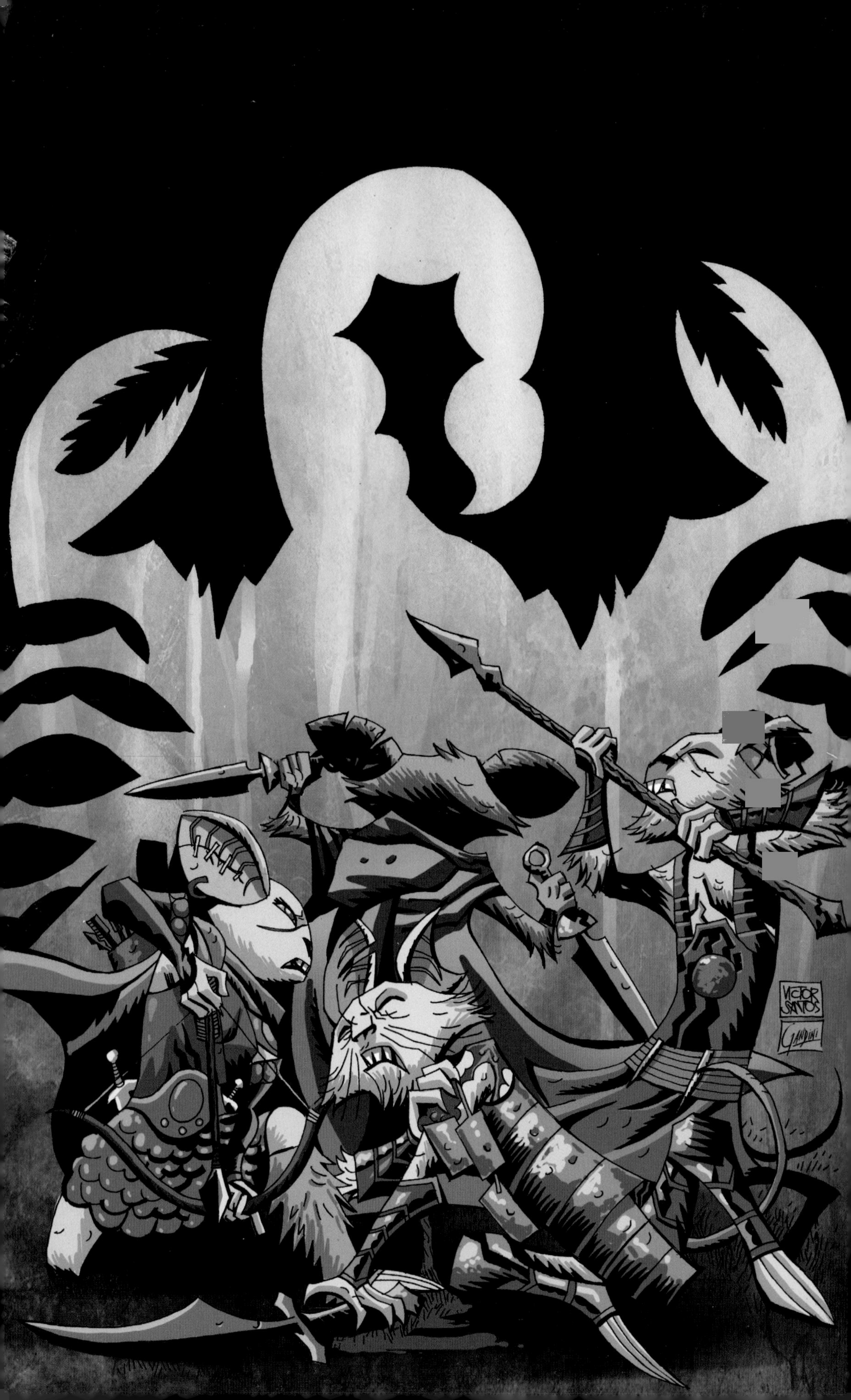
VICTOR SANTOS
GANDINI

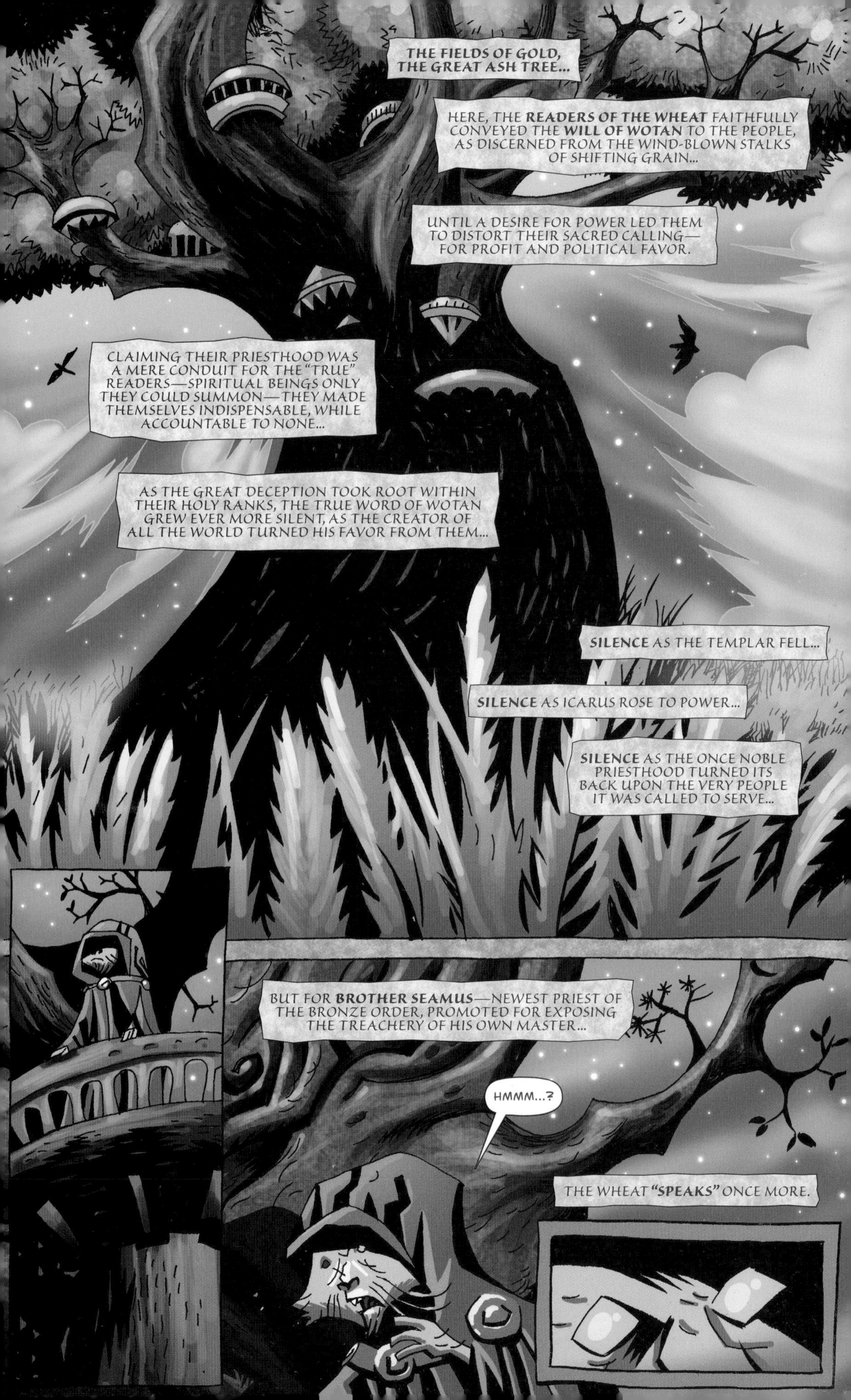
THE FIELDS OF GOLD, THE GREAT ASH TREE...
HERE, THE READERS OF THE WHEAT FAITHFULLY CONVEYED THE WILL OF WOTAN TO THE PEOPLE, AS DISCERNED FROM THE WIND-BLOWN STALKS OF SHIFTING GRAIN...
UNTIL A DESIRE FOR POWER LED THEM TO DISTORT THEIR SACRED CALLING— FOR PROFIT AND POLITICAL FAVOR.
CLAIMING THEIR PRIESTHOOD WAS A MERE CONDUIT FOR THE "TRUE" READERS—SPIRITUAL BEINGS ONLY THEY COULD SUMMON—THEY MADE THEMSELVES INDISPENSABLE, WHILE ACCOUNTABLE TO NONE...
AS THE GREAT DECEPTION TOOK ROOT WITHIN THEIR HOLY RANKS, THE TRUE WORD OF WOTAN GREW EVER MORE SILENT, AS THE CREATOR OF ALL THE WORLD TURNED HIS FAVOR FROM THEM...
SILENCE AS THE TEMPLAR FELL...
SILENCE AS ICARUS ROSE TO POWER...
SILENCE AS THE ONCE NOBLE PRIESTHOOD TURNED ITS BACK UPON THE VERY PEOPLE IT WAS CALLED TO SERVE...
BUT FOR BROTHER SEAMUS—NEWEST PRIEST OF THE BRONZE ORDER, PROMOTED FOR EXPOSING THE TREACHERY OF HIS OWN MASTER...
HMMM...?
THE WHEAT "SPEAKS" ONCE MORE.

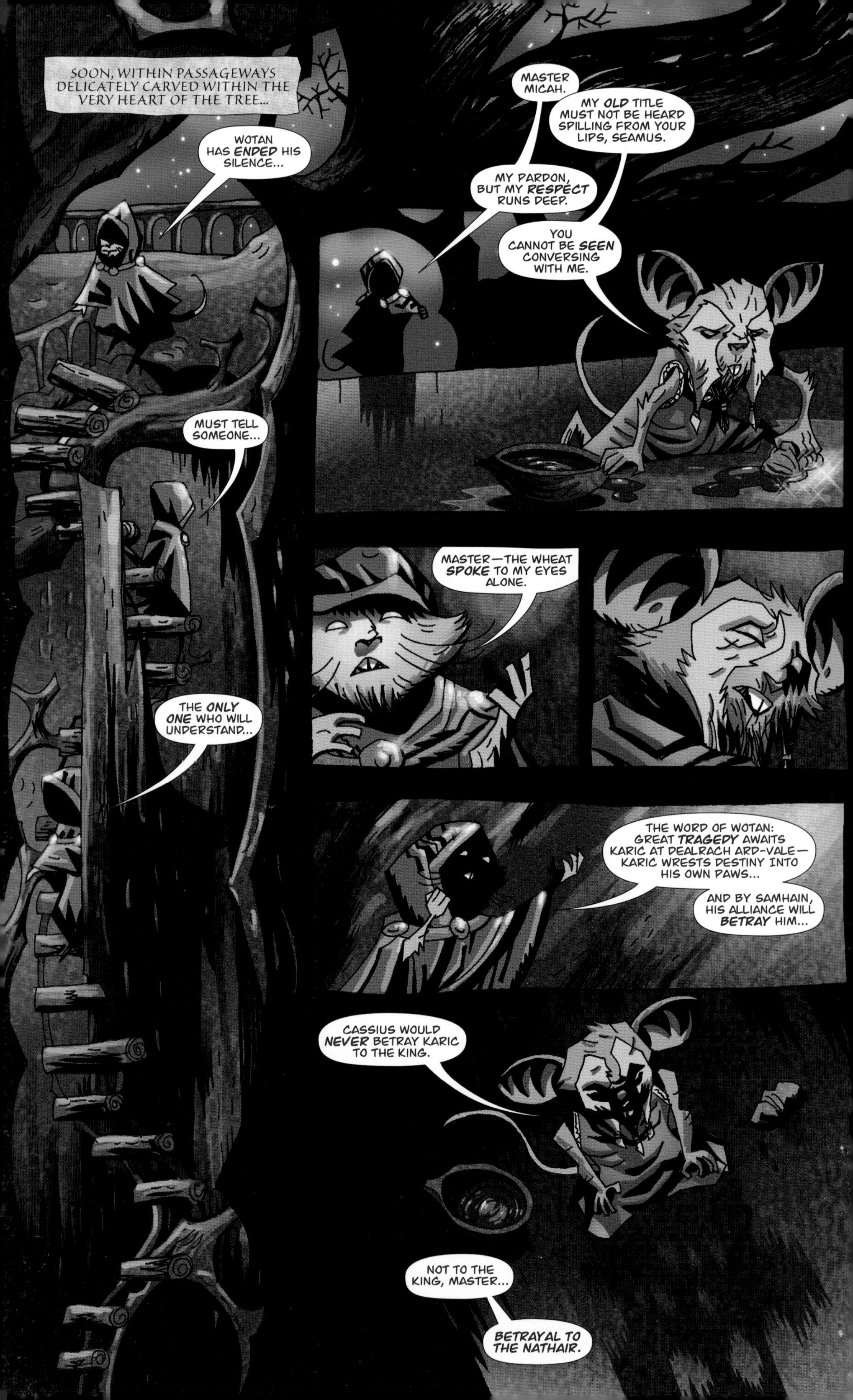
SOON, WITHIN PASSAGEWAYS DELICATELY CARVED WITHIN THE VERY HEART OF THE TREE...
WOTAN HAS ENDED HIS SILENCE...
MUST TELL SOMEONE...
THE ONLY ONE WHO WILL UNDERSTAND...
MASTER MICAH.
MY OLD TITLE MUST NOT BE HEARD SPILLING FROM YOUR LIPS, SEAMUS.
MY PARDON, BUT MY RESPECT RUNS DEEP.
YOU CANNOT BE SEEN CONVERSING WITH ME.
MASTER—THE WHEAT SPOKE TO MY EYES ALONE.
THE WORD OF WOTAN: GREAT TRAGEDY AWAITS KARIC AT DEALRACH ARD-VALE—KARIC WRESTS DESTINY INTO HIS OWN PAWS...
AND BY SAMHAIN, HIS ALLIANCE WILL BETRAY HIM...
CASSIUS WOULD NEVER BETRAY KARIC TO THE KING.
NOT TO THE KING, MASTER...
BETRAYAL TO THE NATHAIR.

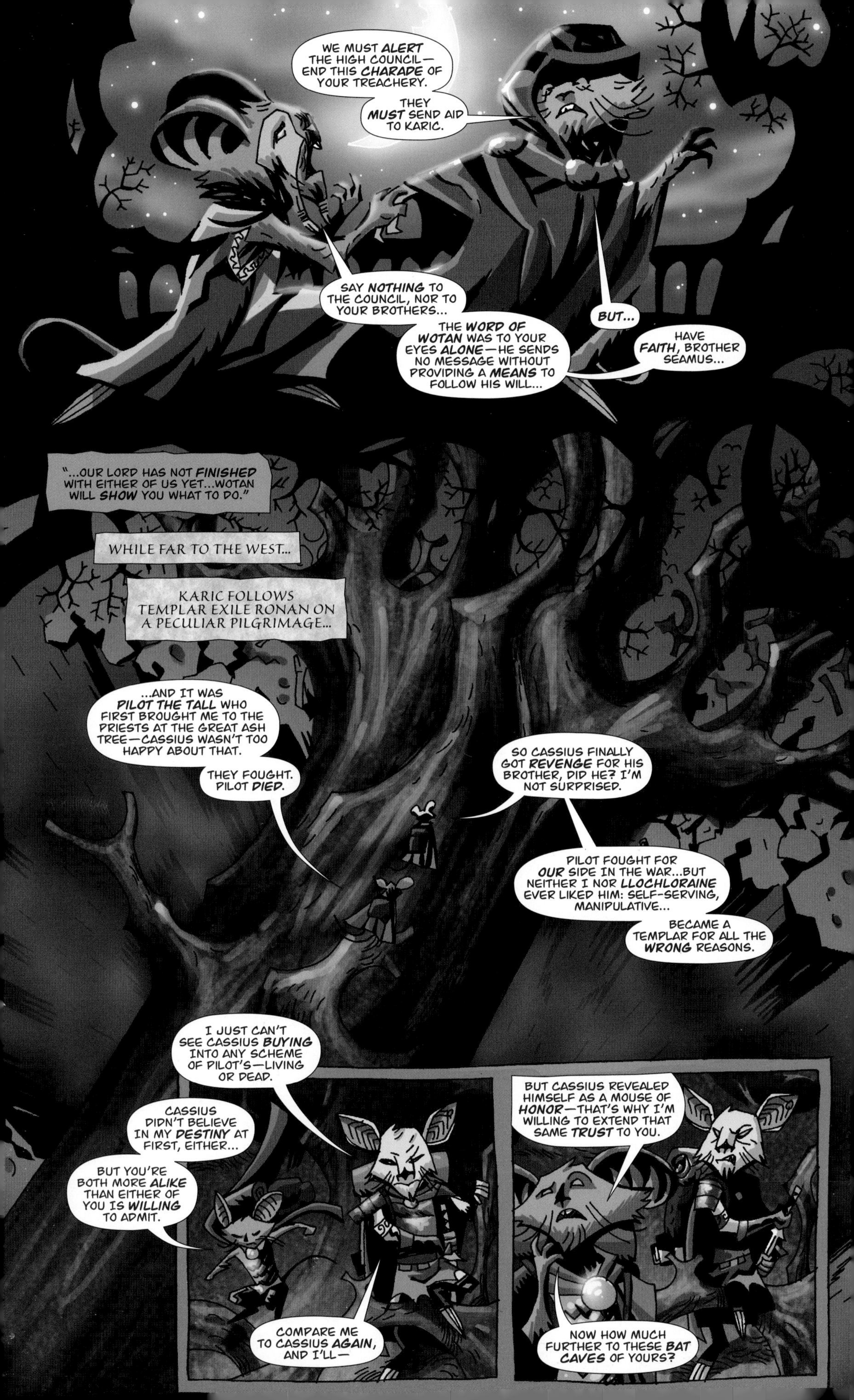
WE MUST ALERT THE HIGH COUNCIL—END THIS CHARADE OF YOUR TREACHERY.
THEY MUST SEND AID TO KARIC.
SAY NOTHING TO THE COUNCIL, NOR TO YOUR BROTHERS...
THE WORD OF WOTAN WAS TO YOUR EYES ALONE—HE SENDS NO MESSAGE WITHOUT PROVIDING A MEANS TO FOLLOW HIS WILL...
BUT...
HAVE FAITH, BROTHER SEAMUS...
"...OUR LORD HAS NOT FINISHED WITH EITHER OF US YET...WOTAN WILL SHOW YOU WHAT TO DO."
WHILE FAR TO THE WEST...
KARIC FOLLOWS TEMPLAR EXILE RONAN ON A PECULIAR PILGRIMAGE...
...AND IT WAS PILOT THE TALL WHO FIRST BROUGHT ME TO THE PRIESTS AT THE GREAT ASH TREE—CASSIUS WASN'T TOO HAPPY ABOUT THAT.
THEY FOUGHT. PILOT DIED.
SO CASSIUS FINALLY GOT REVENGE FOR HIS BROTHER, DID HE? I'M NOT SURPRISED.
PILOT FOUGHT FOR OUR SIDE IN THE WAR...BUT NEITHER I NOR LLOCHLORAINE EVER LIKED HIM: SELF-SERVING, MANIPULATIVE...
BECAME A TEMPLAR FOR ALL THE WRONG REASONS.
I JUST CAN'T SEE CASSIUS BUYING INTO ANY SCHEME OF PILOT'S—LIVING OR DEAD.
CASSIUS DIDN'T BELIEVE IN MY DESTINY AT FIRST, EITHER...
BUT YOU'RE BOTH MORE ALIKE THAN EITHER OF YOU IS WILLING TO ADMIT.
COMPARE ME TO CASSIUS AGAIN, AND I'LL—
BUT CASSIUS REVEALED HIMSELF AS A MOUSE OF HONOR—THAT'S WHY I'M WILLING TO EXTEND THAT SAME TRUST TO YOU.
NOW HOW MUCH FURTHER TO THESE BAT CAVES OF YOURS?

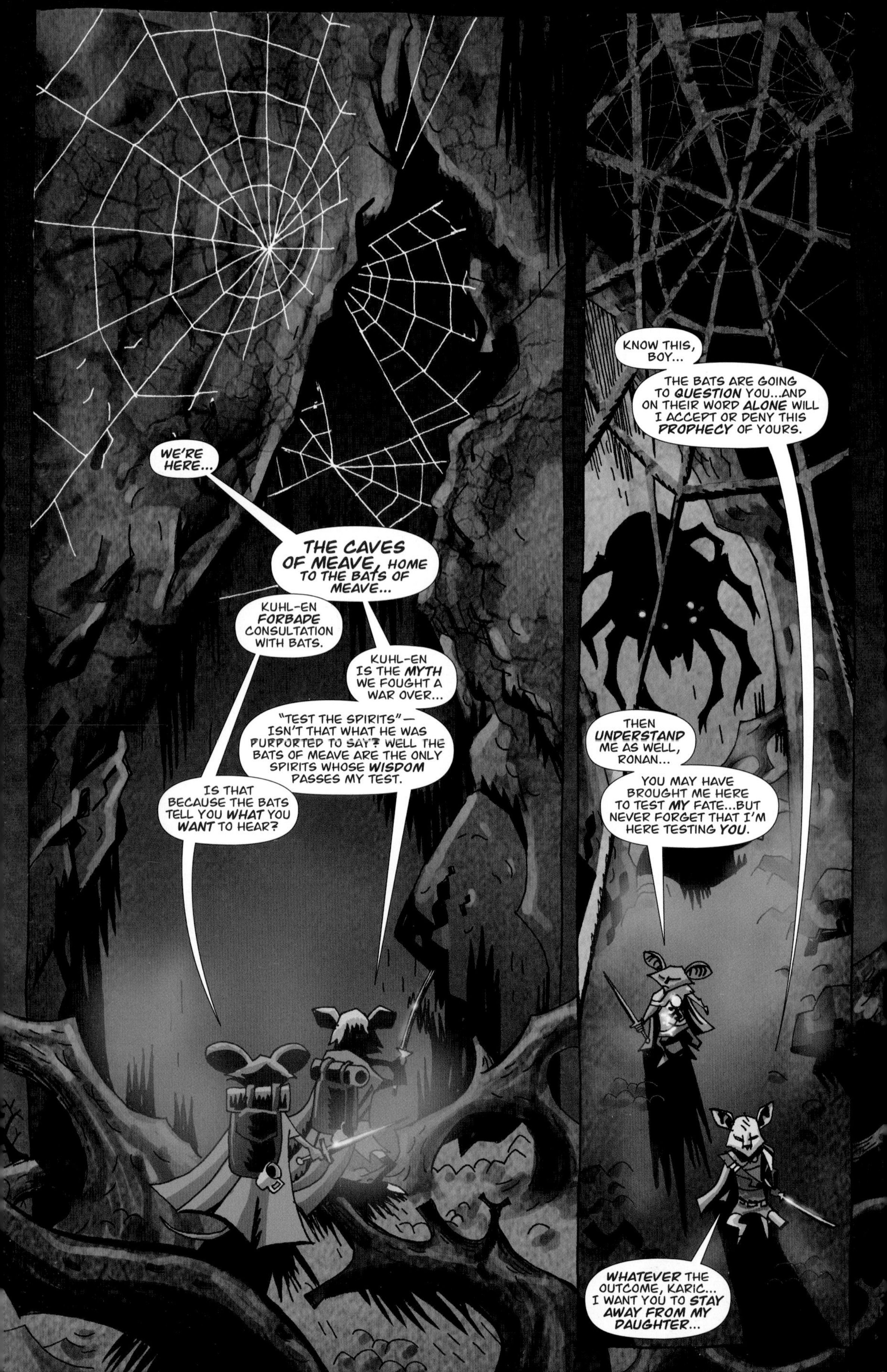

WE'RE HERE...
THE CAVES OF MEAVE, HOME TO THE BATS OF MEAVE...
KUHL-EN FORBADE CONSULTATION WITH BATS.
KUHL-EN IS THE MYTH WE FOUGHT A WAR OVER...
"TEST THE SPIRITS"—ISN'T THAT WHAT HE WAS PURPORTED TO SAY? WELL THE BATS OF MEAVE ARE THE ONLY SPIRITS WHOSE WISDOM PASSES MY TEST.
IS THAT BECAUSE THE BATS TELL YOU WHAT YOU WANT TO HEAR?
KNOW THIS, BOY...
THE BATS ARE GOING TO QUESTION YOU...AND ON THEIR WORD ALONE WILL I ACCEPT OR DENY THIS PROPHECY OF YOURS.
THEN UNDERSTAND ME AS WELL, RONAN...
YOU MAY HAVE BROUGHT ME HERE TO TEST MY FATE...BUT NEVER FORGET THAT I'M HERE TESTING YOU.
WHATEVER THE OUTCOME, KARIC... I WANT YOU TO STAY AWAY FROM MY DAUGHTER...

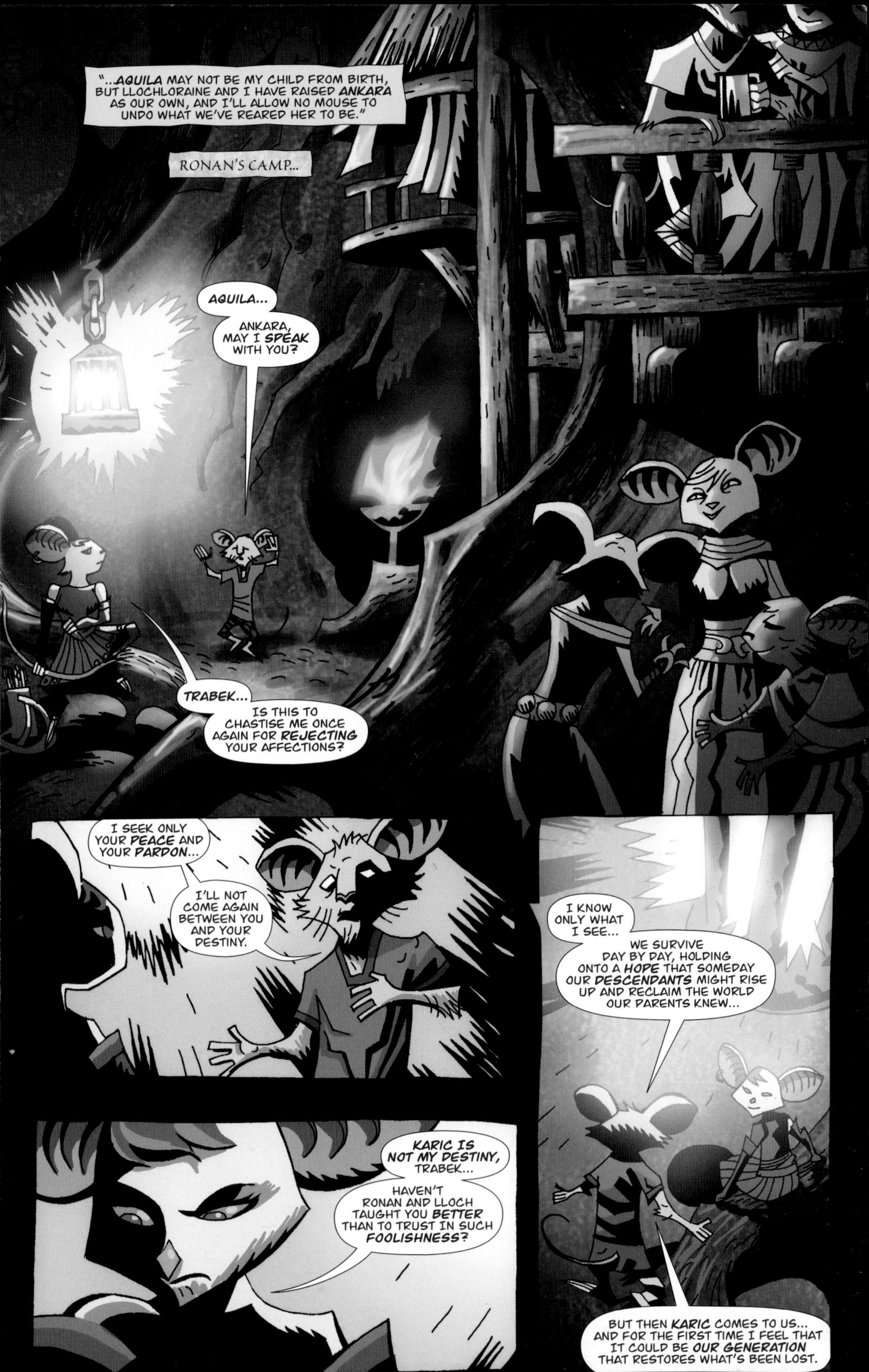
"...AQUILA MAY NOT BE MY CHILD FROM BIRTH, BUT LLOCHLORAINE AND I HAVE RAISED ANKARA AS OUR OWN, AND I'LL ALLOW NO MOUSE TO UNDO WHAT WE'VE REARED HER TO BE."
RONAN'S CAMP...
AQUILA...
ANKARA, MAY I SPEAK WITH YOU?
TRABEK...
IS THIS TO CHASTISE ME ONCE AGAIN FOR REJECTING YOUR AFFECTIONS?
I SEEK ONLY YOUR PEACE AND YOUR PARDON...
I'LL NOT COME AGAIN BETWEEN YOU AND YOUR DESTINY.
KARIC IS NOT MY DESTINY, TRABEK...
HAVEN'T RONAN AND LLOCH TAUGHT YOU BETTER THAN TO TRUST IN SUCH FOOLISHNESS?
I KNOW ONLY WHAT I SEE...
WE SURVIVE DAY BY DAY, HOLDING ONTO A HOPE THAT SOMEDAY OUR DESCENDANTS MIGHT RISE UP AND RECLAIM THE WORLD OUR PARENTS KNEW...
BUT THEN KARIC COMES TO US... AND FOR THE FIRST TIME I FEEL THAT IT COULD BE OUR GENERATION THAT RESTORES WHAT'S BEEN LOST.

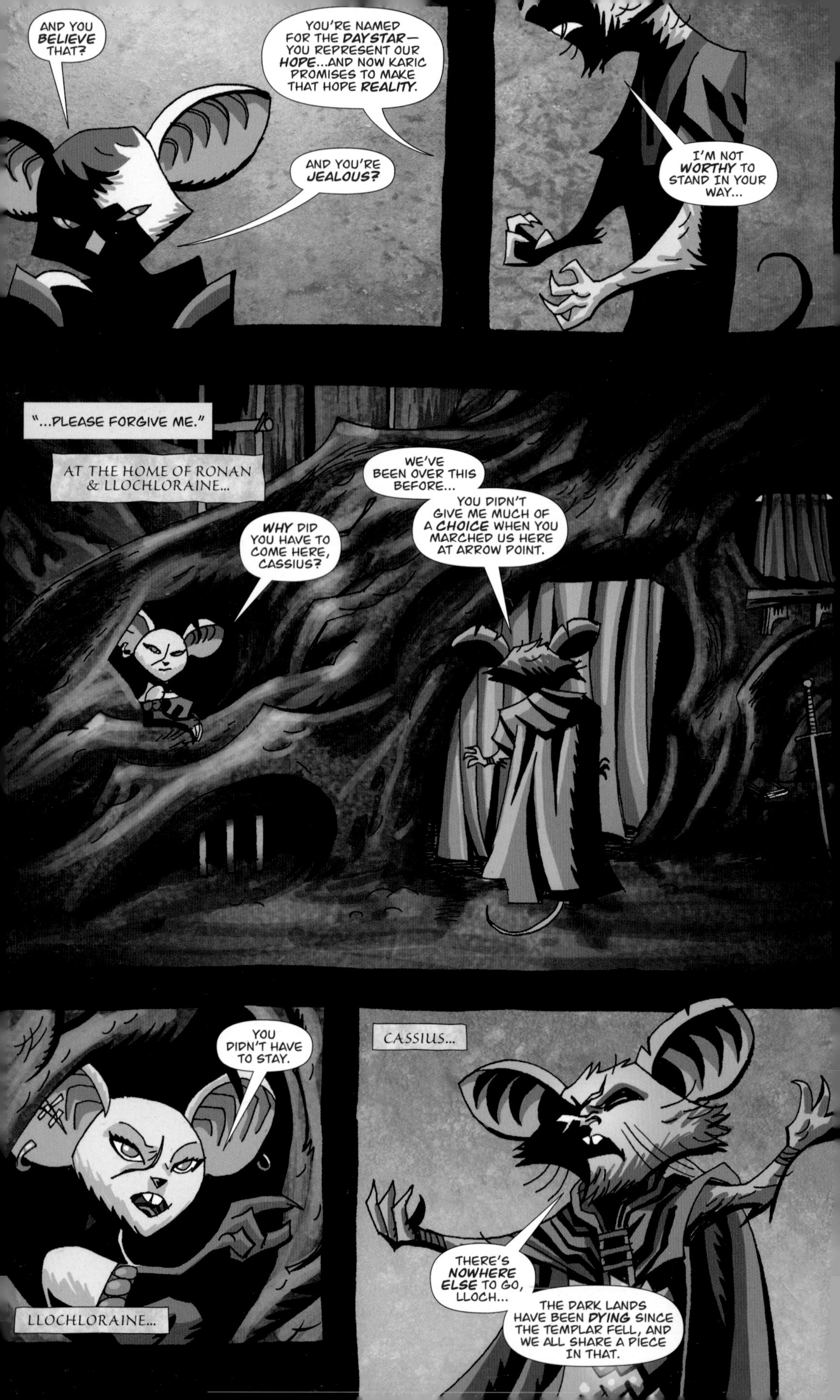
AND YOU BELIEVE THAT?
YOU'RE NAMED FOR THE DAYSTAR— YOU REPRESENT OUR HOPE...AND NOW KARIC PROMISES TO MAKE THAT HOPE REALITY.
AND YOU'RE JEALOUS?
I'M NOT WORTHY TO STAND IN YOUR WAY...
"...PLEASE FORGIVE ME."
AT THE HOME OF RONAN & LLOCHLORAINE...
WHY DID YOU HAVE TO COME HERE, CASSIUS?
WE'VE BEEN OVER THIS BEFORE...
YOU DIDN'T GIVE ME MUCH OF A CHOICE WHEN YOU MARCHED US HERE AT ARROW POINT.
YOU DIDN'T HAVE TO STAY.
LLOCHLORAINE...
CASSIUS...
THERE'S NOWHERE ELSE TO GO, LLOCH...
THE DARK LANDS HAVE BEEN DYING SINCE THE TEMPLAR FELL, AND WE ALL SHARE A PIECE IN THAT.

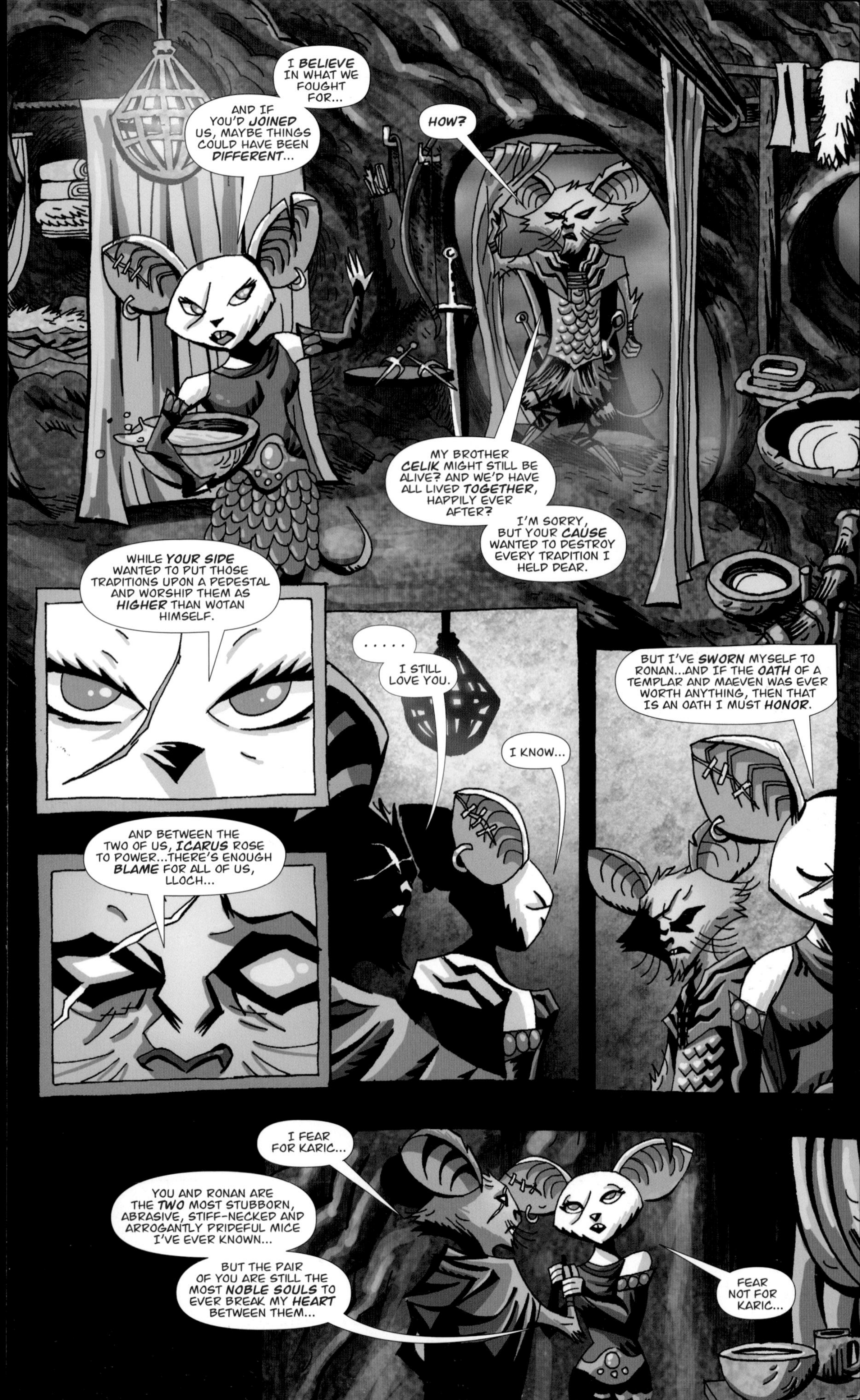
I BELIEVE IN WHAT WE FOUGHT FOR...
AND IF YOU'D JOINED US, MAYBE THINGS COULD HAVE BEEN DIFFERENT...
HOW?
MY BROTHER CELIK MIGHT STILL BE ALIVE? AND WE'D HAVE ALL LIVED TOGETHER, HAPPILY EVER AFTER?
I'M SORRY, BUT YOUR CAUSE WANTED TO DESTROY EVERY TRADITION I HELD DEAR.
WHILE YOUR SIDE WANTED TO PUT THOSE TRADITIONS UPON A PEDESTAL AND WORSHIP THEM AS HIGHER THAN WOTAN HIMSELF.
AND BETWEEN THE TWO OF US, ICARUS ROSE TO POWER...THERE'S ENOUGH BLAME FOR ALL OF US, LLOCH...
. . . . .
I STILL LOVE YOU.
I KNOW...
BUT I'VE SWORN MYSELF TO RONAN...AND IF THE OATH OF A TEMPLAR AND MAEVEN WAS EVER WORTH ANYTHING, THEN THAT IS AN OATH I MUST HONOR.
I FEAR FOR KARIC...
YOU AND RONAN ARE THE TWO MOST STUBBORN, ABRASIVE, STIFF-NECKED AND ARROGANTLY PRIDEFUL MICE I'VE EVER KNOWN...
BUT THE PAIR OF YOU ARE STILL THE MOST NOBLE SOULS TO EVER BREAK MY HEART BETWEEN THEM...
FEAR NOT FOR KARIC...

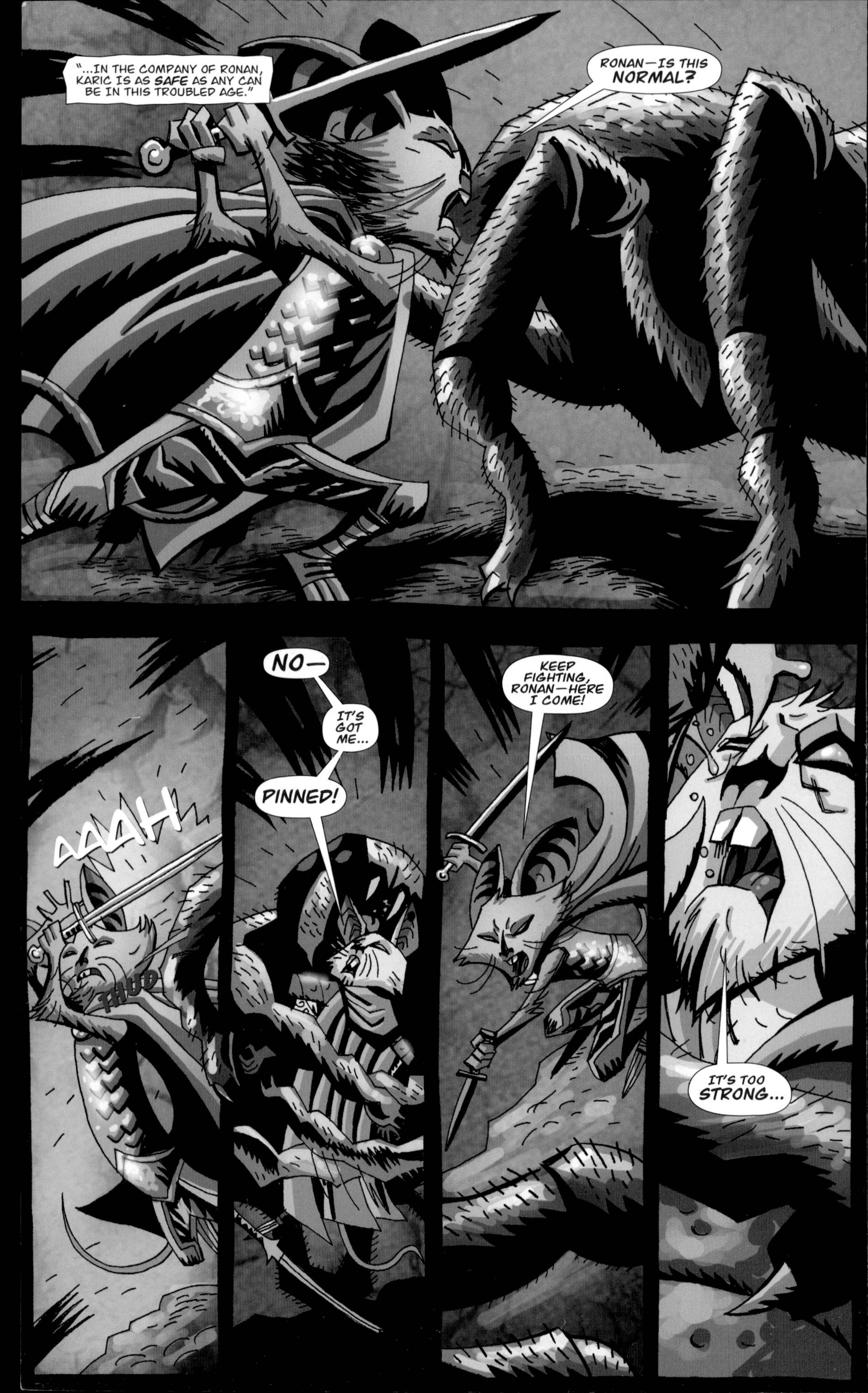
"...IN THE COMPANY OF RONAN, KARIC IS AS SAFE AS ANY CAN BE IN THIS TROUBLED AGE."
RONAN—IS THIS NORMAL?
AAAH
THUD
NO—
IT'S GOT ME...
PINNED!
KEEP FIGHTING, RONAN—HERE I COME!
IT'S TOO STRONG...

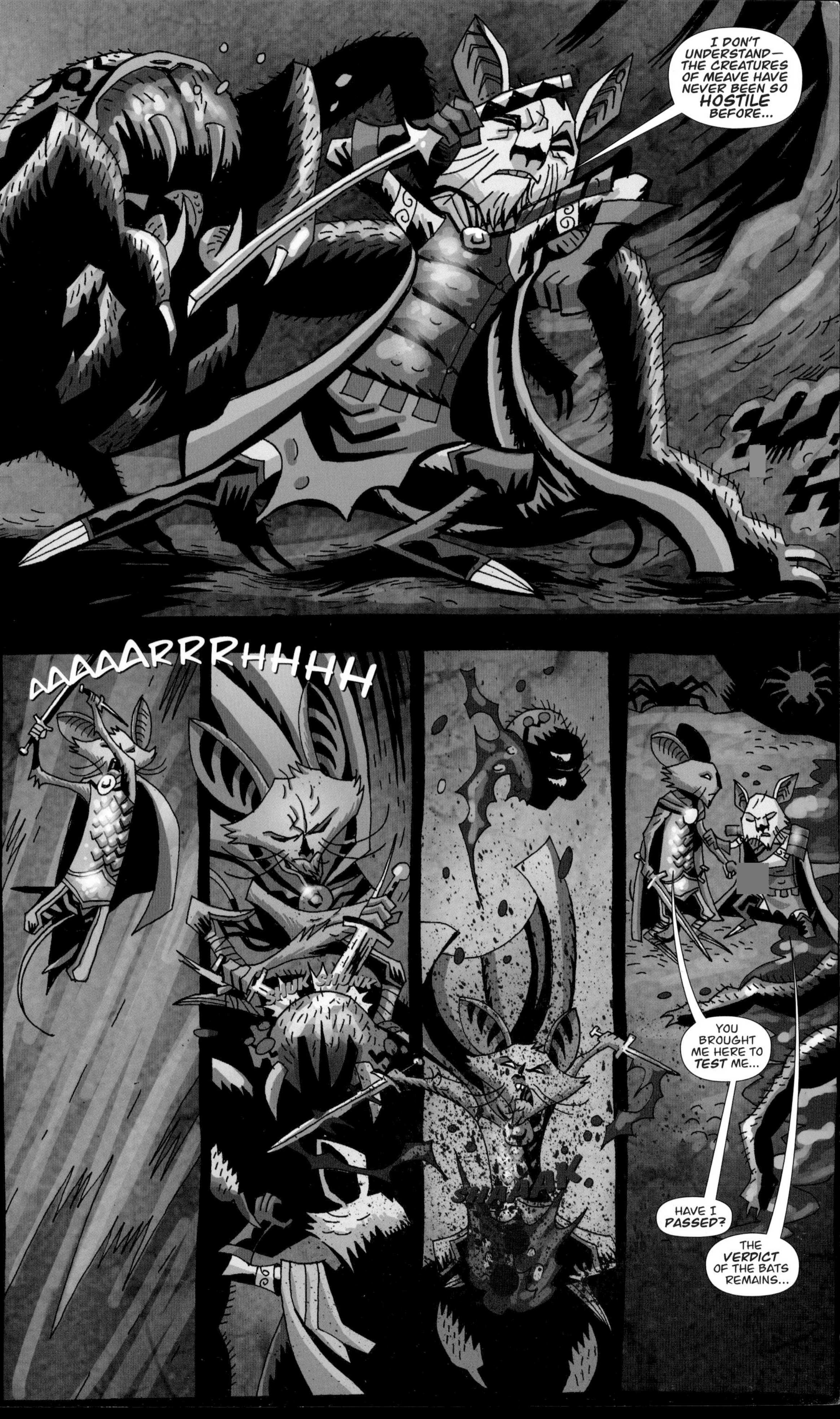
I DON'T UNDERSTAND—THE CREATURES OF MEAVE HAVE NEVER BEEN SO HOSTILE BEFORE...
AAAAARRRRHHHHH
SHUK SHUNK
SHHHAAK
YOU BROUGHT ME HERE TO TEST ME...
HAVE I PASSED?
THE VERDICT OF THE BATS REMAINS...

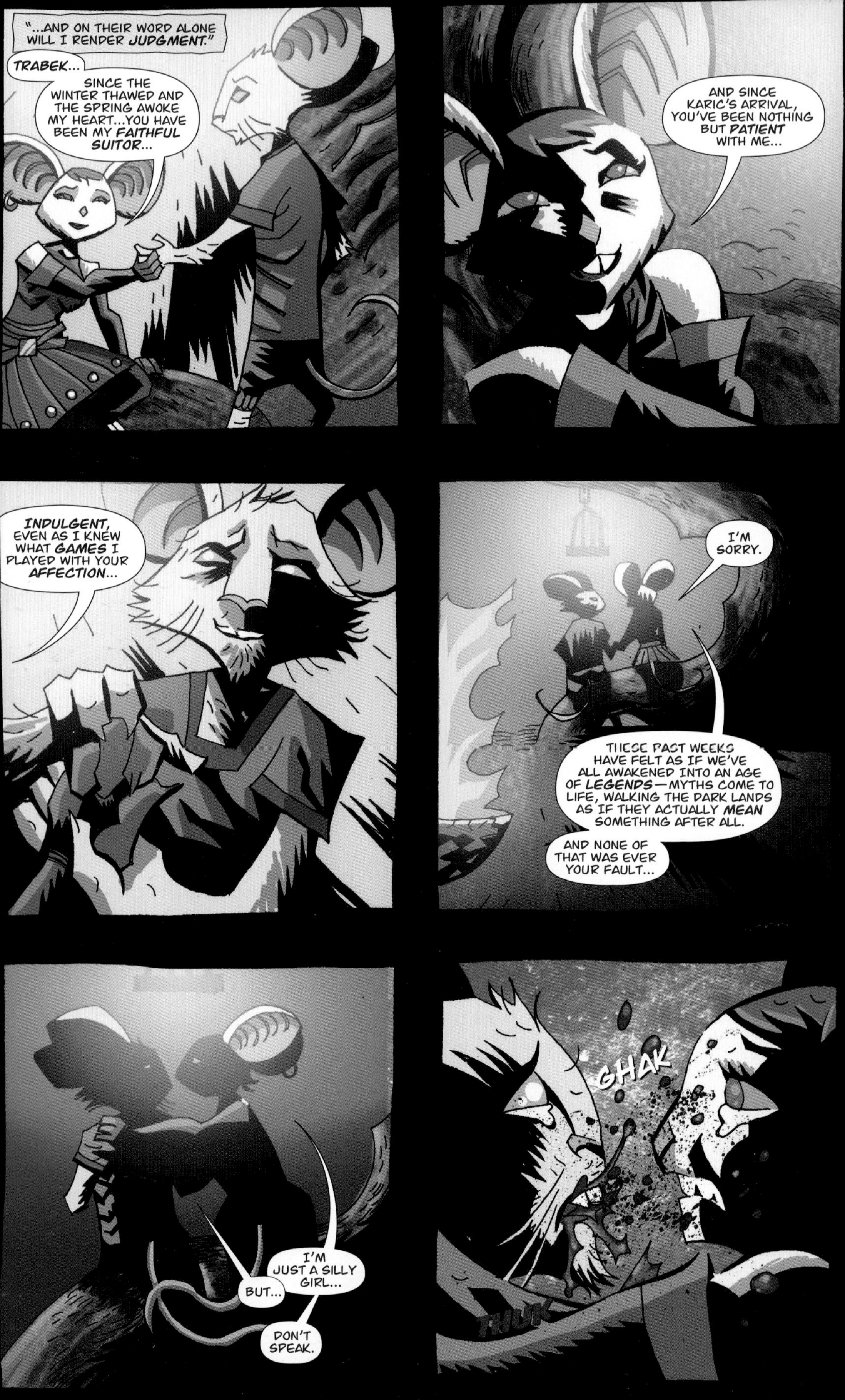
"...AND ON THEIR WORD ALONE WILL I RENDER **JUDGMENT.**"
TRABEK...
SINCE THE WINTER THAWED AND THE SPRING AWOKE MY HEART...YOU HAVE BEEN MY **FAITHFUL SUITOR...**
AND SINCE KARIC'S ARRIVAL, YOU'VE BEEN NOTHING BUT **PATIENT** WITH ME...
INDULGENT, EVEN AS I KNEW WHAT **GAMES** I PLAYED WITH YOUR **AFFECTION...**
I'M SORRY.
THESE PAST WEEKS HAVE FELT AS IF WE'VE ALL AWAKENED INTO AN AGE OF **LEGENDS**—MYTHS COME TO LIFE, WALKING THE DARK LANDS AS IF THEY ACTUALLY **MEAN** SOMETHING AFTER ALL.
AND NONE OF THAT WAS EVER YOUR FAULT...
I'M JUST A SILLY GIRL...
BUT...
DON'T SPEAK.
GHAK
THUK

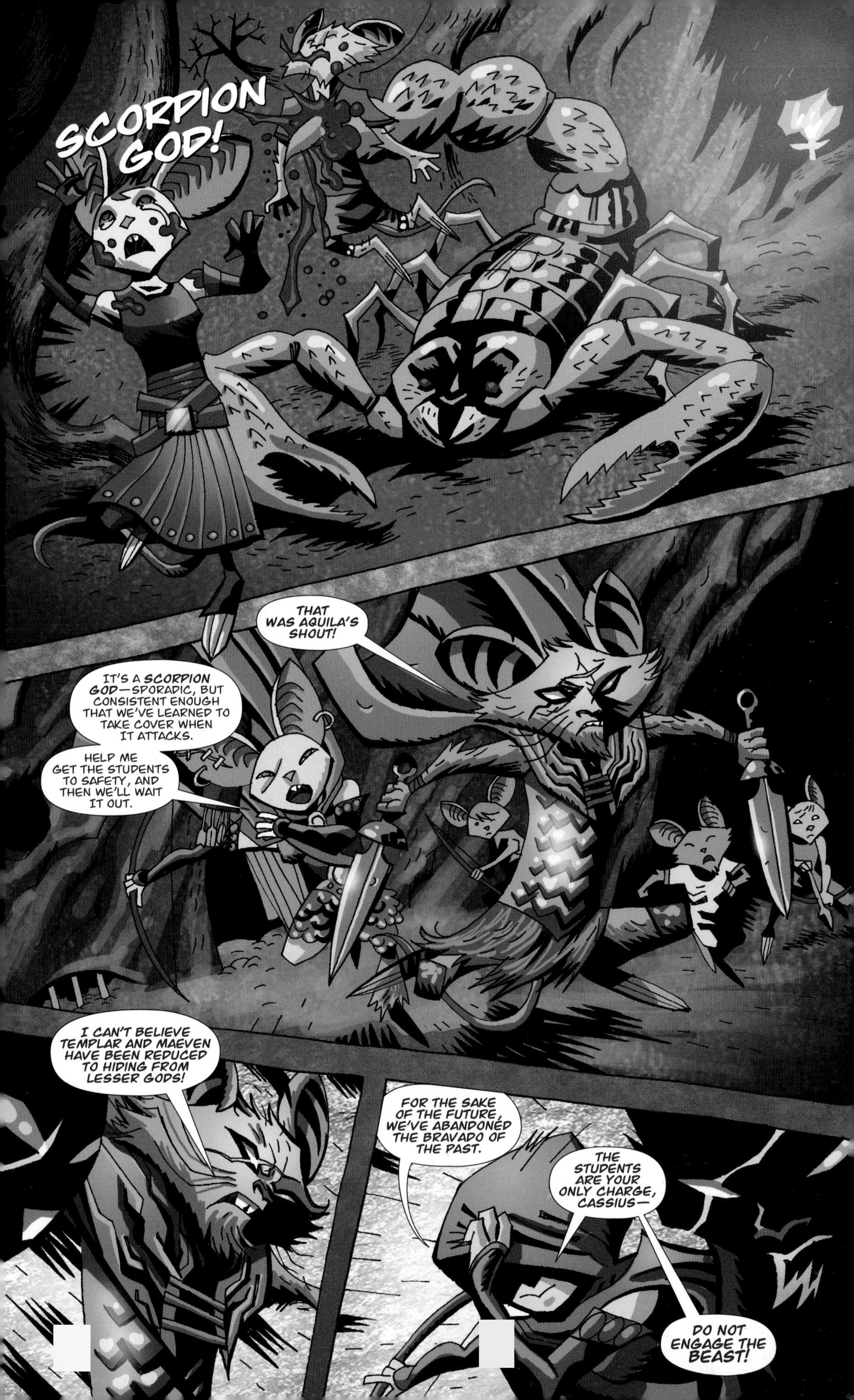
SCORPION GOD!
THAT WAS AQUILA'S SHOUT!
IT'S A SCORPION GOD—SPORADIC, BUT CONSISTENT ENOUGH THAT WE'VE LEARNED TO TAKE COVER WHEN IT ATTACKS.
HELP ME GET THE STUDENTS TO SAFETY, AND THEN WE'LL WAIT IT OUT.
I CAN'T BELIEVE TEMPLAR AND MAEVEN HAVE BEEN REDUCED TO HIDING FROM LESSER GODS!
FOR THE SAKE OF THE FUTURE, WE'VE ABANDONED THE BRAVADO OF THE PAST.
THE STUDENTS ARE YOUR ONLY CHARGE, CASSIUS—
DO NOT ENGAGE THE BEAST!

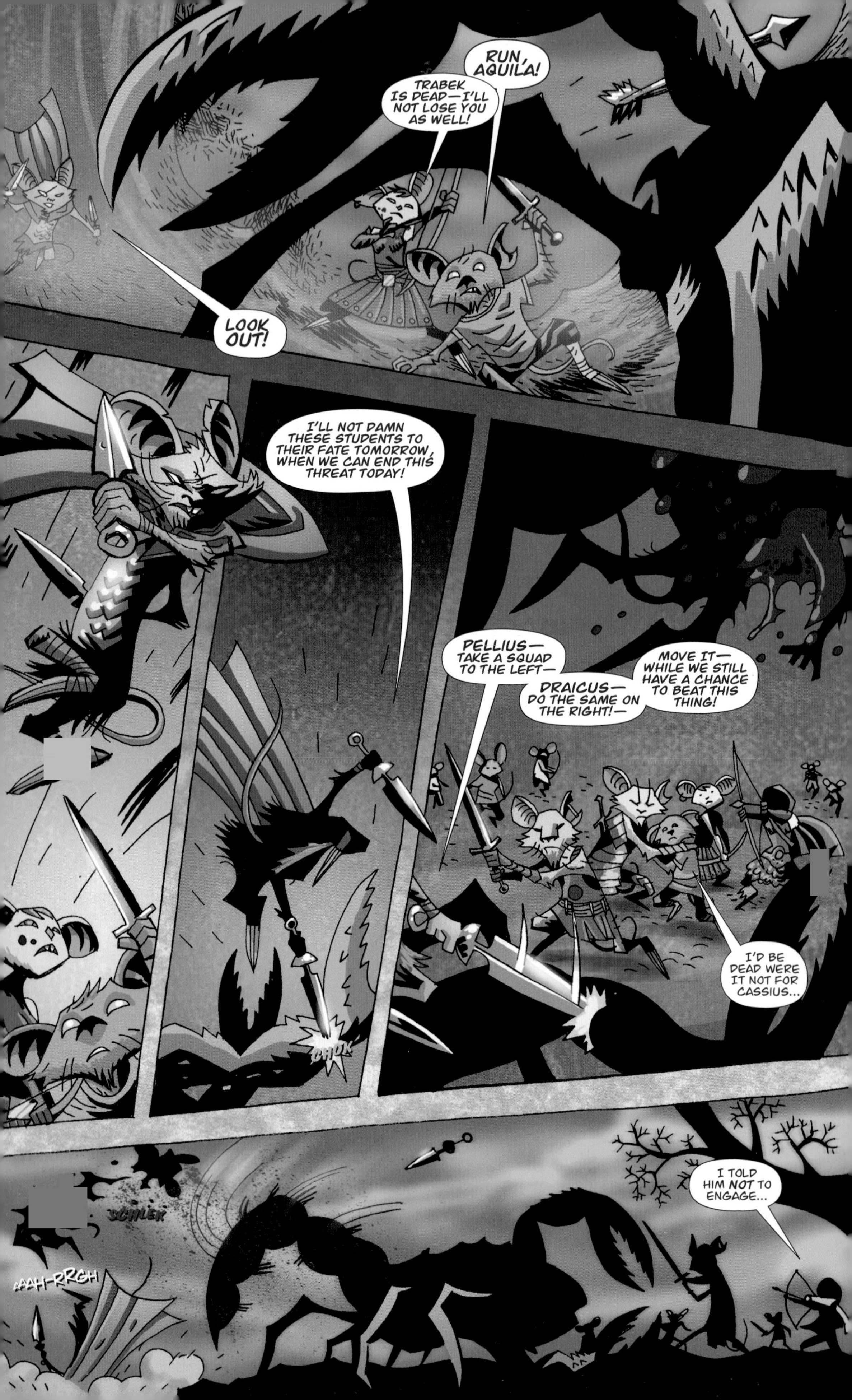
RUN, AQUILA!
TRABEK IS DEAD—I'LL NOT LOSE YOU AS WELL!
LOOK OUT!
I'LL NOT DAMN THESE STUDENTS TO THEIR FATE TOMORROW, WHEN WE CAN END THIS THREAT TODAY!
CHOK
PELLIUS—TAKE A SQUAD TO THE LEFT—
DRAICUS—DO THE SAME ON THE RIGHT!—
MOVE IT—WHILE WE STILL HAVE A CHANCE TO BEAT THIS THING!
I'D BE DEAD WERE IT NOT FOR CASSIUS...
SCHLEK
AAAH-RRGH
I TOLD HIM NOT TO ENGAGE...

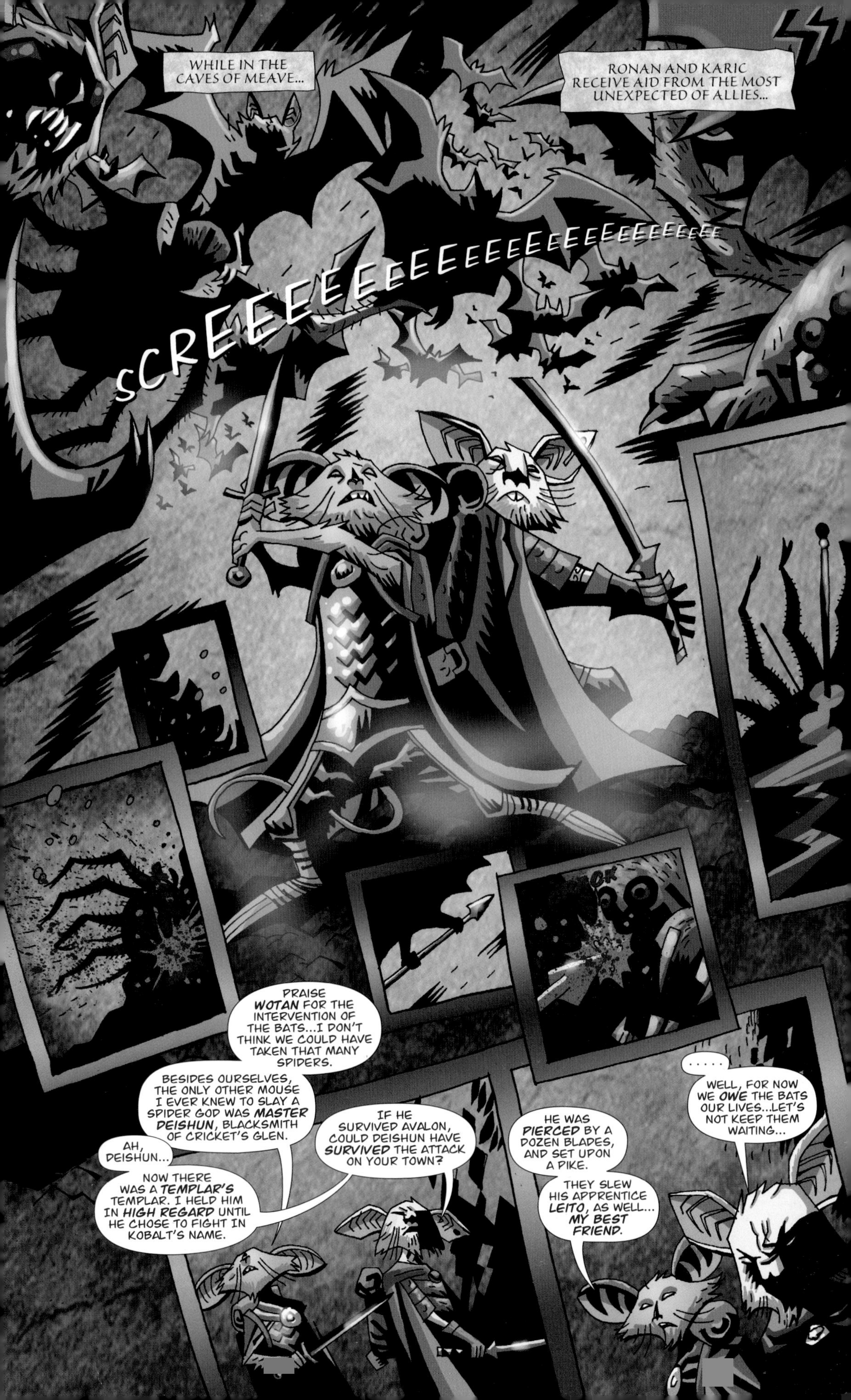
WHILE IN THE CAVES OF MEAVE...
RONAN AND KARIC RECEIVE AID FROM THE MOST UNEXPECTED OF ALLIES...
sCREEEEEEEEEEEEEEEEEEEEEEEEEE
PRAISE WOTAN FOR THE INTERVENTION OF THE BATS...I DON'T THINK WE COULD HAVE TAKEN THAT MANY SPIDERS.
BESIDES OURSELVES, THE ONLY OTHER MOUSE I EVER KNEW TO SLAY A SPIDER GOD WAS MASTER DEISHUN, BLACKSMITH OF CRICKET'S GLEN.
AH, DEISHUN...
NOW THERE WAS A TEMPLAR'S TEMPLAR. I HELD HIM IN HIGH REGARD UNTIL HE CHOSE TO FIGHT IN KOBALT'S NAME.
IF HE SURVIVED AVALON, COULD DEISHUN HAVE SURVIVED THE ATTACK ON YOUR TOWN?
HE WAS PIERCED BY A DOZEN BLADES, AND SET UPON A PIKE.
THEY SLEW HIS APPRENTICE LEITO, AS WELL... MY BEST FRIEND.
. . . . .
WELL, FOR NOW WE OWE THE BATS OUR LIVES...LET'S NOT KEEP THEM WAITING...

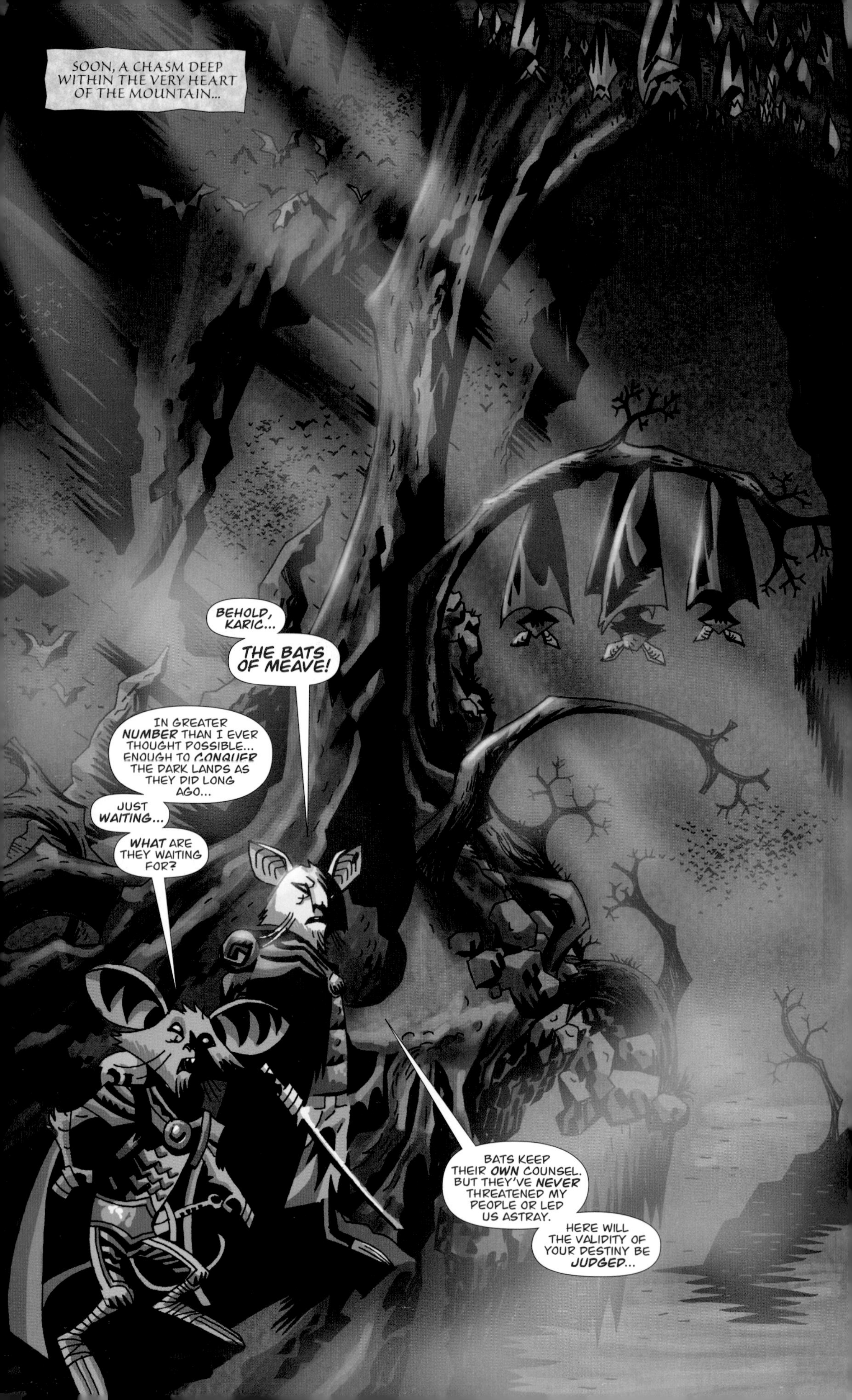
SOON, A CHASM DEEP WITHIN THE VERY HEART OF THE MOUNTAIN...
BEHOLD, KARIC...
THE BATS OF MEAVE!
IN GREATER NUMBER THAN I EVER THOUGHT POSSIBLE... ENOUGH TO CONQUER THE DARK LANDS AS THEY DID LONG AGO...
JUST WAITING...
WHAT ARE THEY WAITING FOR?
BATS KEEP THEIR OWN COUNSEL. BUT THEY'VE NEVER THREATENED MY PEOPLE OR LED US ASTRAY.
HERE WILL THE VALIDITY OF YOUR DESTINY BE JUDGED...

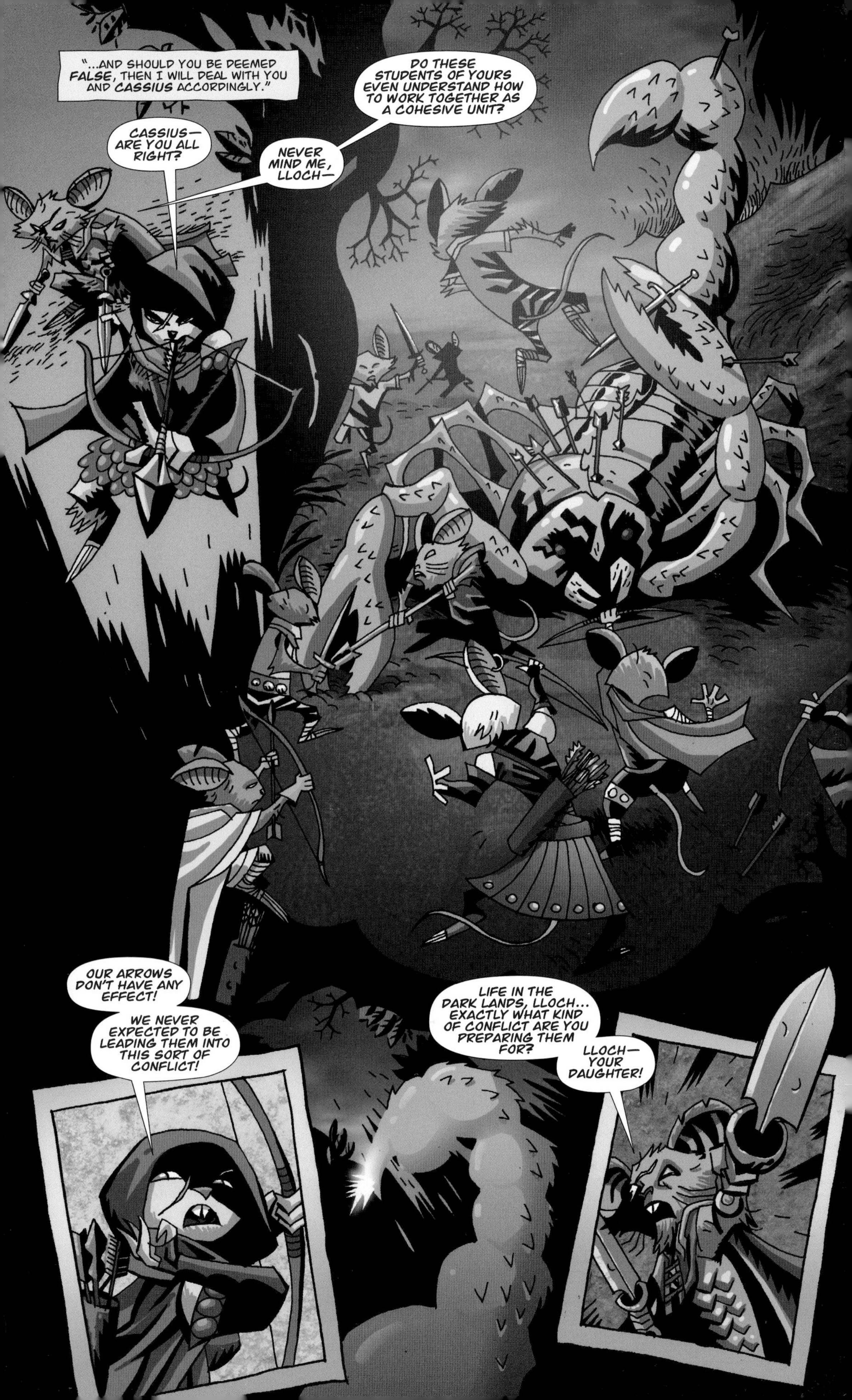
"...AND SHOULD YOU BE DEEMED **FALSE**, THEN I WILL DEAL WITH YOU AND **CASSIUS** ACCORDINGLY."
CASSIUS— ARE YOU ALL RIGHT?
NEVER MIND ME, LLOCH—
DO THESE STUDENTS OF YOURS EVEN UNDERSTAND HOW TO WORK TOGETHER AS A COHESIVE UNIT?
OUR ARROWS DON'T HAVE ANY EFFECT!
WE NEVER EXPECTED TO BE LEADING THEM INTO THIS SORT OF CONFLICT!
LIFE IN THE DARK LANDS, LLOCH... EXACTLY WHAT KIND OF CONFLICT ARE YOU PREPARING THEM FOR?
LLOCH— YOUR DAUGHTER!

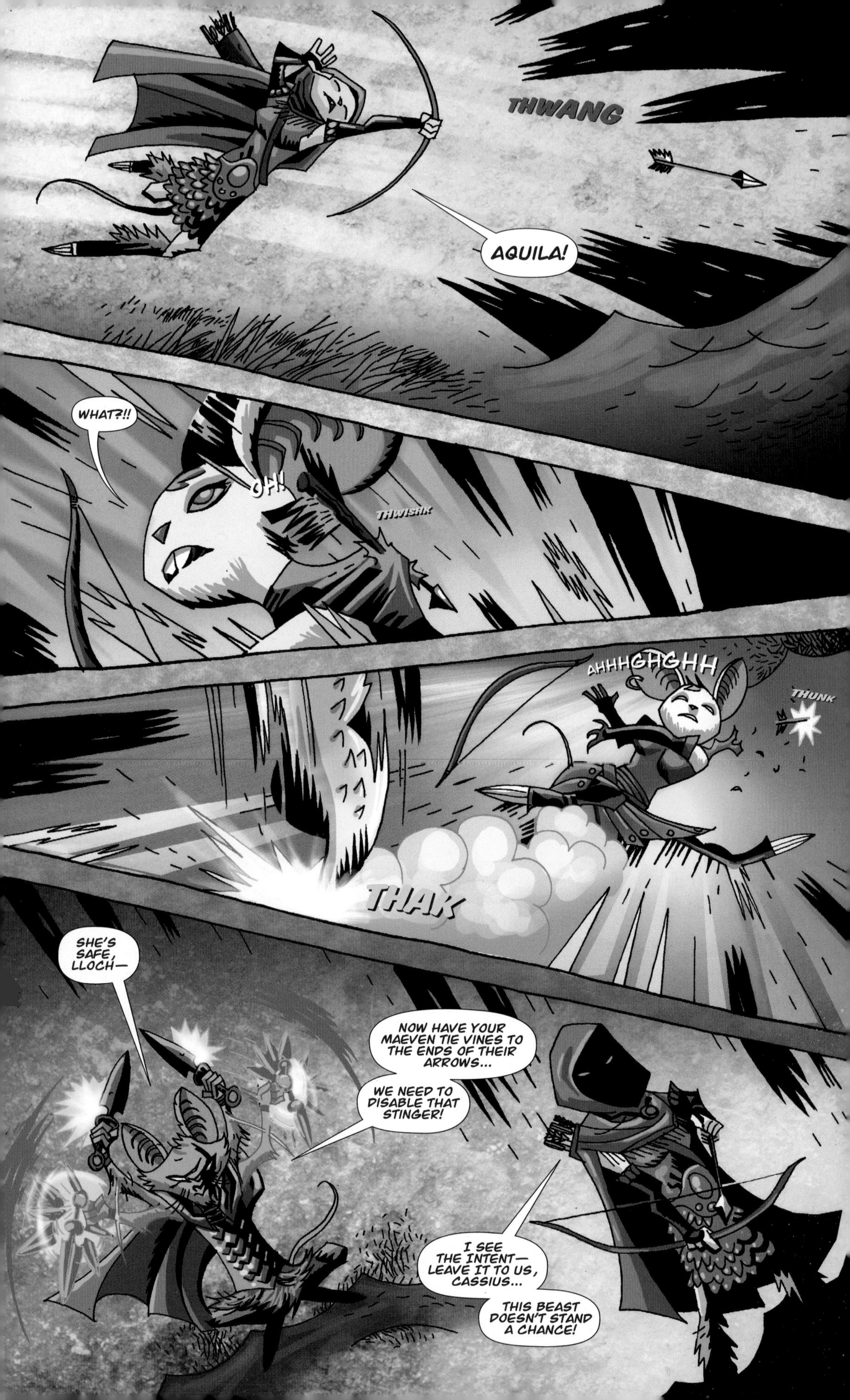
THWANG
AQUILA!
WHAT?!!
OH!
THWISHK
AHHHGHGHH
THUNK
THAK
SHE'S SAFE, LLOCH—
NOW HAVE YOUR MAEVEN TIE VINES TO THE ENDS OF THEIR ARROWS...
WE NEED TO DISABLE THAT STINGER!
I SEE THE INTENT— LEAVE IT TO US, CASSIUS...
THIS BEAST DOESN'T STAND A CHANCE!

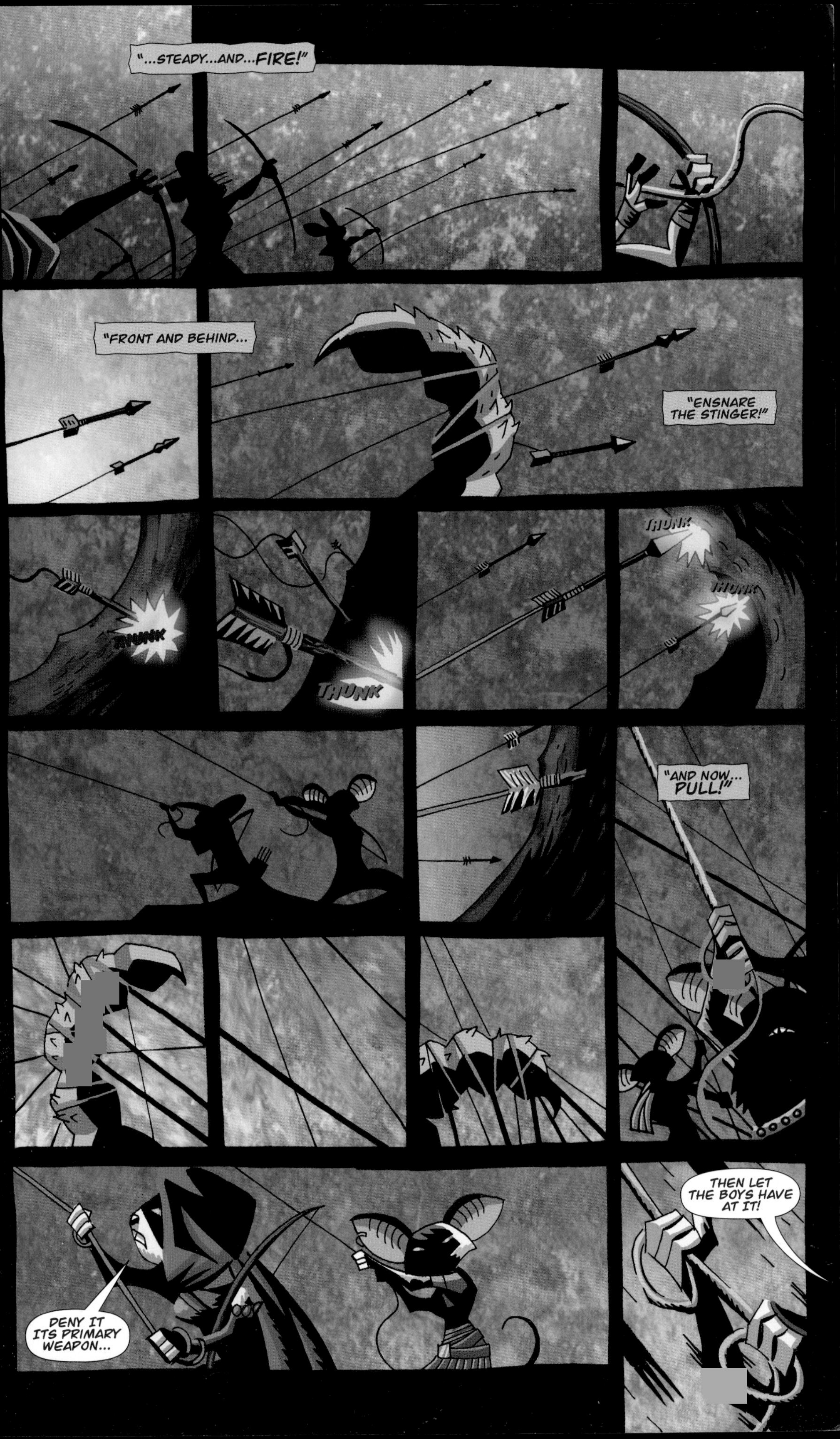
"...STEADY...AND...FIRE!"
"FRONT AND BEHIND...
"ENSNARE THE STINGER!"
THUNK
THUNK
THUNK
THUNK
"AND NOW... PULL!"
DENY IT ITS PRIMARY WEAPON...
THEN LET THE BOYS HAVE AT IT!

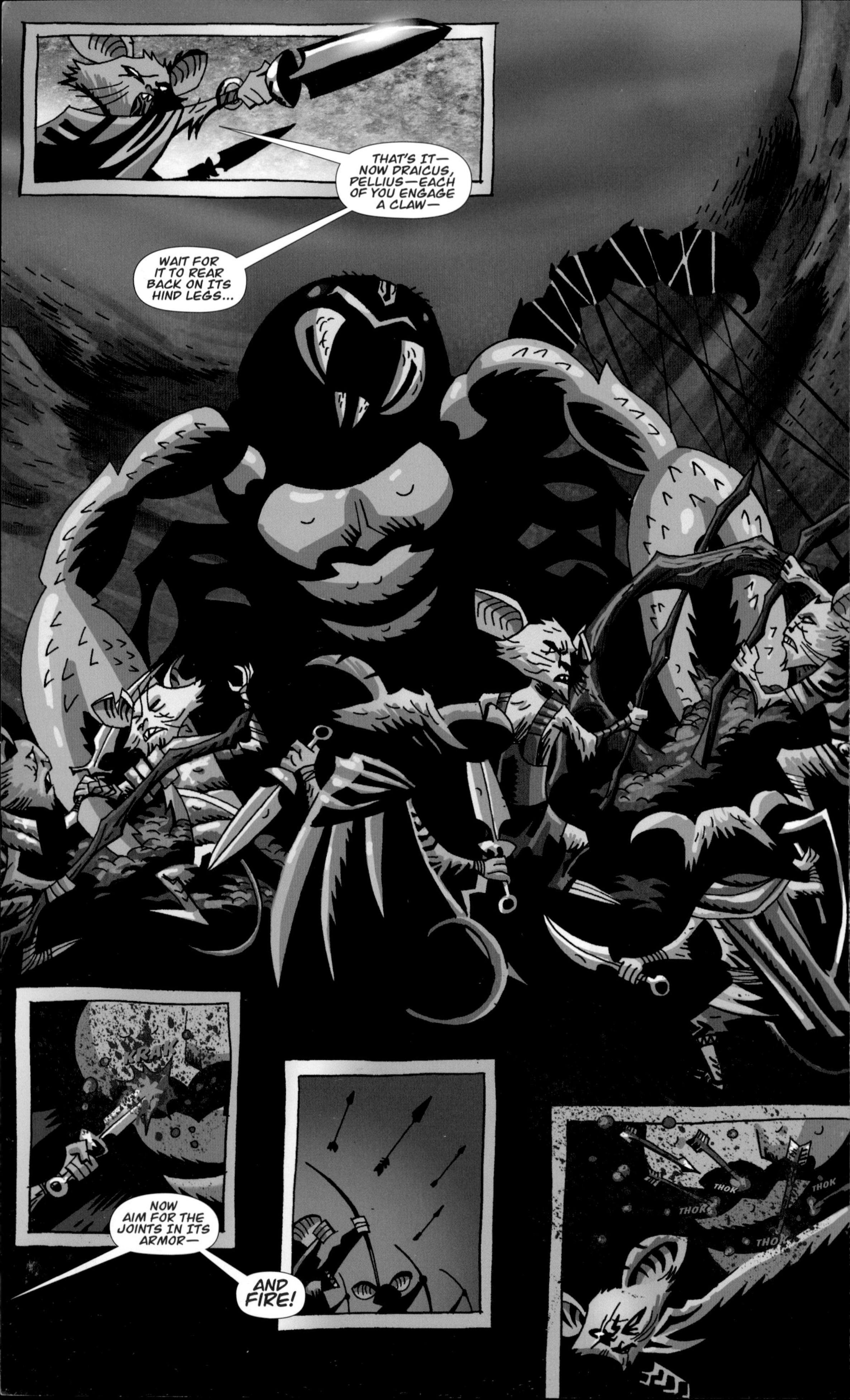
THAT'S IT—NOW DRAICUS, PELLIUS—EACH OF YOU ENGAGE A CLAW—
WAIT FOR IT TO REAR BACK ON ITS HIND LEGS...
KRAK
NOW AIM FOR THE JOINTS IN ITS ARMOR—
AND FIRE!
THOK
THOK
THOK
THOK

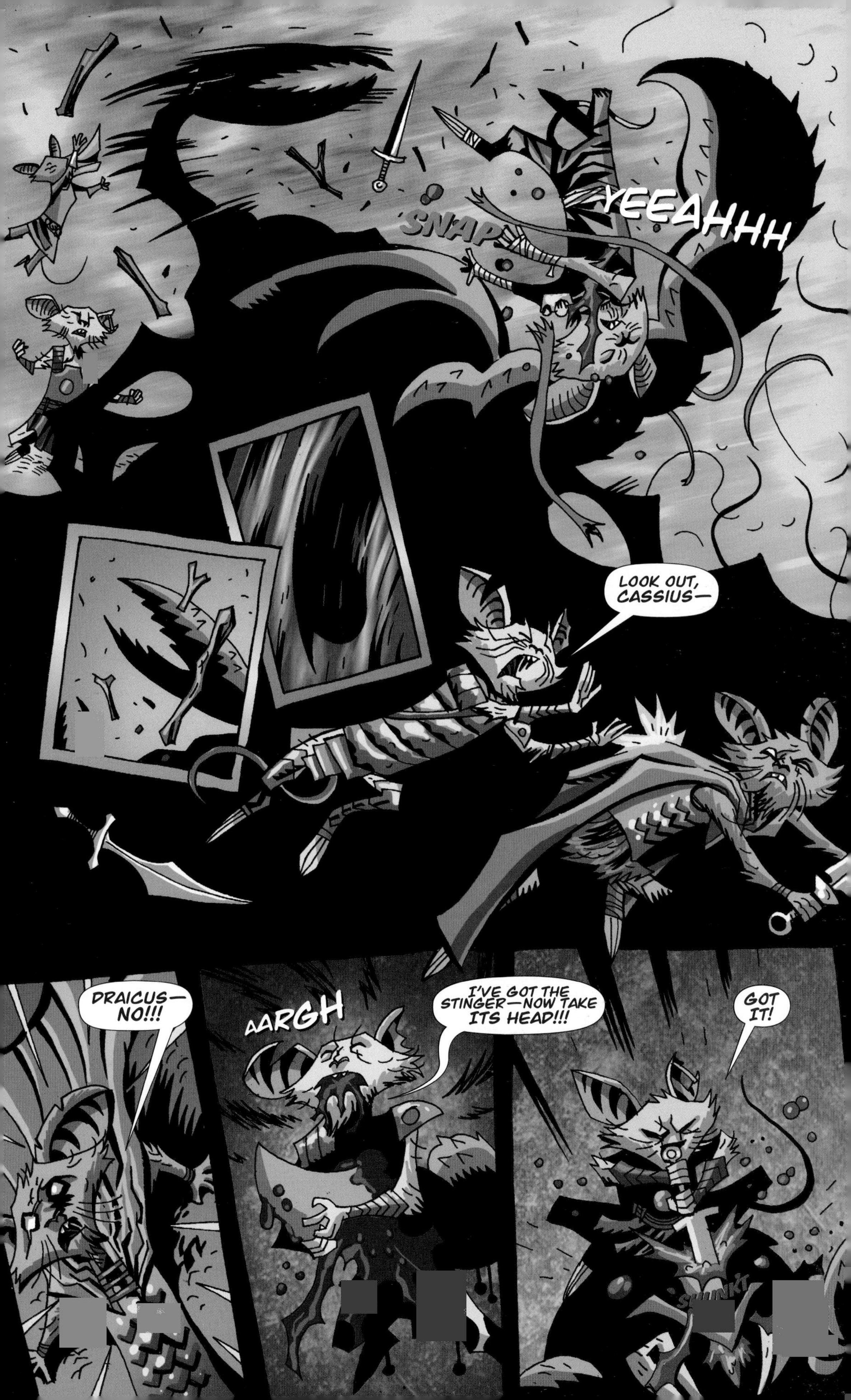

SNAP
YEEAHHH
LOOK OUT, CASSIUS—
DRAICUS—NO!!!
AARGH
I'VE GOT THE STINGER—NOW TAKE ITS HEAD!!!
GOT IT!
SHUNKT

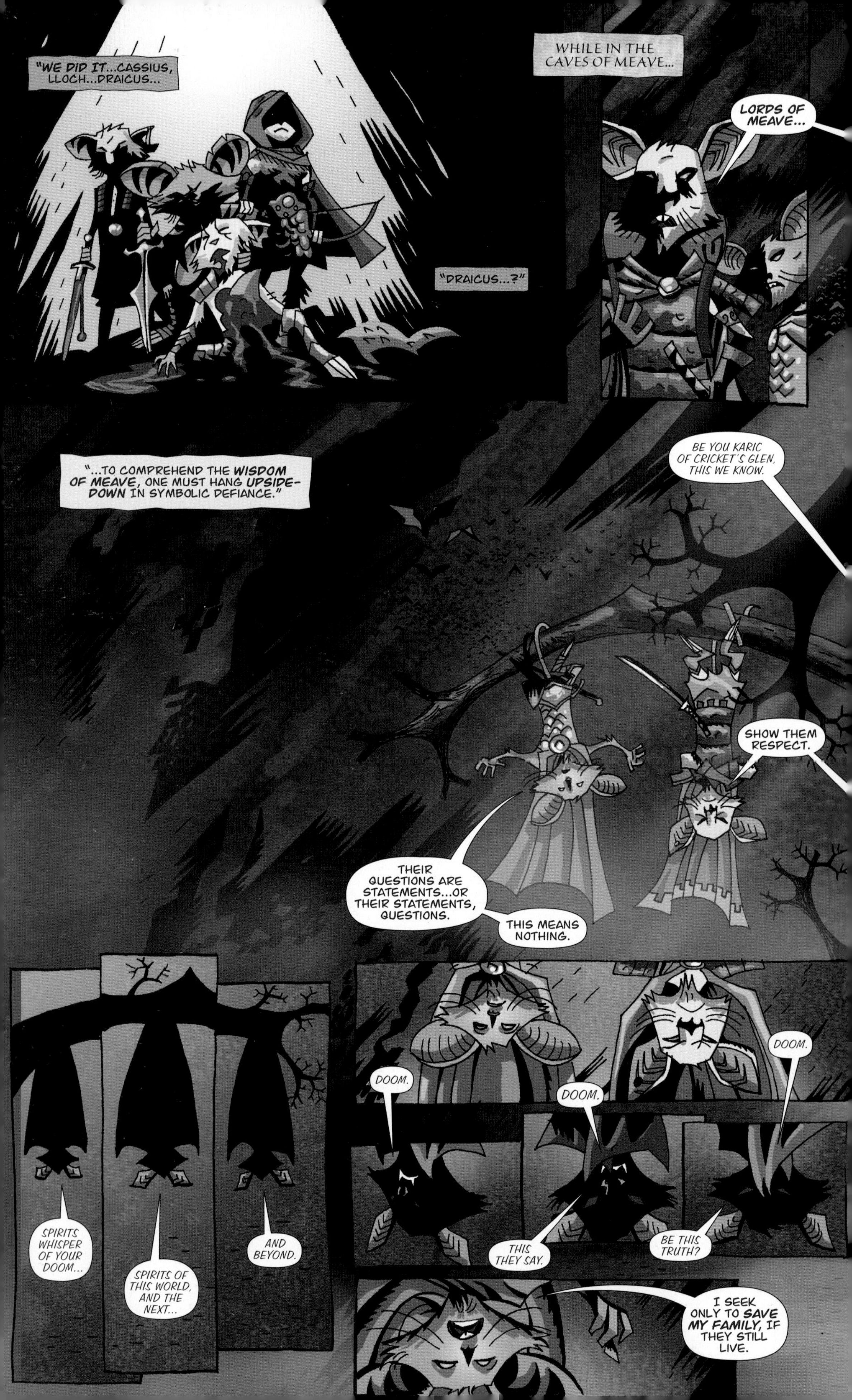
"WE DID IT...CASSIUS, LLOCH...DRAICUS...
"DRAICUS...?"
WHILE IN THE CAVES OF MEAVE...
LORDS OF MEAVE...
"...TO COMPREHEND THE WISDOM OF MEAVE, ONE MUST HANG UPSIDE-DOWN IN SYMBOLIC DEFIANCE."
BE YOU KARIC OF CRICKET'S GLEN, THIS WE KNOW.
SHOW THEM RESPECT.
THEIR QUESTIONS ARE STATEMENTS...OR THEIR STATEMENTS, QUESTIONS.
THIS MEANS NOTHING.
SPIRITS WHISPER OF YOUR DOOM...
SPIRITS OF THIS WORLD, AND THE NEXT...
AND BEYOND.
DOOM.
DOOM.
DOOM.
THIS THEY SAY.
BE THIS TRUTH?
I SEEK ONLY TO SAVE MY FAMILY, IF THEY STILL LIVE.

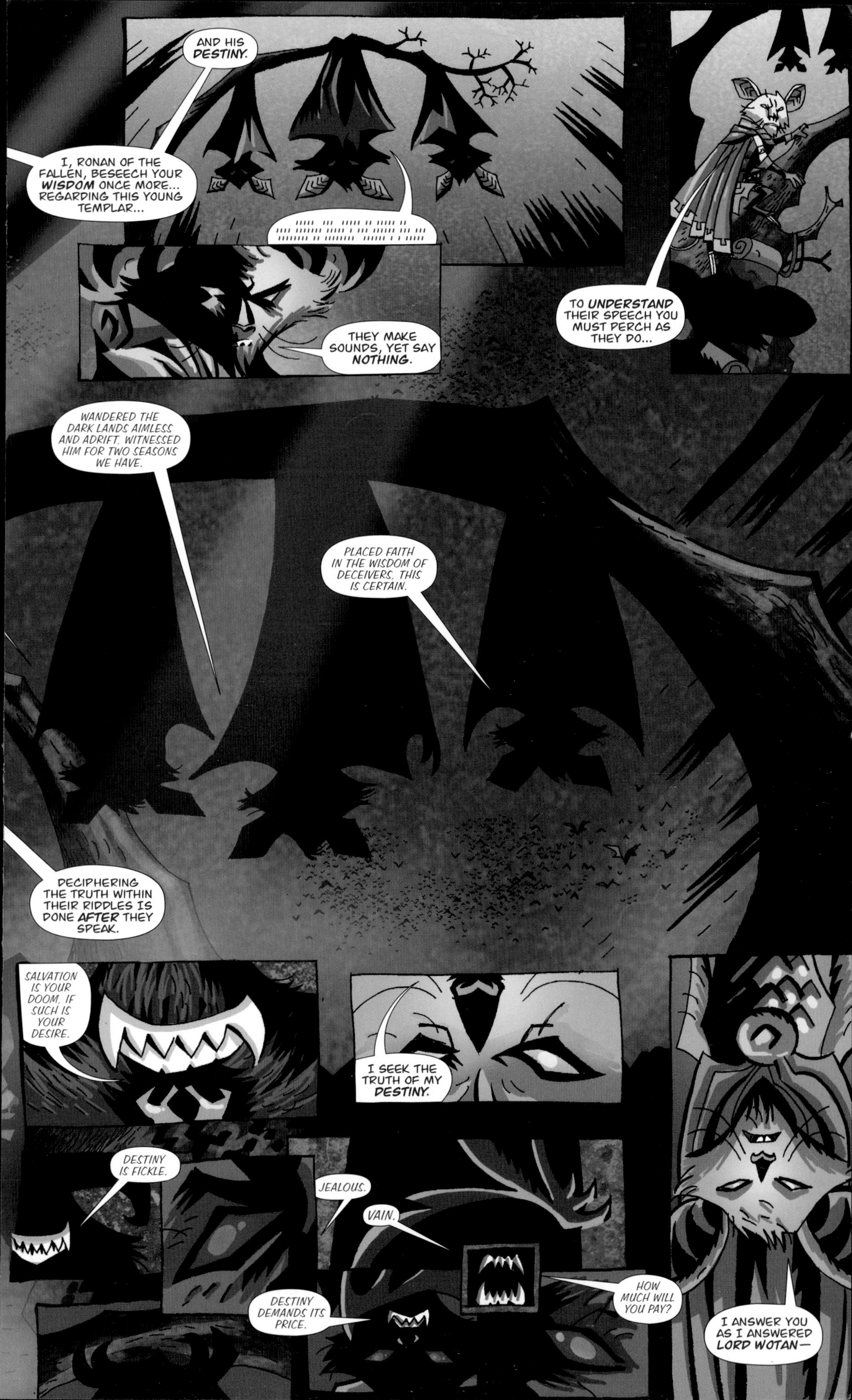
AND HIS DESTINY.
I, RONAN OF THE FALLEN, BESEECH YOUR WISDOM ONCE MORE... REGARDING THIS YOUNG TEMPLAR...
TO UNDERSTAND THEIR SPEECH YOU MUST PERCH AS THEY DO...
THEY MAKE SOUNDS, YET SAY NOTHING.
WANDERED THE DARK LANDS AIMLESS AND ADRIFT, WITNESSED HIM FOR TWO SEASONS WE HAVE.
PLACED FAITH IN THE WISDOM OF DECEIVERS, THIS IS CERTAIN.
DECIPHERING THE TRUTH WITHIN THEIR RIDDLES IS DONE AFTER THEY SPEAK.
SALVATION IS YOUR DOOM, IF SUCH IS YOUR DESIRE.
I SEEK THE TRUTH OF MY DESTINY.
DESTINY IS FICKLE.
JEALOUS.
VAIN.
DESTINY DEMANDS ITS PRICE.
HOW MUCH WILL YOU PAY?
I ANSWER YOU AS I ANSWERED LORD WOTAN—

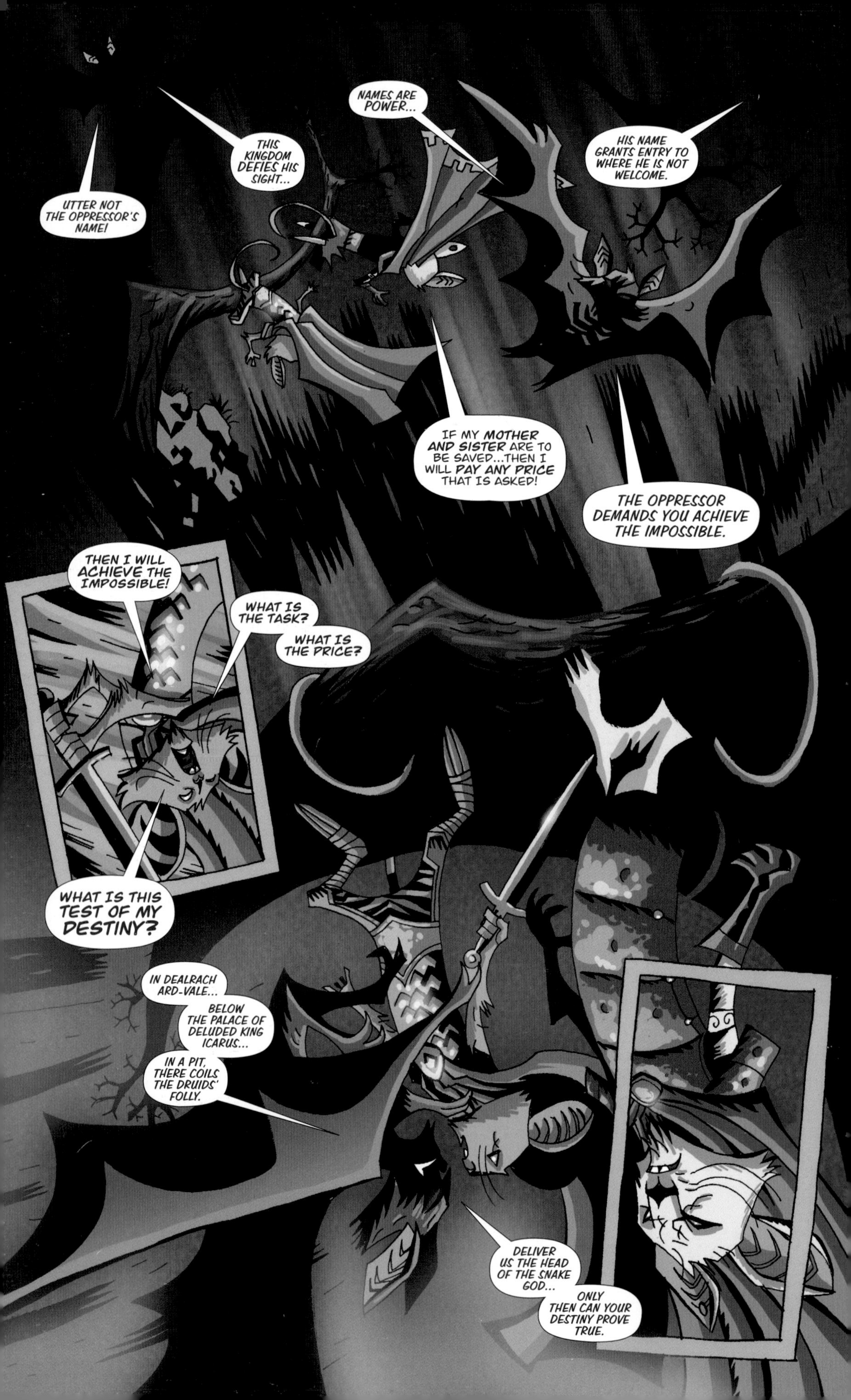
UTTER NOT THE OPPRESSOR'S NAME!
THIS KINGDOM DEFIES HIS SIGHT...
NAMES ARE POWER...
HIS NAME GRANTS ENTRY TO WHERE HE IS NOT WELCOME.
IF MY MOTHER AND SISTER ARE TO BE SAVED...THEN I WILL PAY ANY PRICE THAT IS ASKED!
THE OPPRESSOR DEMANDS YOU ACHIEVE THE IMPOSSIBLE.
THEN I WILL ACHIEVE THE IMPOSSIBLE!
WHAT IS THE TASK?
WHAT IS THE PRICE?
WHAT IS THIS TEST OF MY DESTINY?
IN DEALRACH ARD-VALE...
BELOW THE PALACE OF DELUDED KING ICARUS...
IN A PIT, THERE COILS THE DRUIDS' FOLLY.
DELIVER US THE HEAD OF THE SNAKE GOD...
ONLY THEN CAN YOUR DESTINY PROVE TRUE.

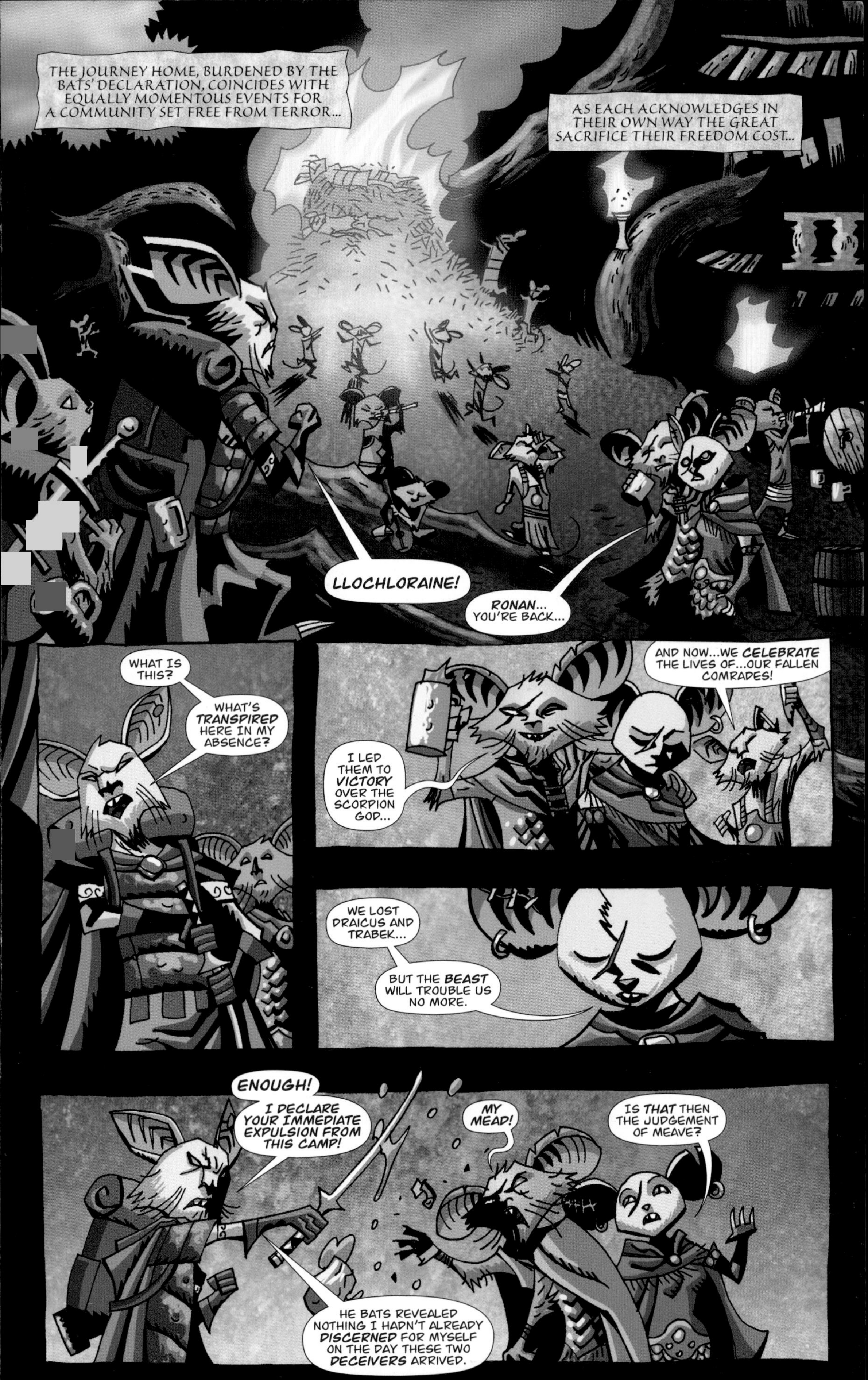
THE JOURNEY HOME, BURDENED BY THE BATS' DECLARATION, COINCIDES WITH EQUALLY MOMENTOUS EVENTS FOR A COMMUNITY SET FREE FROM TERROR...
AS EACH ACKNOWLEDGES IN THEIR OWN WAY THE GREAT SACRIFICE THEIR FREEDOM COST...
LLOCHLORAINE!
RONAN... YOU'RE BACK...
WHAT IS THIS?
WHAT'S TRANSPIRED HERE IN MY ABSENCE?
I LED THEM TO VICTORY OVER THE SCORPION GOD...
AND NOW...WE CELEBRATE THE LIVES OF...OUR FALLEN COMRADES!
WE LOST DRAICUS AND TRABEK...
BUT THE BEAST WILL TROUBLE US NO MORE.
ENOUGH!
I DECLARE YOUR IMMEDIATE EXPULSION FROM THIS CAMP!
MY MEAD!
IS THAT THEN THE JUDGEMENT OF MEAVE?
HE BATS REVEALED NOTHING I HADN'T ALREADY DISCERNED FOR MYSELF ON THE DAY THESE TWO DECEIVERS ARRIVED.

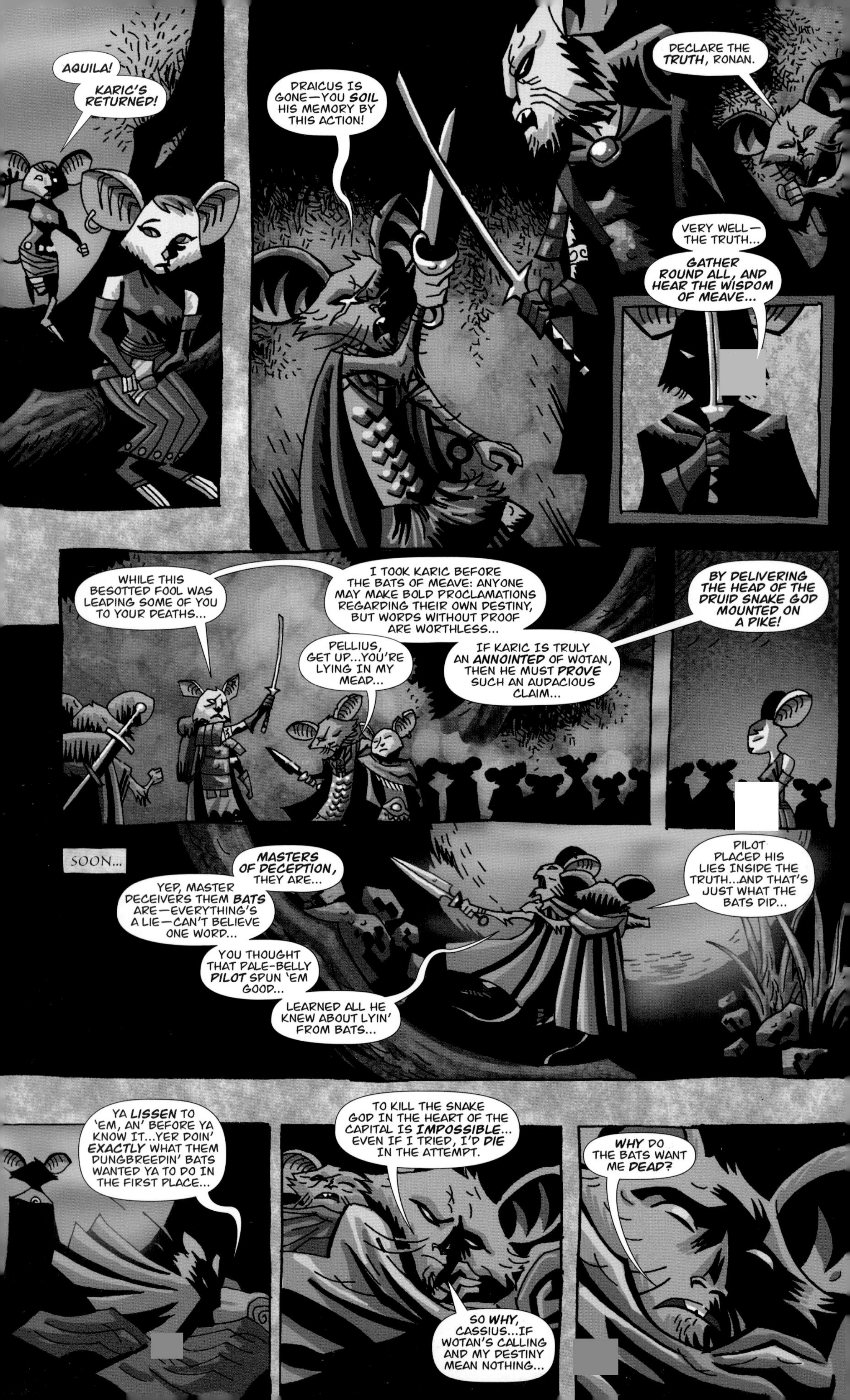
AQUILA!
KARIC'S RETURNED!
DRAICUS IS GONE—YOU SOIL HIS MEMORY BY THIS ACTION!
DECLARE THE TRUTH, RONAN.
VERY WELL— THE TRUTH...
GATHER ROUND ALL, AND HEAR THE WISDOM OF MEAVE...
WHILE THIS BESOTTED FOOL WAS LEADING SOME OF YOU TO YOUR DEATHS...
I TOOK KARIC BEFORE THE BATS OF MEAVE: ANYONE MAY MAKE BOLD PROCLAMATIONS REGARDING THEIR OWN DESTINY, BUT WORDS WITHOUT PROOF ARE WORTHLESS...
PELLIUS, GET UP...YOU'RE LYING IN MY MEAD...
IF KARIC IS TRULY AN ANNOINTED OF WOTAN, THEN HE MUST PROVE SUCH AN AUDACIOUS CLAIM...
BY DELIVERING THE HEAD OF THE DRUID SNAKE GOD MOUNTED ON A PIKE!
SOON...
MASTERS OF DECEPTION, THEY ARE...
YEP, MASTER DECEIVERS THEM BATS ARE—EVERYTHING'S A LIE—CAN'T BELIEVE ONE WORD...
YOU THOUGHT THAT PALE-BELLY PILOT SPUN 'EM GOOD...
LEARNED ALL HE KNEW ABOUT LYIN' FROM BATS...
PILOT PLACED HIS LIES INSIDE THE TRUTH...AND THAT'S JUST WHAT THE BATS DID...
YA LISSEN TO 'EM, AN' BEFORE YA KNOW IT...YER DOIN' EXACTLY WHAT THEM DUNGBREEDIN' BATS WANTED YA TO DO IN THE FIRST PLACE...
TO KILL THE SNAKE GOD IN THE HEART OF THE CAPITAL IS IMPOSSIBLE... EVEN IF I TRIED, I'D DIE IN THE ATTEMPT.
SO WHY, CASSIUS...IF WOTAN'S CALLING AND MY DESTINY MEAN NOTHING...
WHY DO THE BATS WANT ME DEAD?

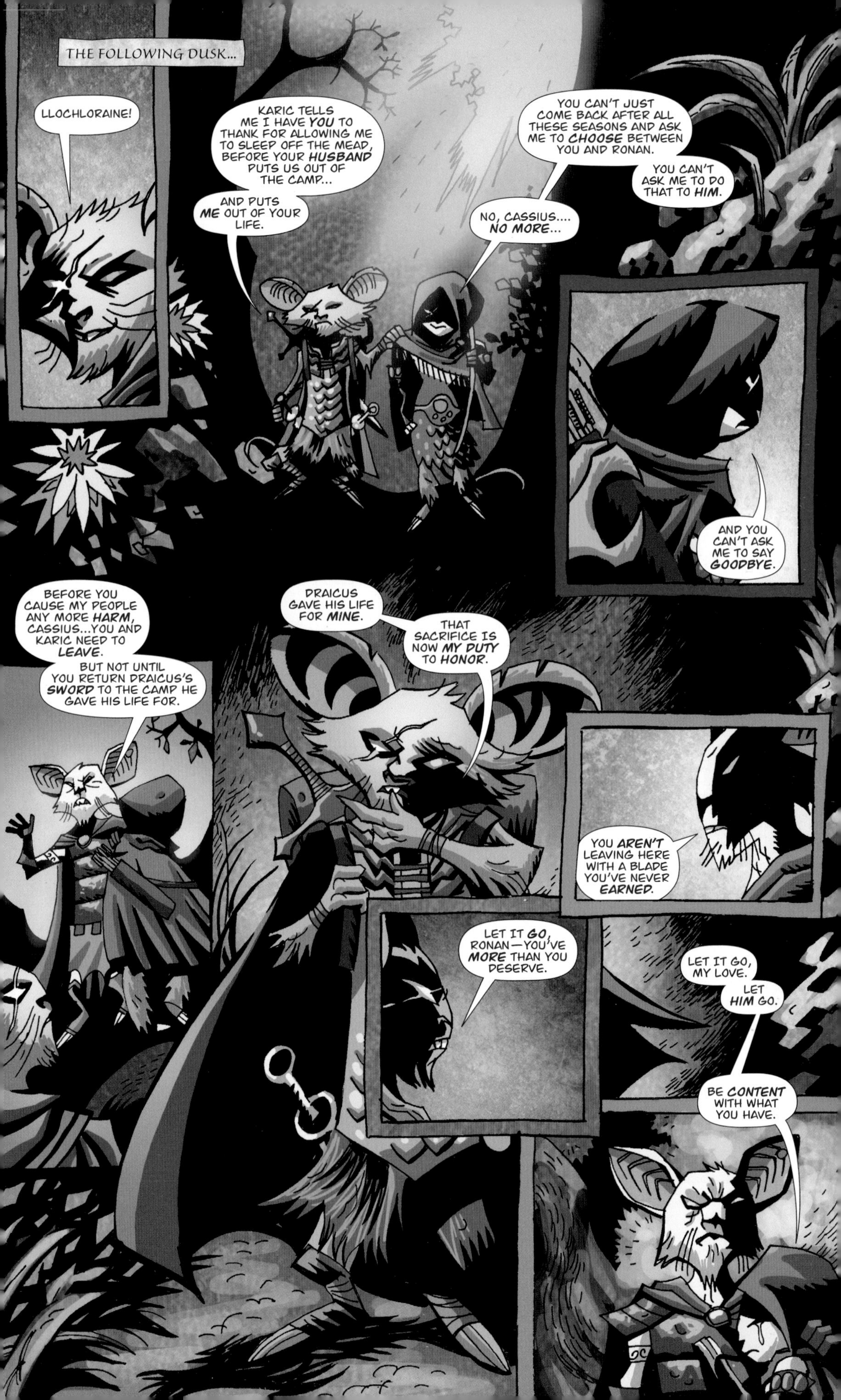
THE FOLLOWING DUSK...
LLOCHLORAINE!
KARIC TELLS ME I HAVE YOU TO THANK FOR ALLOWING ME TO SLEEP OFF THE MEAD, BEFORE YOUR HUSBAND PUTS US OUT OF THE CAMP...
AND PUTS ME OUT OF YOUR LIFE.
NO, CASSIUS.... NO MORE...
YOU CAN'T JUST COME BACK AFTER ALL THESE SEASONS AND ASK ME TO CHOOSE BETWEEN YOU AND RONAN.
YOU CAN'T ASK ME TO DO THAT TO HIM.
AND YOU CAN'T ASK ME TO SAY GOODBYE.
BEFORE YOU CAUSE MY PEOPLE ANY MORE HARM, CASSIUS...YOU AND KARIC NEED TO LEAVE.
BUT NOT UNTIL YOU RETURN DRAICUS'S SWORD TO THE CAMP HE GAVE HIS LIFE FOR.
DRAICUS GAVE HIS LIFE FOR MINE.
THAT SACRIFICE IS NOW MY DUTY TO HONOR.
YOU AREN'T LEAVING HERE WITH A BLADE YOU'VE NEVER EARNED.
LET IT GO, RONAN—YOU'VE MORE THAN YOU DESERVE.
LET IT GO, MY LOVE.
LET HIM GO.
BE CONTENT WITH WHAT YOU HAVE.

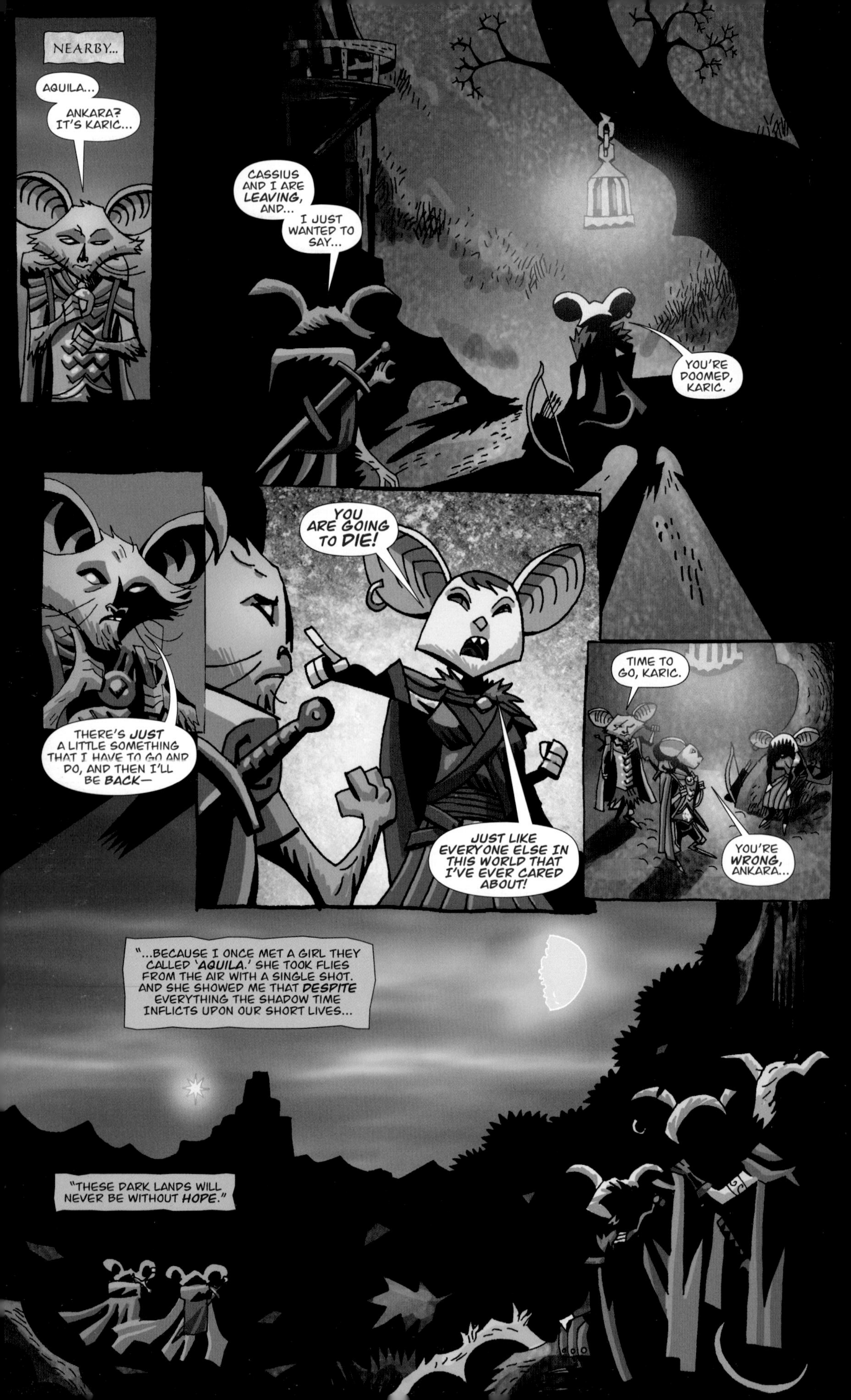
NEARBY...
AQUILA...
ANKARA? IT'S KARIC...
CASSIUS AND I ARE LEAVING, AND...
I JUST WANTED TO SAY...
YOU'RE DOOMED, KARIC.
THERE'S JUST A LITTLE SOMETHING THAT I HAVE TO GO AND DO, AND THEN I'LL BE BACK—
YOU ARE GOING TO DIE!
JUST LIKE EVERYONE ELSE IN THIS WORLD THAT I'VE EVER CARED ABOUT!
TIME TO GO, KARIC.
YOU'RE WRONG, ANKARA...
"...BECAUSE I ONCE MET A GIRL THEY CALLED 'AQUILA.' SHE TOOK FLIES FROM THE AIR WITH A SINGLE SHOT. AND SHE SHOWED ME THAT DESPITE EVERYTHING THE SHADOW TIME INFLICTS UPON OUR SHORT LIVES...
"THESE DARK LANDS WILL NEVER BE WITHOUT HOPE."

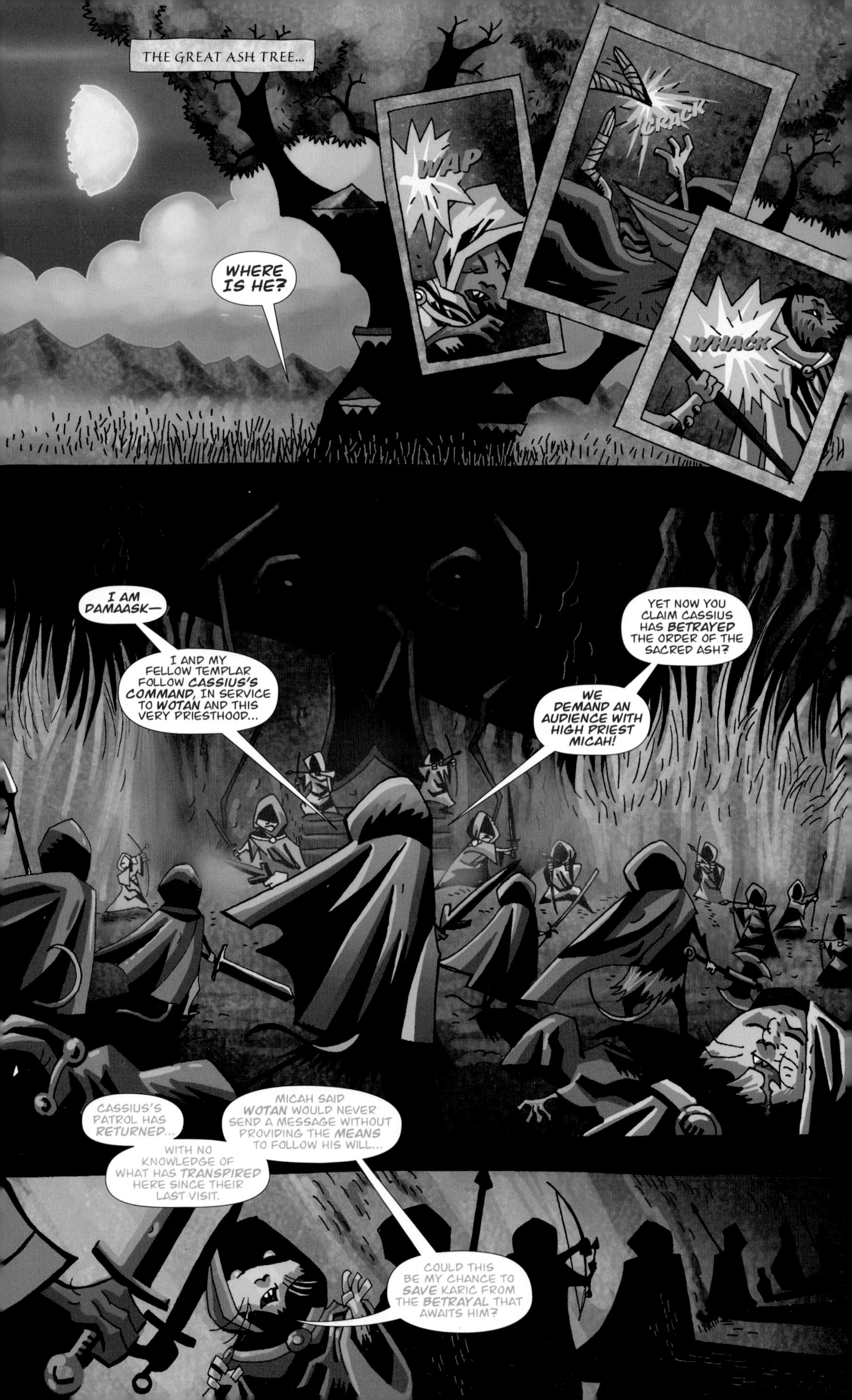
THE GREAT ASH TREE...
WAP
CRACK
WHACK
WHERE IS HE?
I AM DAMAASK—
I AND MY FELLOW TEMPLAR FOLLOW CASSIUS'S COMMAND, IN SERVICE TO WOTAN AND THIS VERY PRIESTHOOD...
YET NOW YOU CLAIM CASSIUS HAS BETRAYED THE ORDER OF THE SACRED ASH?
WE DEMAND AN AUDIENCE WITH HIGH PRIEST MICAH!
CASSIUS'S PATROL HAS RETURNED...
WITH NO KNOWLEDGE OF WHAT HAS TRANSPIRED HERE SINCE THEIR LAST VISIT.
MICAH SAID WOTAN WOULD NEVER SEND A MESSAGE WITHOUT PROVIDING THE MEANS TO FOLLOW HIS WILL...
COULD THIS BE MY CHANCE TO SAVE KARIC FROM THE BETRAYAL THAT AWAITS HIM?

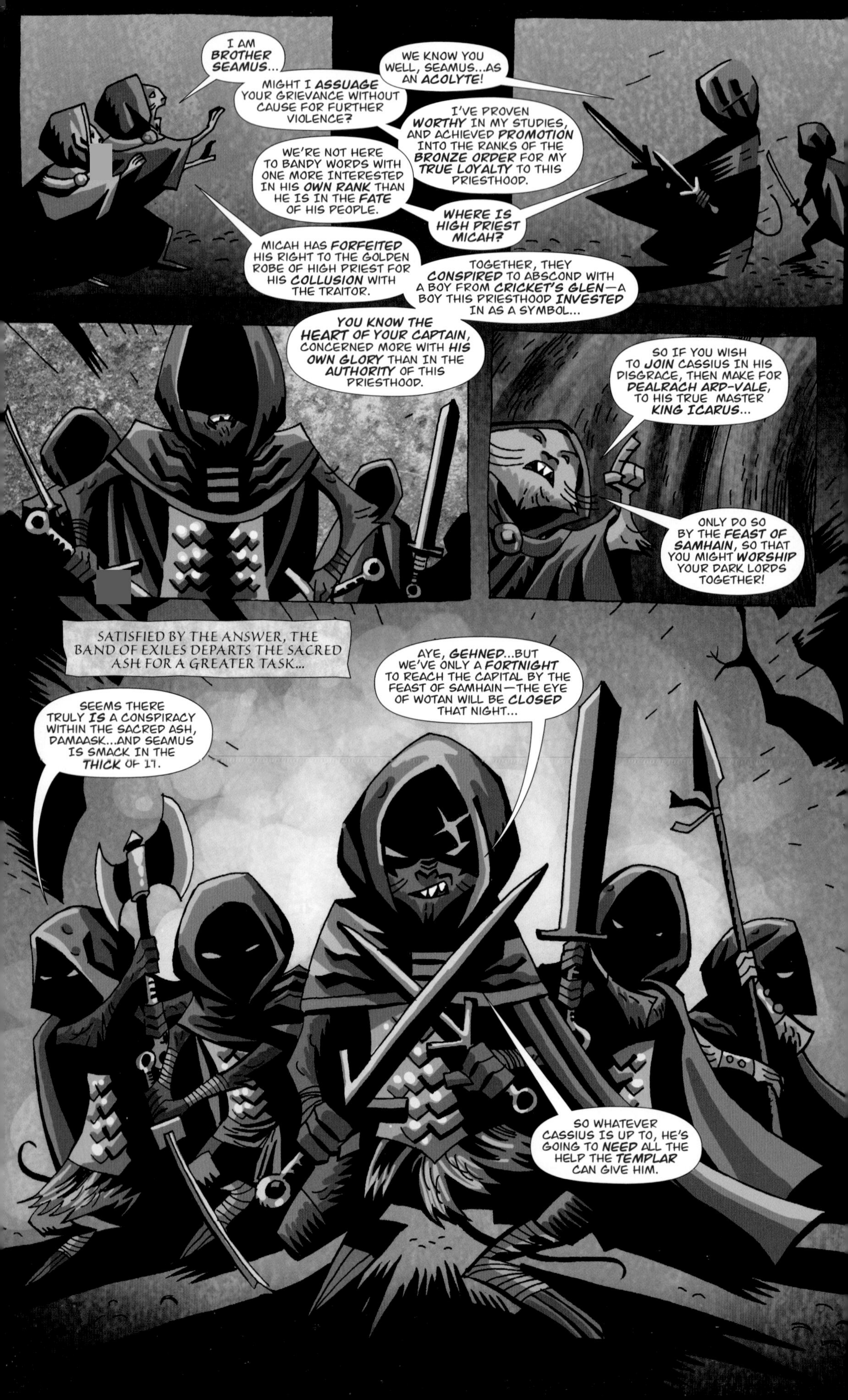
I AM BROTHER SEAMUS... MIGHT I ASSUAGE YOUR GRIEVANCE WITHOUT CAUSE FOR FURTHER VIOLENCE?
WE KNOW YOU WELL, SEAMUS...AS AN ACOLYTE!
I'VE PROVEN WORTHY IN MY STUDIES, AND ACHIEVED PROMOTION INTO THE RANKS OF THE BRONZE ORDER FOR MY TRUE LOYALTY TO THIS PRIESTHOOD.
WE'RE NOT HERE TO BANDY WORDS WITH ONE MORE INTERESTED IN HIS OWN RANK THAN HE IS IN THE FATE OF HIS PEOPLE.
WHERE IS HIGH PRIEST MICAH?
MICAH HAS FORFEITED HIS RIGHT TO THE GOLDEN ROBE OF HIGH PRIEST FOR HIS COLLUSION WITH THE TRAITOR.
TOGETHER, THEY CONSPIRED TO ABSCOND WITH A BOY FROM CRICKET'S GLEN—A BOY THIS PRIESTHOOD INVESTED IN AS A SYMBOL...
YOU KNOW THE HEART OF YOUR CAPTAIN, CONCERNED MORE WITH HIS OWN GLORY THAN IN THE AUTHORITY OF THIS PRIESTHOOD.
SO IF YOU WISH TO JOIN CASSIUS IN HIS DISGRACE, THEN MAKE FOR DEALRACH ARD-VALE, TO HIS TRUE MASTER KING ICARUS...
ONLY DO SO BY THE FEAST OF SAMHAIN, SO THAT YOU MIGHT WORSHIP YOUR DARK LORDS TOGETHER!
SATISFIED BY THE ANSWER, THE BAND OF EXILES DEPARTS THE SACRED ASH FOR A GREATER TASK...
SEEMS THERE TRULY IS A CONSPIRACY WITHIN THE SACRED ASH, DAMAASK...AND SEAMUS IS SMACK IN THE THICK OF IT.
AYE, GEHNED...BUT WE'VE ONLY A FORTNIGHT TO REACH THE CAPITAL BY THE FEAST OF SAMHAIN—THE EYE OF WOTAN WILL BE CLOSED THAT NIGHT...
SO WHATEVER CASSIUS IS UP TO, HE'S GOING TO NEED ALL THE HELP THE TEMPLAR CAN GIVE HIM.

CHAPTER SEVEN

SEIZING DESTINY

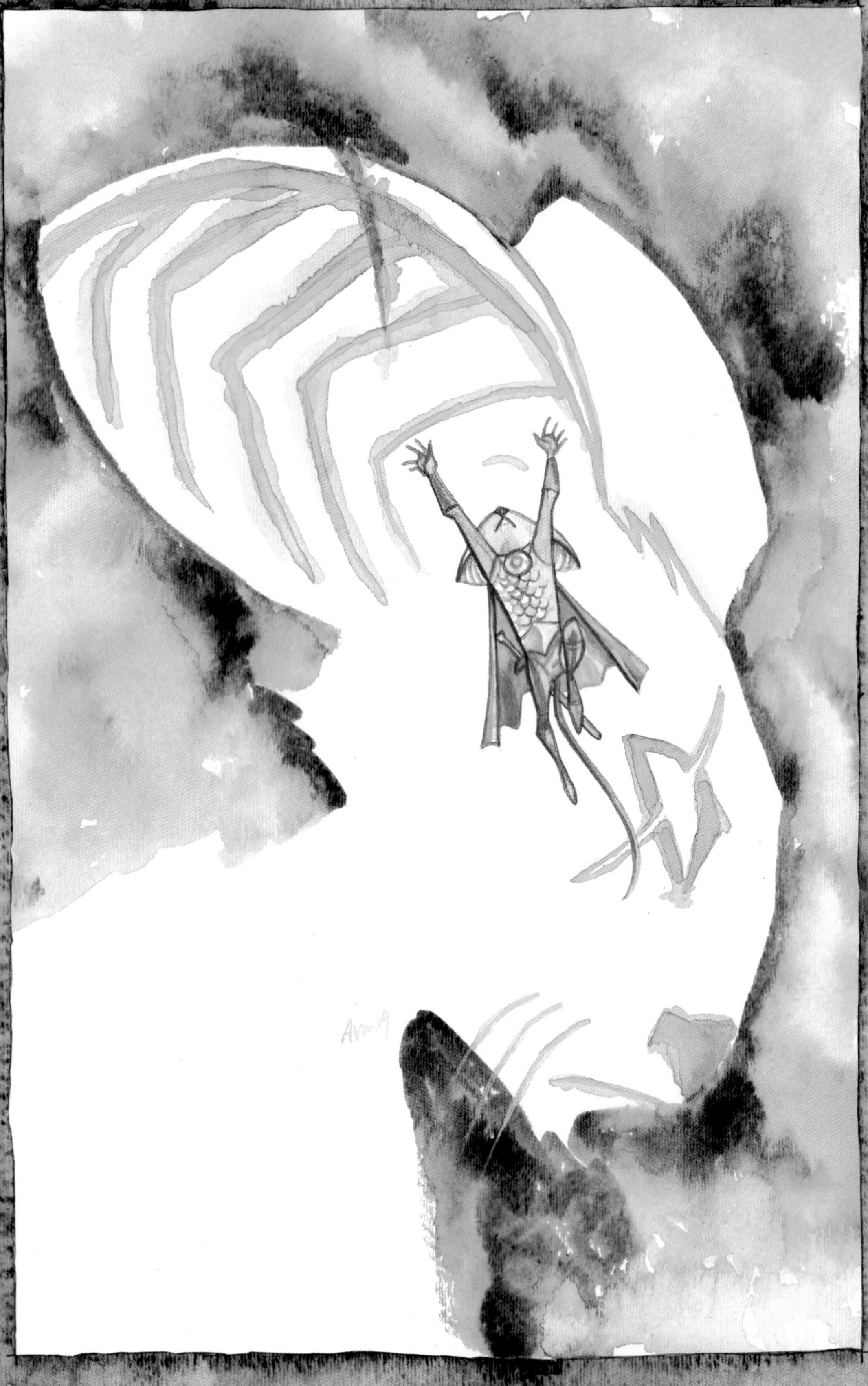

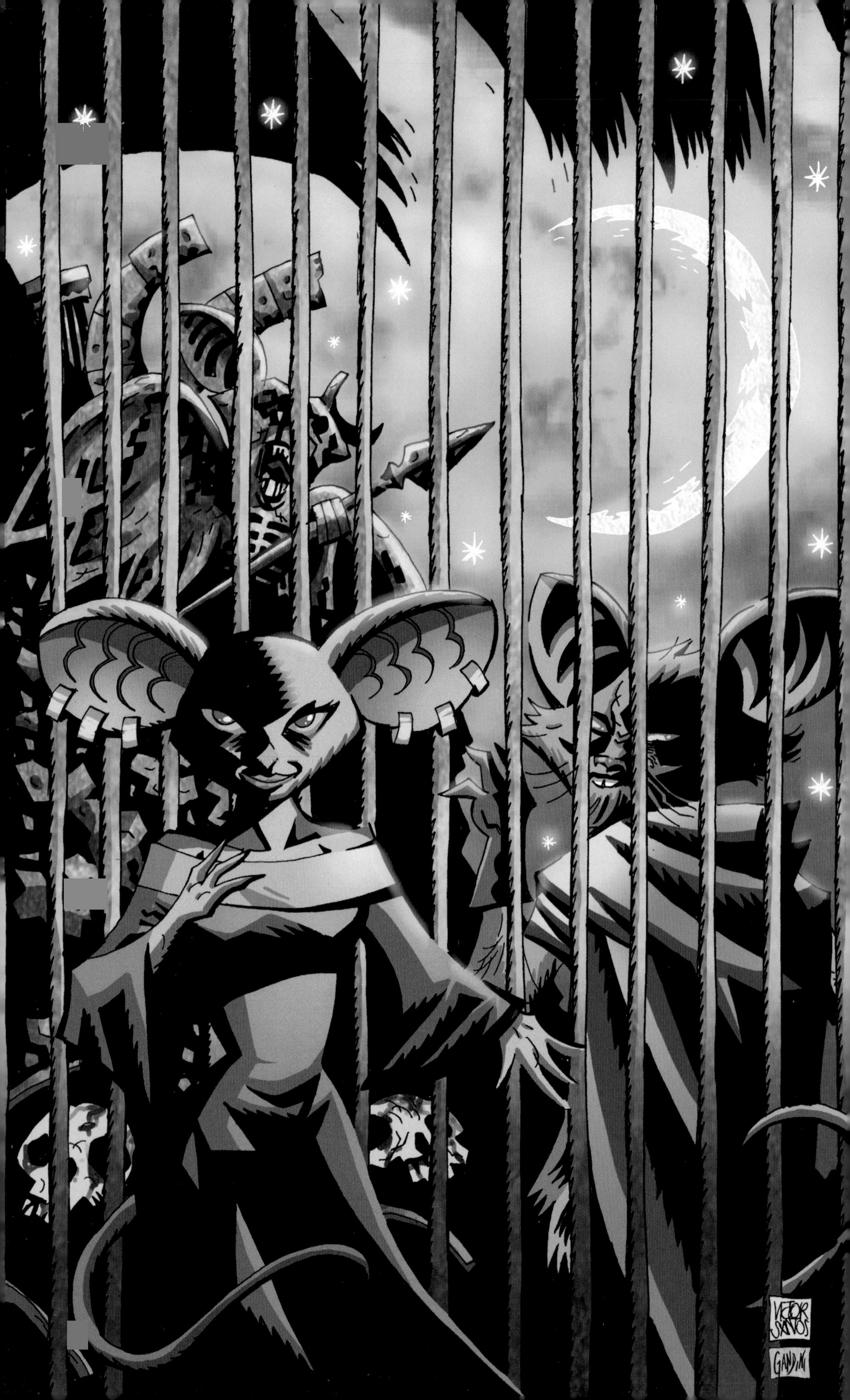
VICTOR SANTOS
GANDINI

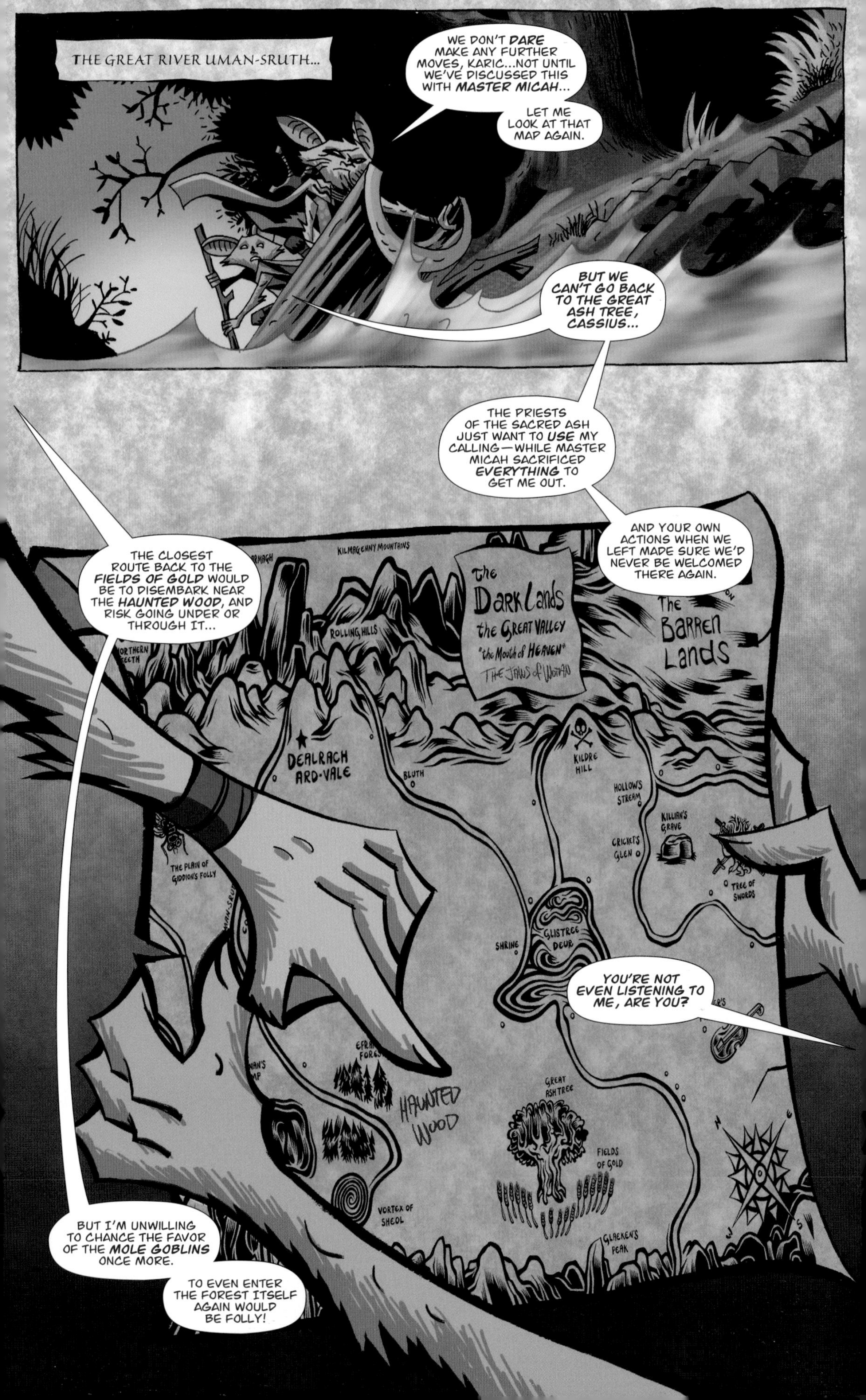
THE GREAT RIVER UMAN-SRUTH...
WE DON'T DARE MAKE ANY FURTHER MOVES, KARIC...NOT UNTIL WE'VE DISCUSSED THIS WITH MASTER MICAH...
LET ME LOOK AT THAT MAP AGAIN.
BUT WE CAN'T GO BACK TO THE GREAT ASH TREE, CASSIUS...
THE PRIESTS OF THE SACRED ASH JUST WANT TO USE MY CALLING—WHILE MASTER MICAH SACRIFICED EVERYTHING TO GET ME OUT.
AND YOUR OWN ACTIONS WHEN WE LEFT MADE SURE WE'D NEVER BE WELCOMED THERE AGAIN.
THE CLOSEST ROUTE BACK TO THE FIELDS OF GOLD WOULD BE TO DISEMBARK NEAR THE HAUNTED WOOD, AND RISK GOING UNDER OR THROUGH IT...
KILMAGENNY MOUNTAINS
the DarkLands
the GREAT VALLEY
"the Mouth of HEAVEN"
THE JAWS of WORAN
The BARREN Lands
ROLLING HILLS
DEALRACH ARD-VALE
BLUTH
KILDRE HILL
HOLLOWS STREAM
KILLIAN'S GRAVE
CRICKET'S GLEN
TREE OF SWORDS
THE PLAIN OF GIDDION'S FOLLY
SHRINE
GLISTREE DEUR
YOU'RE NOT EVEN LISTENING TO ME, ARE YOU?
HAUNTED WOOD
GREAT ASH TREE
FIELDS OF GOLD
VORTEX OF SHEOL
GLAEKEN'S PEAK
BUT I'M UNWILLING TO CHANCE THE FAVOR OF THE MOLE GOBLINS ONCE MORE.
TO EVEN ENTER THE FOREST ITSELF AGAIN WOULD BE FOLLY!

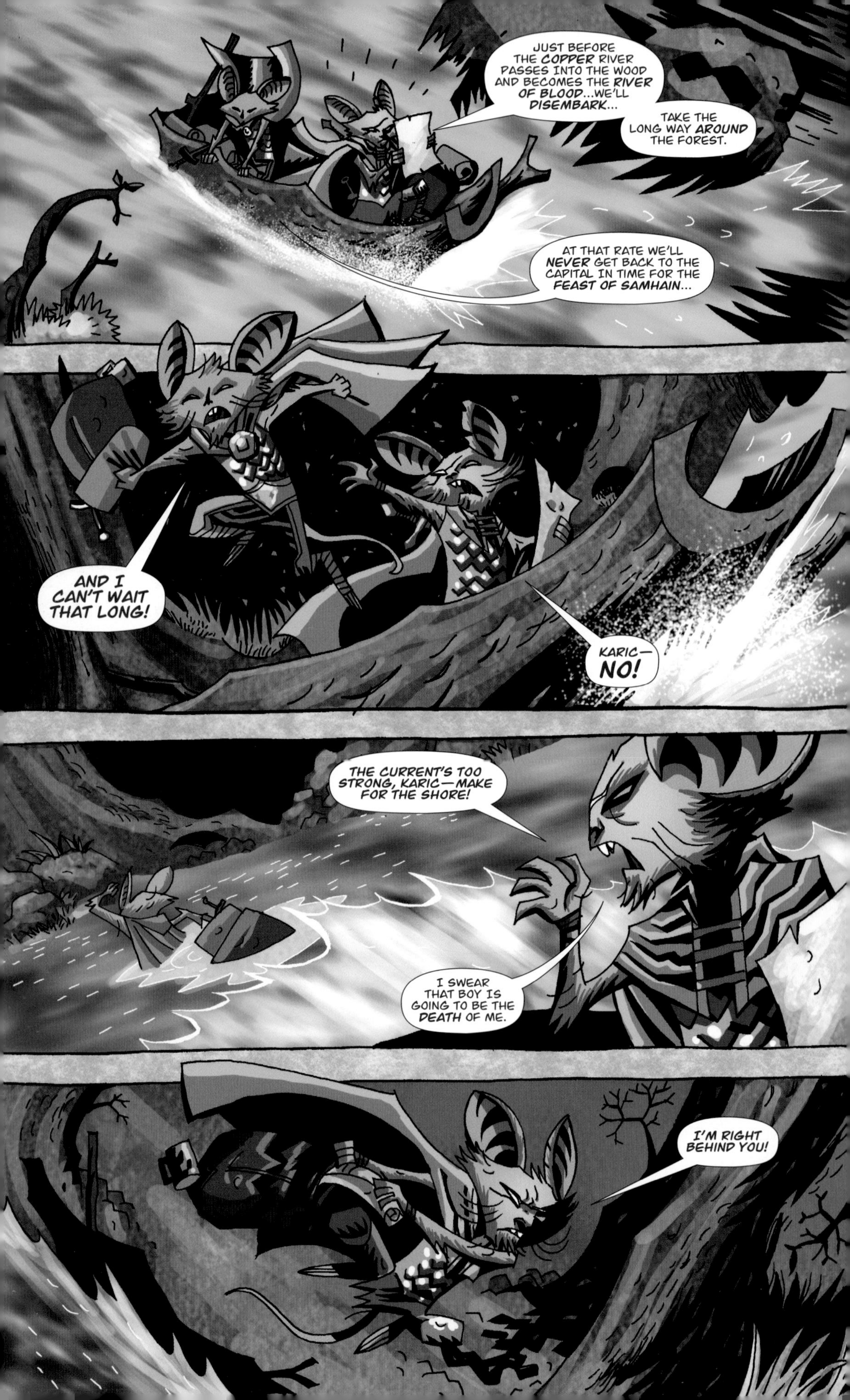
JUST BEFORE THE COPPER RIVER PASSES INTO THE WOOD AND BECOMES THE RIVER OF BLOOD...WE'LL DISEMBARK...
TAKE THE LONG WAY AROUND THE FOREST.
AT THAT RATE WE'LL NEVER GET BACK TO THE CAPITAL IN TIME FOR THE FEAST OF SAMHAIN...
AND I CAN'T WAIT THAT LONG!
KARIC— NO!
THE CURRENT'S TOO STRONG, KARIC—MAKE FOR THE SHORE!
I SWEAR THAT BOY IS GOING TO BE THE DEATH OF ME.
I'M RIGHT BEHIND YOU!

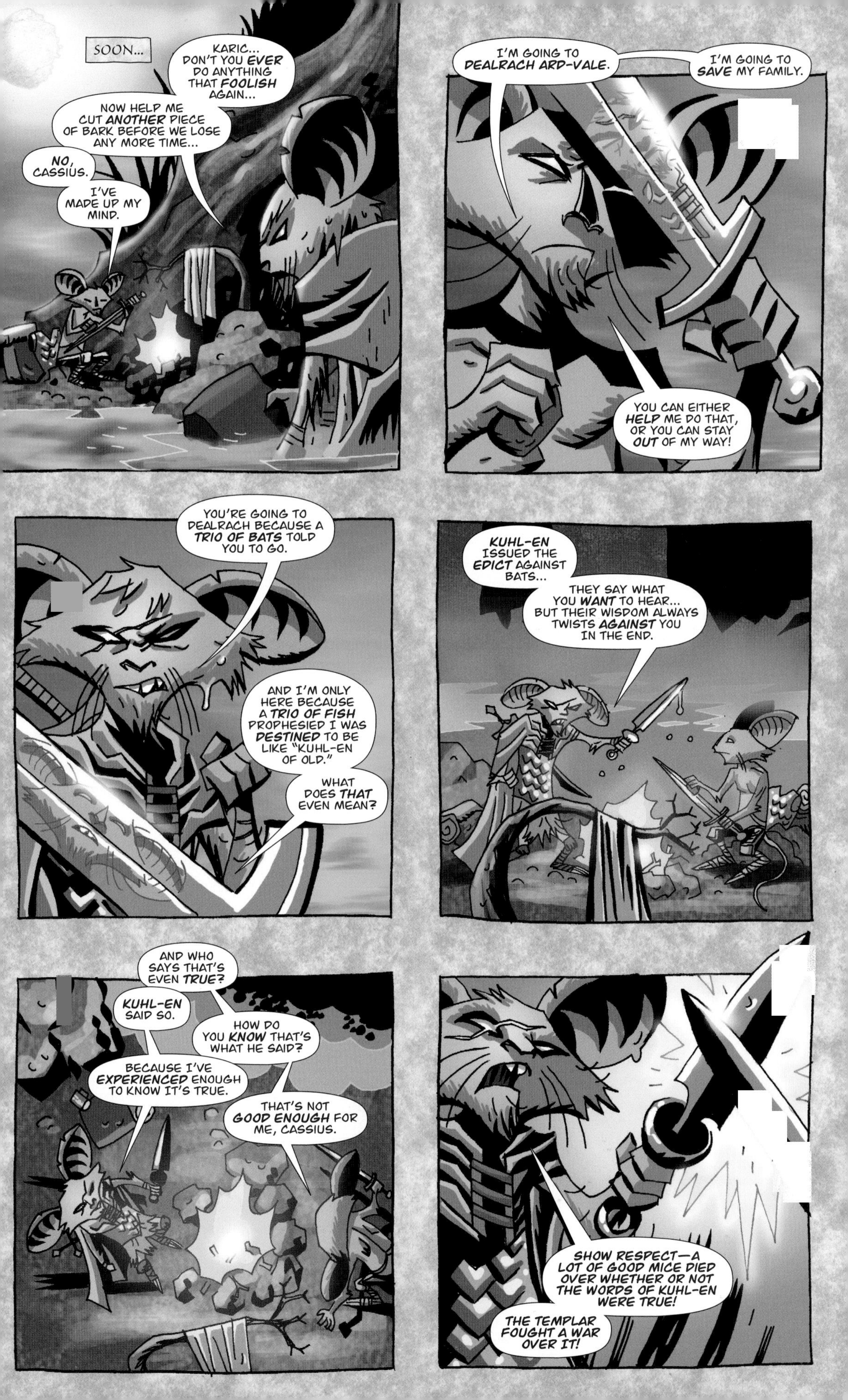
SOON...
KARIC... DON'T YOU EVER DO ANYTHING THAT FOOLISH AGAIN...
NOW HELP ME CUT ANOTHER PIECE OF BARK BEFORE WE LOSE ANY MORE TIME...
NO, CASSIUS.
I'VE MADE UP MY MIND.
I'M GOING TO DEALRACH ARD-VALE.
I'M GOING TO SAVE MY FAMILY.
YOU CAN EITHER HELP ME DO THAT, OR YOU CAN STAY OUT OF MY WAY!
YOU'RE GOING TO DEALRACH BECAUSE A TRIO OF BATS TOLD YOU TO GO.
AND I'M ONLY HERE BECAUSE A TRIO OF FISH PROPHESIED I WAS DESTINED TO BE LIKE "KUHL-EN OF OLD."
WHAT DOES THAT EVEN MEAN?
KUHL-EN ISSUED THE EDICT AGAINST BATS...
THEY SAY WHAT YOU WANT TO HEAR... BUT THEIR WISDOM ALWAYS TWISTS AGAINST YOU IN THE END.
AND WHO SAYS THAT'S EVEN TRUE?
KUHL-EN SAID SO.
HOW DO YOU KNOW THAT'S WHAT HE SAID?
BECAUSE I'VE EXPERIENCED ENOUGH TO KNOW IT'S TRUE.
THAT'S NOT GOOD ENOUGH FOR ME, CASSIUS.
SHOW RESPECT—A LOT OF GOOD MICE DIED OVER WHETHER OR NOT THE WORDS OF KUHL-EN WERE TRUE!
THE TEMPLAR FOUGHT A WAR OVER IT!

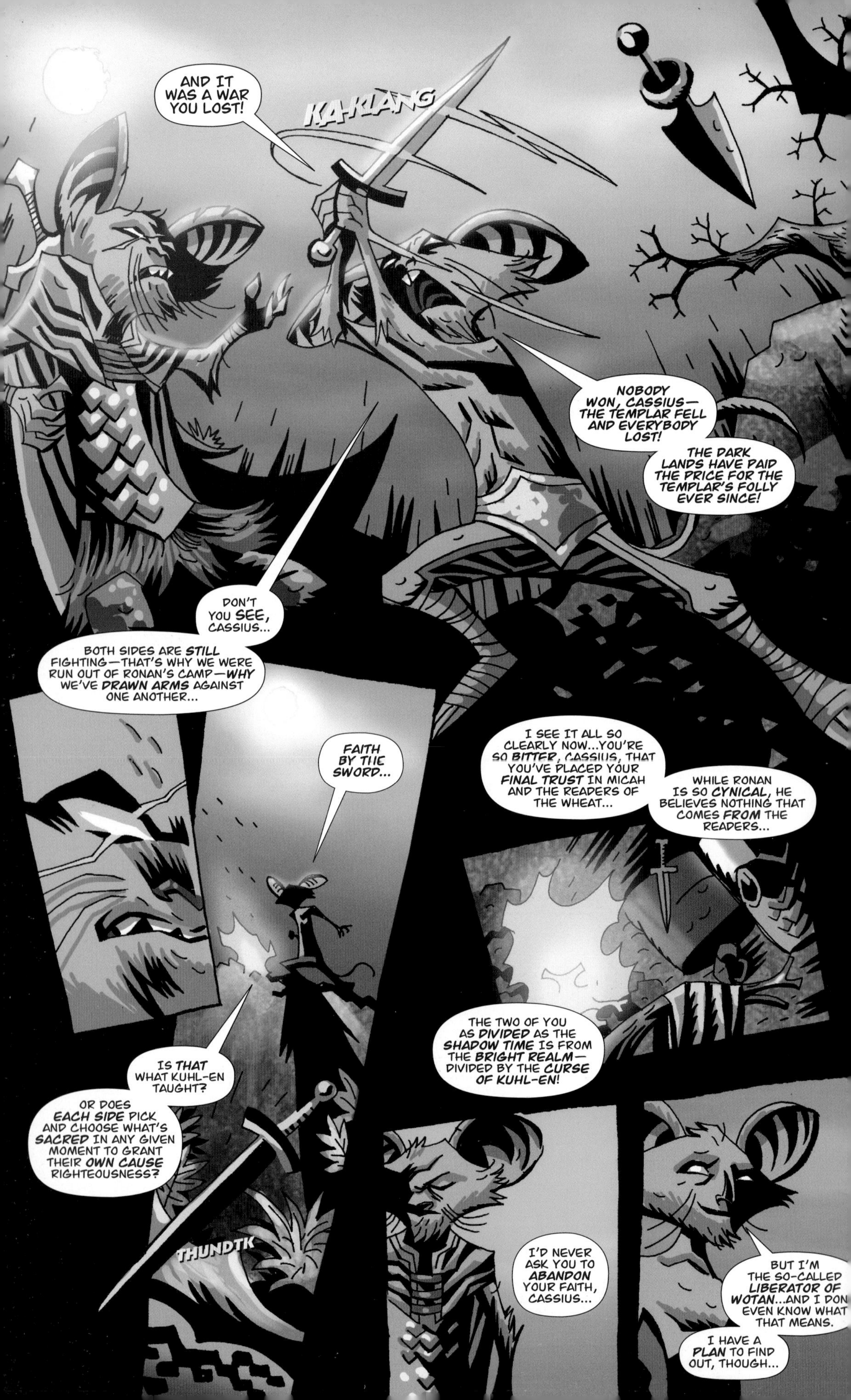

AND IT WAS A WAR YOU LOST!
KA-KLANG
NOBODY WON, CASSIUS— THE TEMPLAR FELL AND EVERYBODY LOST!
THE DARK LANDS HAVE PAID THE PRICE FOR THE TEMPLAR'S FOLLY EVER SINCE!
DON'T YOU SEE, CASSIUS...
BOTH SIDES ARE STILL FIGHTING—THAT'S WHY WE WERE RUN OUT OF RONAN'S CAMP—WHY WE'VE DRAWN ARMS AGAINST ONE ANOTHER...
FAITH BY THE SWORD...
I SEE IT ALL SO CLEARLY NOW...YOU'RE SO BITTER, CASSIUS, THAT YOU'VE PLACED YOUR FINAL TRUST IN MICAH AND THE READERS OF THE WHEAT...
WHILE RONAN IS SO CYNICAL, HE BELIEVES NOTHING THAT COMES FROM THE READERS...
THE TWO OF YOU AS DIVIDED AS THE SHADOW TIME IS FROM THE BRIGHT REALM— DIVIDED BY THE CURSE OF KUHL-EN!
IS THAT WHAT KUHL-EN TAUGHT?
OR DOES EACH SIDE PICK AND CHOOSE WHAT'S SACRED IN ANY GIVEN MOMENT TO GRANT THEIR OWN CAUSE RIGHTEOUSNESS?
THUNDTK
I'D NEVER ASK YOU TO ABANDON YOUR FAITH, CASSIUS...
BUT I'M THE SO-CALLED LIBERATOR OF WOTAN...AND I DON EVEN KNOW WHAT THAT MEANS.
I HAVE A PLAN TO FIND OUT, THOUGH...

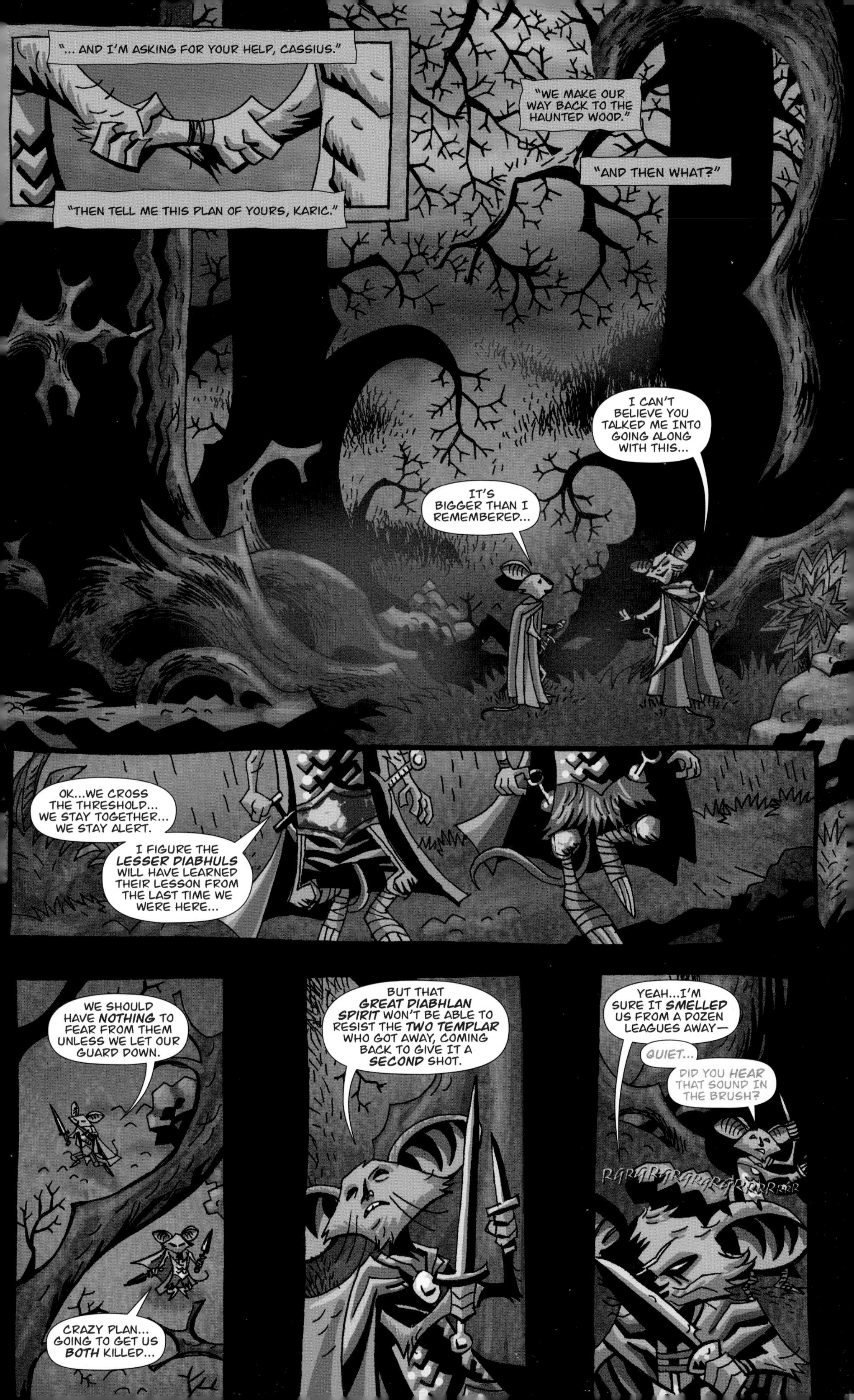
"... AND I'M ASKING FOR YOUR HELP, CASSIUS."
"THEN TELL ME THIS PLAN OF YOURS, KARIC."
"WE MAKE OUR WAY BACK TO THE HAUNTED WOOD."
"AND THEN WHAT?"
I CAN'T BELIEVE YOU TALKED ME INTO GOING ALONG WITH THIS...
IT'S BIGGER THAN I REMEMBERED...
OK...WE CROSS THE THRESHOLD... WE STAY TOGETHER... WE STAY ALERT.
I FIGURE THE LESSER DIABHULS WILL HAVE LEARNED THEIR LESSON FROM THE LAST TIME WE WERE HERE...
WE SHOULD HAVE NOTHING TO FEAR FROM THEM UNLESS WE LET OUR GUARD DOWN.
CRAZY PLAN... GOING TO GET US BOTH KILLED...
BUT THAT GREAT DIABHLAN SPIRIT WON'T BE ABLE TO RESIST THE TWO TEMPLAR WHO GOT AWAY, COMING BACK TO GIVE IT A SECOND SHOT.
YEAH...I'M SURE IT SMELLED US FROM A DOZEN LEAGUES AWAY—
QUIET...
DID YOU HEAR THAT SOUND IN THE BRUSH?
RGRGRGRGRGRGRGRRRRR

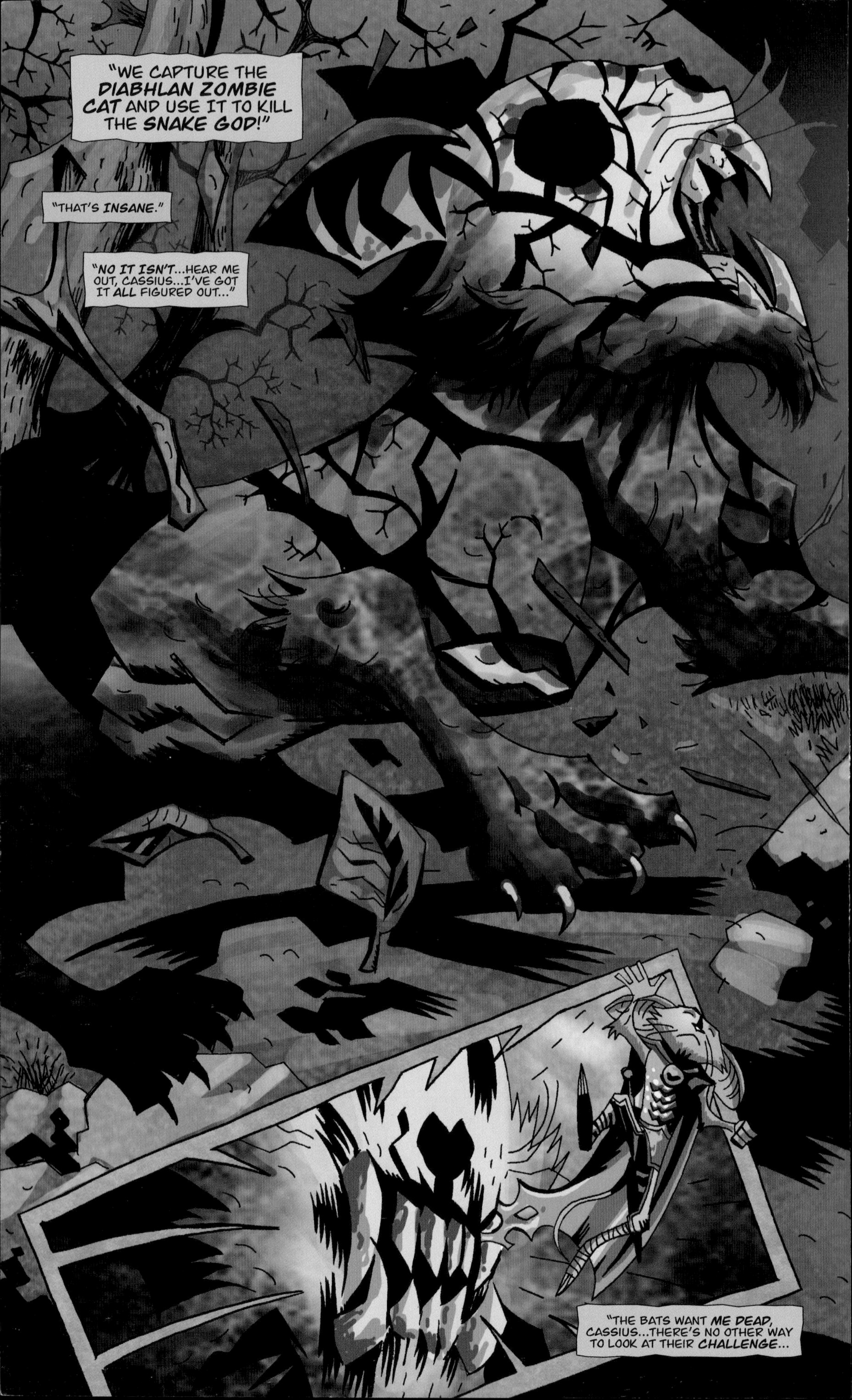
"WE CAPTURE THE DIABHLAN ZOMBIE CAT AND USE IT TO KILL THE SNAKE GOD!"
"THAT'S INSANE."
"NO IT ISN'T...HEAR ME OUT, CASSIUS...I'VE GOT IT ALL FIGURED OUT..."
"THE BATS WANT ME DEAD, CASSIUS...THERE'S NO OTHER WAY TO LOOK AT THEIR CHALLENGE...

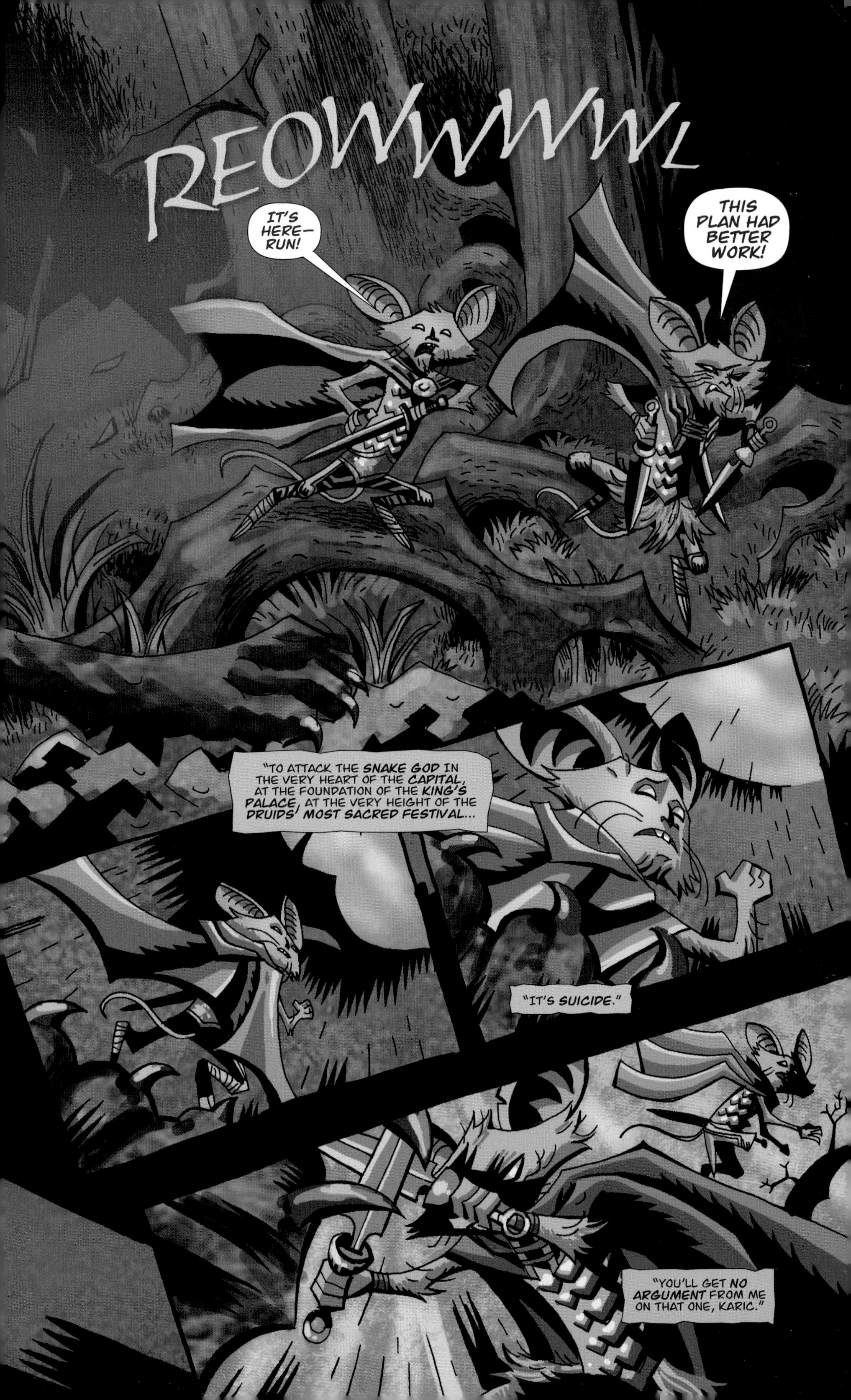
REOWWWWL
IT'S HERE—RUN!
THIS PLAN HAD BETTER WORK!
"TO ATTACK THE SNAKE GOD IN THE VERY HEART OF THE CAPITAL, AT THE FOUNDATION OF THE KING'S PALACE, AT THE VERY HEIGHT OF THE DRUIDS' MOST SACRED FESTIVAL...
"IT'S SUICIDE."
"YOU'LL GET NO ARGUMENT FROM ME ON THAT ONE, KARIC."

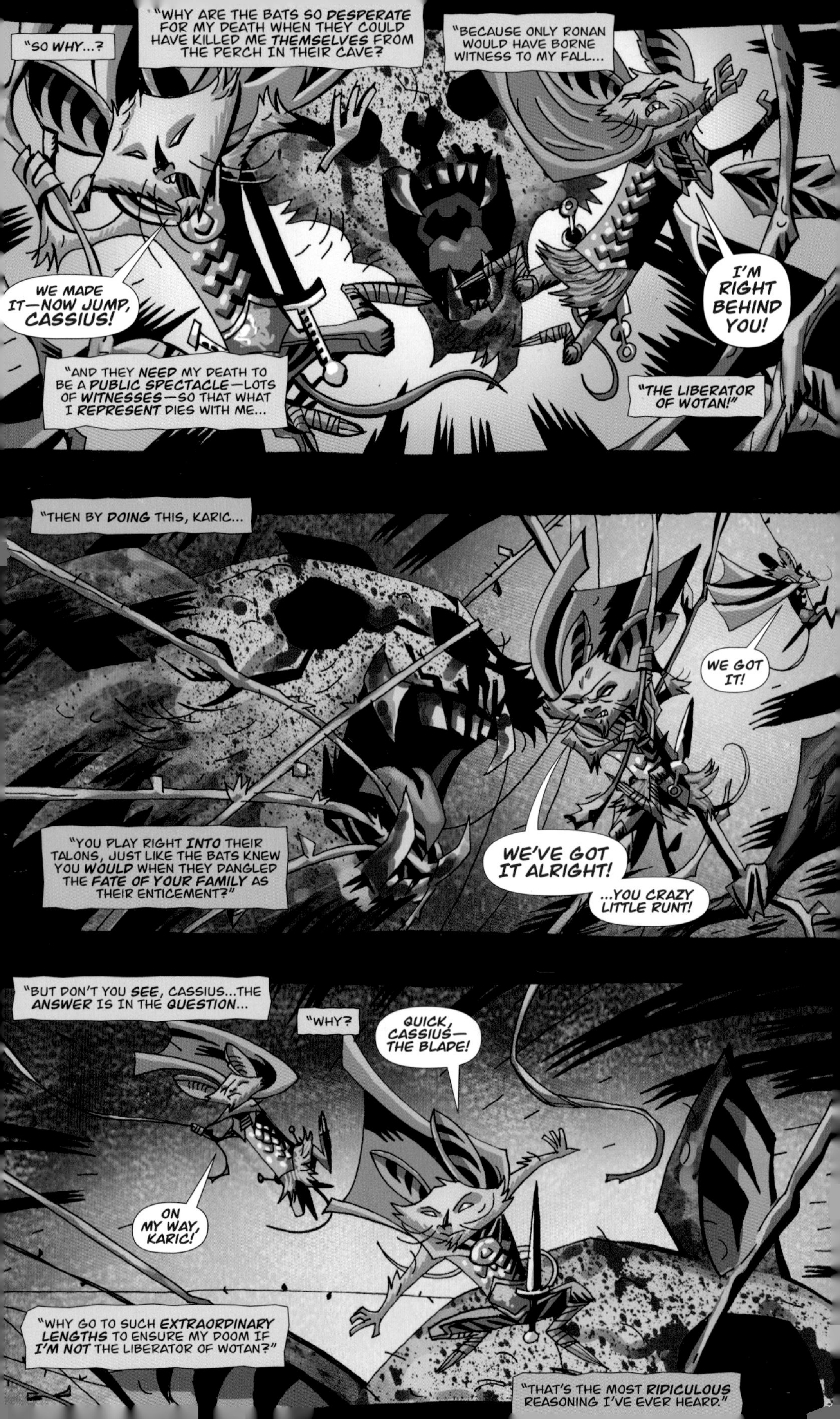

"SO WHY...?
"WHY ARE THE BATS SO DESPERATE FOR MY DEATH WHEN THEY COULD HAVE KILLED ME THEMSELVES FROM THE PERCH IN THEIR CAVE?
"BECAUSE ONLY RONAN WOULD HAVE BORNE WITNESS TO MY FALL...
WE MADE IT—NOW JUMP, CASSIUS!
I'M RIGHT BEHIND YOU!
"AND THEY NEED MY DEATH TO BE A PUBLIC SPECTACLE—LOTS OF WITNESSES—SO THAT WHAT I REPRESENT DIES WITH ME...
"THE LIBERATOR OF WOTAN!"
"THEN BY DOING THIS, KARIC...
WE GOT IT!
"YOU PLAY RIGHT INTO THEIR TALONS, JUST LIKE THE BATS KNEW YOU WOULD WHEN THEY DANGLED THE FATE OF YOUR FAMILY AS THEIR ENTICEMENT?"
WE'VE GOT IT ALRIGHT!
...YOU CRAZY LITTLE RUNT!
"BUT DON'T YOU SEE, CASSIUS...THE ANSWER IS IN THE QUESTION...
"WHY?
QUICK, CASSIUS—THE BLADE!
ON MY WAY, KARIC!
"WHY GO TO SUCH EXTRAORDINARY LENGTHS TO ENSURE MY DOOM IF I'M NOT THE LIBERATOR OF WOTAN?"
"THAT'S THE MOST RIDICULOUS REASONING I'VE EVER HEARD."

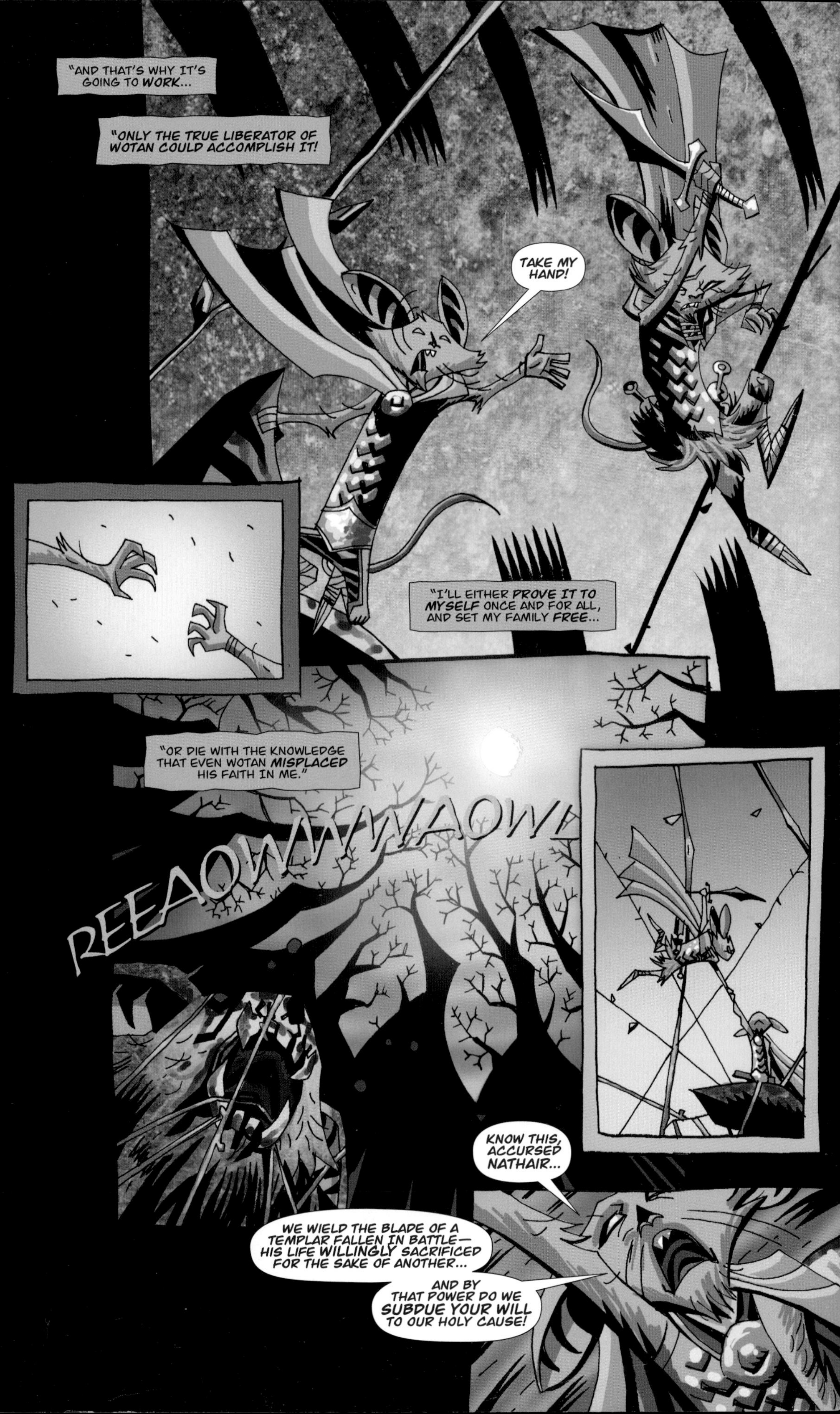
"AND THAT'S WHY IT'S GOING TO WORK...
"ONLY THE TRUE LIBERATOR OF WOTAN COULD ACCOMPLISH IT!
TAKE MY HAND!
"I'LL EITHER PROVE IT TO MYSELF ONCE AND FOR ALL, AND SET MY FAMILY FREE...
"OR DIE WITH THE KNOWLEDGE THAT EVEN WOTAN MISPLACED HIS FAITH IN ME."
REEAOWWWAOWL
KNOW THIS, ACCURSED NATHAIR...
WE WIELD THE BLADE OF A TEMPLAR FALLEN IN BATTLE— HIS LIFE WILLINGLY SACRIFICED FOR THE SAKE OF ANOTHER...
AND BY THAT POWER DO WE SUBDUE YOUR WILL TO OUR HOLY CAUSE!

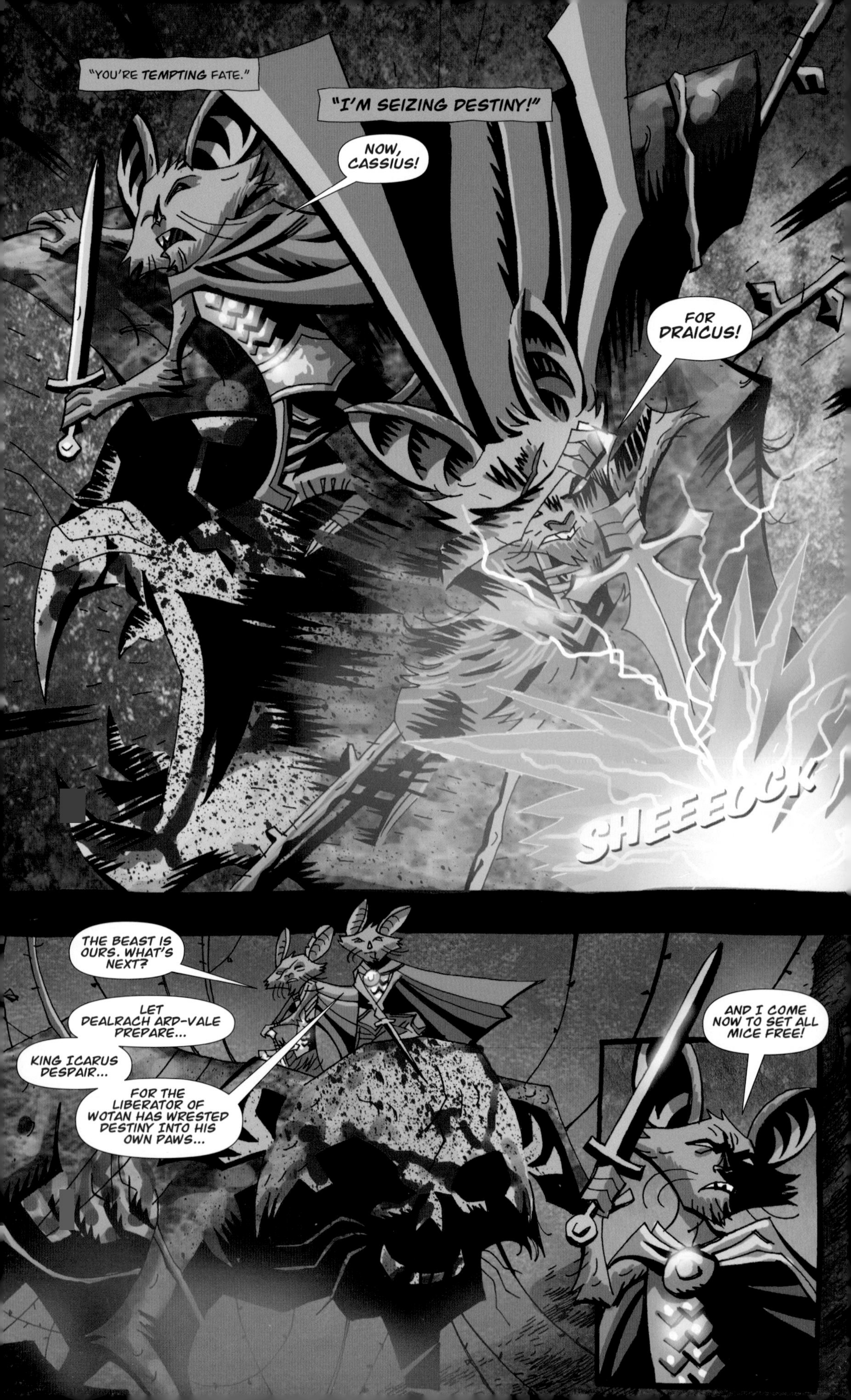
"YOU'RE TEMPTING FATE."
"I'M SEIZING DESTINY!"
NOW, CASSIUS!
FOR DRAICUS!
SHEEEOCK
THE BEAST IS OURS. WHAT'S NEXT?
LET DEALRACH ARD-VALE PREPARE...
KING ICARUS DESPAIR...
FOR THE LIBERATOR OF WOTAN HAS WRESTED DESTINY INTO HIS OWN PAWS...
AND I COME NOW TO SET ALL MICE FREE!

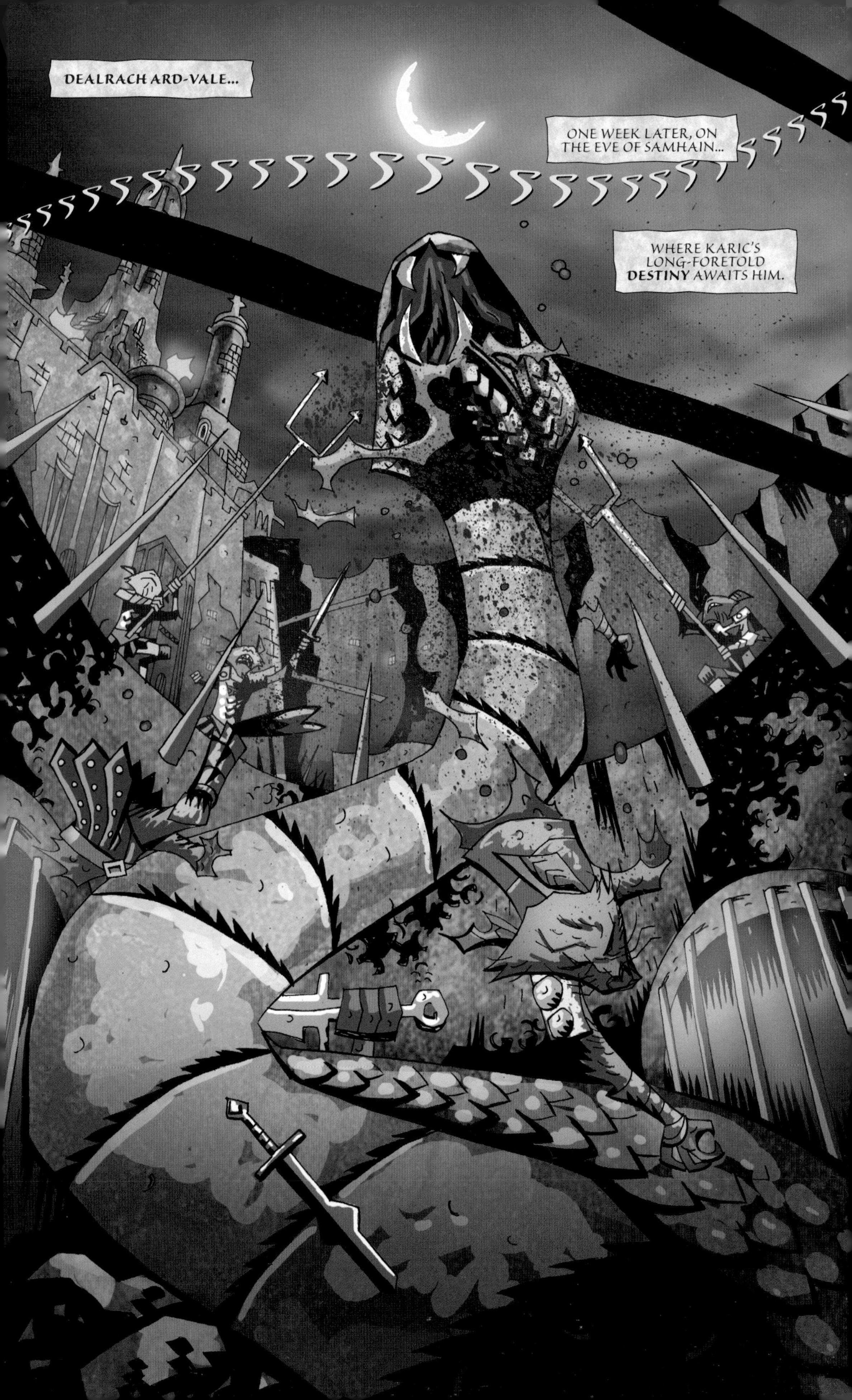
DEALRACH ARD-VALE...
ONE WEEK LATER, ON THE EVE OF SAMHAIN...
SSSSSSSSSSSSSSSSSSSSSSSSSSSSSSSSSSSSSS
WHERE KARIC'S LONG-FORETOLD DESTINY AWAITS HIM.

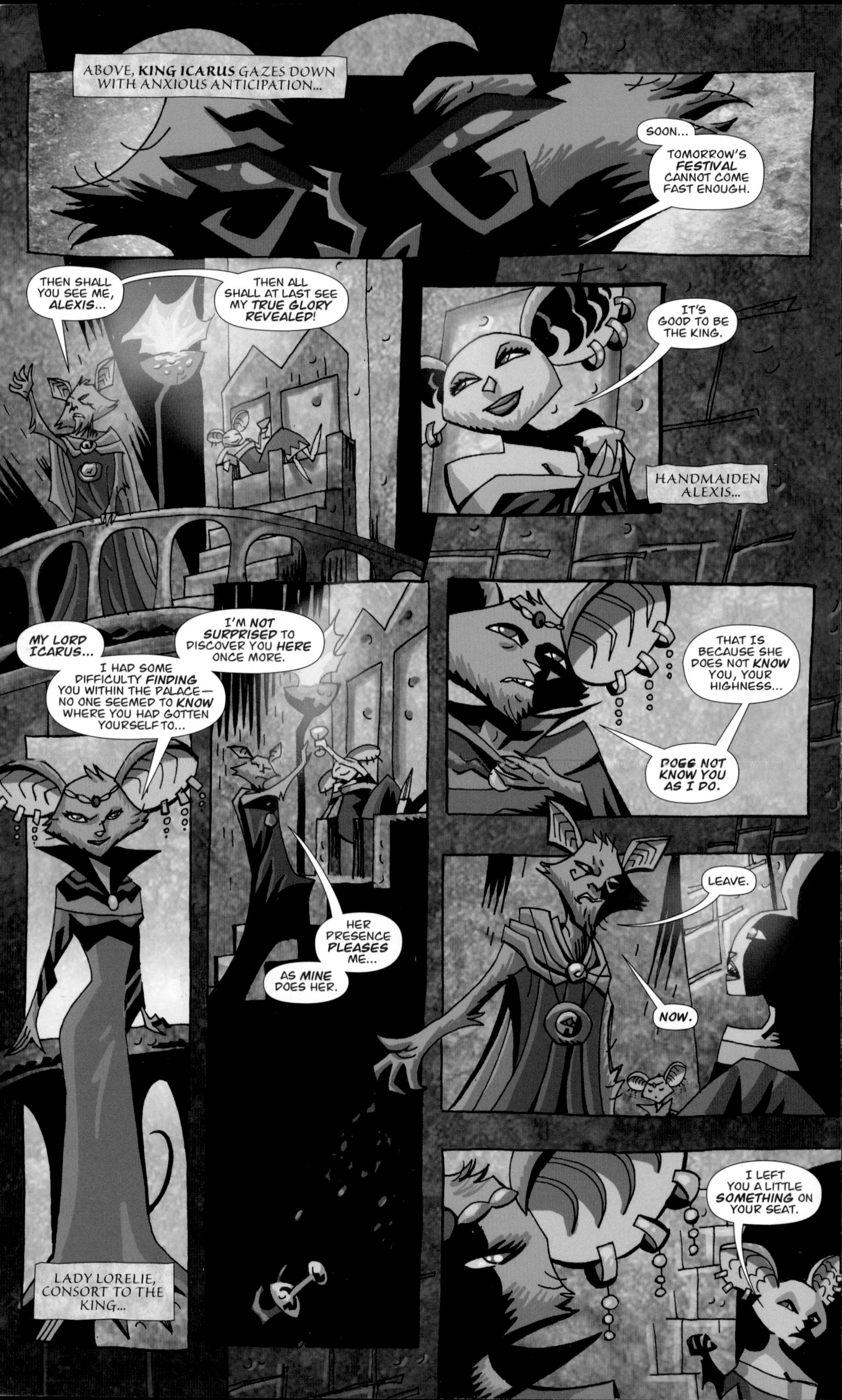
ABOVE, KING ICARUS GAZES DOWN WITH ANXIOUS ANTICIPATION...
SOON...
TOMORROW'S FESTIVAL CANNOT COME FAST ENOUGH.
THEN SHALL YOU SEE ME, ALEXIS...
THEN ALL SHALL AT LAST SEE MY TRUE GLORY REVEALED!
IT'S GOOD TO BE THE KING.
HANDMAIDEN ALEXIS...
MY LORD ICARUS...
I HAD SOME DIFFICULTY FINDING YOU WITHIN THE PALACE— NO ONE SEEMED TO KNOW WHERE YOU HAD GOTTEN YOURSELF TO...
I'M NOT SURPRISED TO DISCOVER YOU HERE ONCE MORE.
LADY LORELIE, CONSORT TO THE KING...
HER PRESENCE PLEASES ME...
AS MINE DOES HER.
THAT IS BECAUSE SHE DOES NOT KNOW YOU, YOUR HIGHNESS...
DOES NOT KNOW YOU AS I DO.
LEAVE.
NOW.
I LEFT YOU A LITTLE SOMETHING ON YOUR SEAT.

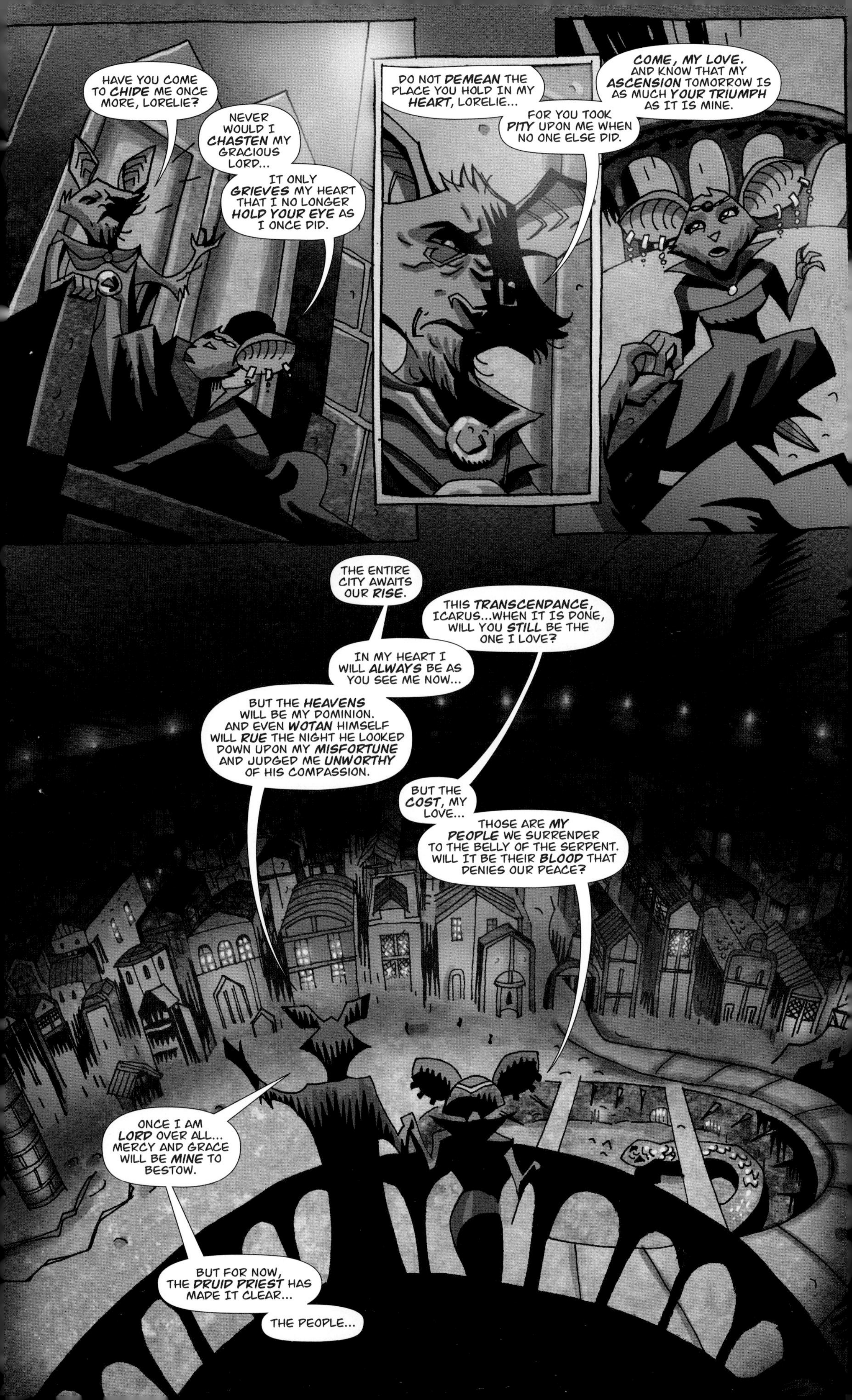
HAVE YOU COME TO CHIDE ME ONCE MORE, LORELIE?
NEVER WOULD I CHASTEN MY GRACIOUS LORD...
IT ONLY GRIEVES MY HEART THAT I NO LONGER HOLD YOUR EYE AS I ONCE DID.
DO NOT DEMEAN THE PLACE YOU HOLD IN MY HEART, LORELIE...
FOR YOU TOOK PITY UPON ME WHEN NO ONE ELSE DID.
COME, MY LOVE. AND KNOW THAT MY ASCENSION TOMORROW IS AS MUCH YOUR TRIUMPH AS IT IS MINE.
THE ENTIRE CITY AWAITS OUR RISE.
THIS TRANSCENDANCE, ICARUS...WHEN IT IS DONE, WILL YOU STILL BE THE ONE I LOVE?
IN MY HEART I WILL ALWAYS BE AS YOU SEE ME NOW...
BUT THE HEAVENS WILL BE MY DOMINION. AND EVEN WOTAN HIMSELF WILL RUE THE NIGHT HE LOOKED DOWN UPON MY MISFORTUNE AND JUDGED ME UNWORTHY OF HIS COMPASSION.
BUT THE COST, MY LOVE...
THOSE ARE MY PEOPLE WE SURRENDER TO THE BELLY OF THE SERPENT. WILL IT BE THEIR BLOOD THAT DENIES OUR PEACE?
ONCE I AM LORD OVER ALL... MERCY AND GRACE WILL BE MINE TO BESTOW.
BUT FOR NOW, THE DRUID PRIEST HAS MADE IT CLEAR...
THE PEOPLE...

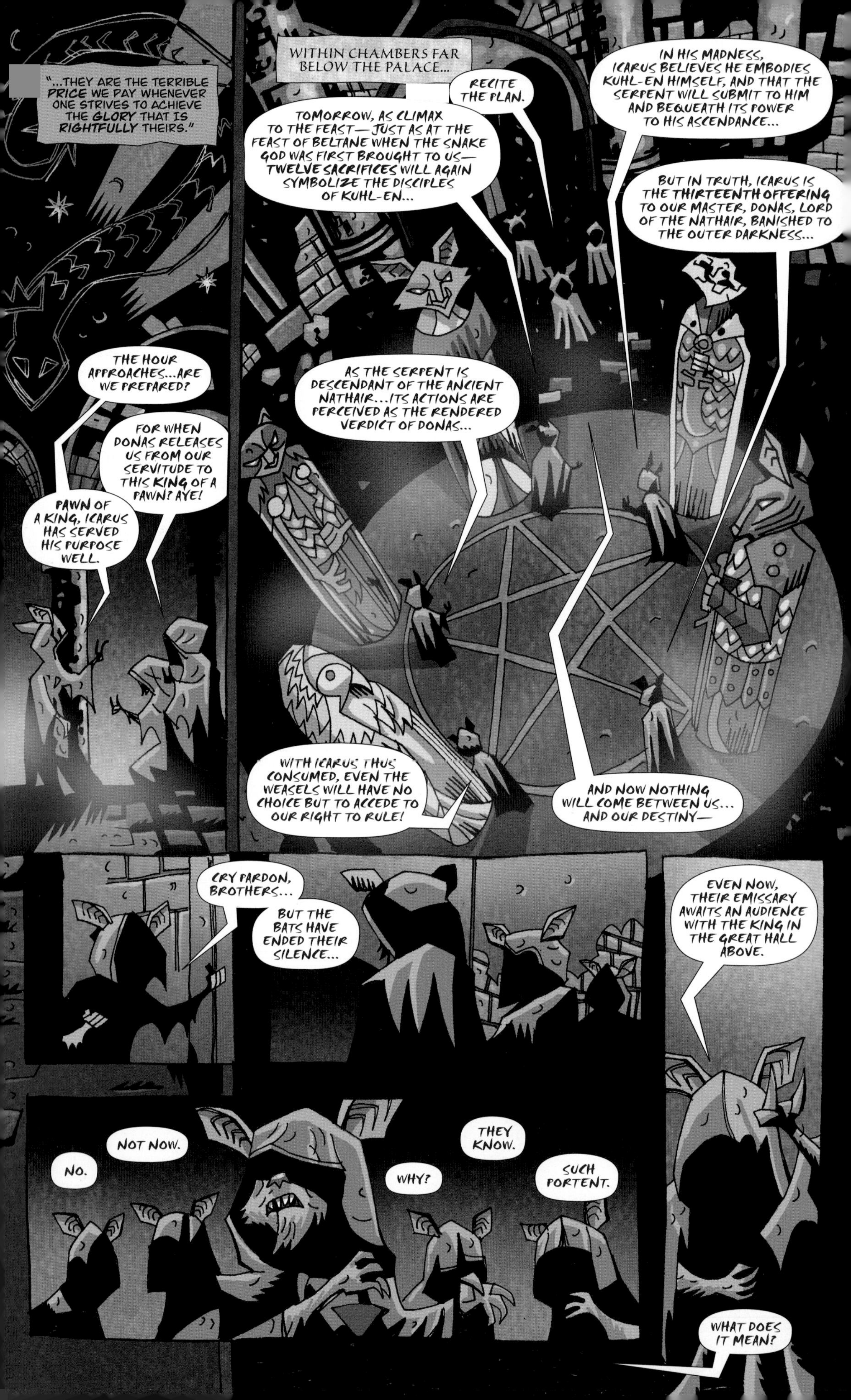
"...THEY ARE THE TERRIBLE PRICE WE PAY WHENEVER ONE STRIVES TO ACHIEVE THE GLORY THAT IS RIGHTFULLY THEIRS."
WITHIN CHAMBERS FAR BELOW THE PALACE...
RECITE THE PLAN.
TOMORROW, AS CLIMAX TO THE FEAST—JUST AS AT THE FEAST OF BELTANE WHEN THE SNAKE GOD WAS FIRST BROUGHT TO US—TWELVE SACRIFICES WILL AGAIN SYMBOLIZE THE DISCIPLES OF KUHL-EN...
IN HIS MADNESS, ICARUS BELIEVES HE EMBODIES KUHL-EN HIMSELF, AND THAT THE SERPENT WILL SUBMIT TO HIM AND BEQUEATH ITS POWER TO HIS ASCENDANCE...
BUT IN TRUTH, ICARUS IS THE THIRTEENTH OFFERING TO OUR MASTER, DONAS, LORD OF THE NATHAIR, BANISHED TO THE OUTER DARKNESS...
THE HOUR APPROACHES...ARE WE PREPARED?
FOR WHEN DONAS RELEASES US FROM OUR SERVITUDE TO THIS KING OF A PAWN? AYE!
PAWN OF A KING, ICARUS HAS SERVED HIS PURPOSE WELL.
AS THE SERPENT IS DESCENDANT OF THE ANCIENT NATHAIR...ITS ACTIONS ARE PERCEIVED AS THE RENDERED VERDICT OF DONAS...
WITH ICARUS THUS CONSUMED, EVEN THE WEASELS WILL HAVE NO CHOICE BUT TO ACCEDE TO OUR RIGHT TO RULE!
AND NOW NOTHING WILL COME BETWEEN US... AND OUR DESTINY—
CRY PARDON, BROTHERS...
BUT THE BATS HAVE ENDED THEIR SILENCE...
EVEN NOW, THEIR EMISSARY AWAITS AN AUDIENCE WITH THE KING IN THE GREAT HALL ABOVE.
NO.
NOT NOW.
WHY?
THEY KNOW.
SUCH PORTENT.
WHAT DOES IT MEAN?

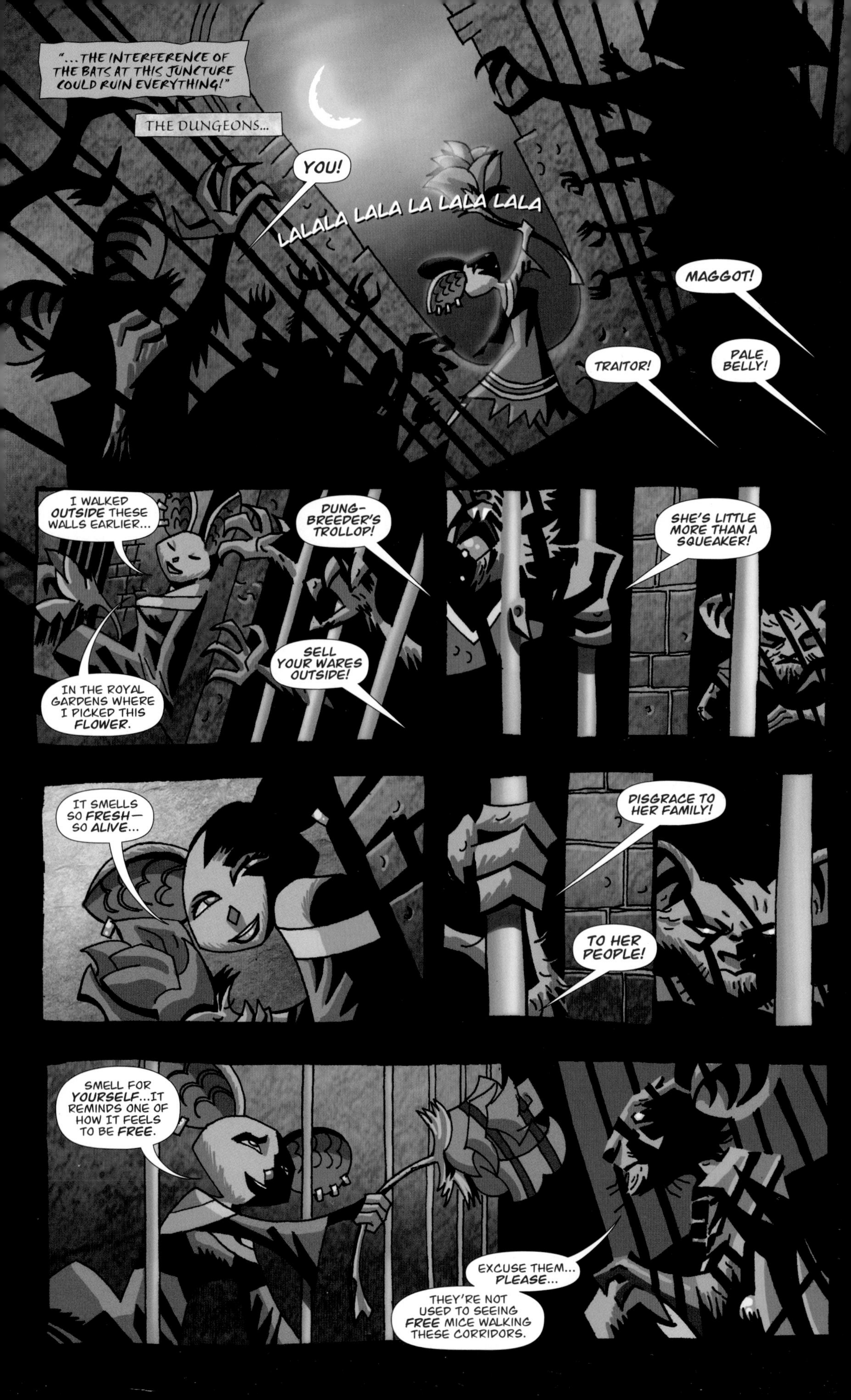
"...THE INTERFERENCE OF THE BATS AT THIS JUNCTURE COULD RUIN EVERYTHING!"
THE DUNGEONS...
YOU!
LALALA LALA LA LALA LALA
MAGGOT!
TRAITOR!
PALE BELLY!
I WALKED OUTSIDE THESE WALLS EARLIER...
IN THE ROYAL GARDENS WHERE I PICKED THIS FLOWER.
DUNG-BREEDER'S TROLLOP!
SELL YOUR WARES OUTSIDE!
SHE'S LITTLE MORE THAN A SQUEAKER!
IT SMELLS SO FRESH— SO ALIVE...
DISGRACE TO HER FAMILY!
TO HER PEOPLE!
SMELL FOR YOURSELF...IT REMINDS ONE OF HOW IT FEELS TO BE FREE.
EXCUSE THEM... PLEASE...
THEY'RE NOT USED TO SEEING FREE MICE WALKING THESE CORRIDORS.

AND *YOU* ARE?

I'M LEITO.

ALEXIS.

SO LEITO, WHAT'D YOU DO TO GET *LOCKED UP* IN HERE WITH THE REST OF THIS RIFF-RAFF?

LIKE MOST HERE, I DID *NOTHING* TO WARRANT THIS...

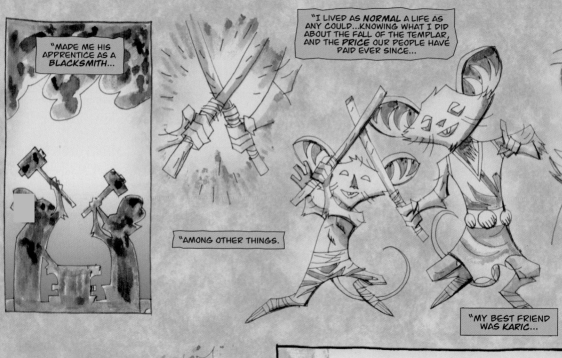

"MADE ME HIS APPRENTICE AS A *BLACKSMITH*...

"I LIVED AS *NORMAL* A LIFE AS ANY COULD...KNOWING WHAT I DID ABOUT THE FALL OF THE TEMPLAR, AND THE *PRICE* OUR PEOPLE HAVE PAID EVER SINCE...

"AMONG OTHER THINGS.

"MY BEST FRIEND WAS *KARIC*...

"BUT ALL THAT ENDED WHEN *CAPTAIN TOSK* LED A RAT RAIDING PARTY TO OUR TOWN...

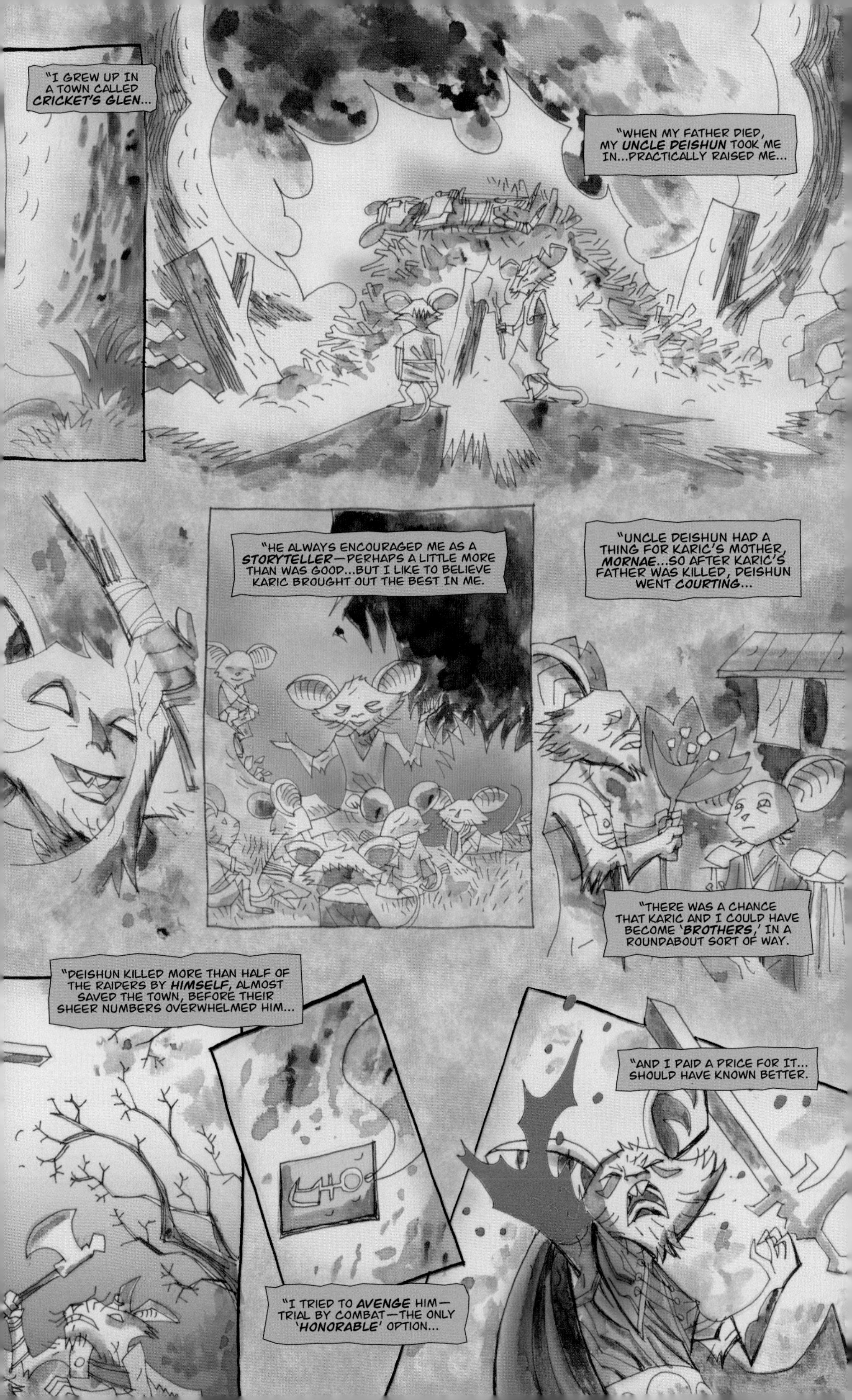
"I GREW UP IN A TOWN CALLED CRICKET'S GLEN...
"WHEN MY FATHER DIED, MY UNCLE DEISHUN TOOK ME IN...PRACTICALLY RAISED ME...
"HE ALWAYS ENCOURAGED ME AS A STORYTELLER—PERHAPS A LITTLE MORE THAN WAS GOOD...BUT I LIKE TO BELIEVE KARIC BROUGHT OUT THE BEST IN ME.
"UNCLE DEISHUN HAD A THING FOR KARIC'S MOTHER, MORNAE...SO AFTER KARIC'S FATHER WAS KILLED, DEISHUN WENT COURTING...
"THERE WAS A CHANCE THAT KARIC AND I COULD HAVE BECOME 'BROTHERS,' IN A ROUNDABOUT SORT OF WAY.
"DEISHUN KILLED MORE THAN HALF OF THE RAIDERS BY HIMSELF, ALMOST SAVED THE TOWN, BEFORE THEIR SHEER NUMBERS OVERWHELMED HIM...
"I TRIED TO AVENGE HIM—TRIAL BY COMBAT—THE ONLY 'HONORABLE' OPTION...
"AND I PAID A PRICE FOR IT... SHOULD HAVE KNOWN BETTER.

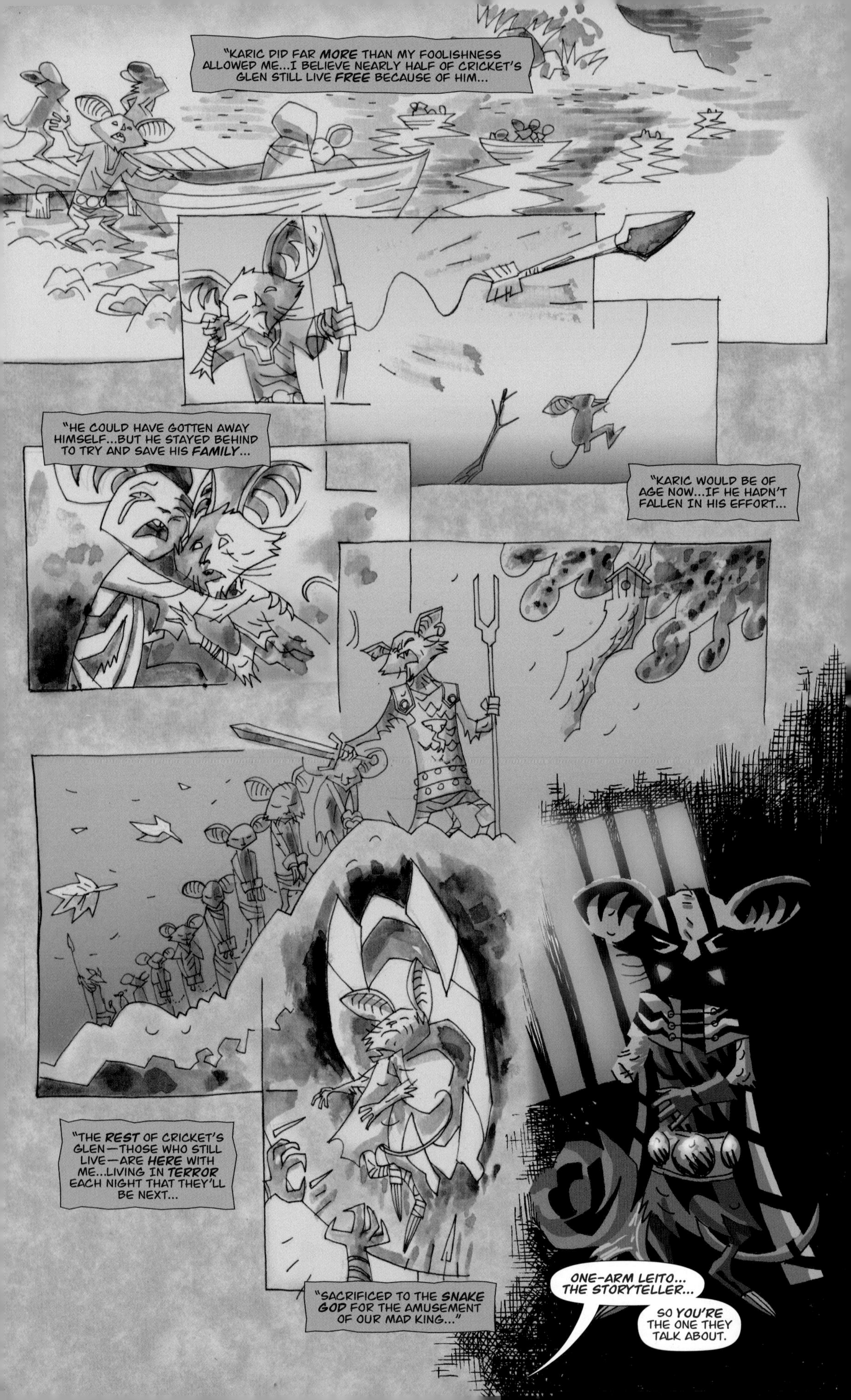
"KARIC DID FAR MORE THAN MY FOOLISHNESS ALLOWED ME...I BELIEVE NEARLY HALF OF CRICKET'S GLEN STILL LIVE FREE BECAUSE OF HIM...
"HE COULD HAVE GOTTEN AWAY HIMSELF...BUT HE STAYED BEHIND TO TRY AND SAVE HIS FAMILY...
"KARIC WOULD BE OF AGE NOW...IF HE HADN'T FALLEN IN HIS EFFORT...
"THE REST OF CRICKET'S GLEN—THOSE WHO STILL LIVE—ARE HERE WITH ME...LIVING IN TERROR EACH NIGHT THAT THEY'LL BE NEXT...
"SACRIFICED TO THE SNAKE GOD FOR THE AMUSEMENT OF OUR MAD KING..."
ONE-ARM LEITO... THE STORYTELLER...
SO YOU'RE THE ONE THEY TALK ABOUT.

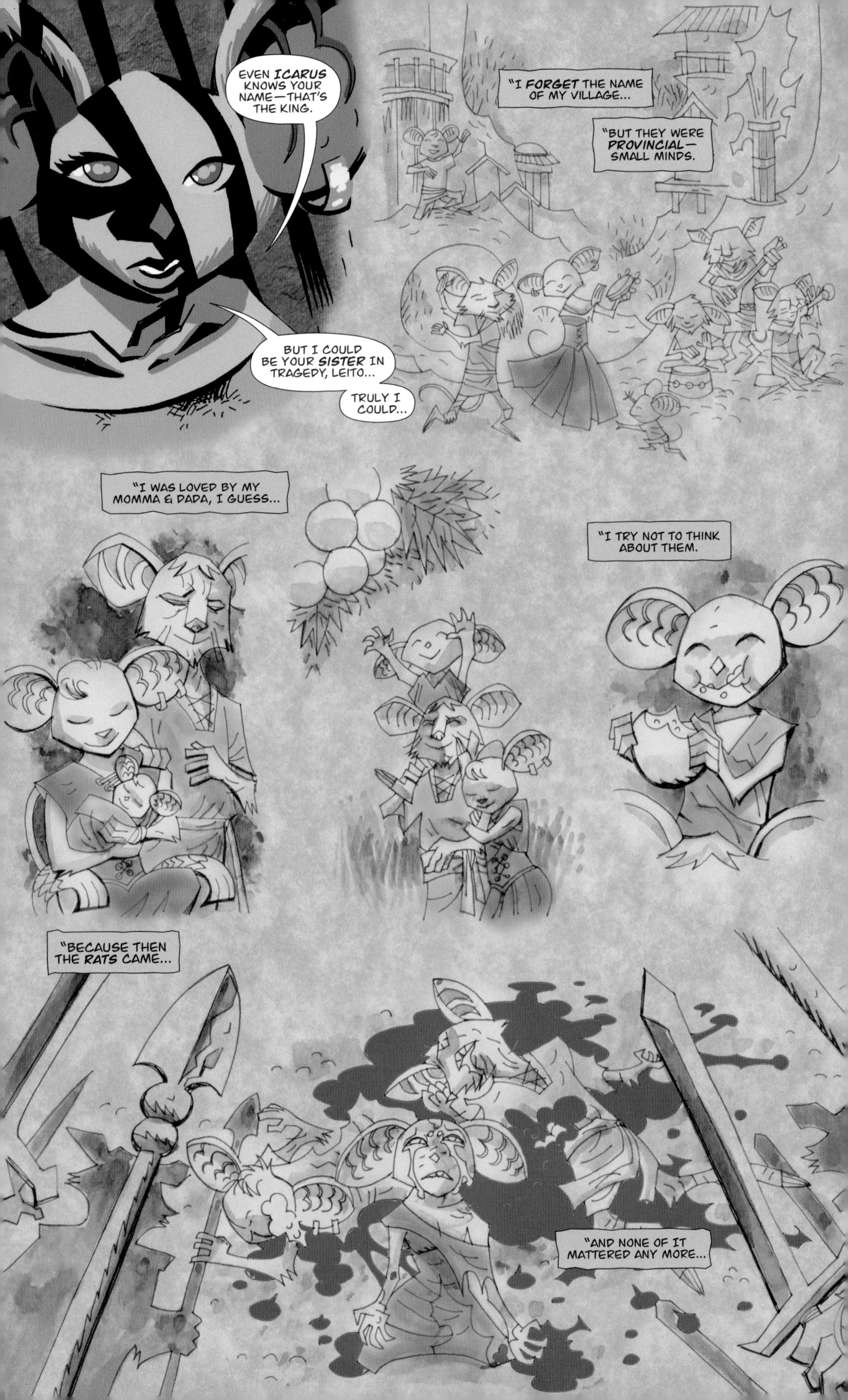
EVEN ICARUS KNOWS YOUR NAME—THAT'S THE KING.
"I FORGET THE NAME OF MY VILLAGE...
"BUT THEY WERE PROVINCIAL—SMALL MINDS.
BUT I COULD BE YOUR SISTER IN TRAGEDY, LEITO...
TRULY I COULD...
"I WAS LOVED BY MY MOMMA & DADA, I GUESS...
"I TRY NOT TO THINK ABOUT THEM.
"BECAUSE THEN THE RATS CAME...
"AND NONE OF IT MATTERED ANY MORE...

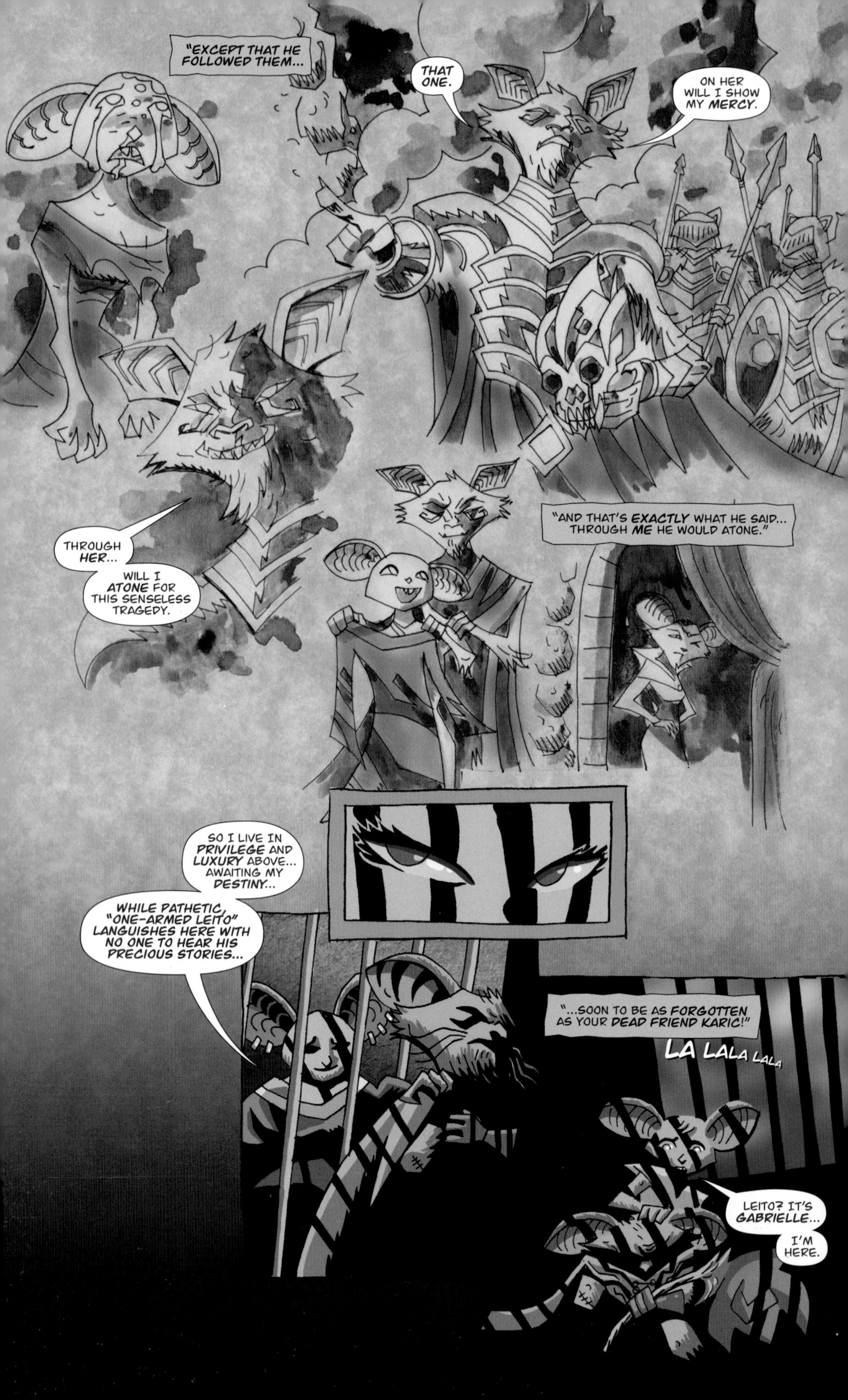
"EXCEPT THAT HE FOLLOWED THEM...
THAT ONE.
ON HER WILL I SHOW MY MERCY.
THROUGH HER...
WILL I ATONE FOR THIS SENSELESS TRAGEDY.
"AND THAT'S EXACTLY WHAT HE SAID... THROUGH ME HE WOULD ATONE."
SO I LIVE IN PRIVILEGE AND LUXURY ABOVE... AWAITING MY DESTINY...
WHILE PATHETIC, "ONE-ARMED LEITO" LANGUISHES HERE WITH NO ONE TO HEAR HIS PRECIOUS STORIES...
"...SOON TO BE AS FORGOTTEN AS YOUR DEAD FRIEND KARIC!"
LA LALA LALA
LEITO? IT'S GABRIELLE...
I'M HERE.

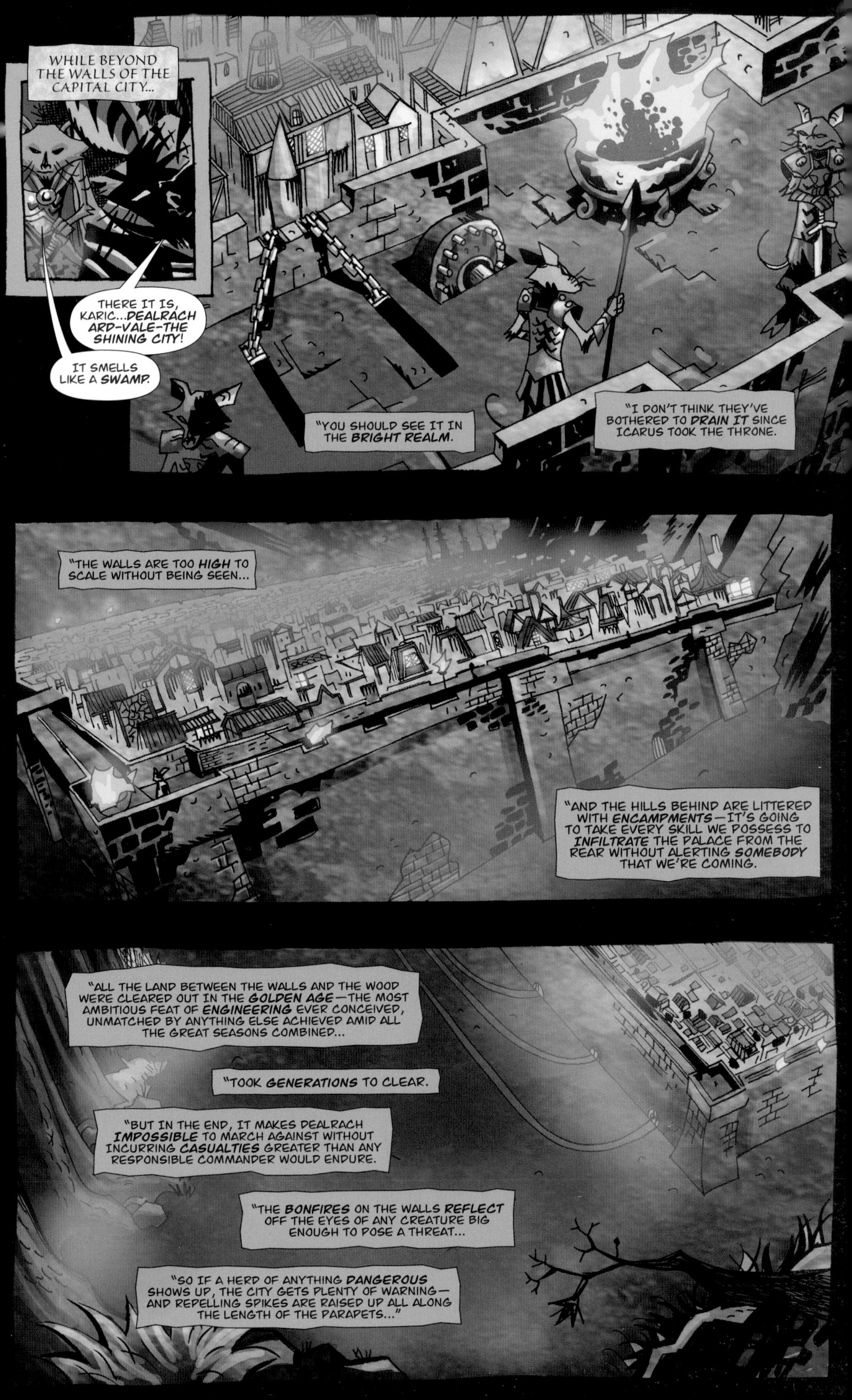
WHILE BEYOND THE WALLS OF THE CAPITAL CITY...
THERE IT IS, KARIC...DEALRACH ARD-VALE-THE SHINING CITY!
IT SMELLS LIKE A SWAMP.
"YOU SHOULD SEE IT IN THE BRIGHT REALM.
"I DON'T THINK THEY'VE BOTHERED TO DRAIN IT SINCE ICARUS TOOK THE THRONE.
"THE WALLS ARE TOO HIGH TO SCALE WITHOUT BEING SEEN...
"AND THE HILLS BEHIND ARE LITTERED WITH ENCAMPMENTS—IT'S GOING TO TAKE EVERY SKILL WE POSSESS TO INFILTRATE THE PALACE FROM THE REAR WITHOUT ALERTING SOMEBODY THAT WE'RE COMING.
"ALL THE LAND BETWEEN THE WALLS AND THE WOOD WERE CLEARED OUT IN THE GOLDEN AGE—THE MOST AMBITIOUS FEAT OF ENGINEERING EVER CONCEIVED, UNMATCHED BY ANYTHING ELSE ACHIEVED AMID ALL THE GREAT SEASONS COMBINED...
"TOOK GENERATIONS TO CLEAR.
"BUT IN THE END, IT MAKES DEALRACH IMPOSSIBLE TO MARCH AGAINST WITHOUT INCURRING CASUALTIES GREATER THAN ANY RESPONSIBLE COMMANDER WOULD ENDURE.
"THE BONFIRES ON THE WALLS REFLECT OFF THE EYES OF ANY CREATURE BIG ENOUGH TO POSE A THREAT...
"SO IF A HERD OF ANYTHING DANGEROUS SHOWS UP, THE CITY GETS PLENTY OF WARNING—AND REPELLING SPIKES ARE RAISED UP ALL ALONG THE LENGTH OF THE PARAPETS..."

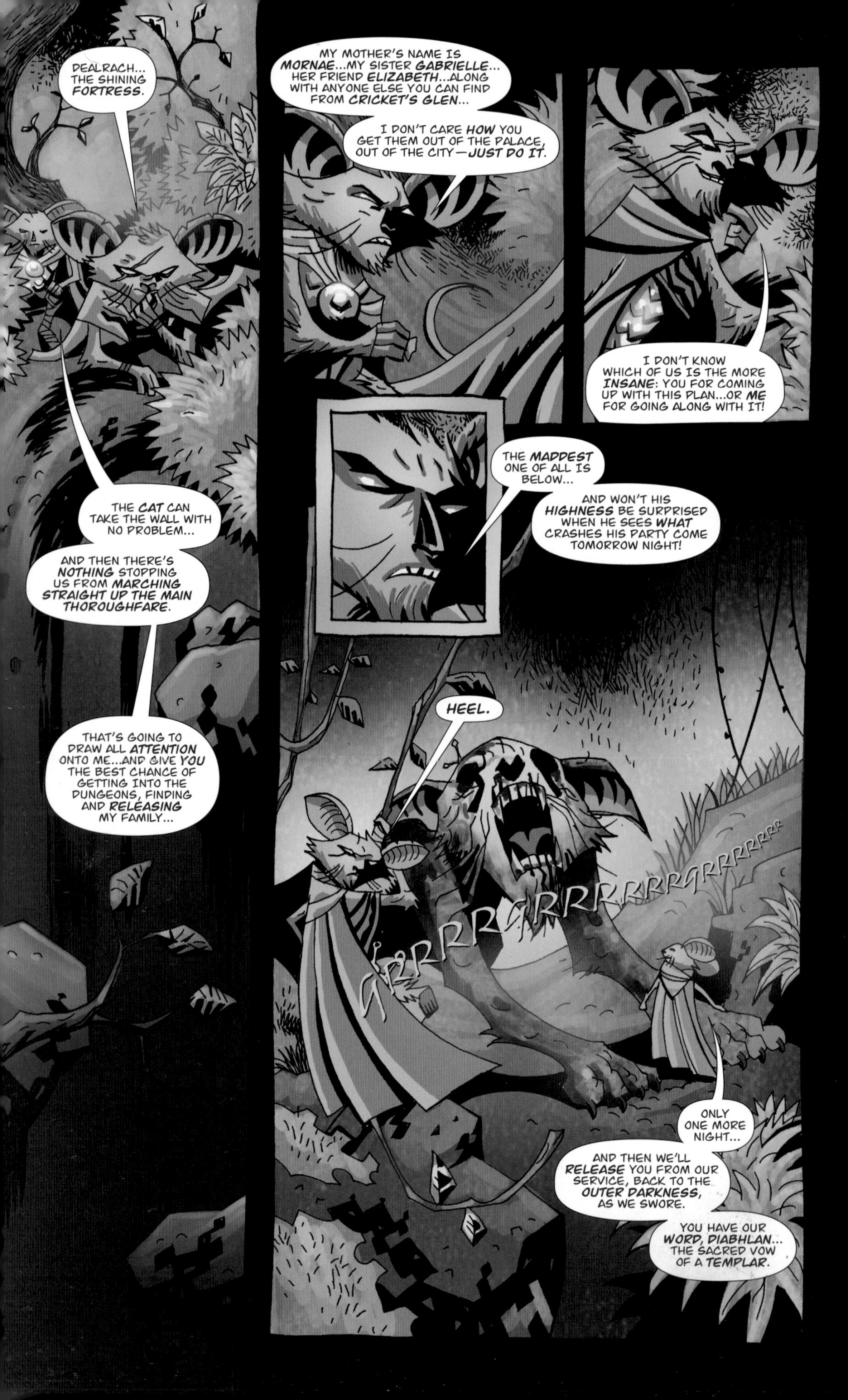

DEALRACH... THE SHINING FORTRESS.
THE CAT CAN TAKE THE WALL WITH NO PROBLEM...
AND THEN THERE'S NOTHING STOPPING US FROM MARCHING STRAIGHT UP THE MAIN THOROUGHFARE.
THAT'S GOING TO DRAW ALL ATTENTION ONTO ME...AND GIVE YOU THE BEST CHANCE OF GETTING INTO THE DUNGEONS, FINDING AND RELEASING MY FAMILY...
MY MOTHER'S NAME IS MORNAE...MY SISTER GABRIELLE... HER FRIEND ELIZABETH...ALONG WITH ANYONE ELSE YOU CAN FIND FROM CRICKET'S GLEN...
I DON'T CARE HOW YOU GET THEM OUT OF THE PALACE, OUT OF THE CITY—JUST DO IT.
I DON'T KNOW WHICH OF US IS THE MORE INSANE: YOU FOR COMING UP WITH THIS PLAN...OR ME FOR GOING ALONG WITH IT!
THE MADDEST ONE OF ALL IS BELOW...
AND WON'T HIS HIGHNESS BE SURPRISED WHEN HE SEES WHAT CRASHES HIS PARTY COME TOMORROW NIGHT!
HEEL.
GRRRRRGRRRRRRRRGRRRRRRRR
ONLY ONE MORE NIGHT...
AND THEN WE'LL RELEASE YOU FROM OUR SERVICE, BACK TO THE OUTER DARKNESS, AS WE SWORE.
YOU HAVE OUR WORD, DIABHLAN... THE SACRED VOW OF A TEMPLAR.

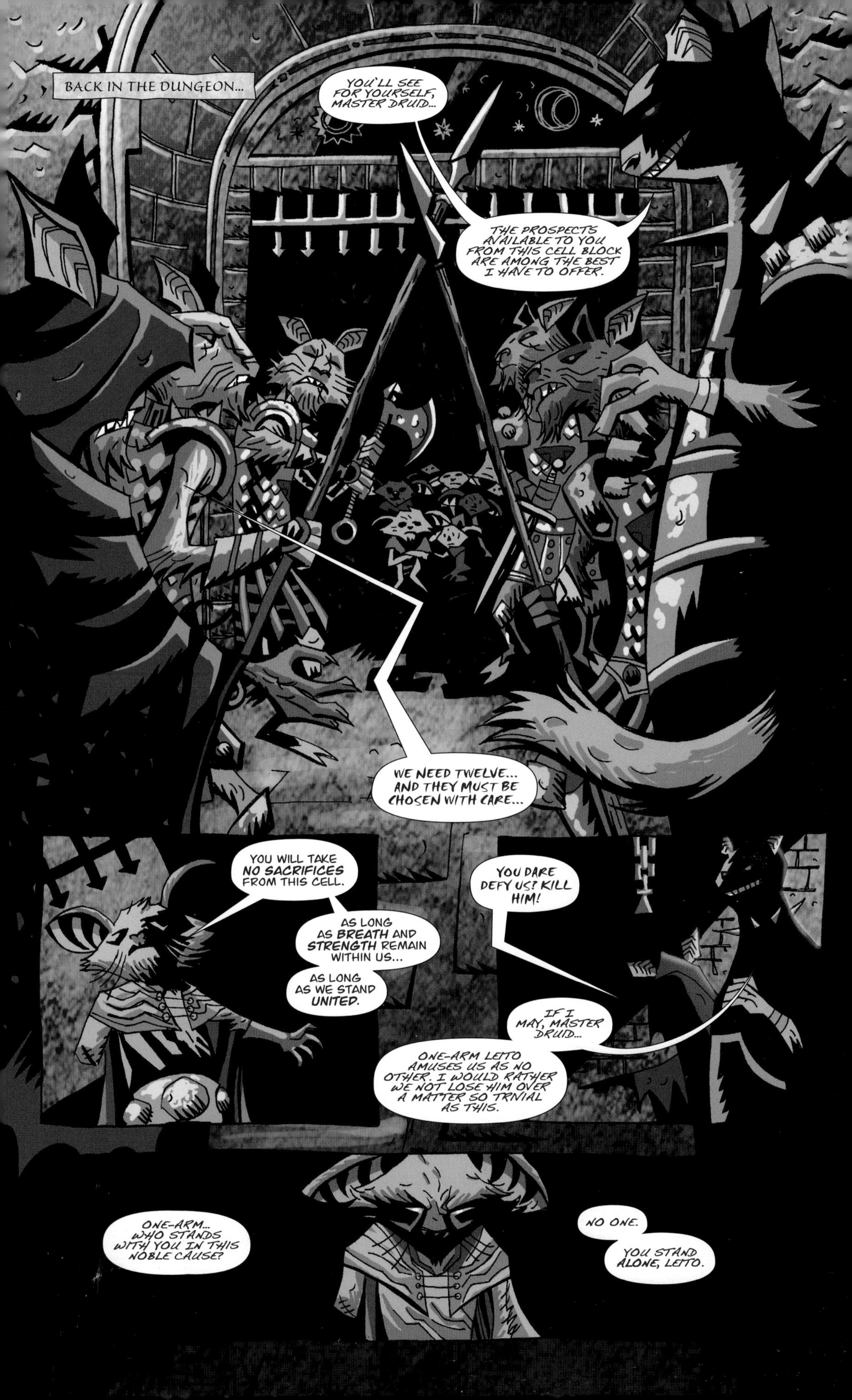
BACK IN THE DUNGEON...
YOU'LL SEE FOR YOURSELF, MASTER DRUID...
THE PROSPECTS AVAILABLE TO YOU FROM THIS CELL BLOCK ARE AMONG THE BEST I HAVE TO OFFER.
WE NEED TWELVE... AND THEY MUST BE CHOSEN WITH CARE...
YOU WILL TAKE NO SACRIFICES FROM THIS CELL.
AS LONG AS BREATH AND STRENGTH REMAIN WITHIN US...
AS LONG AS WE STAND UNITED.
YOU DARE DEFY US? KILL HIM!
IF I MAY, MASTER DRUID...
ONE-ARM LEITO AMUSES US AS NO OTHER. I WOULD RATHER WE NOT LOSE HIM OVER A MATTER SO TRIVIAL AS THIS.
ONE-ARM... WHO STANDS WITH YOU IN THIS NOBLE CAUSE?
NO ONE.
YOU STAND ALONE, LEITO.

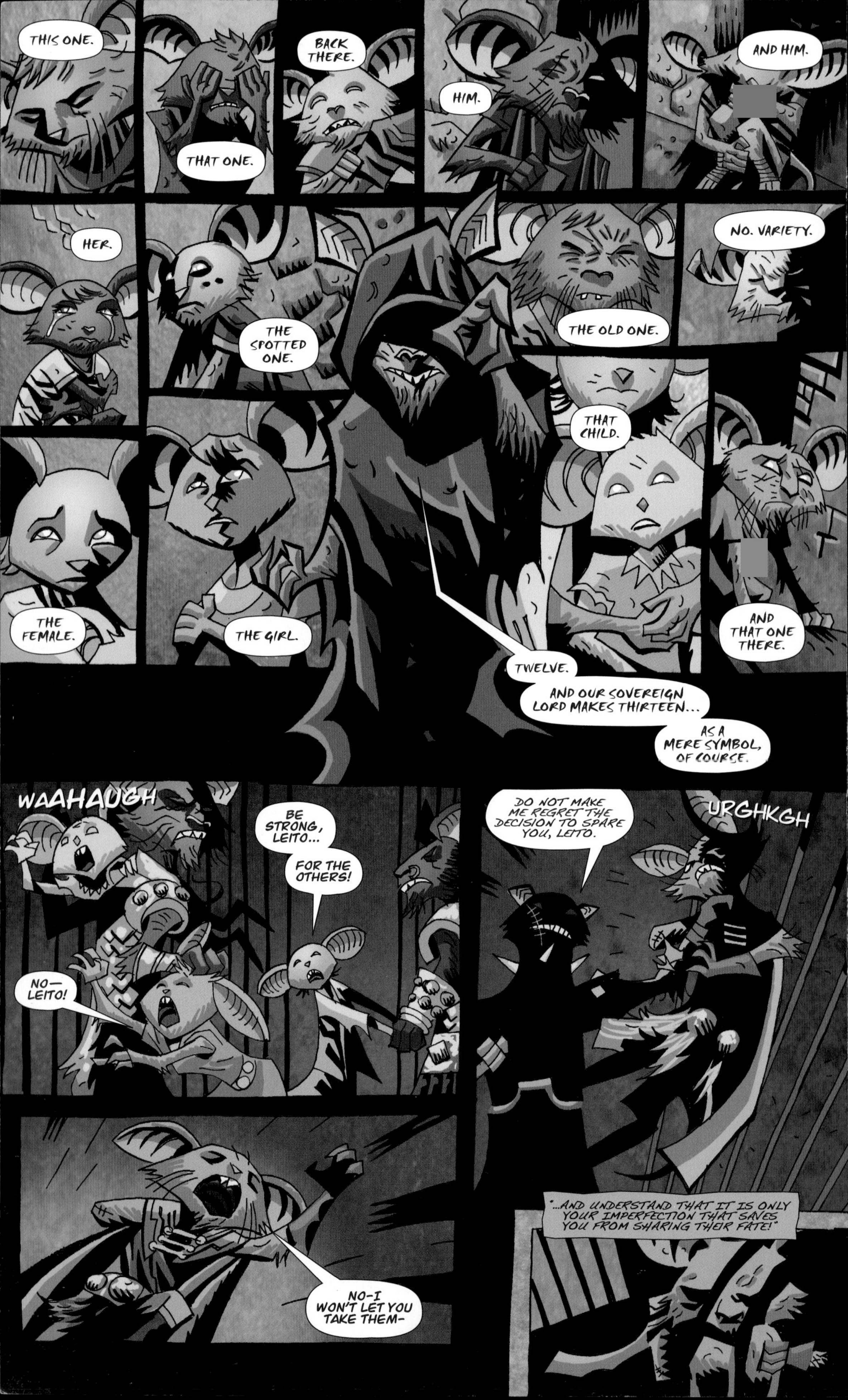
THIS ONE.
THAT ONE.
BACK THERE.
HIM.
AND HIM.
HER.
THE SPOTTED ONE.
THE OLD ONE.
NO. VARIETY.
THAT CHILD.
THE FEMALE.
THE GIRL.
AND THAT ONE THERE.
TWELVE.
AND OUR SOVEREIGN LORD MAKES THIRTEEN...
AS A MERE SYMBOL, OF COURSE.
WAAHAUGH
BE STRONG, LEITO...
FOR THE OTHERS!
NO— LEITO!
NO-I WON'T LET YOU TAKE THEM-
DO NOT MAKE ME REGRET THE DECISION TO SPARE YOU, LEITO.
URGHKGH
"...AND UNDERSTAND THAT IT IS ONLY YOUR IMPERFECTION THAT SAVES YOU FROM SHARING THEIR FATE!"

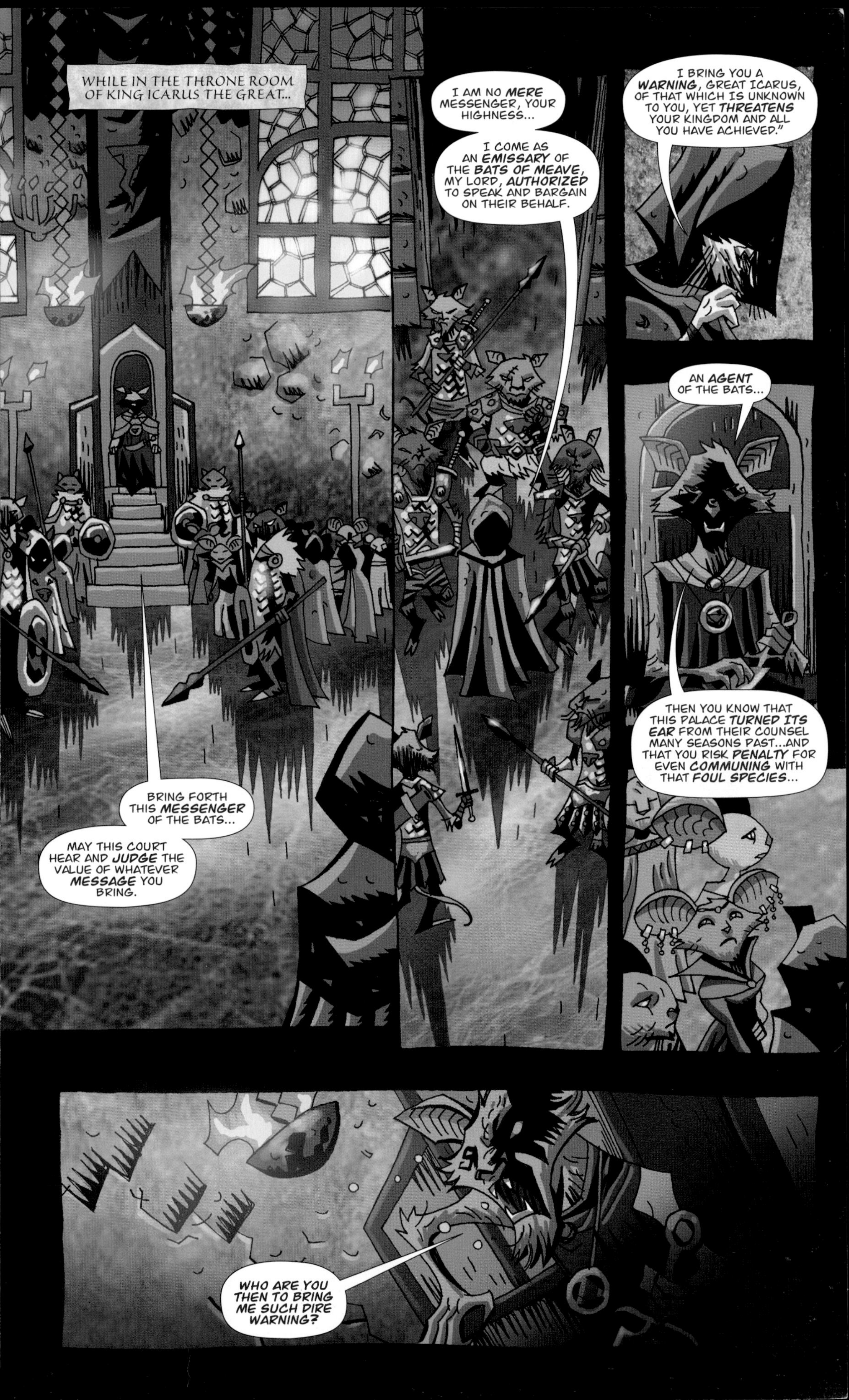
WHILE IN THE THRONE ROOM OF KING ICARUS THE GREAT...
BRING FORTH THIS MESSENGER OF THE BATS...
MAY THIS COURT HEAR AND JUDGE THE VALUE OF WHATEVER MESSAGE YOU BRING.
I AM NO MERE MESSENGER, YOUR HIGHNESS...
I COME AS AN EMISSARY OF THE BATS OF MEAVE, MY LORD, AUTHORIZED TO SPEAK AND BARGAIN ON THEIR BEHALF.
I BRING YOU A WARNING, GREAT ICARUS, OF THAT WHICH IS UNKNOWN TO YOU, YET THREATENS YOUR KINGDOM AND ALL YOU HAVE ACHIEVED."
AN AGENT OF THE BATS...
THEN YOU KNOW THAT THIS PALACE TURNED ITS EAR FROM THEIR COUNSEL MANY SEASONS PAST...AND THAT YOU RISK PENALTY FOR EVEN COMMUNING WITH THAT FOUL SPECIES...
WHO ARE YOU THEN TO BRING ME SUCH DIRE WARNING?

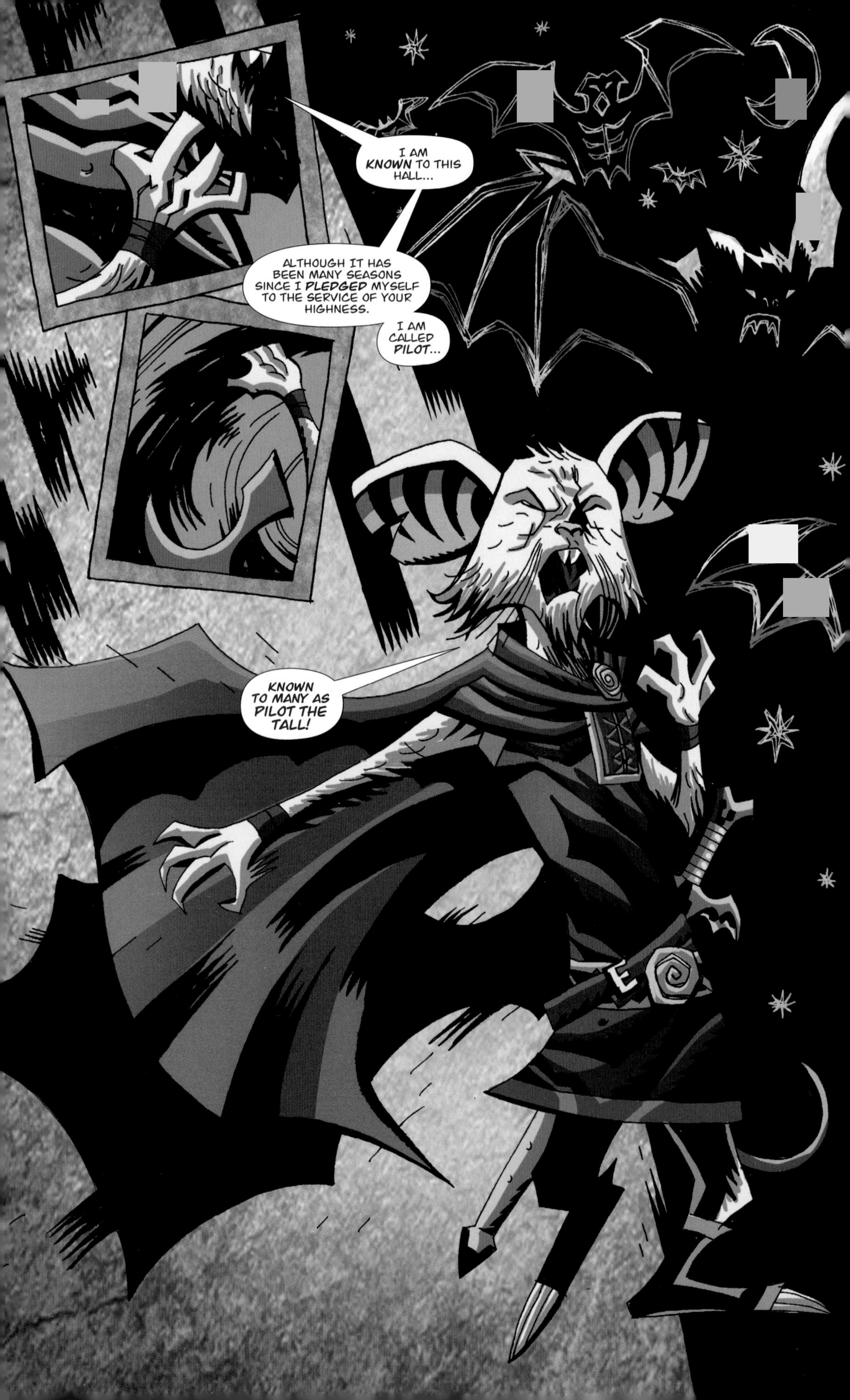
I AM KNOWN TO THIS HALL...
ALTHOUGH IT HAS BEEN MANY SEASONS SINCE I PLEDGED MYSELF TO THE SERVICE OF YOUR HIGHNESS.
I AM CALLED PILOT...
KNOWN TO MANY AS PILOT THE TALL!

CHAPTER EIGHT

THE FESTIVAL OF SAMHAIN

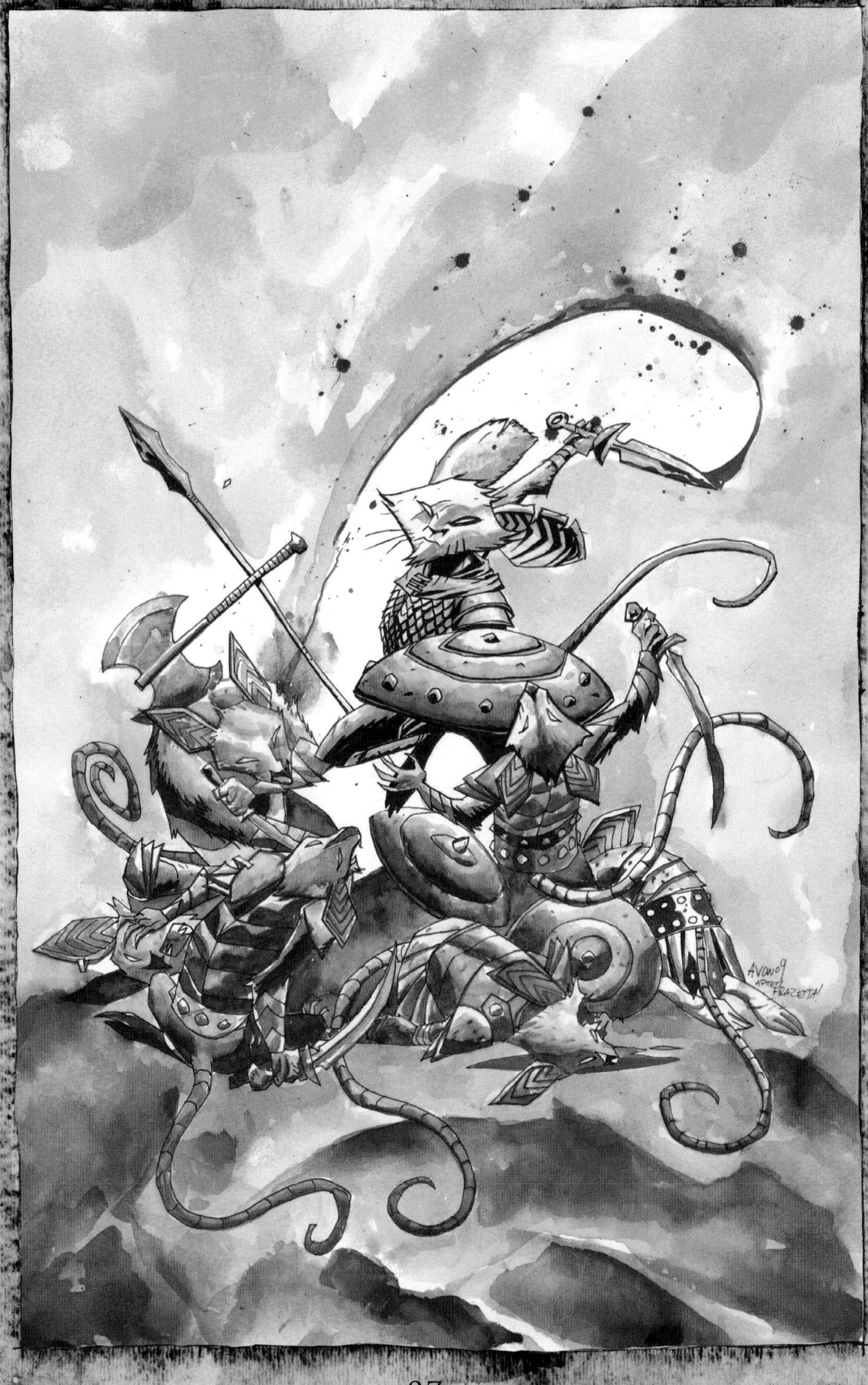

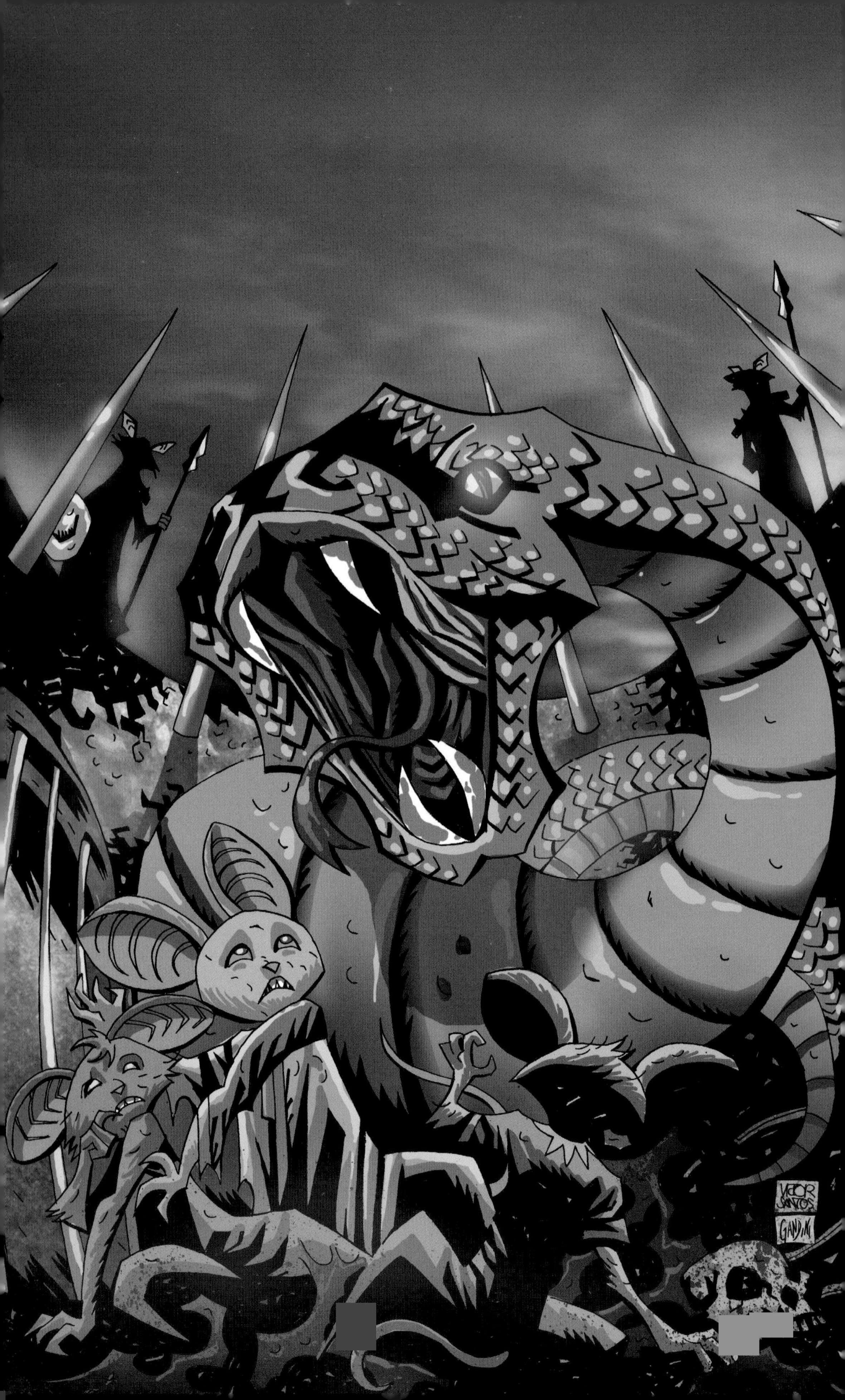
VICTOR SANTOS
GANDINI

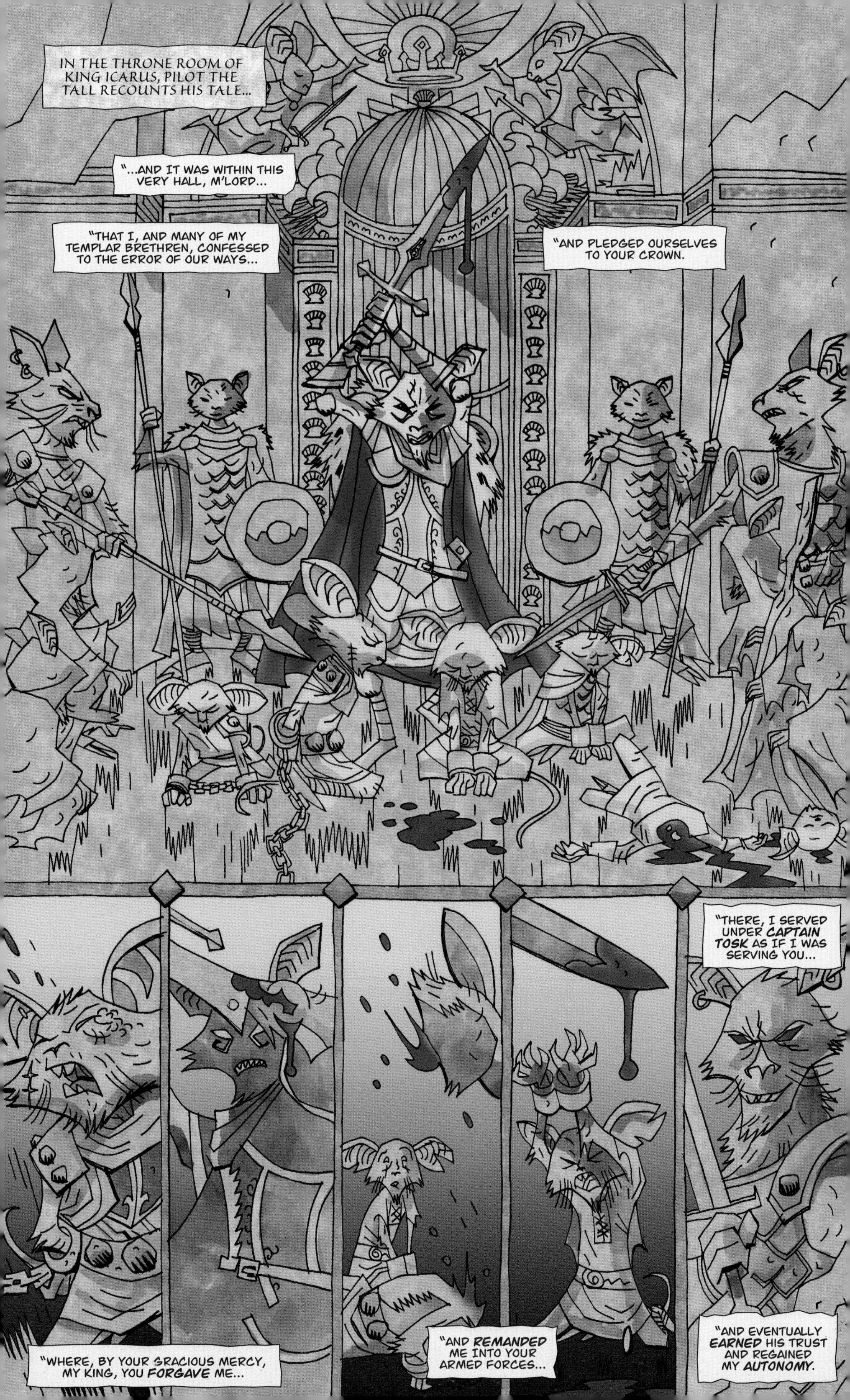

IN THE THRONE ROOM OF KING ICARUS, PILOT THE TALL RECOUNTS HIS TALE...
"...AND IT WAS WITHIN THIS VERY HALL, M'LORD...
"THAT I, AND MANY OF MY TEMPLAR BRETHREN, CONFESSED TO THE ERROR OF OUR WAYS...
"AND PLEDGED OURSELVES TO YOUR CROWN.
"WHERE, BY YOUR GRACIOUS MERCY, MY KING, YOU FORGAVE ME...
"AND REMANDED ME INTO YOUR ARMED FORCES...
"THERE, I SERVED UNDER CAPTAIN TOSK AS IF I WAS SERVING YOU...
"AND EVENTUALLY EARNED HIS TRUST AND REGAINED MY AUTONOMY.

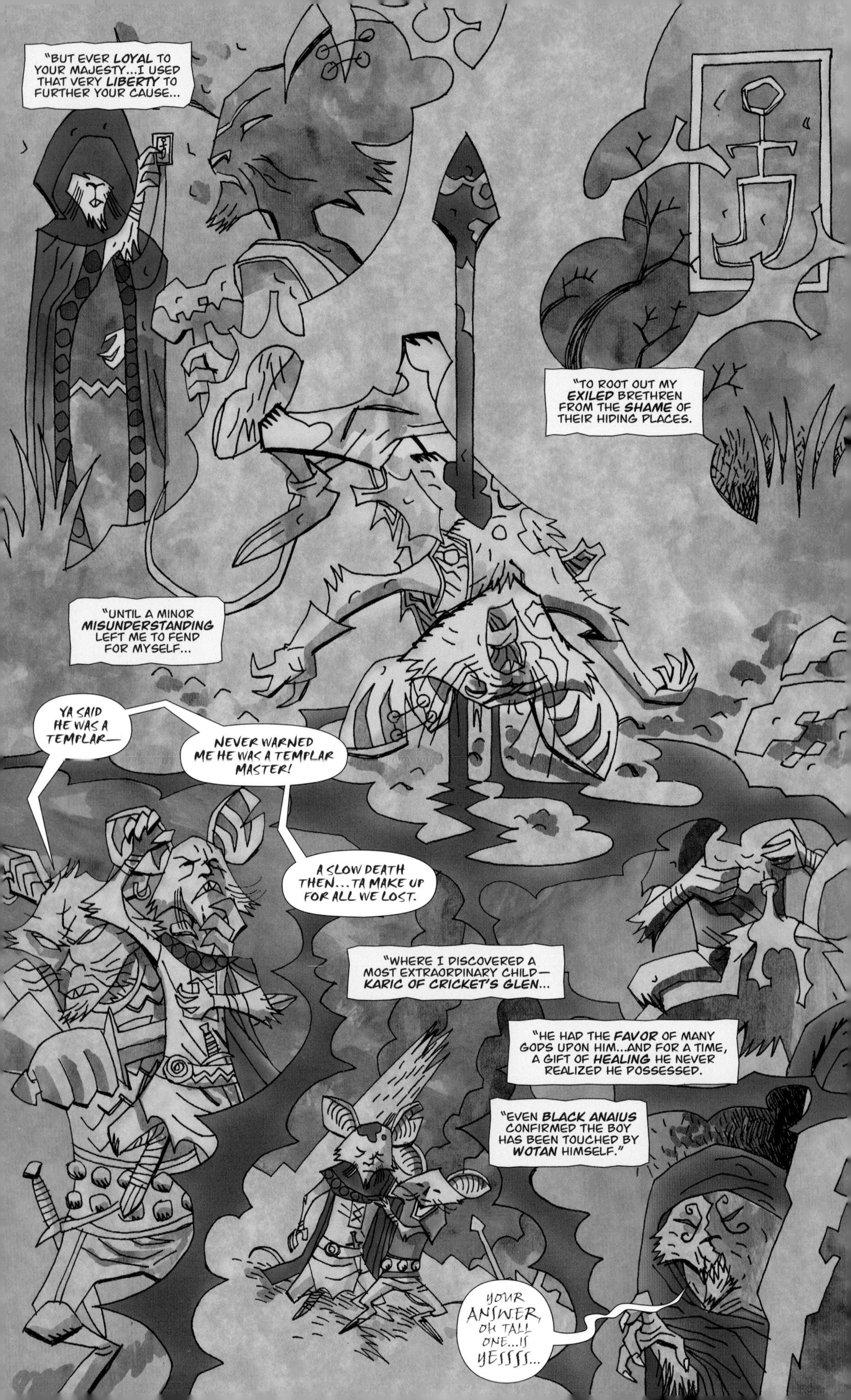
"BUT EVER LOYAL TO YOUR MAJESTY...I USED THAT VERY LIBERTY TO FURTHER YOUR CAUSE...
"TO ROOT OUT MY EXILED BRETHREN FROM THE SHAME OF THEIR HIDING PLACES.
"UNTIL A MINOR MISUNDERSTANDING LEFT ME TO FEND FOR MYSELF...
YA SAID HE WAS A TEMPLAR—
NEVER WARNED ME HE WAS A TEMPLAR MASTER!
A SLOW DEATH THEN... TA MAKE UP FOR ALL WE LOST.
"WHERE I DISCOVERED A MOST EXTRAORDINARY CHILD— KARIC OF CRICKET'S GLEN...
"HE HAD THE FAVOR OF MANY GODS UPON HIM...AND FOR A TIME, A GIFT OF HEALING HE NEVER REALIZED HE POSSESSED.
"EVEN BLACK ANAIUS CONFIRMED THE BOY HAS BEEN TOUCHED BY WOTAN HIMSELF."
YOUR ANSWER, OH TALL ONE...IS YESSSS...

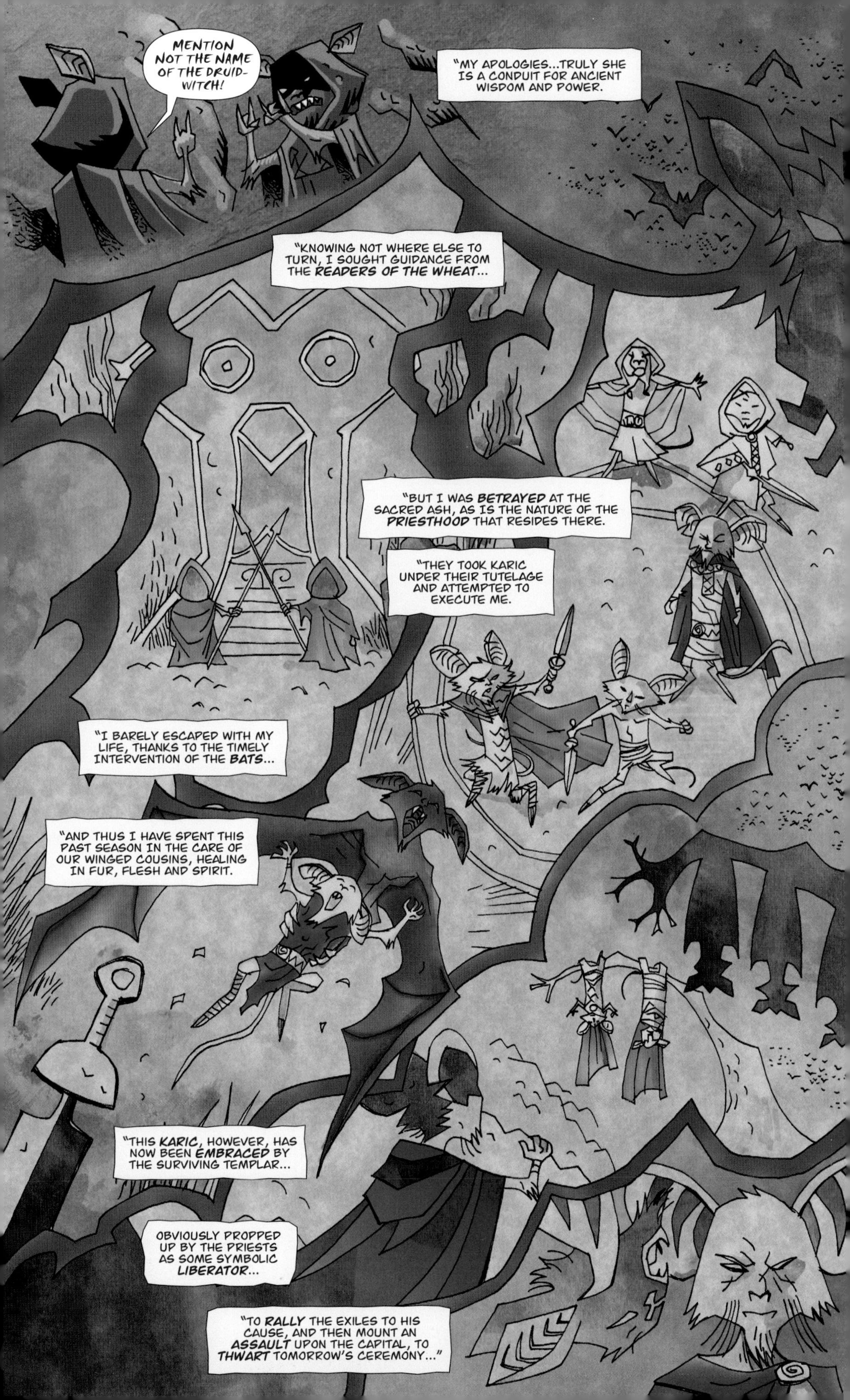
MENTION NOT THE NAME OF THE DRUID-WITCH!
"MY APOLOGIES...TRULY SHE IS A CONDUIT FOR ANCIENT WISDOM AND POWER.
"KNOWING NOT WHERE ELSE TO TURN, I SOUGHT GUIDANCE FROM THE READERS OF THE WHEAT...
"BUT I WAS BETRAYED AT THE SACRED ASH, AS IS THE NATURE OF THE PRIESTHOOD THAT RESIDES THERE.
"THEY TOOK KARIC UNDER THEIR TUTELAGE AND ATTEMPTED TO EXECUTE ME.
"I BARELY ESCAPED WITH MY LIFE, THANKS TO THE TIMELY INTERVENTION OF THE BATS...
"AND THUS I HAVE SPENT THIS PAST SEASON IN THE CARE OF OUR WINGED COUSINS, HEALING IN FUR, FLESH AND SPIRIT.
"THIS KARIC, HOWEVER, HAS NOW BEEN EMBRACED BY THE SURVIVING TEMPLAR...
OBVIOUSLY PROPPED UP BY THE PRIESTS AS SOME SYMBOLIC LIBERATOR...
"TO RALLY THE EXILES TO HIS CAUSE, AND THEN MOUNT AN ASSAULT UPON THE CAPITAL, TO THWART TOMORROW'S CEREMONY..."

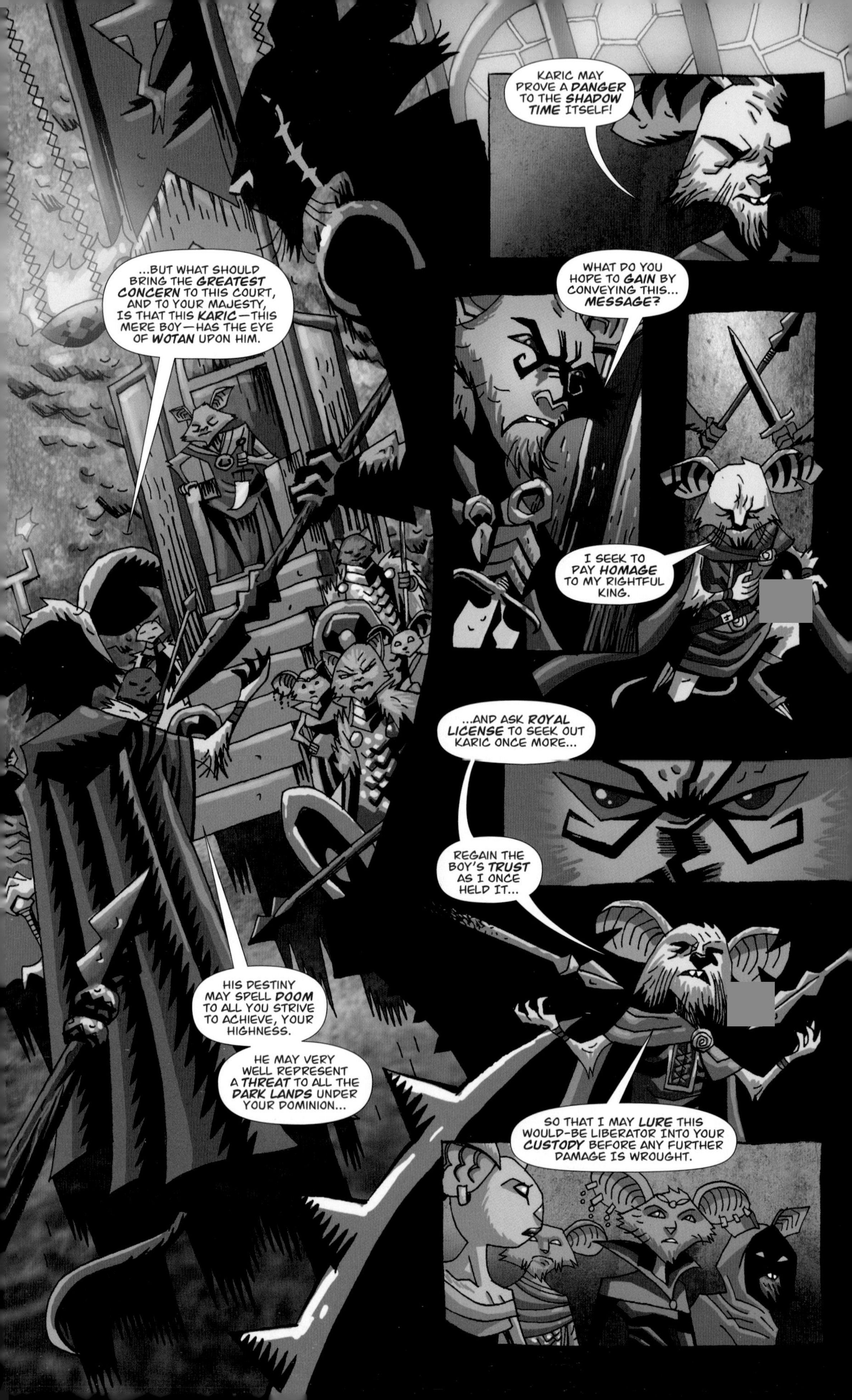

...BUT WHAT SHOULD BRING THE GREATEST CONCERN TO THIS COURT, AND TO YOUR MAJESTY, IS THAT THIS KARIC—THIS MERE BOY—HAS THE EYE OF WOTAN UPON HIM.
HIS DESTINY MAY SPELL DOOM TO ALL YOU STRIVE TO ACHIEVE, YOUR HIGHNESS.
HE MAY VERY WELL REPRESENT A THREAT TO ALL THE DARK LANDS UNDER YOUR DOMINION...
KARIC MAY PROVE A DANGER TO THE SHADOW TIME ITSELF!
WHAT DO YOU HOPE TO GAIN BY CONVEYING THIS... MESSAGE?
I SEEK TO PAY HOMAGE TO MY RIGHTFUL KING.
...AND ASK ROYAL LICENSE TO SEEK OUT KARIC ONCE MORE...
REGAIN THE BOY'S TRUST AS I ONCE HELD IT...
SO THAT I MAY LURE THIS WOULD-BE LIBERATOR INTO YOUR CUSTODY BEFORE ANY FURTHER DAMAGE IS WROUGHT.

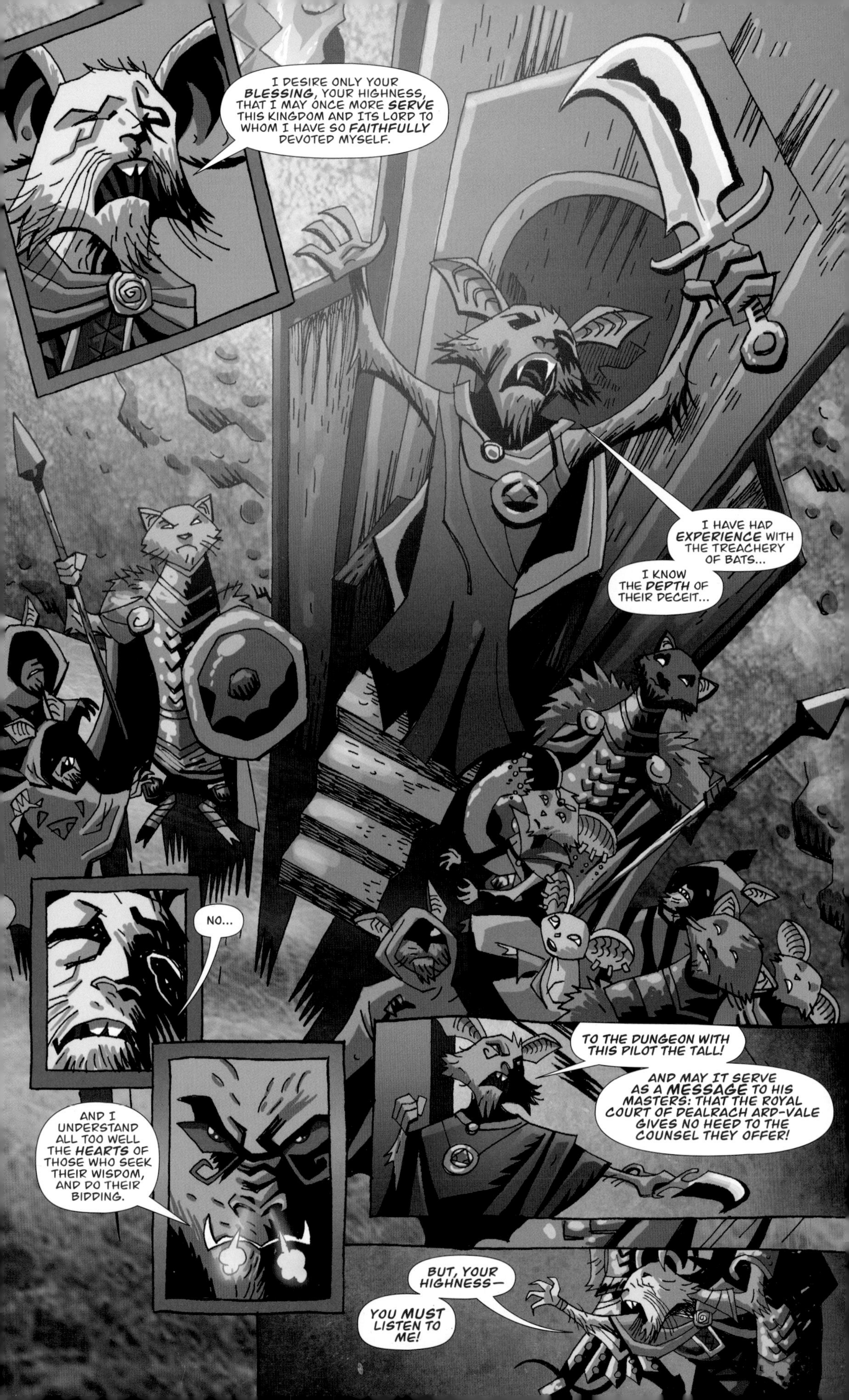
I DESIRE ONLY YOUR BLESSING, YOUR HIGHNESS, THAT I MAY ONCE MORE SERVE THIS KINGDOM AND ITS LORD TO WHOM I HAVE SO FAITHFULLY DEVOTED MYSELF.
I HAVE HAD EXPERIENCE WITH THE TREACHERY OF BATS...
I KNOW THE DEPTH OF THEIR DECEIT...
NO...
AND I UNDERSTAND ALL TOO WELL THE HEARTS OF THOSE WHO SEEK THEIR WISDOM, AND DO THEIR BIDDING.
TO THE DUNGEON WITH THIS PILOT THE TALL!
AND MAY IT SERVE AS A MESSAGE TO HIS MASTERS: THAT THE ROYAL COURT OF DEALRACH ARD-VALE GIVES NO HEED TO THE COUNSEL THEY OFFER!
BUT, YOUR HIGHNESS—
YOU MUST LISTEN TO ME!

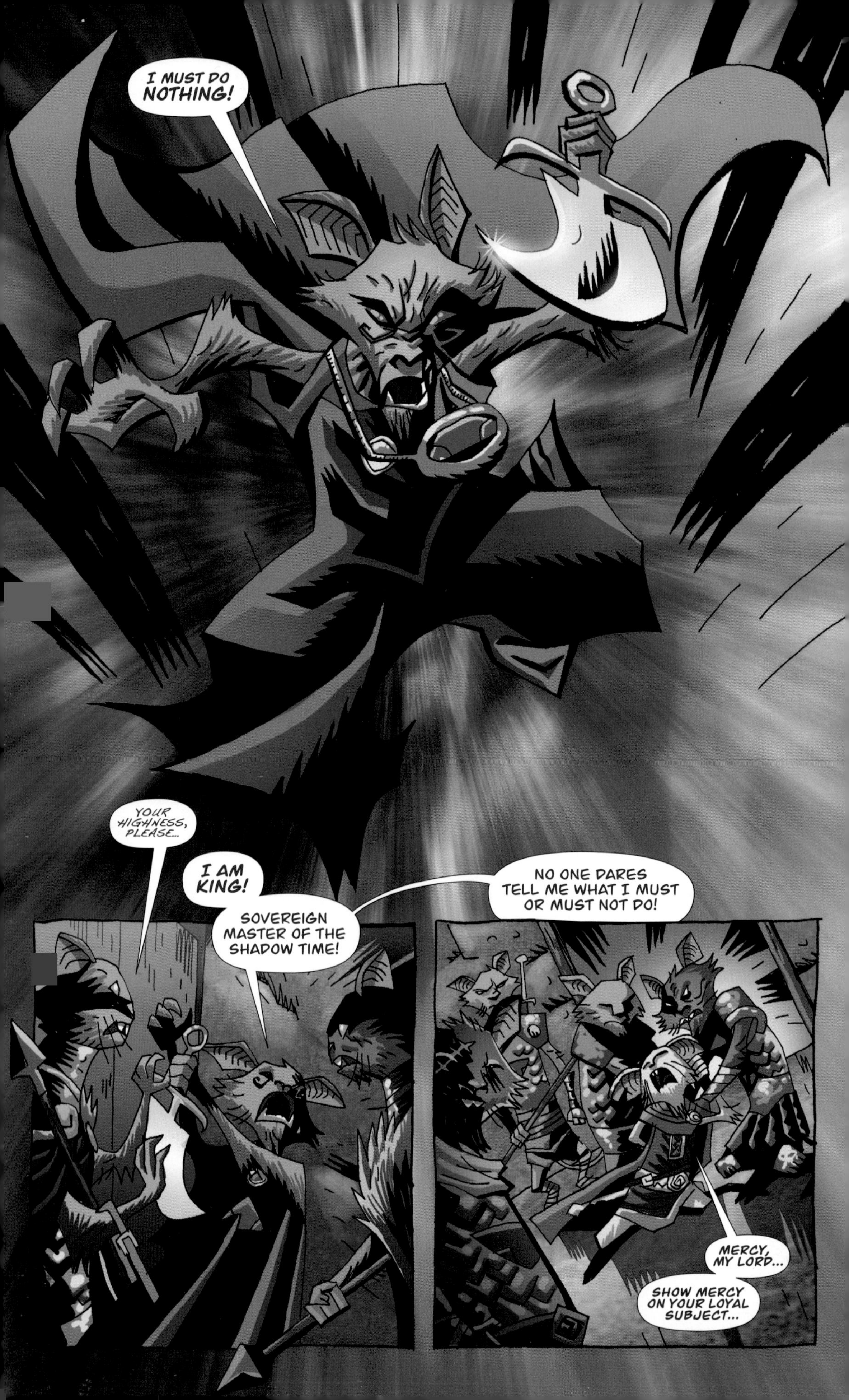
I MUST DO NOTHING!
YOUR HIGHNESS, PLEASE...
I AM KING!
SOVEREIGN MASTER OF THE SHADOW TIME!
NO ONE DARES TELL ME WHAT I MUST OR MUST NOT DO!
MERCY, MY LORD...
SHOW MERCY ON YOUR LOYAL SUBJECT...

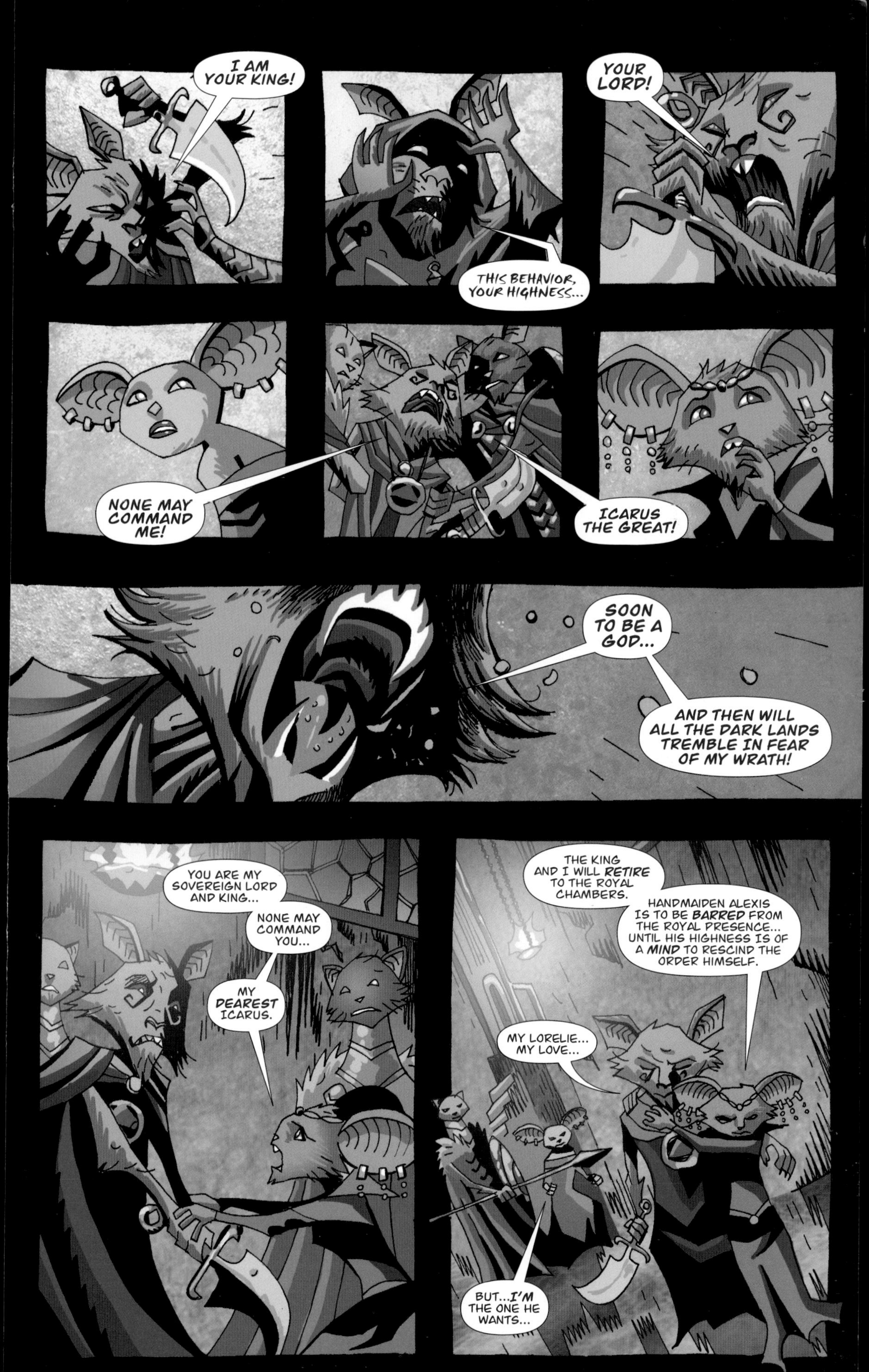
I AM YOUR KING!
THIS BEHAVIOR, YOUR HIGHNESS...
YOUR LORD!
NONE MAY COMMAND ME!
ICARUS THE GREAT!
SOON TO BE A GOD...
AND THEN WILL ALL THE DARK LANDS TREMBLE IN FEAR OF MY WRATH!
YOU ARE MY SOVEREIGN LORD AND KING...
NONE MAY COMMAND YOU...
MY DEAREST ICARUS.
THE KING AND I WILL RETIRE TO THE ROYAL CHAMBERS.
HANDMAIDEN ALEXIS IS TO BE BARRED FROM THE ROYAL PRESENCE... UNTIL HIS HIGHNESS IS OF A MIND TO RESCIND THE ORDER HIMSELF.
MY LORELIE... MY LOVE...
BUT...I'M THE ONE HE WANTS...

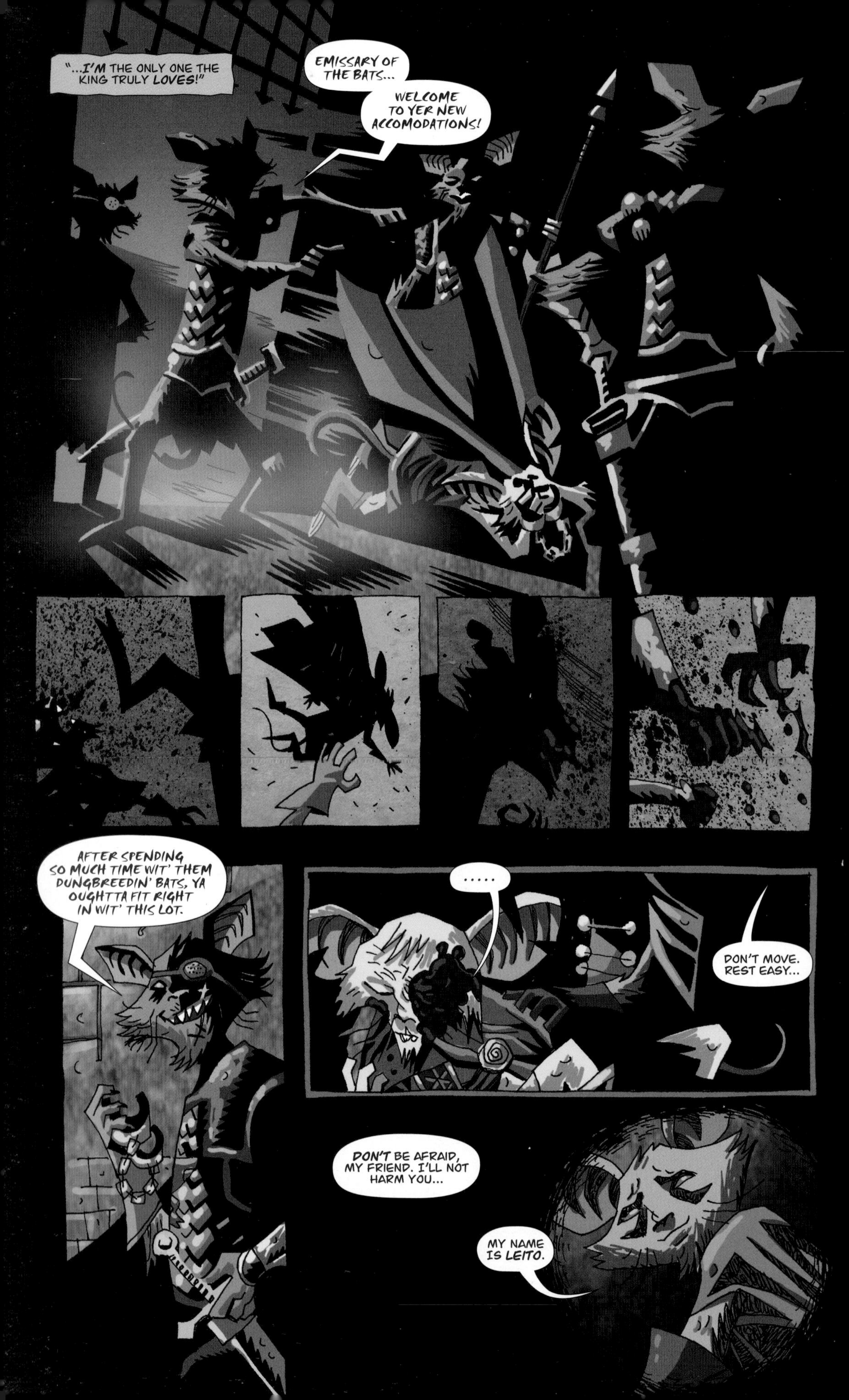
"...I'M THE ONLY ONE THE KING TRULY LOVES!"
EMISSARY OF THE BATS...
WELCOME TO YER NEW ACCOMODATIONS!
AFTER SPENDING SO MUCH TIME WIT' THEM DUNGBREEDIN' BATS, YA OUGHTTA FIT RIGHT IN WIT' THIS LOT.
.....
DON'T MOVE. REST EASY...
DON'T BE AFRAID, MY FRIEND. I'LL NOT HARM YOU...
MY NAME IS LEITO.

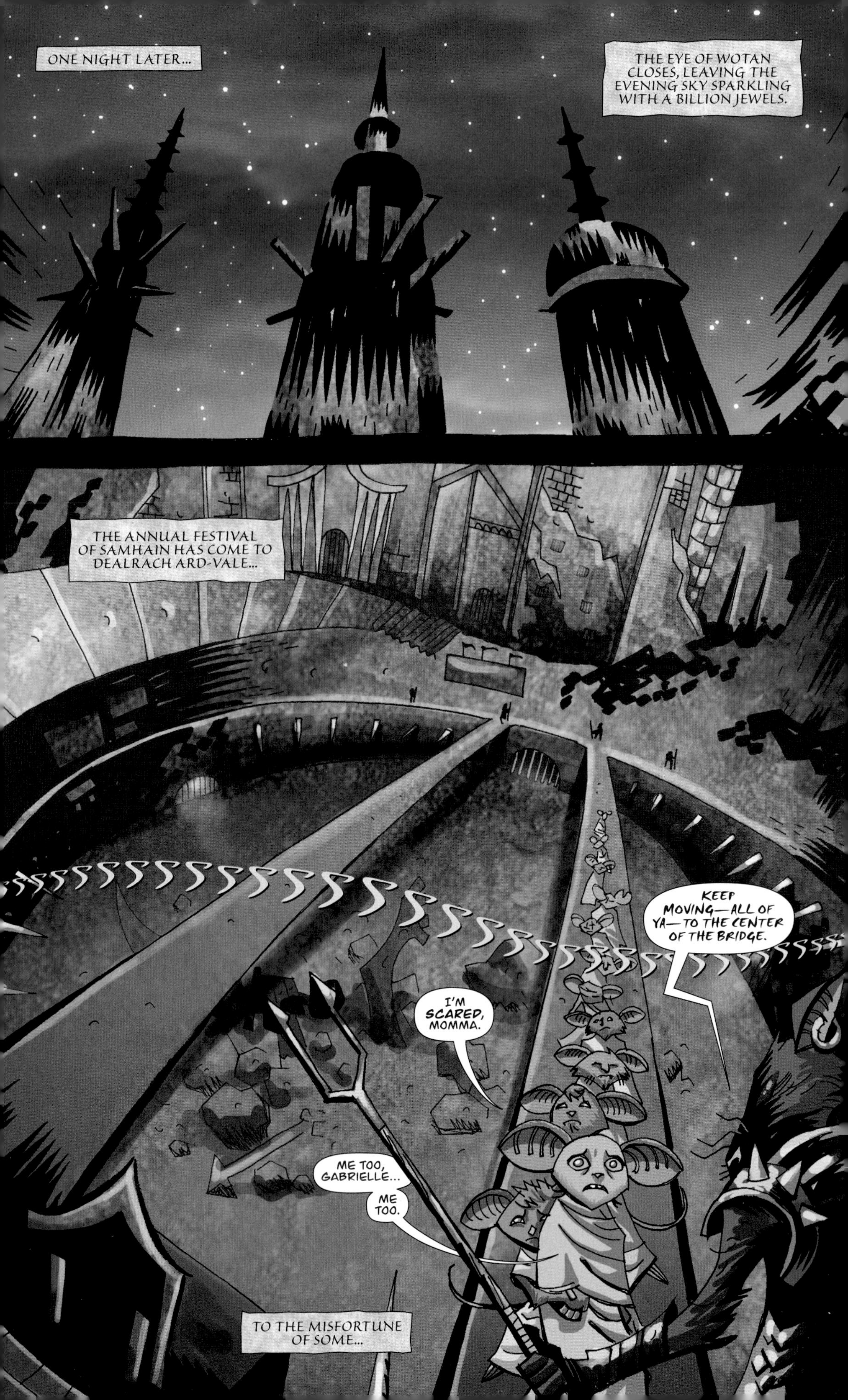

ONE NIGHT LATER...
THE EYE OF WOTAN CLOSES, LEAVING THE EVENING SKY SPARKLING WITH A BILLION JEWELS.
THE ANNUAL FESTIVAL OF SAMHAIN HAS COME TO DEALRACH ARD-VALE...
KEEP MOVING—ALL OF YA—TO THE CENTER OF THE BRIDGE.
I'M SCARED, MOMMA.
ME TOO, GABRIELLE...
ME TOO.
TO THE MISFORTUNE OF SOME...

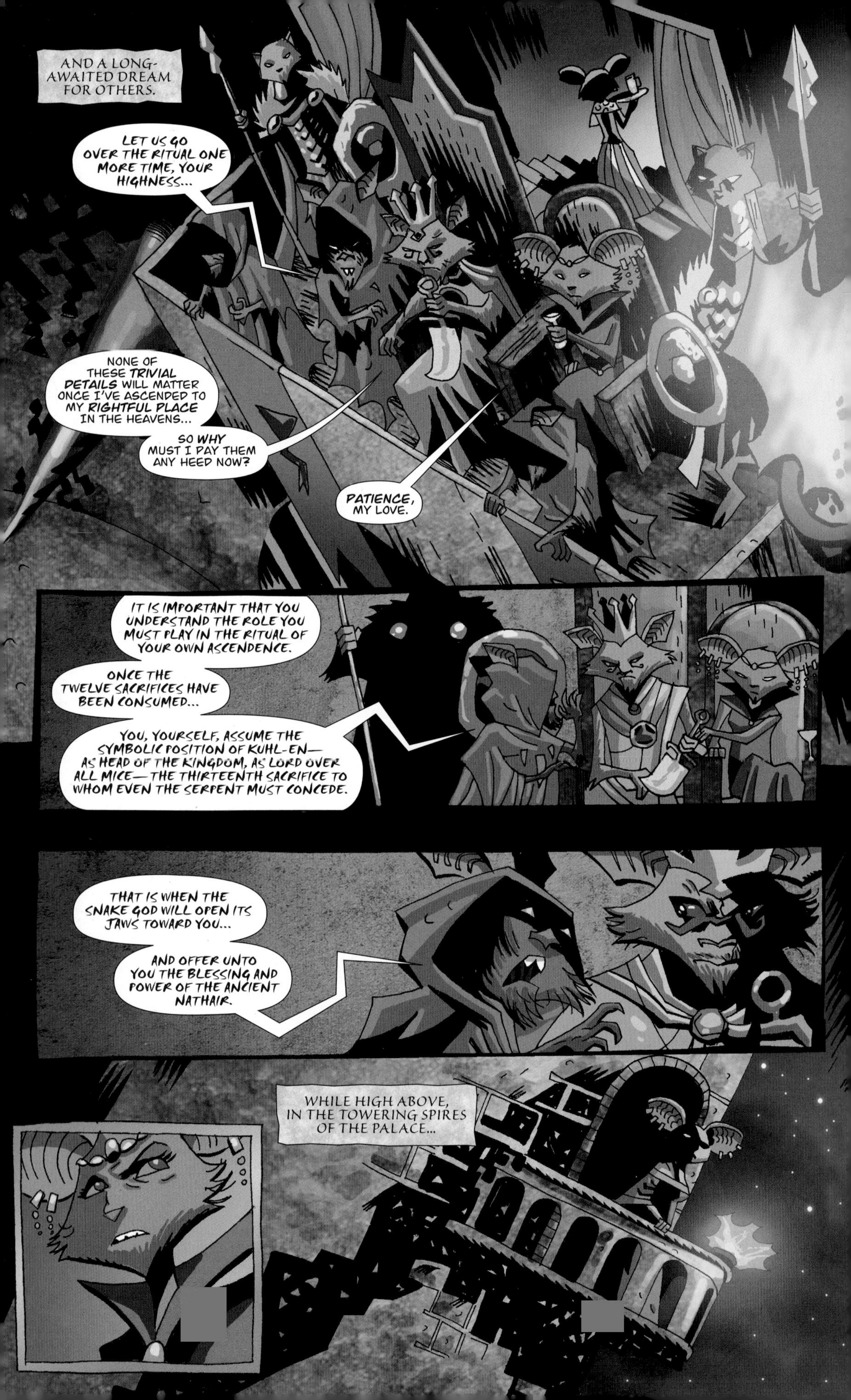
AND A LONG-AWAITED DREAM FOR OTHERS.
LET US GO OVER THE RITUAL ONE MORE TIME, YOUR HIGHNESS...
NONE OF THESE TRIVIAL DETAILS WILL MATTER ONCE I'VE ASCENDED TO MY RIGHTFUL PLACE IN THE HEAVENS...
SO WHY MUST I PAY THEM ANY HEED NOW?
PATIENCE, MY LOVE.
IT IS IMPORTANT THAT YOU UNDERSTAND THE ROLE YOU MUST PLAY IN THE RITUAL OF YOUR OWN ASCENDENCE.
ONCE THE TWELVE SACRIFICES HAVE BEEN CONSUMED...
YOU, YOURSELF, ASSUME THE SYMBOLIC POSITION OF KUHL-EN— AS HEAD OF THE KINGDOM, AS LORD OVER ALL MICE— THE THIRTEENTH SACRIFICE TO WHOM EVEN THE SERPENT MUST CONCEDE.
THAT IS WHEN THE SNAKE GOD WILL OPEN ITS JAWS TOWARD YOU...
AND OFFER UNTO YOU THE BLESSING AND POWER OF THE ANCIENT NATHAIR.
WHILE HIGH ABOVE, IN THE TOWERING SPIRES OF THE PALACE...

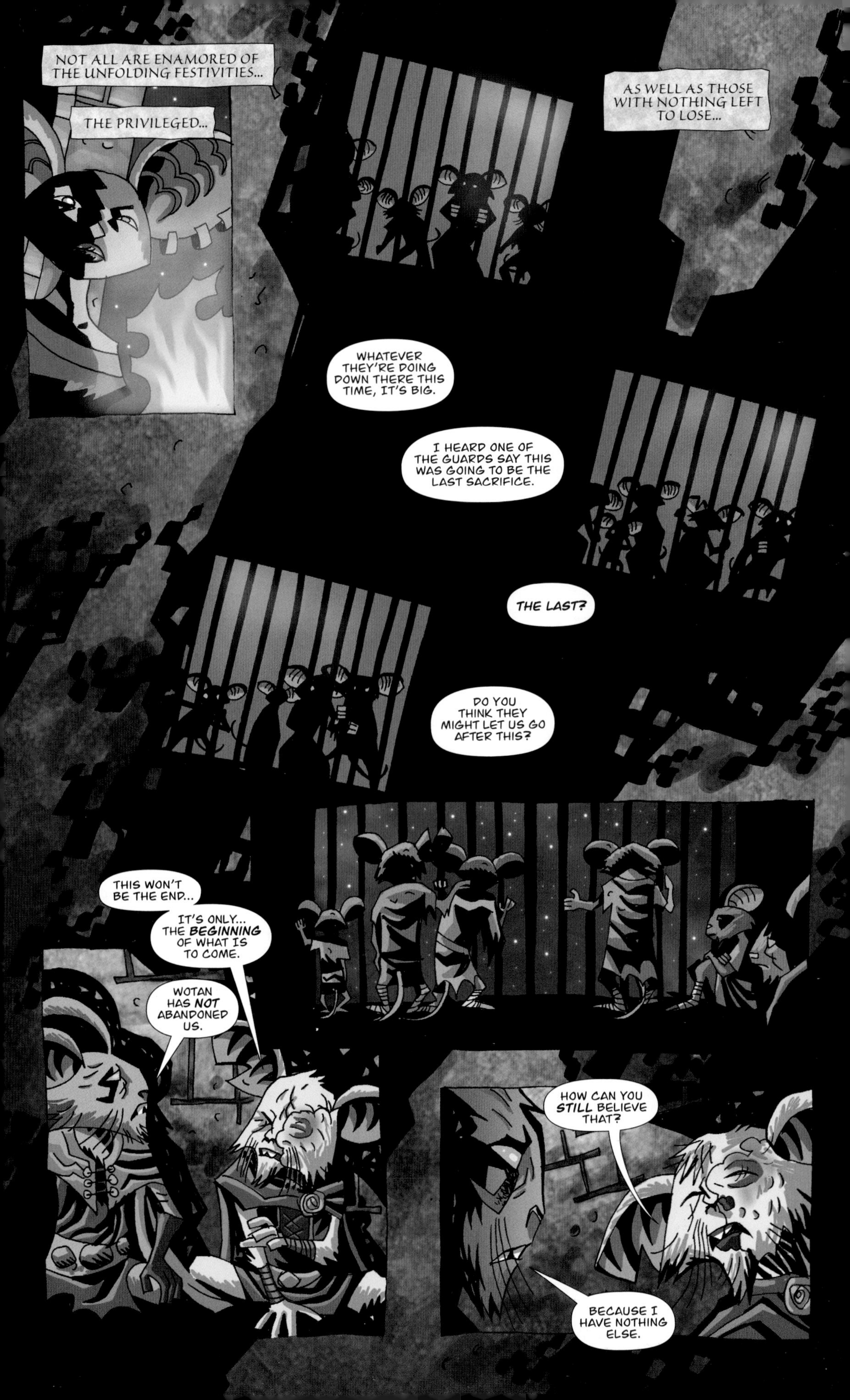
NOT ALL ARE ENAMORED OF THE UNFOLDING FESTIVITIES...
THE PRIVILEGED...
AS WELL AS THOSE WITH NOTHING LEFT TO LOSE...
WHATEVER THEY'RE DOING DOWN THERE THIS TIME, IT'S BIG.
I HEARD ONE OF THE GUARDS SAY THIS WAS GOING TO BE THE LAST SACRIFICE.
THE LAST?
DO YOU THINK THEY MIGHT LET US GO AFTER THIS?
THIS WON'T BE THE END...
IT'S ONLY... THE BEGINNING OF WHAT IS TO COME.
WOTAN HAS NOT ABANDONED US.
HOW CAN YOU STILL BELIEVE THAT?
BECAUSE I HAVE NOTHING ELSE.

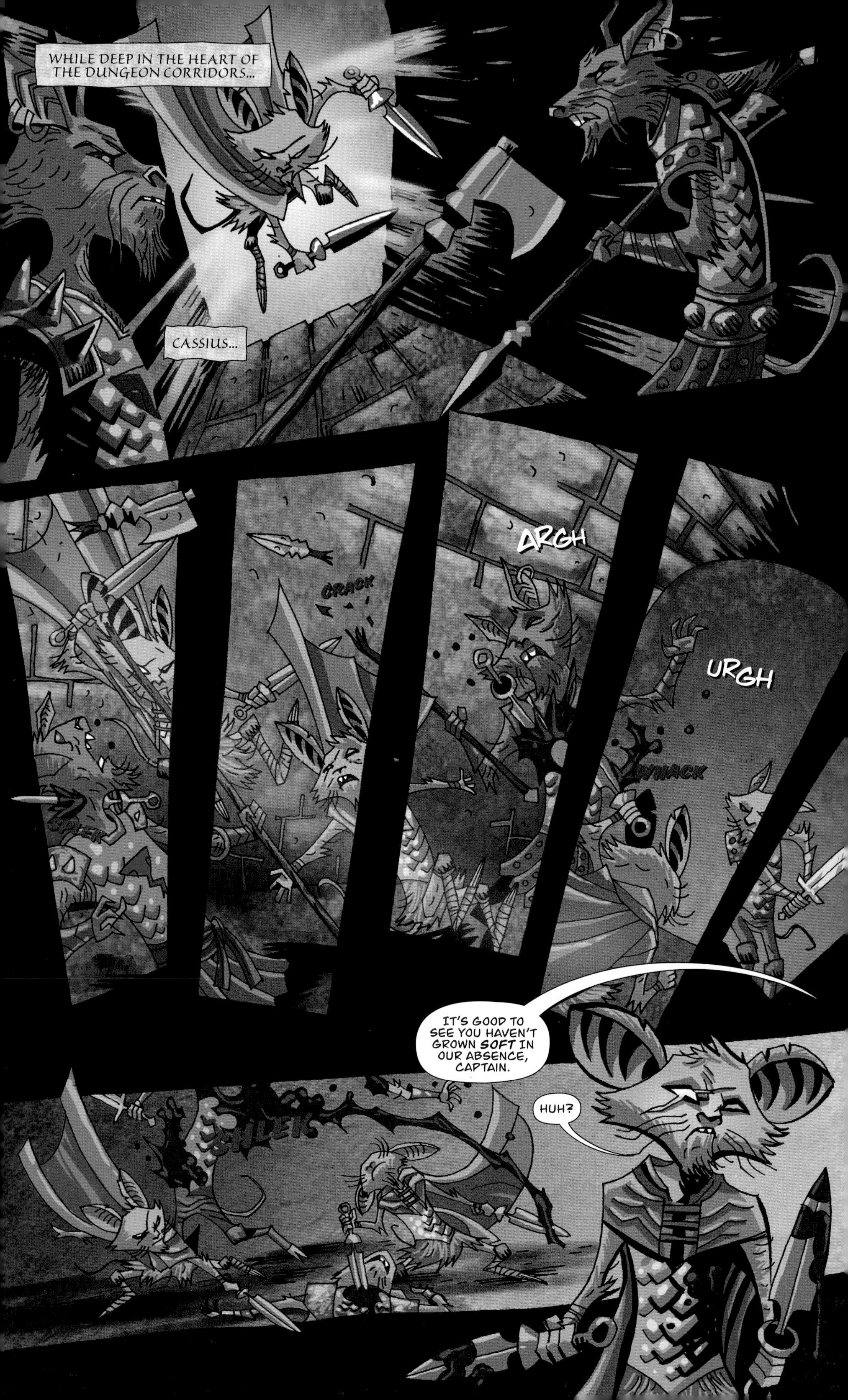

WHILE DEEP IN THE HEART OF THE DUNGEON CORRIDORS...
CASSIUS...
CRACK
ARGH
URGH
WHACK
IT'S GOOD TO SEE YOU HAVEN'T GROWN SOFT IN OUR ABSENCE, CAPTAIN.
HUH?

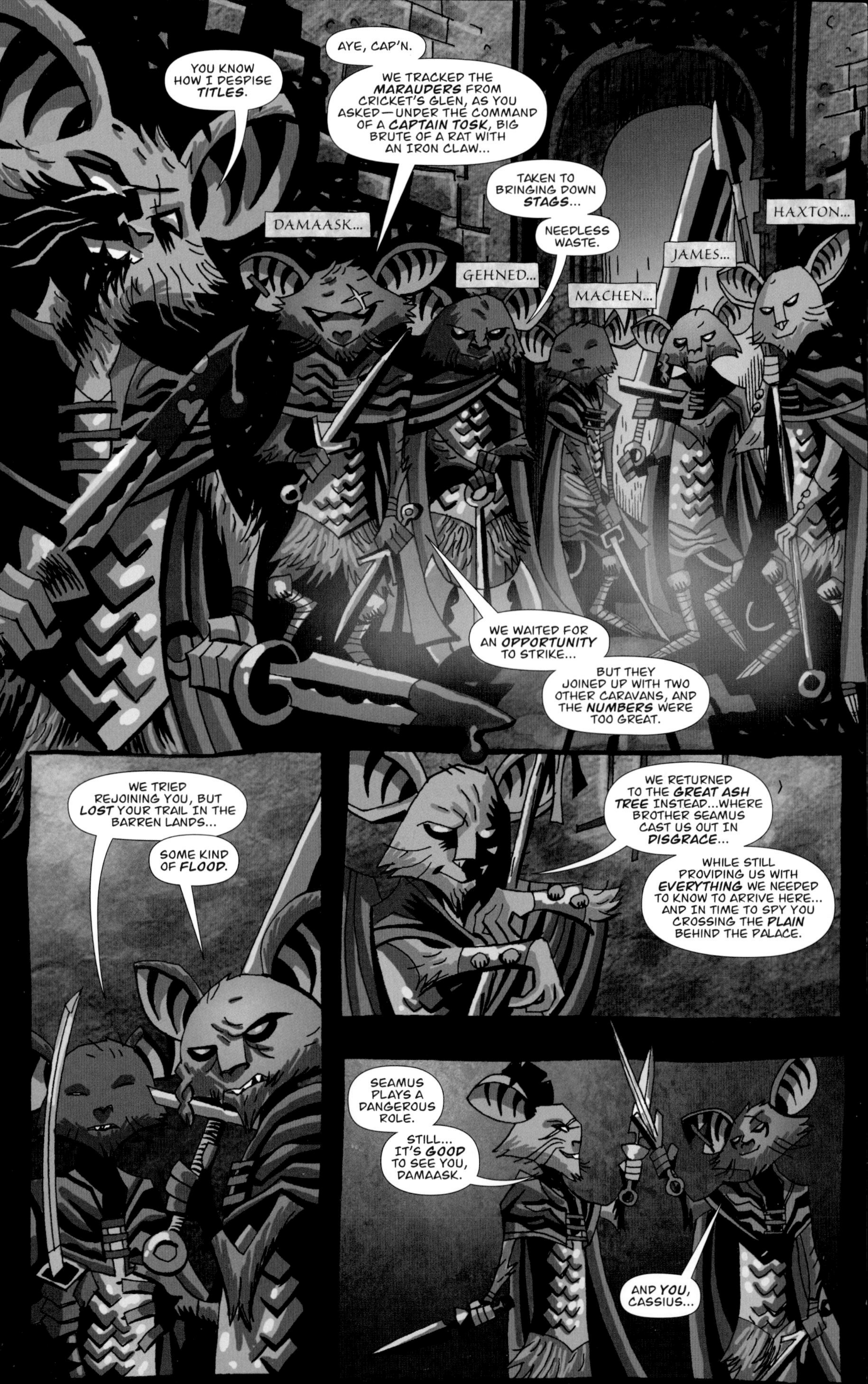
YOU KNOW HOW I DESPISE TITLES.
AYE, CAP'N.
WE TRACKED THE MARAUDERS FROM CRICKET'S GLEN, AS YOU ASKED—UNDER THE COMMAND OF A CAPTAIN TOSK, BIG BRUTE OF A RAT WITH AN IRON CLAW...
TAKEN TO BRINGING DOWN STAGS...
NEEDLESS WASTE.
DAMAASK...
GEHNED...
MACHEN...
JAMES...
HAXTON...
WE WAITED FOR AN OPPORTUNITY TO STRIKE...
BUT THEY JOINED UP WITH TWO OTHER CARAVANS, AND THE NUMBERS WERE TOO GREAT.
WE TRIED REJOINING YOU, BUT LOST YOUR TRAIL IN THE BARREN LANDS...
SOME KIND OF FLOOD.
WE RETURNED TO THE GREAT ASH TREE INSTEAD...WHERE BROTHER SEAMUS CAST US OUT IN DISGRACE...
WHILE STILL PROVIDING US WITH EVERYTHING WE NEEDED TO KNOW TO ARRIVE HERE... AND IN TIME TO SPY YOU CROSSING THE PLAIN BEHIND THE PALACE.
SEAMUS PLAYS A DANGEROUS ROLE.
STILL... IT'S GOOD TO SEE YOU, DAMAASK.
AND YOU, CASSIUS...

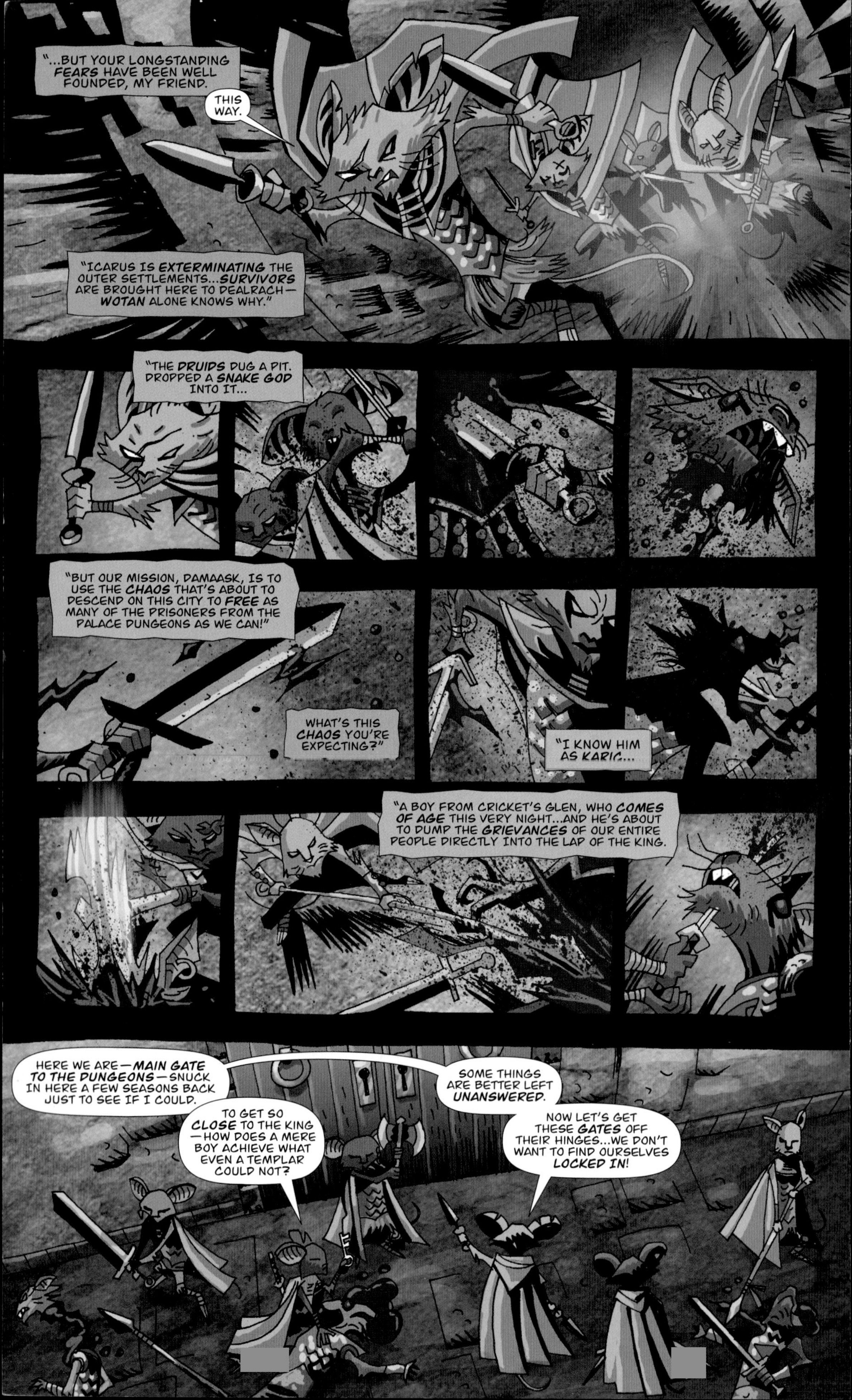
"...BUT YOUR LONGSTANDING FEARS HAVE BEEN WELL FOUNDED, MY FRIEND.
THIS WAY.
"ICARUS IS EXTERMINATING THE OUTER SETTLEMENTS...SURVIVORS ARE BROUGHT HERE TO DEALRACH—WOTAN ALONE KNOWS WHY."
"THE DRUIDS DUG A PIT. DROPPED A SNAKE GOD INTO IT...
"BUT OUR MISSION, DAMAASK, IS TO USE THE CHAOS THAT'S ABOUT TO DESCEND ON THIS CITY TO FREE AS MANY OF THE PRISONERS FROM THE PALACE DUNGEONS AS WE CAN!"
WHAT'S THIS CHAOS YOU'RE EXPECTING?"
"I KNOW HIM AS KARIC...
"A BOY FROM CRICKET'S GLEN, WHO COMES OF AGE THIS VERY NIGHT...AND HE'S ABOUT TO DUMP THE GRIEVANCES OF OUR ENTIRE PEOPLE DIRECTLY INTO THE LAP OF THE KING.
HERE WE ARE—MAIN GATE TO THE DUNGEONS—SNUCK IN HERE A FEW SEASONS BACK JUST TO SEE IF I COULD.
TO GET SO CLOSE TO THE KING—HOW DOES A MERE BOY ACHIEVE WHAT EVEN A TEMPLAR COULD NOT?
SOME THINGS ARE BETTER LEFT UNANSWERED.
NOW LET'S GET THESE GATES OFF THEIR HINGES...WE DON'T WANT TO FIND OURSELVES LOCKED IN!

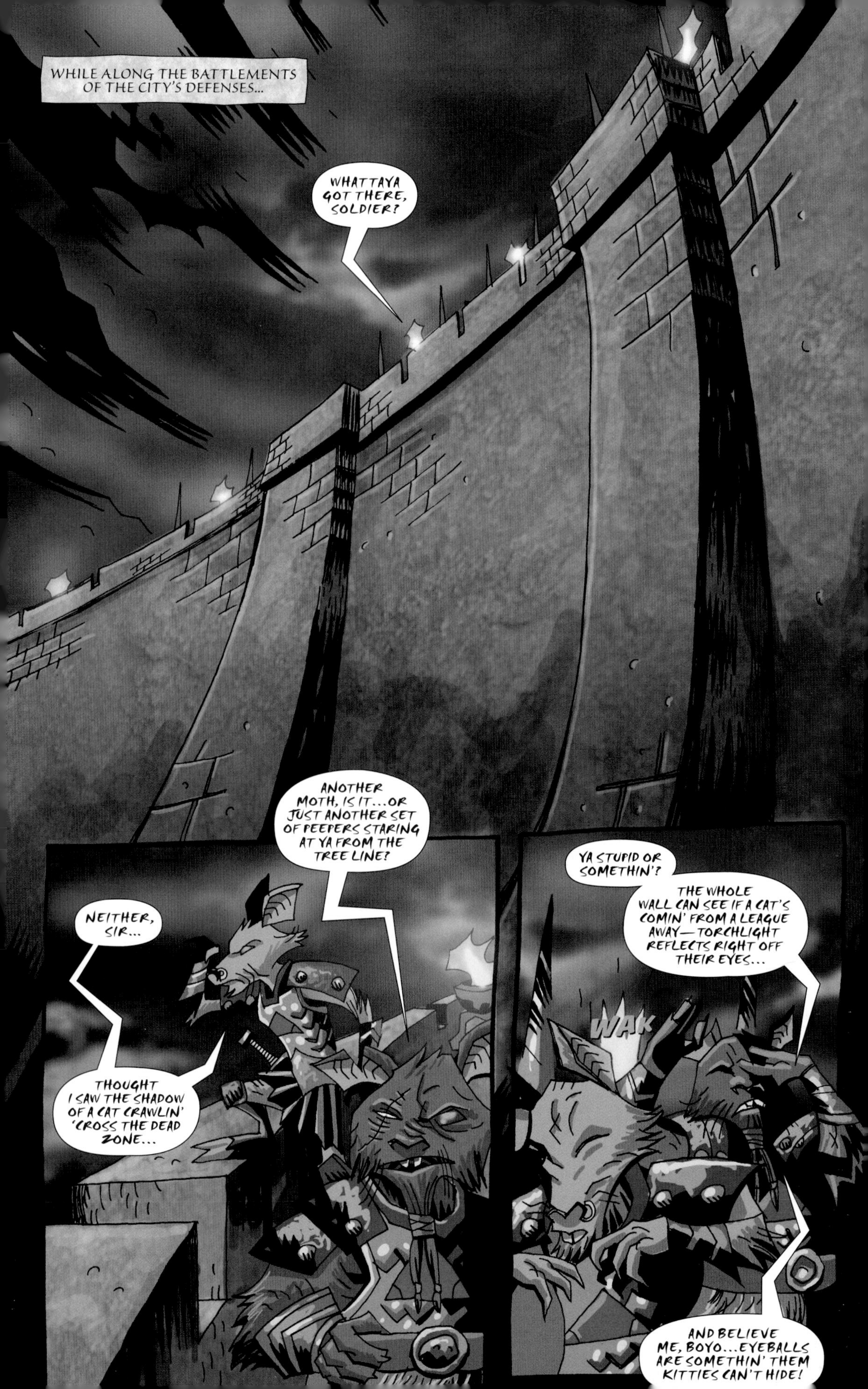
WHILE ALONG THE BATTLEMENTS OF THE CITY'S DEFENSES...
WHATTAYA GOT THERE, SOLDIER?
ANOTHER MOTH, IS IT...OR JUST ANOTHER SET OF PEEPERS STARING AT YA FROM THE TREE LINE?
NEITHER, SIR...
THOUGHT I SAW THE SHADOW OF A CAT CRAWLIN' 'CROSS THE DEAD ZONE...
YA STUPID OR SOMETHIN'?
THE WHOLE WALL CAN SEE IF A CAT'S COMIN' FROM A LEAGUE AWAY—TORCHLIGHT REFLECTS RIGHT OFF THEIR EYES...
WAK
AND BELIEVE ME, BOYO...EYEBALLS ARE SOMETHIN' THEM KITTIES CAN'T HIDE!

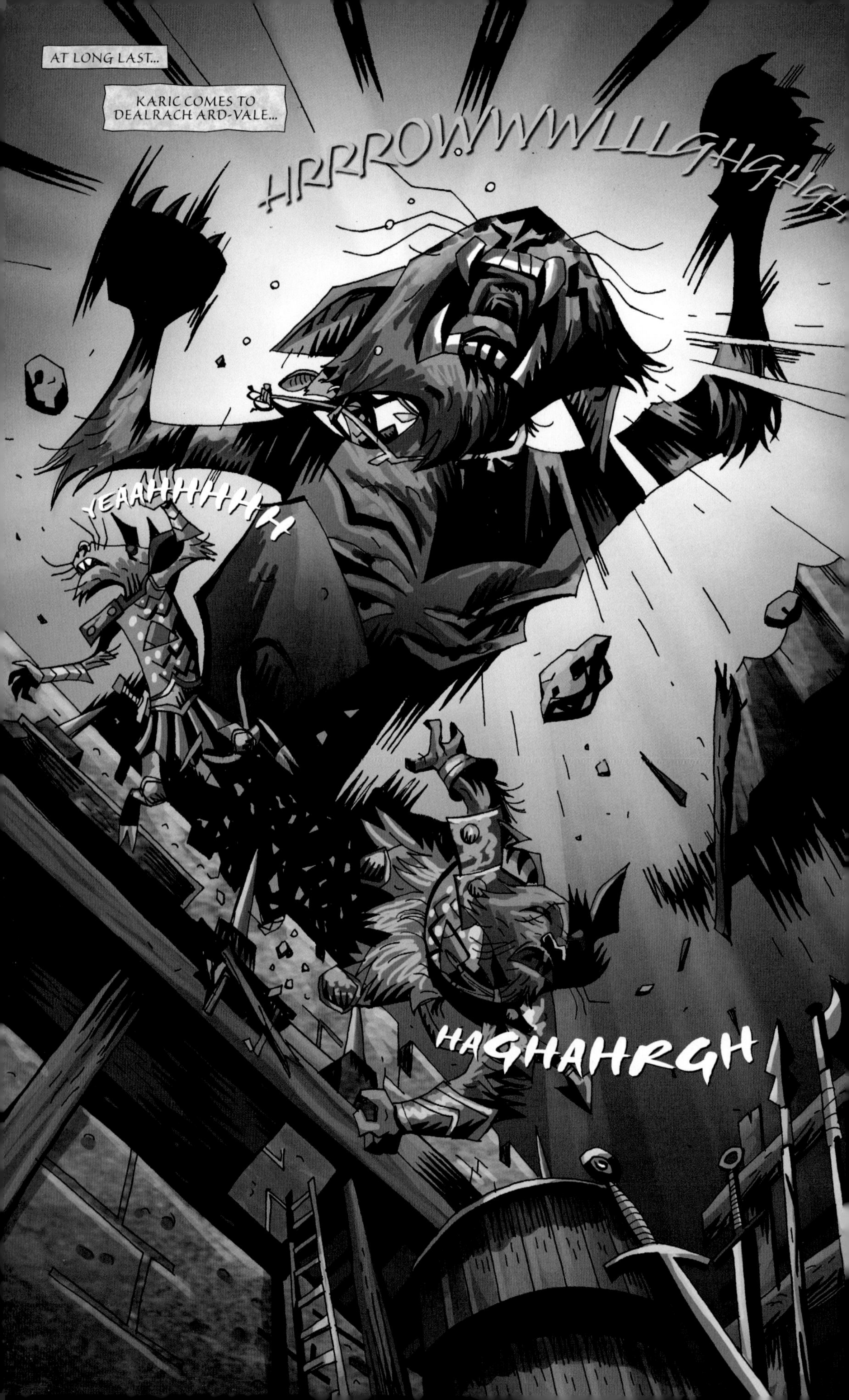
AT LONG LAST...
KARIC COMES TO DEALRACH ARD-VALE...
HRRROWWWLLLGHGHGH
YEAAHHHHHH
HAGHAHRGH

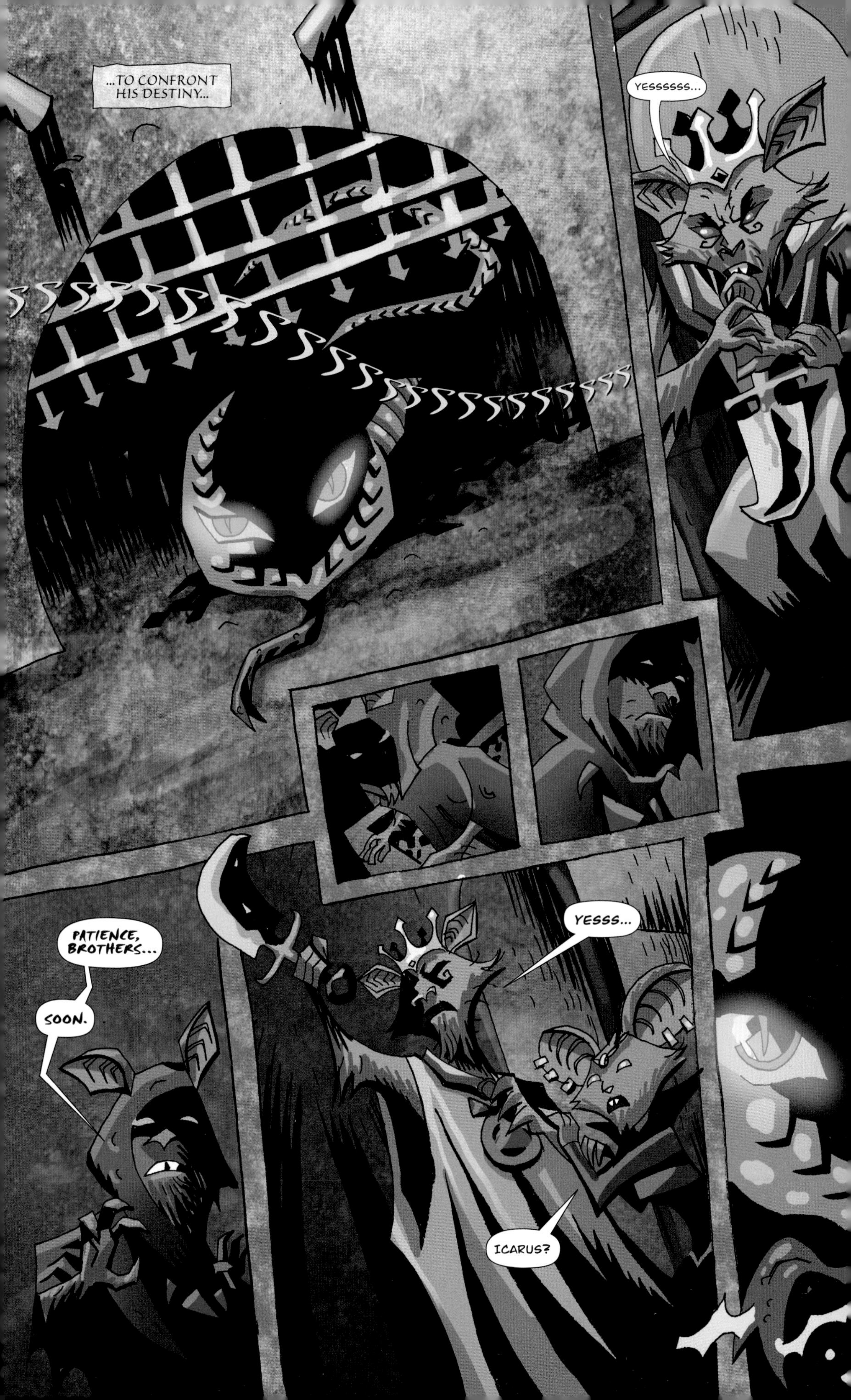
...TO CONFRONT HIS DESTINY...
YESSSSSS...
SSSSSSSSSSSSSSSSSSSSSSSSSSSS
PATIENCE, BROTHERS...
SOON.
YESSS...
ICARUS?

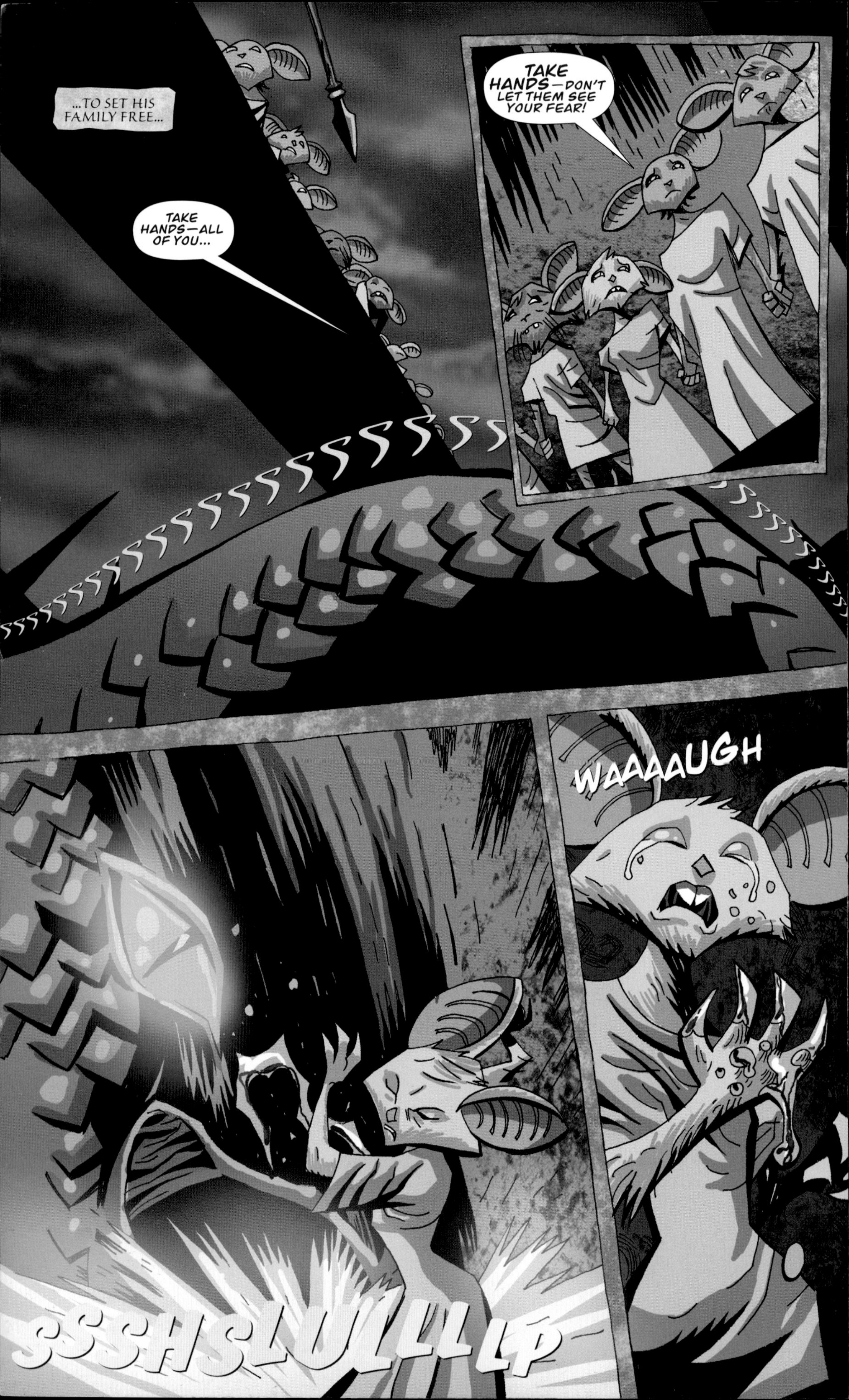
...TO SET HIS FAMILY FREE...
TAKE HANDS—ALL OF YOU...
TAKE HANDS—DON'T LET THEM SEE YOUR FEAR!
SSSSSSSSSSSSSSSSSSSSSSSSSSSSSSSSSSSS
SSSHSLULLLLP
WAAAAUGH

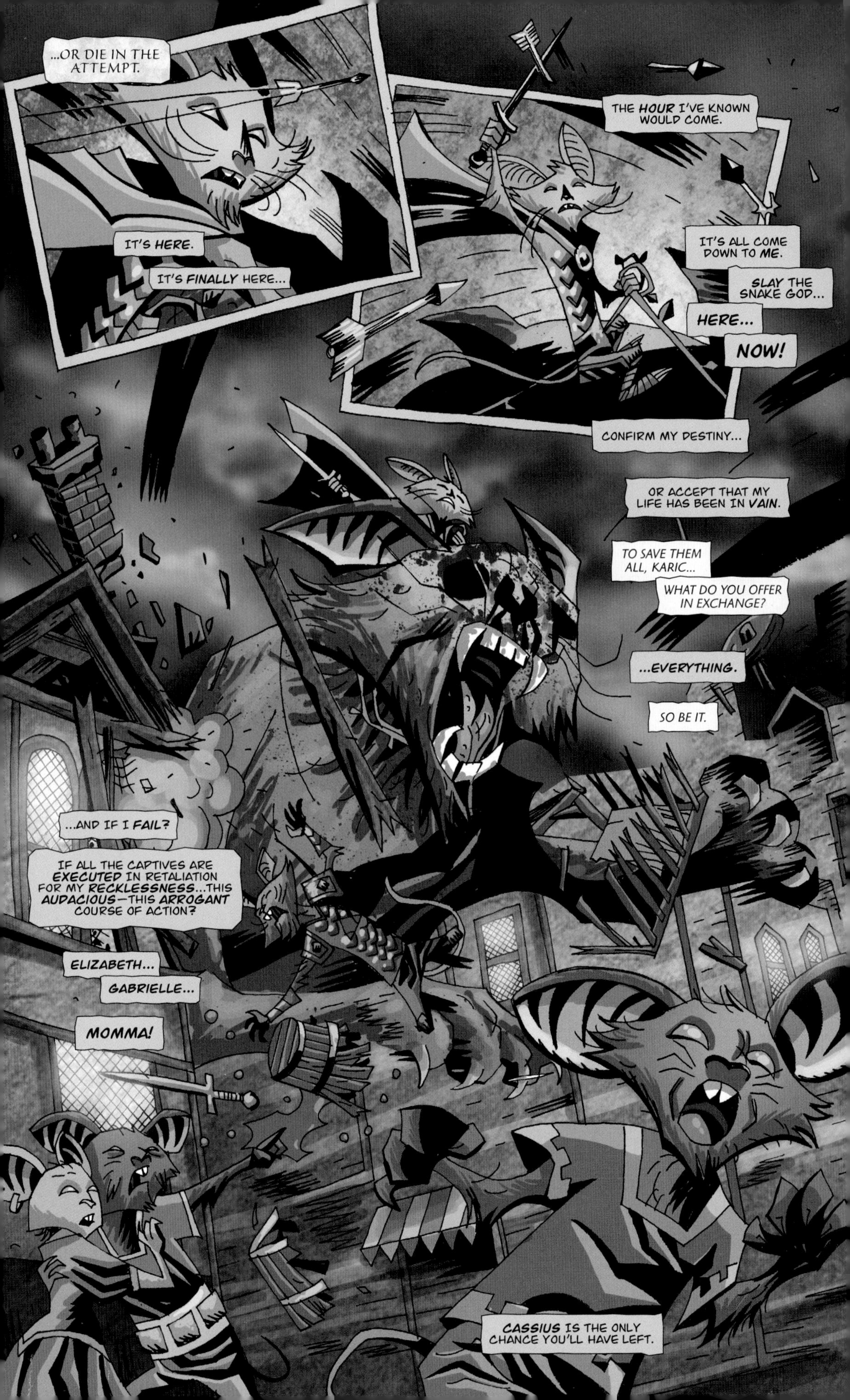
...OR DIE IN THE ATTEMPT.
IT'S HERE.
IT'S FINALLY HERE...
THE HOUR I'VE KNOWN WOULD COME.
IT'S ALL COME DOWN TO ME.
SLAY THE SNAKE GOD...
HERE...
NOW!
CONFIRM MY DESTINY...
OR ACCEPT THAT MY LIFE HAS BEEN IN VAIN.
TO SAVE THEM ALL, KARIC...
WHAT DO YOU OFFER IN EXCHANGE?
...EVERYTHING.
SO BE IT.
...AND IF I FAIL?
IF ALL THE CAPTIVES ARE EXECUTED IN RETALIATION FOR MY RECKLESSNESS...THIS AUDACIOUS—THIS ARROGANT COURSE OF ACTION?
ELIZABETH...
GABRIELLE...
MOMMA!
CASSIUS IS THE ONLY CHANCE YOU'LL HAVE LEFT.

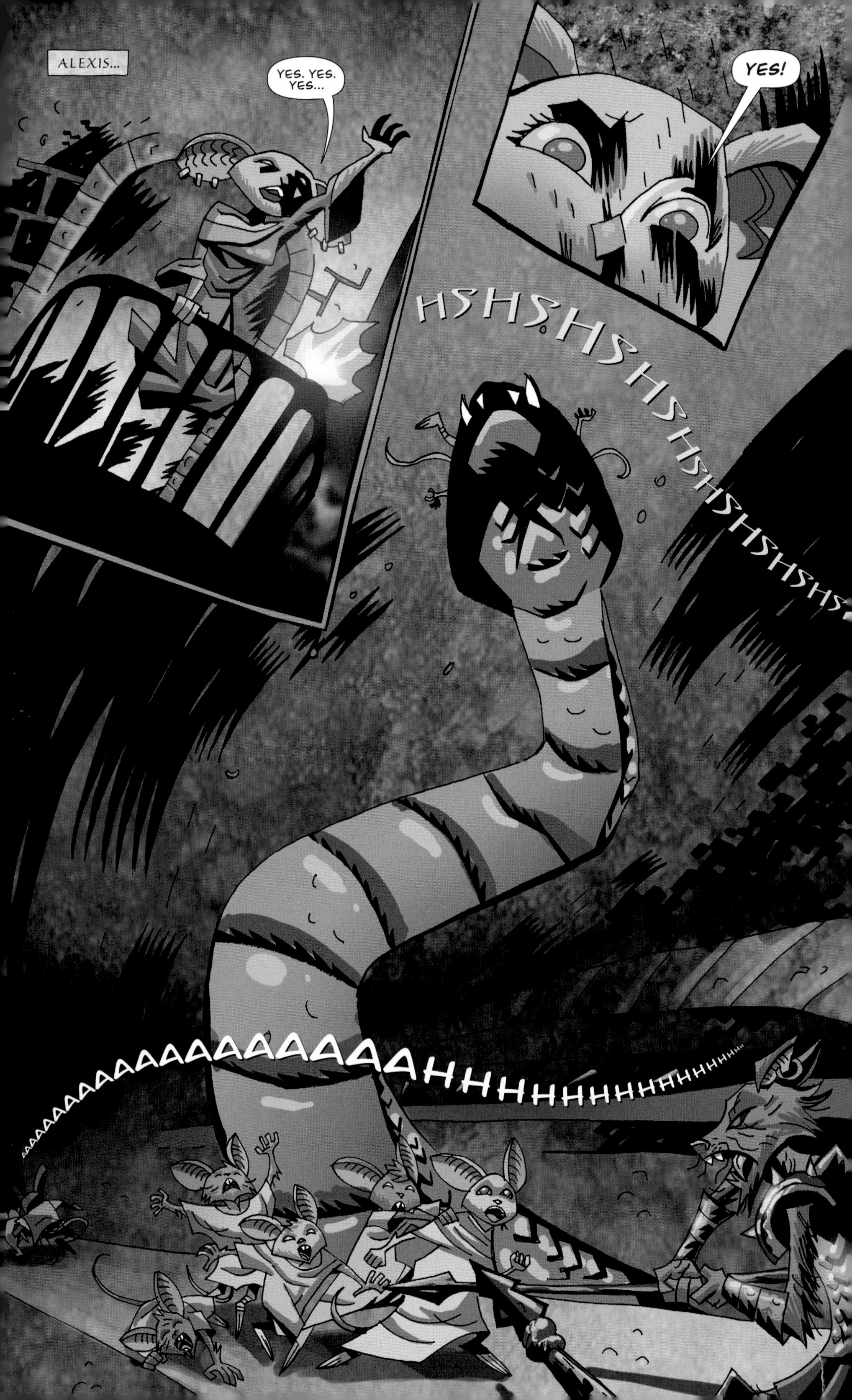
ALEXIS...
YES. YES. YES...
YES!
HSHSHSHSHSHSHSHSHSHSHSHS
AAAAAAAAAAAAAAAAAAAAAHHHHHHHHHHHHHHHHH

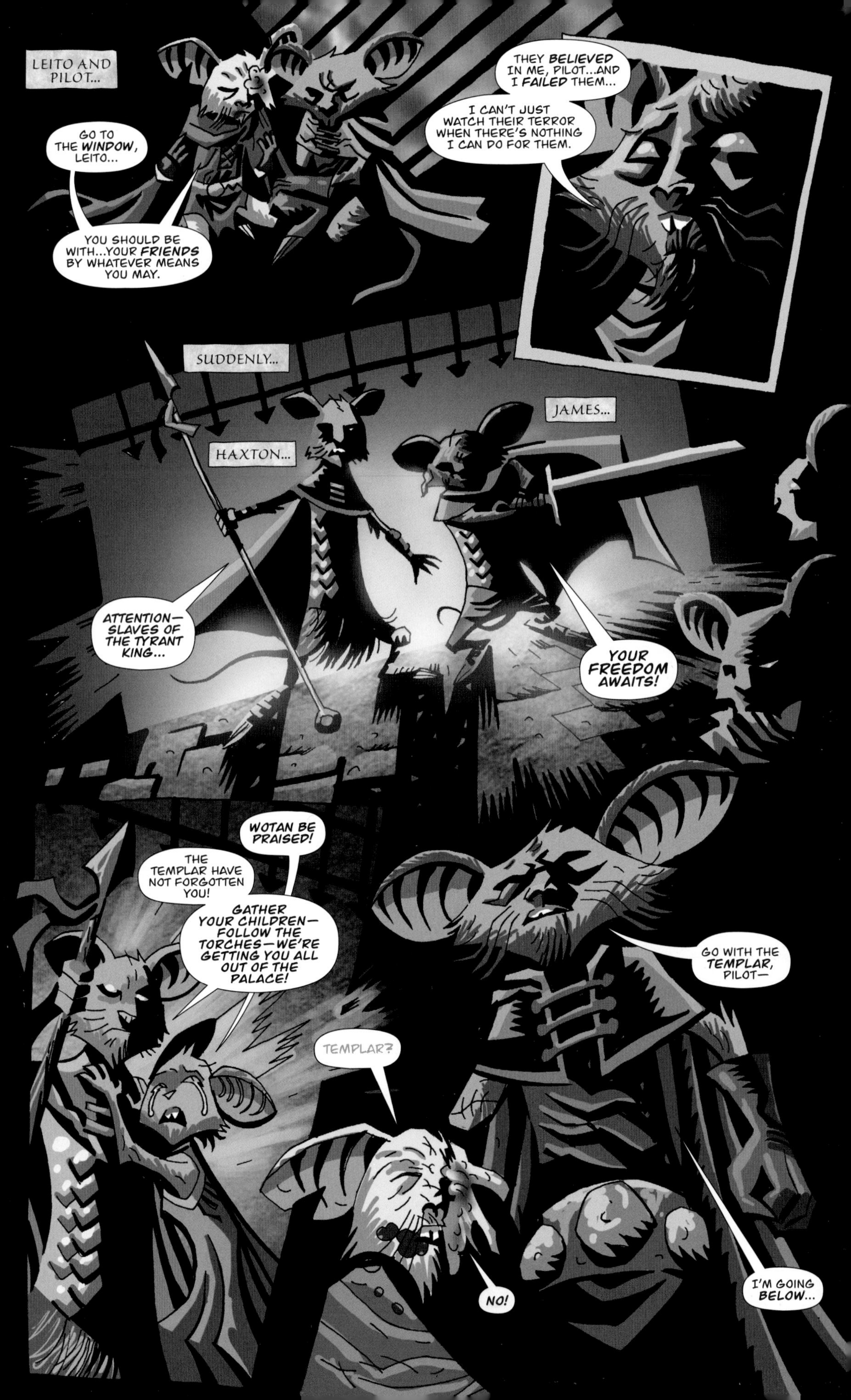

LEITO AND PILOT...
GO TO THE WINDOW, LEITO...
YOU SHOULD BE WITH...YOUR FRIENDS BY WHATEVER MEANS YOU MAY.
THEY BELIEVED IN ME, PILOT...AND I FAILED THEM...
I CAN'T JUST WATCH THEIR TERROR WHEN THERE'S NOTHING I CAN DO FOR THEM.
SUDDENLY...
HAXTON...
JAMES...
ATTENTION— SLAVES OF THE TYRANT KING...
YOUR FREEDOM AWAITS!
WOTAN BE PRAISED!
THE TEMPLAR HAVE NOT FORGOTTEN YOU!
GATHER YOUR CHILDREN— FOLLOW THE TORCHES—WE'RE GETTING YOU ALL OUT OF THE PALACE!
TEMPLAR?
NO!
GO WITH THE TEMPLAR, PILOT—
I'M GOING BELOW...

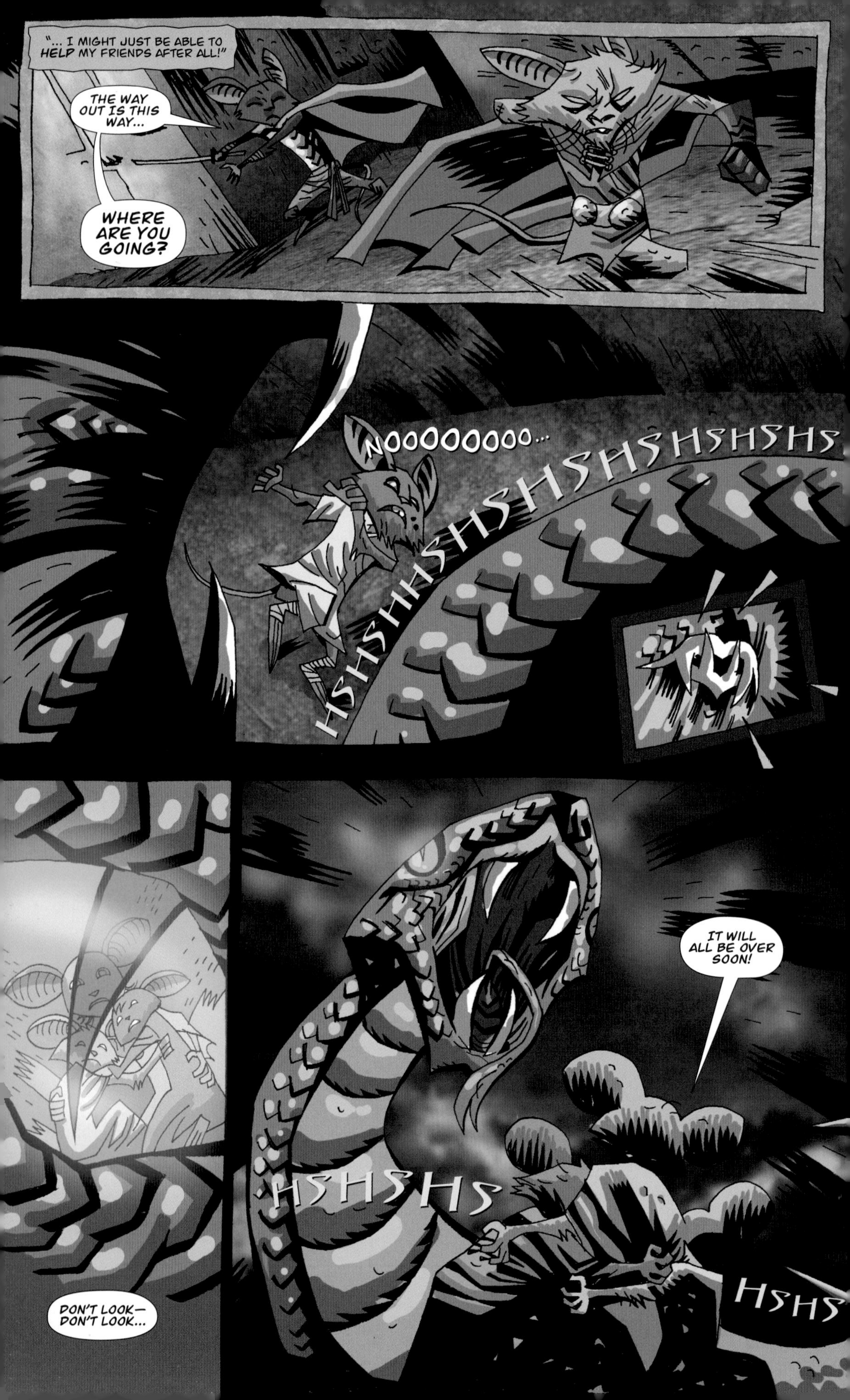
"... I MIGHT JUST BE ABLE TO HELP MY FRIENDS AFTER ALL!"
THE WAY OUT IS THIS WAY...
WHERE ARE YOU GOING?
NOOOOOOOO...
HSHSHSHSHSHSHSHSHS
IT WILL ALL BE OVER SOON!
HSHSHS
HSHS
DON'T LOOK— DON'T LOOK...

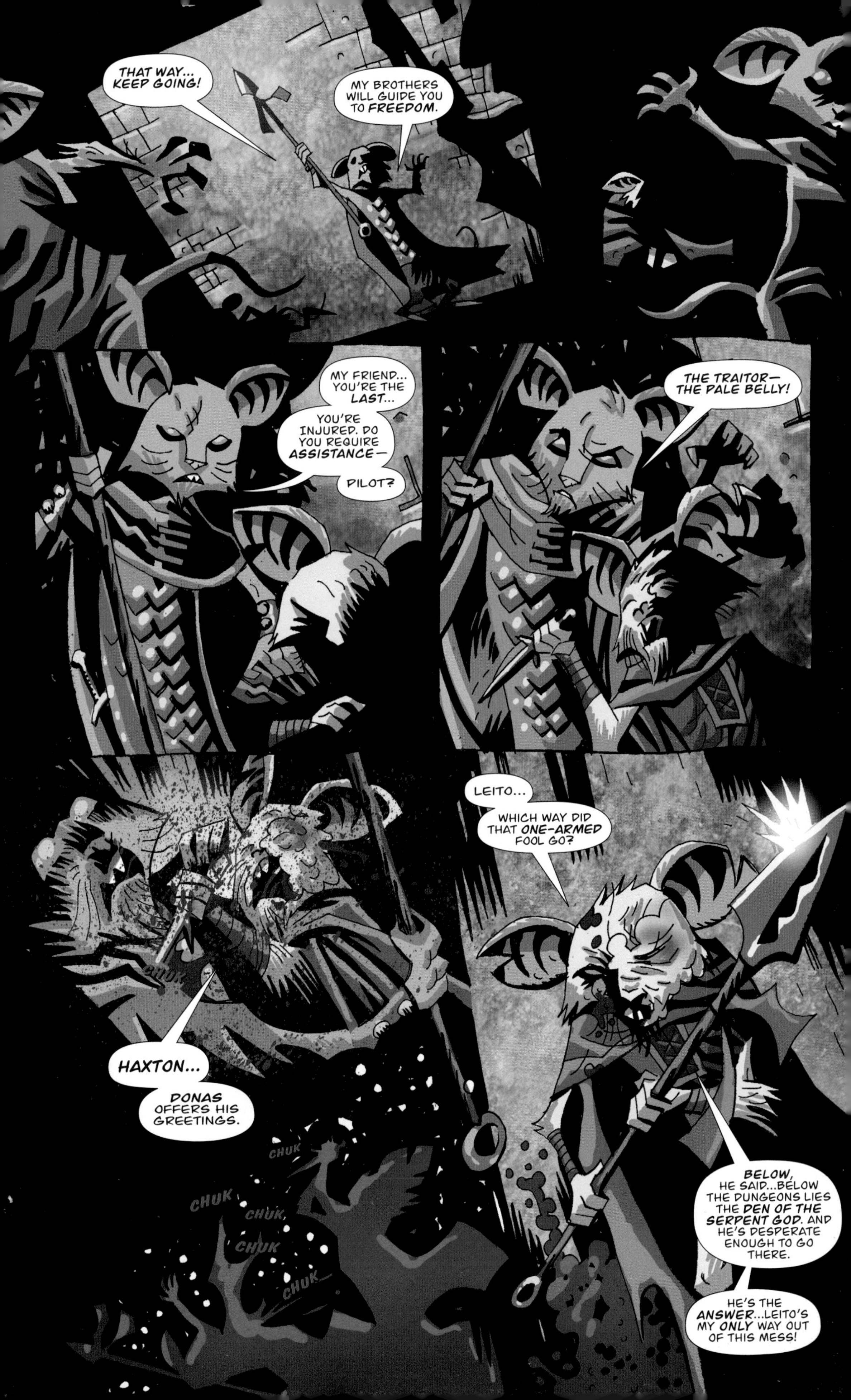
THAT WAY... KEEP GOING!
MY BROTHERS WILL GUIDE YOU TO FREEDOM.
MY FRIEND... YOU'RE THE LAST...
YOU'RE INJURED. DO YOU REQUIRE ASSISTANCE—
PILOT?
THE TRAITOR— THE PALE BELLY!
CHUK
HAXTON...
DONAS OFFERS HIS GREETINGS.
CHUK
CHUK
CHUK
CHUK
CHUK
LEITO...
WHICH WAY DID THAT ONE-ARMED FOOL GO?
BELOW, HE SAID...BELOW THE DUNGEONS LIES THE DEN OF THE SERPENT GOD. AND HE'S DESPERATE ENOUGH TO GO THERE.
HE'S THE ANSWER...LEITO'S MY ONLY WAY OUT OF THIS MESS!

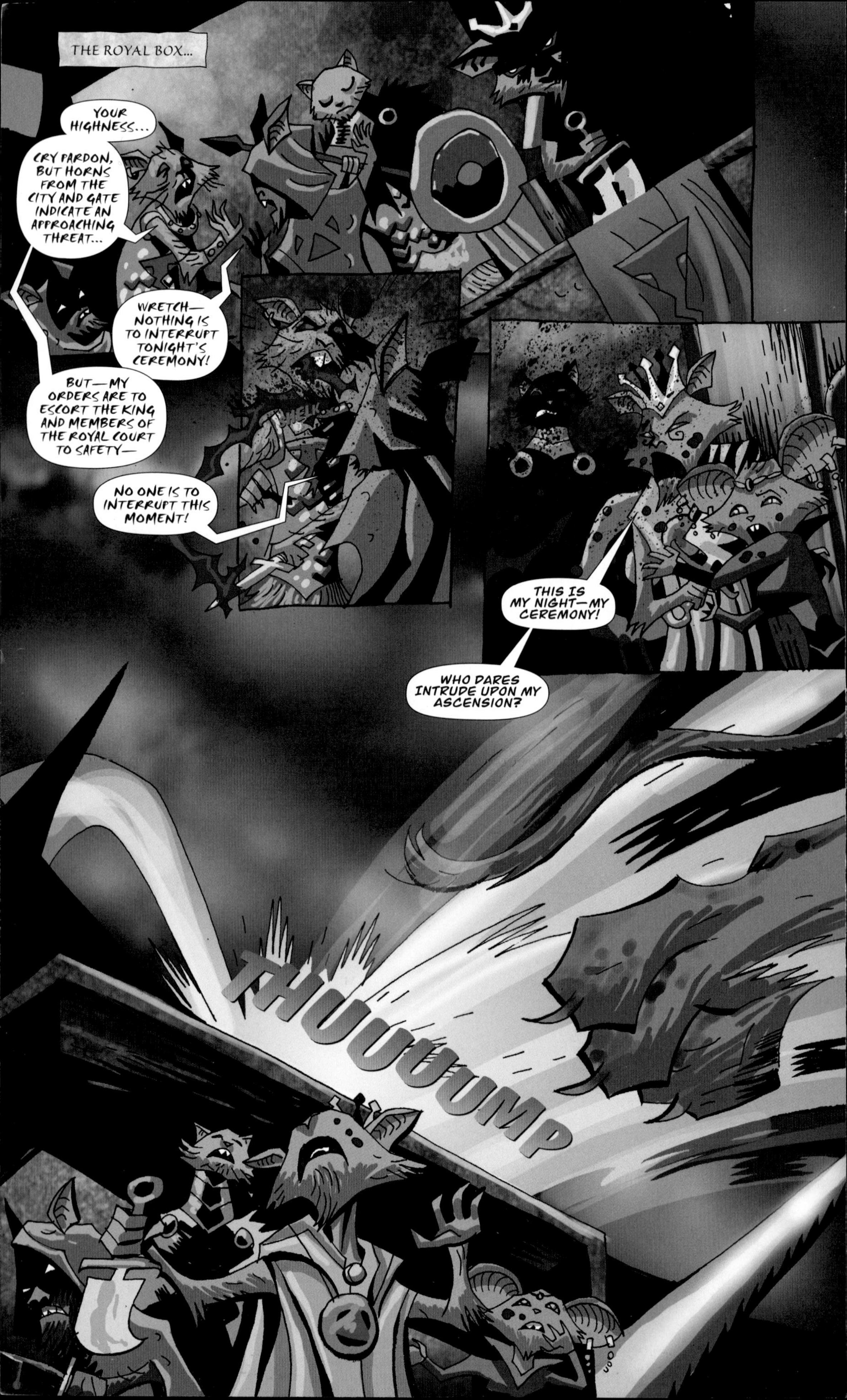
THE ROYAL BOX...
YOUR HIGHNESS...
CRY PARDON, BUT HORNS FROM THE CITY AND GATE INDICATE AN APPROACHING THREAT...
WRETCH—NOTHING IS TO INTERRUPT TONIGHT'S CEREMONY!
BUT—MY ORDERS ARE TO ESCORT THE KING AND MEMBERS OF THE ROYAL COURT TO SAFETY—
SHELK
NO ONE IS TO INTERRUPT THIS MOMENT!
THIS IS MY NIGHT—MY CEREMONY!
WHO DARES INTRUDE UPON MY ASCENSION?
THUUUUMP

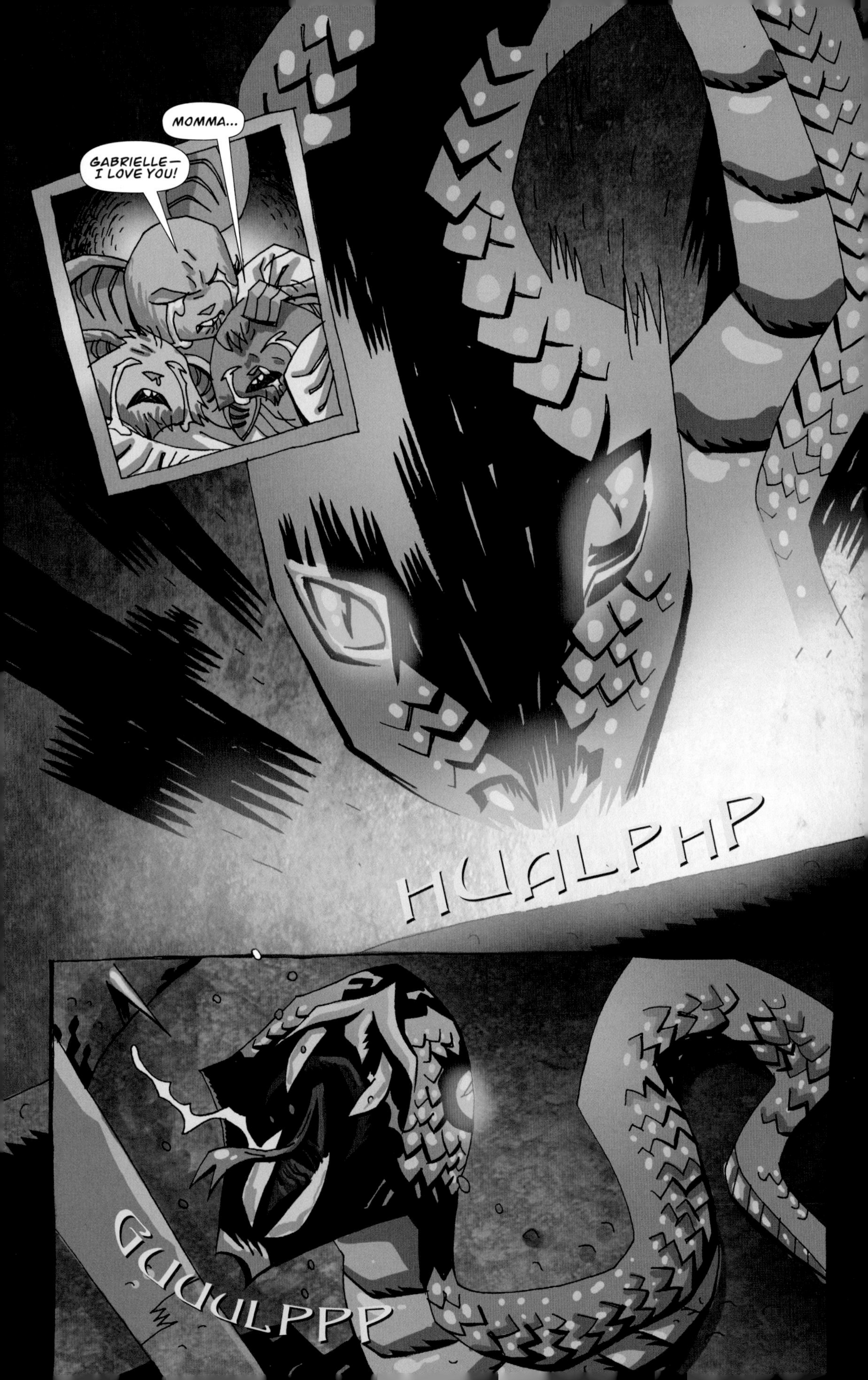
MOMMA...
GABRIELLE— I LOVE YOU!
HUALPHP
GUUULPPP

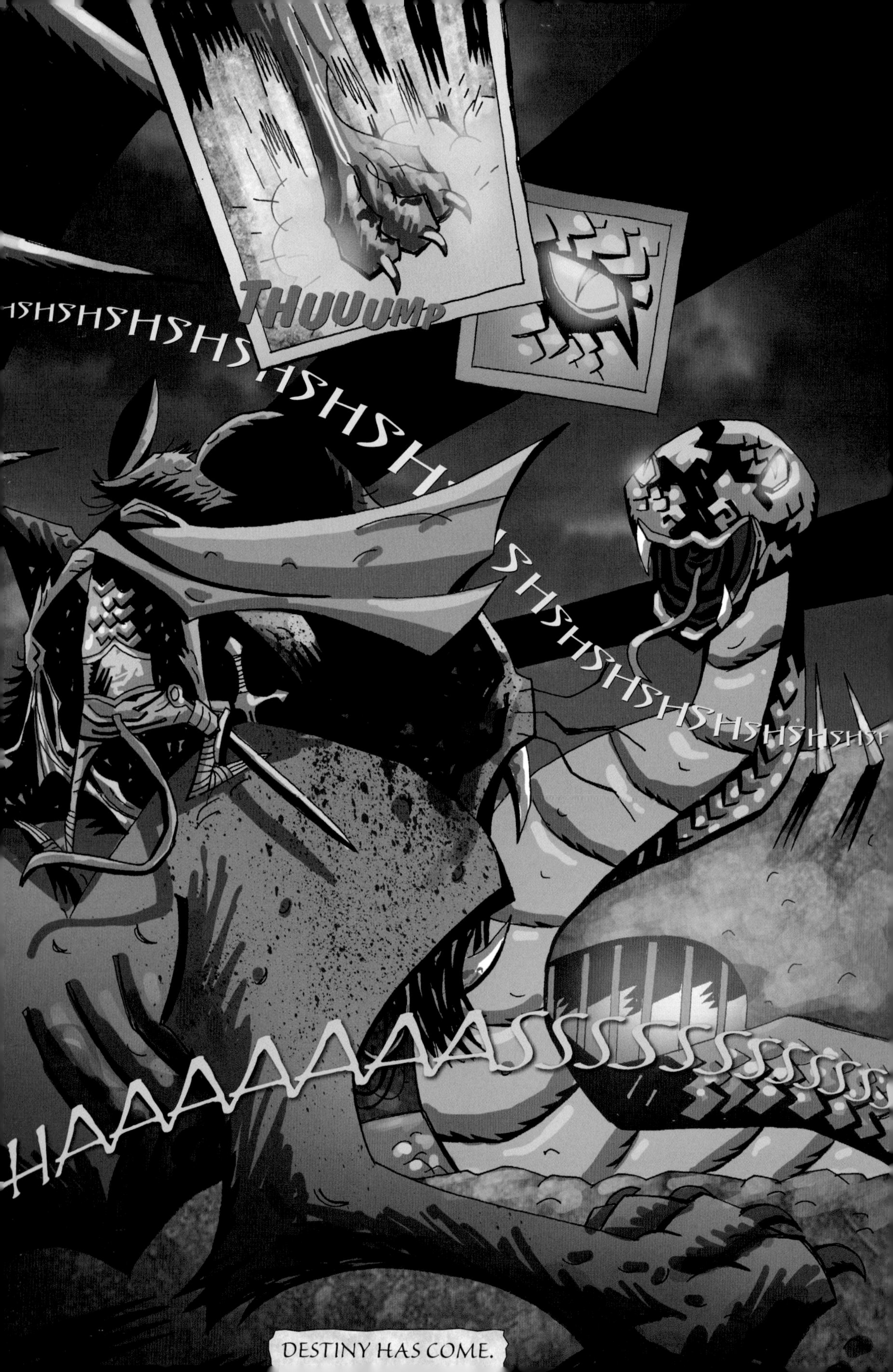
THUUUMP
SHSHSHSHSHSHSHSHSHSHSHSHSHSHSHSHSHSHSHSH
HAAAAAAAAASSSSSSSSSSSS
DESTINY HAS COME.

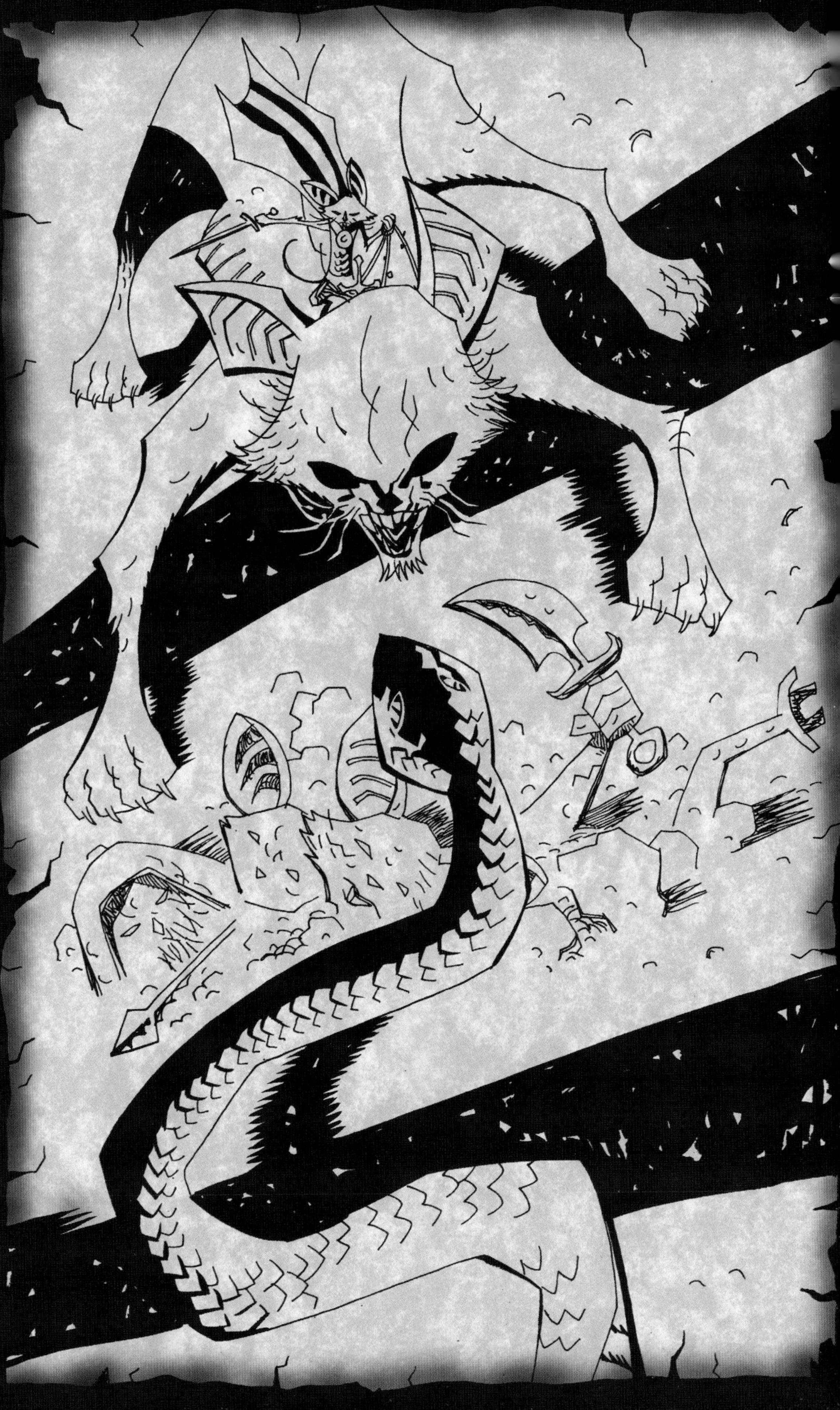

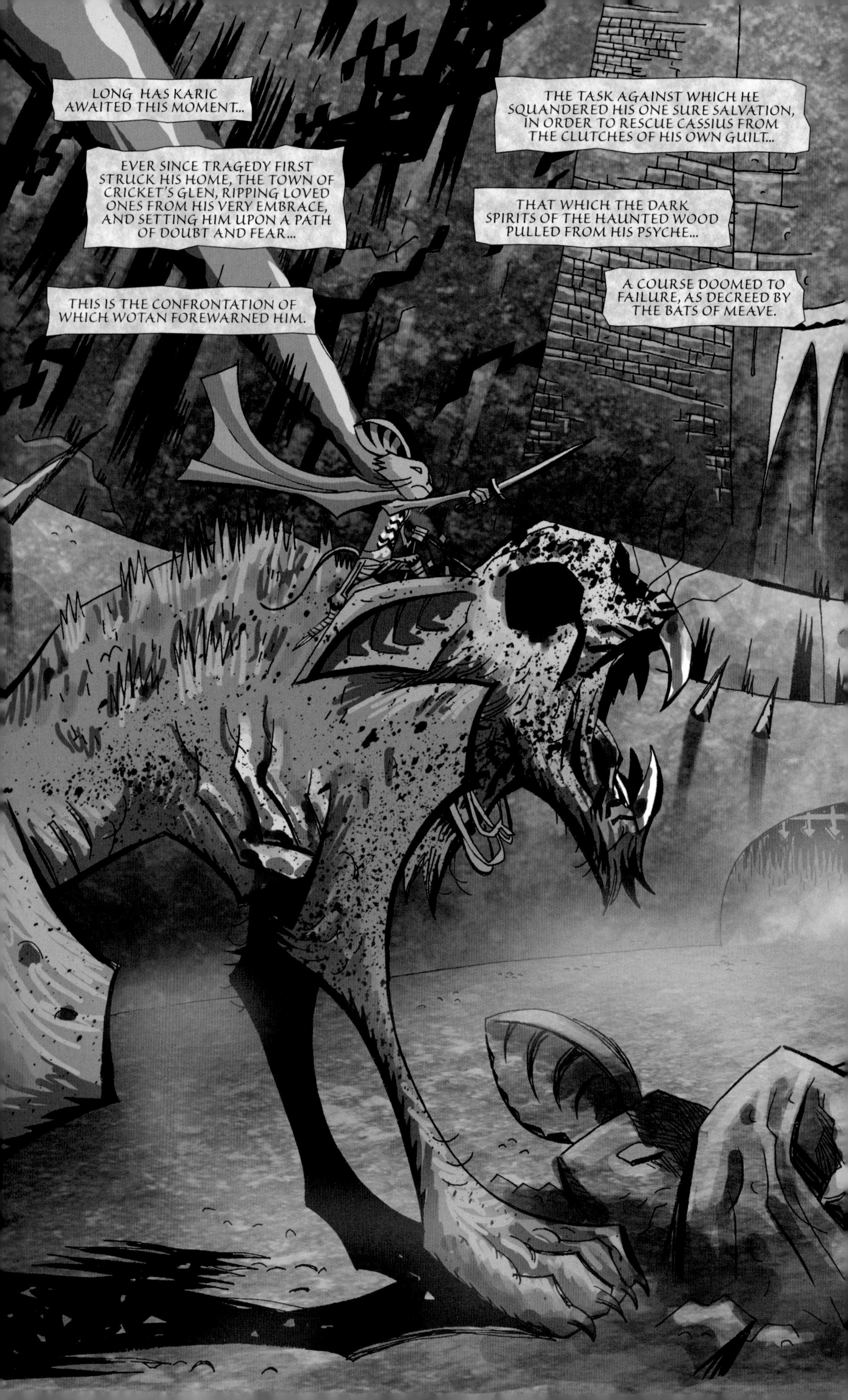
LONG HAS KARIC AWAITED THIS MOMENT...
EVER SINCE TRAGEDY FIRST STRUCK HIS HOME, THE TOWN OF CRICKET'S GLEN, RIPPING LOVED ONES FROM HIS VERY EMBRACE, AND SETTING HIM UPON A PATH OF DOUBT AND FEAR...
THIS IS THE CONFRONTATION OF WHICH WOTAN FOREWARNED HIM.
THE TASK AGAINST WHICH HE SQUANDERED HIS ONE SURE SALVATION, IN ORDER TO RESCUE CASSIUS FROM THE CLUTCHES OF HIS OWN GUILT...
THAT WHICH THE DARK SPIRITS OF THE HAUNTED WOOD PULLED FROM HIS PSYCHE...
A COURSE DOOMED TO FAILURE, AS DECREED BY THE BATS OF MEAVE.

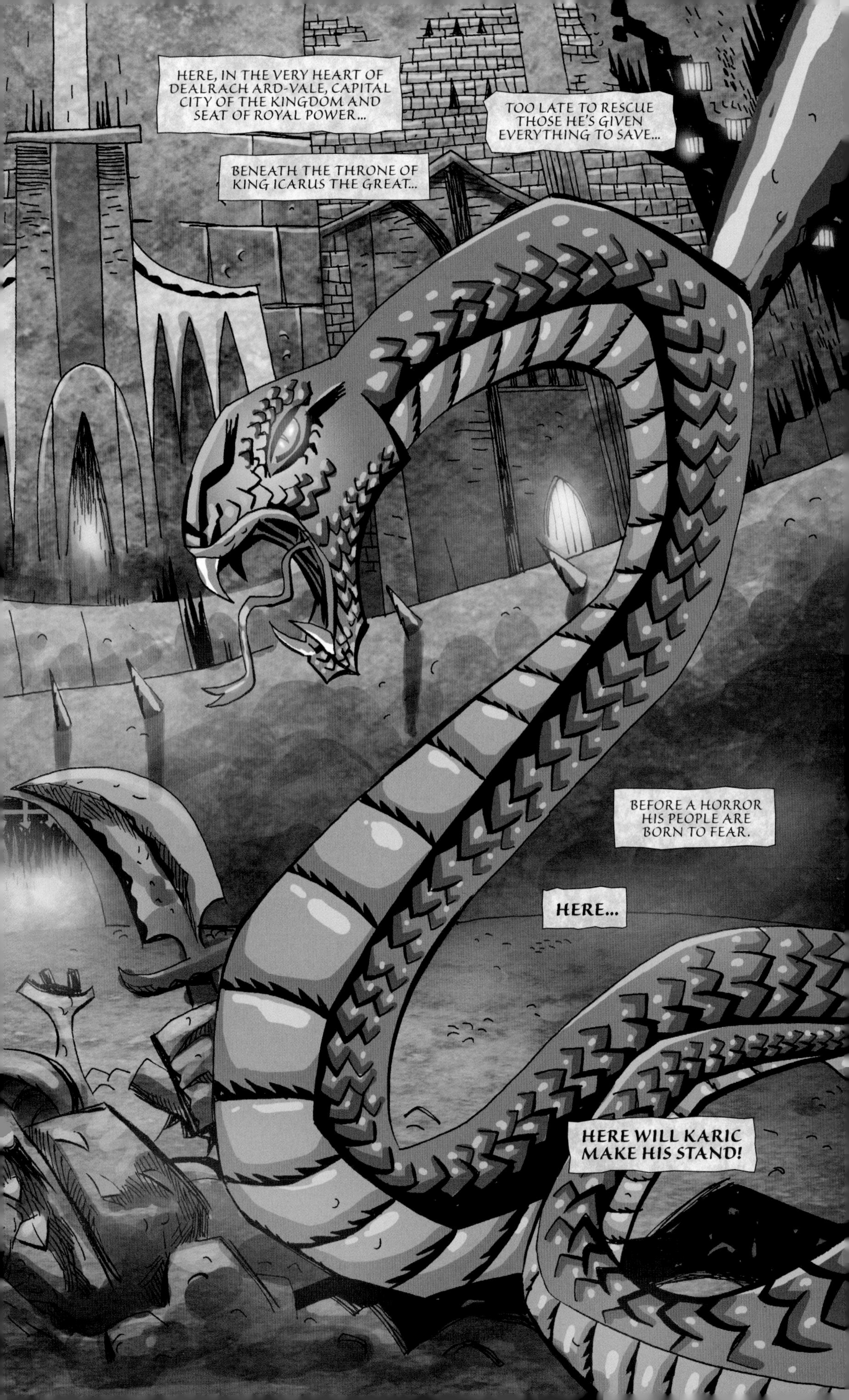
HERE, IN THE VERY HEART OF DEALRACH ARD-VALE, CAPITAL CITY OF THE KINGDOM AND SEAT OF ROYAL POWER...
BENEATH THE THRONE OF KING ICARUS THE GREAT...
TOO LATE TO RESCUE THOSE HE'S GIVEN EVERYTHING TO SAVE...
BEFORE A HORROR HIS PEOPLE ARE BORN TO FEAR.
HERE...
HERE WILL KARIC MAKE HIS STAND!

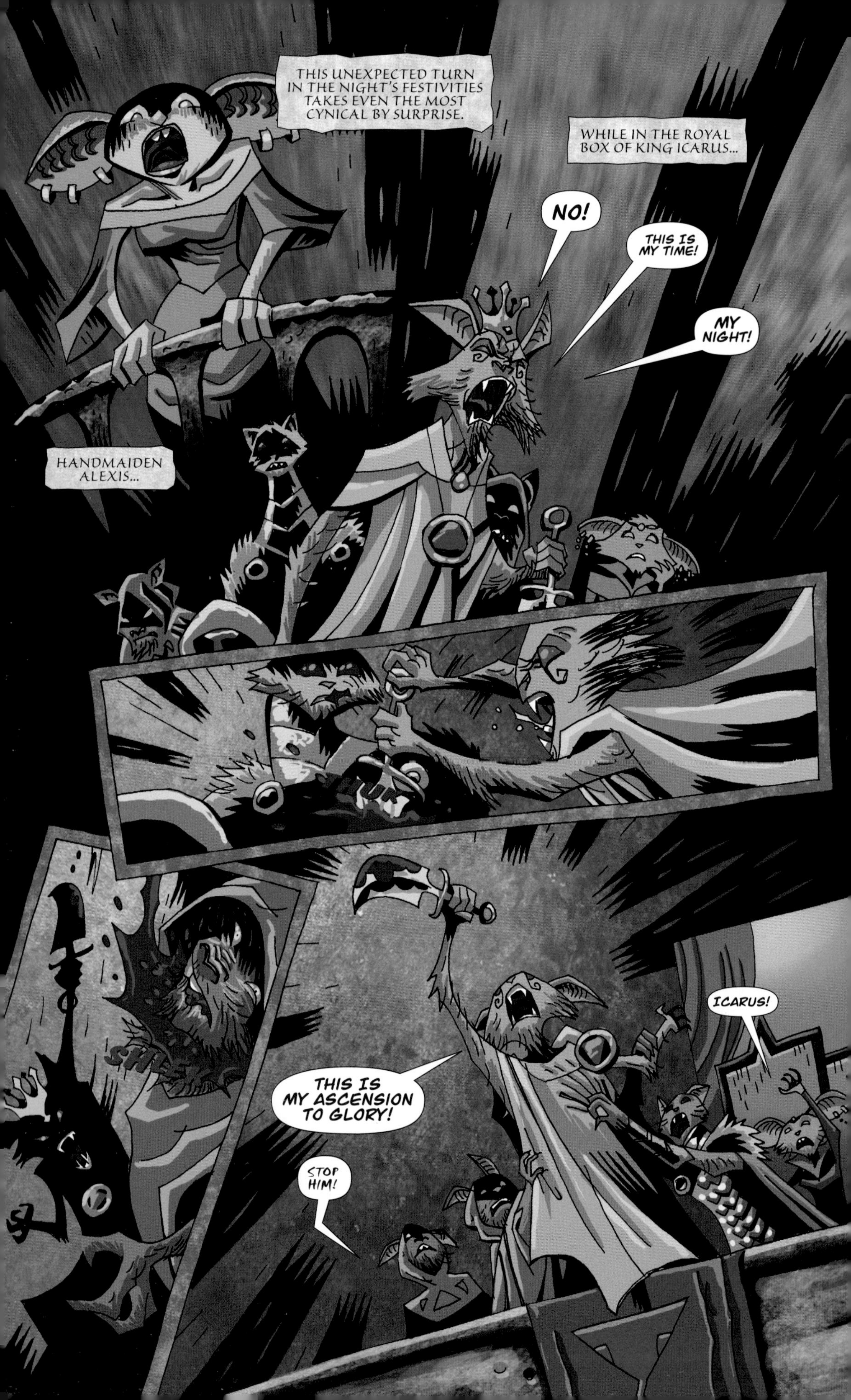
THIS UNEXPECTED TURN IN THE NIGHT'S FESTIVITIES TAKES EVEN THE MOST CYNICAL BY SURPRISE.
HANDMAIDEN ALEXIS...
WHILE IN THE ROYAL BOX OF KING ICARUS...
NO!
THIS IS MY TIME!
MY NIGHT!
THIS IS MY ASCENSION TO GLORY!
ICARUS!
STOP HIM!

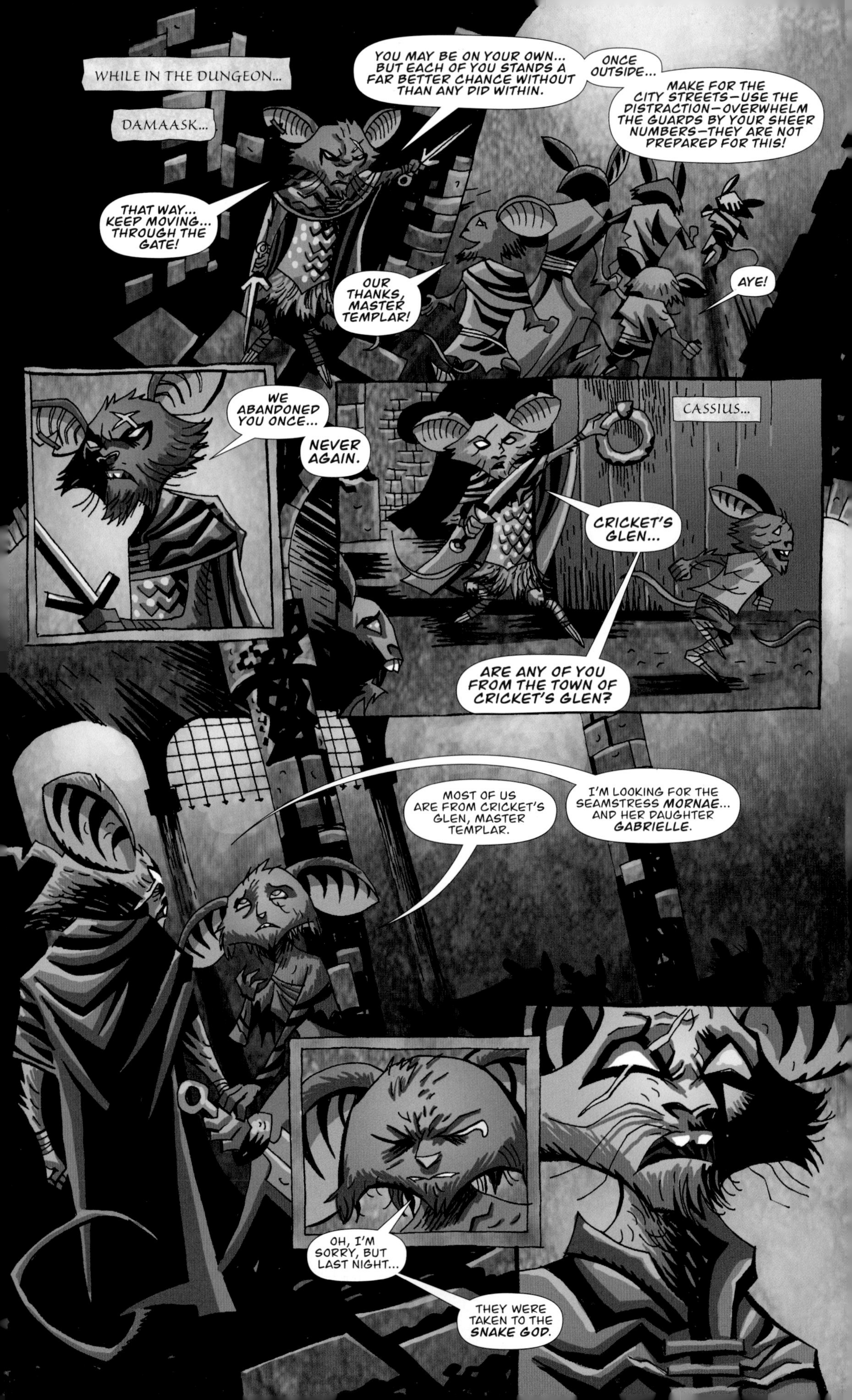
WHILE IN THE DUNGEON...
DAMAASK...
YOU MAY BE ON YOUR OWN... BUT EACH OF YOU STANDS A FAR BETTER CHANCE WITHOUT THAN ANY DID WITHIN.
ONCE OUTSIDE...
MAKE FOR THE CITY STREETS—USE THE DISTRACTION—OVERWHELM THE GUARDS BY YOUR SHEER NUMBERS—THEY ARE NOT PREPARED FOR THIS!
THAT WAY... KEEP MOVING... THROUGH THE GATE!
OUR THANKS, MASTER TEMPLAR!
AYE!
WE ABANDONED YOU ONCE...
NEVER AGAIN.
CASSIUS...
CRICKET'S GLEN...
ARE ANY OF YOU FROM THE TOWN OF CRICKET'S GLEN?
I'M LOOKING FOR THE SEAMSTRESS MORNAE... AND HER DAUGHTER GABRIELLE.
MOST OF US ARE FROM CRICKET'S GLEN, MASTER TEMPLAR.
OH, I'M SORRY, BUT LAST NIGHT...
THEY WERE TAKEN TO THE SNAKE GOD.

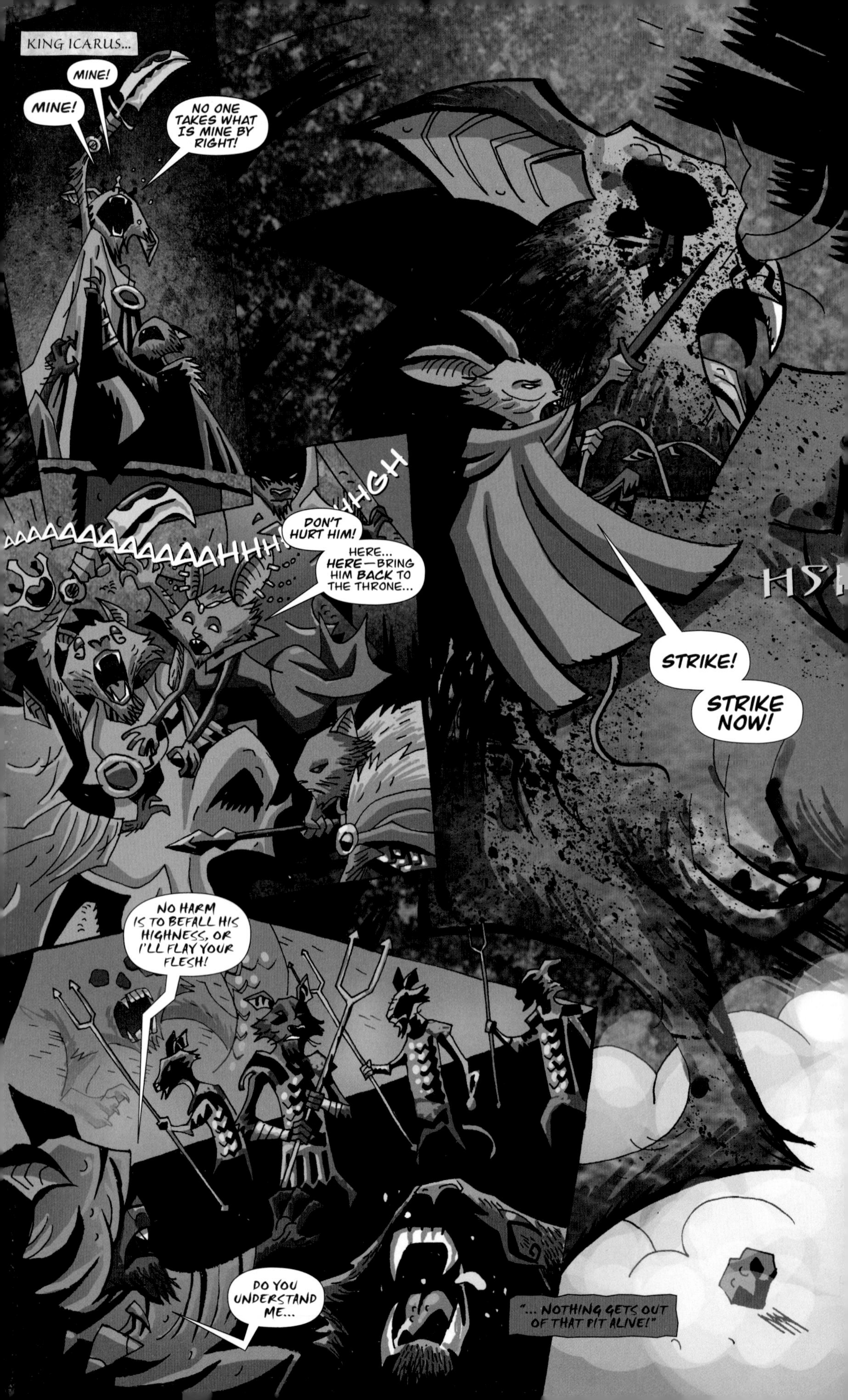
KING ICARUS...
MINE!
MINE!
NO ONE TAKES WHAT IS MINE BY RIGHT!
AAAAAAAAAAAAAAAAAAHHH
DON'T HURT HIM!
HERE... HERE—BRING HIM BACK TO THE THRONE...
STRIKE!
STRIKE NOW!
NO HARM IS TO BEFALL HIS HIGHNESS, OR I'LL FLAY YOUR FLESH!
DO YOU UNDERSTAND ME...
"... NOTHING GETS OUT OF THAT PIT ALIVE!"

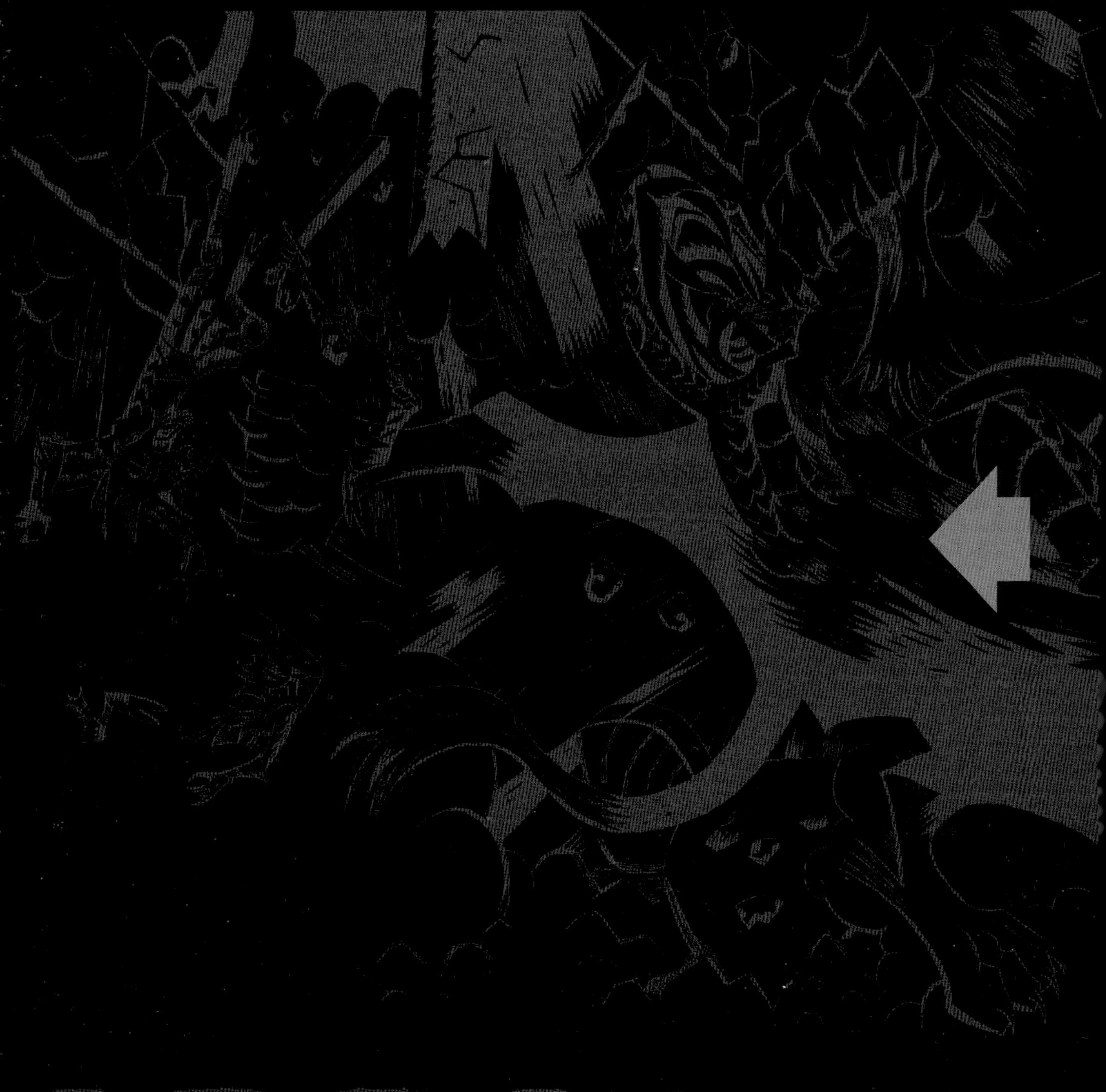

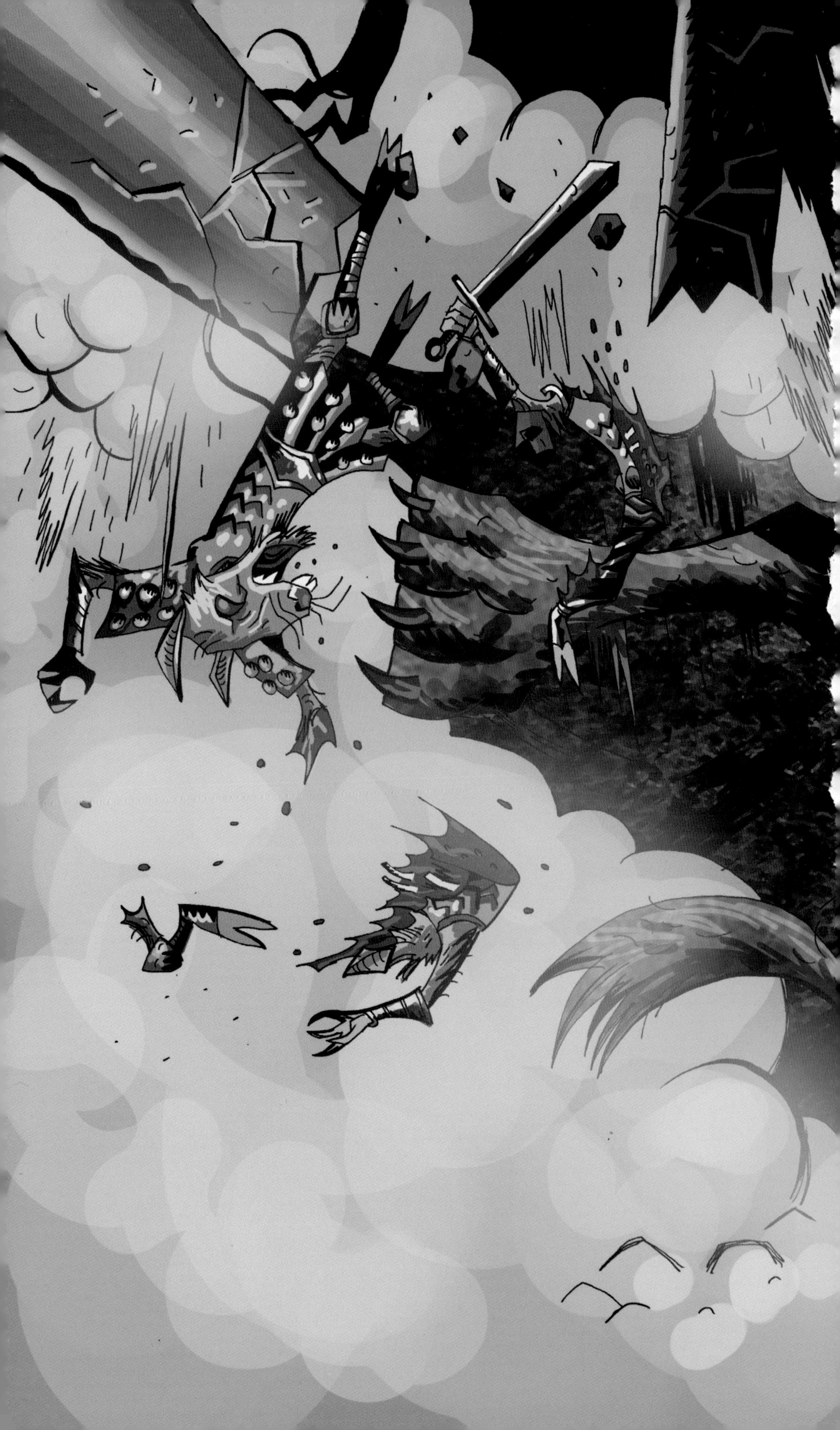

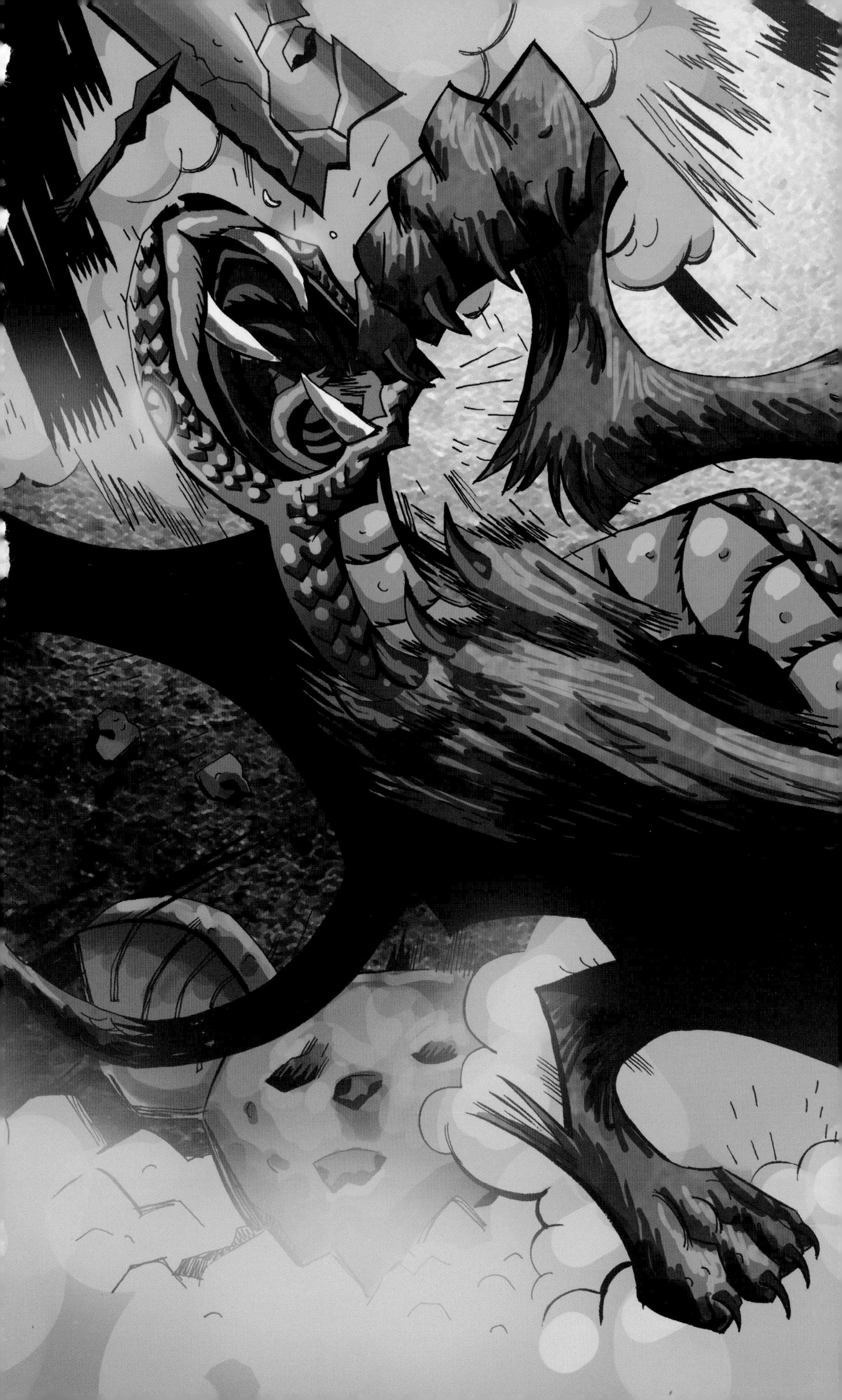

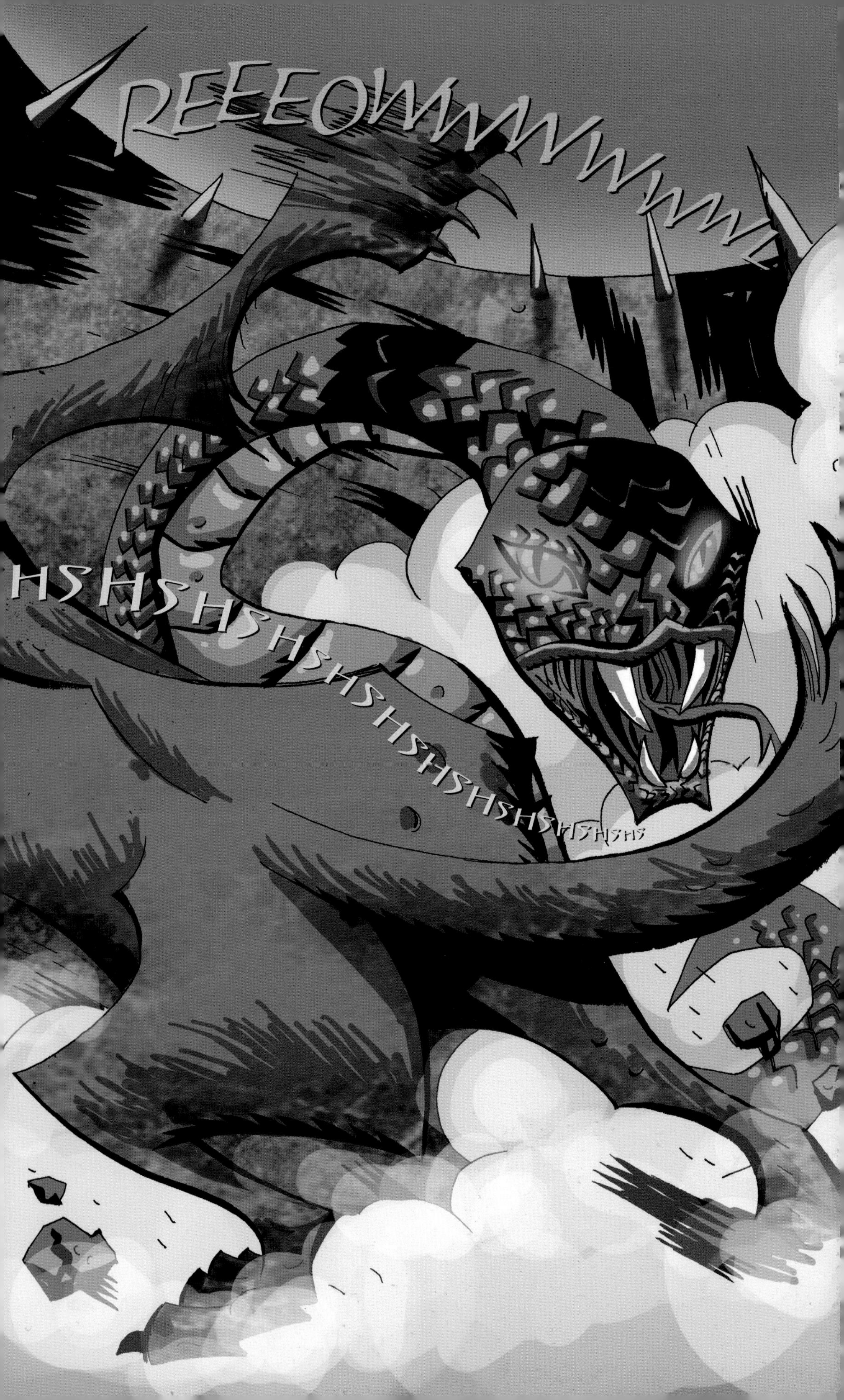
REEEOWWWWWWL
HSHSHSHSHSHSHSHSHSHSHSHSHS

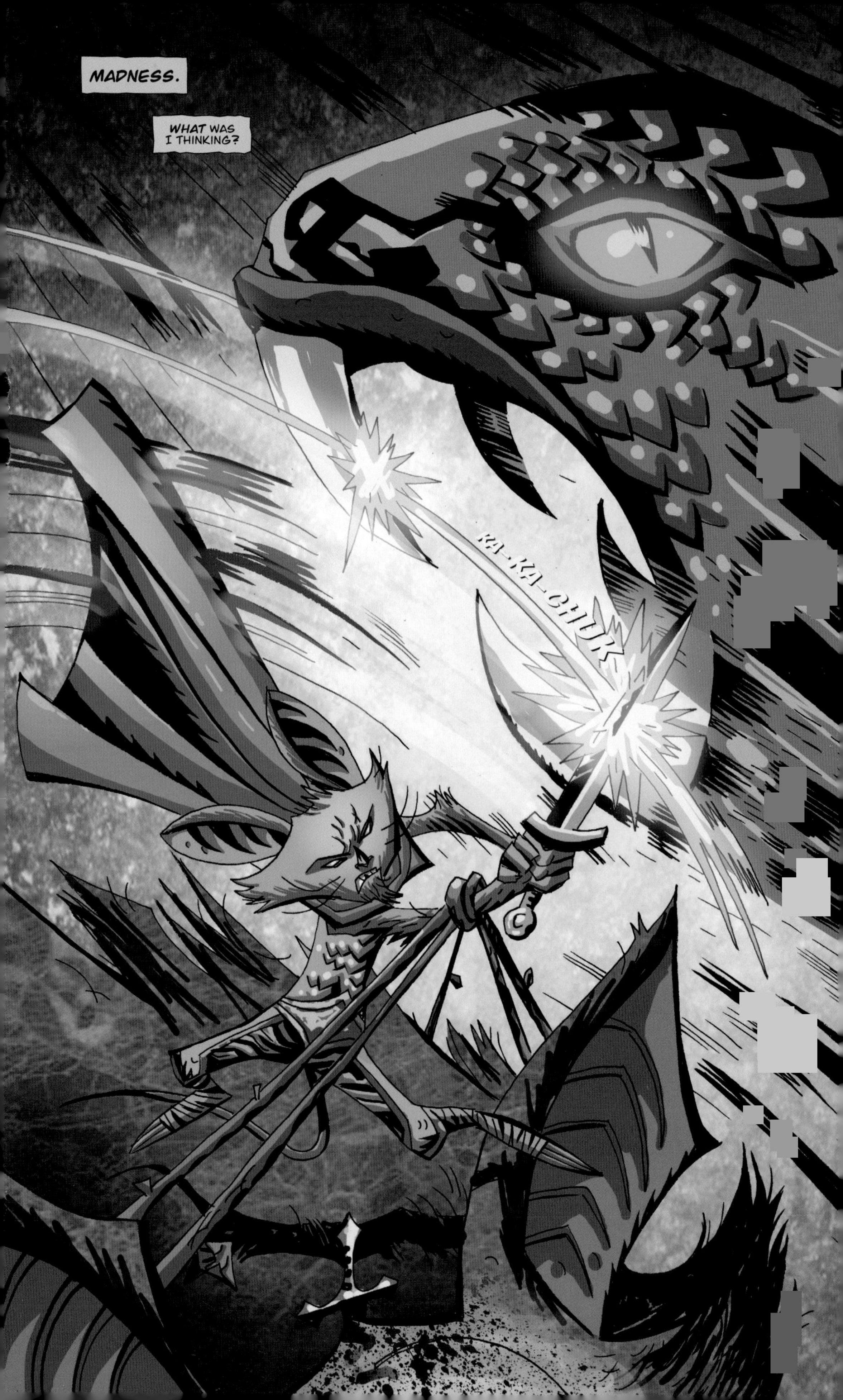
MADNESS.
WHAT WAS I THINKING?
KA-KA-CHUK

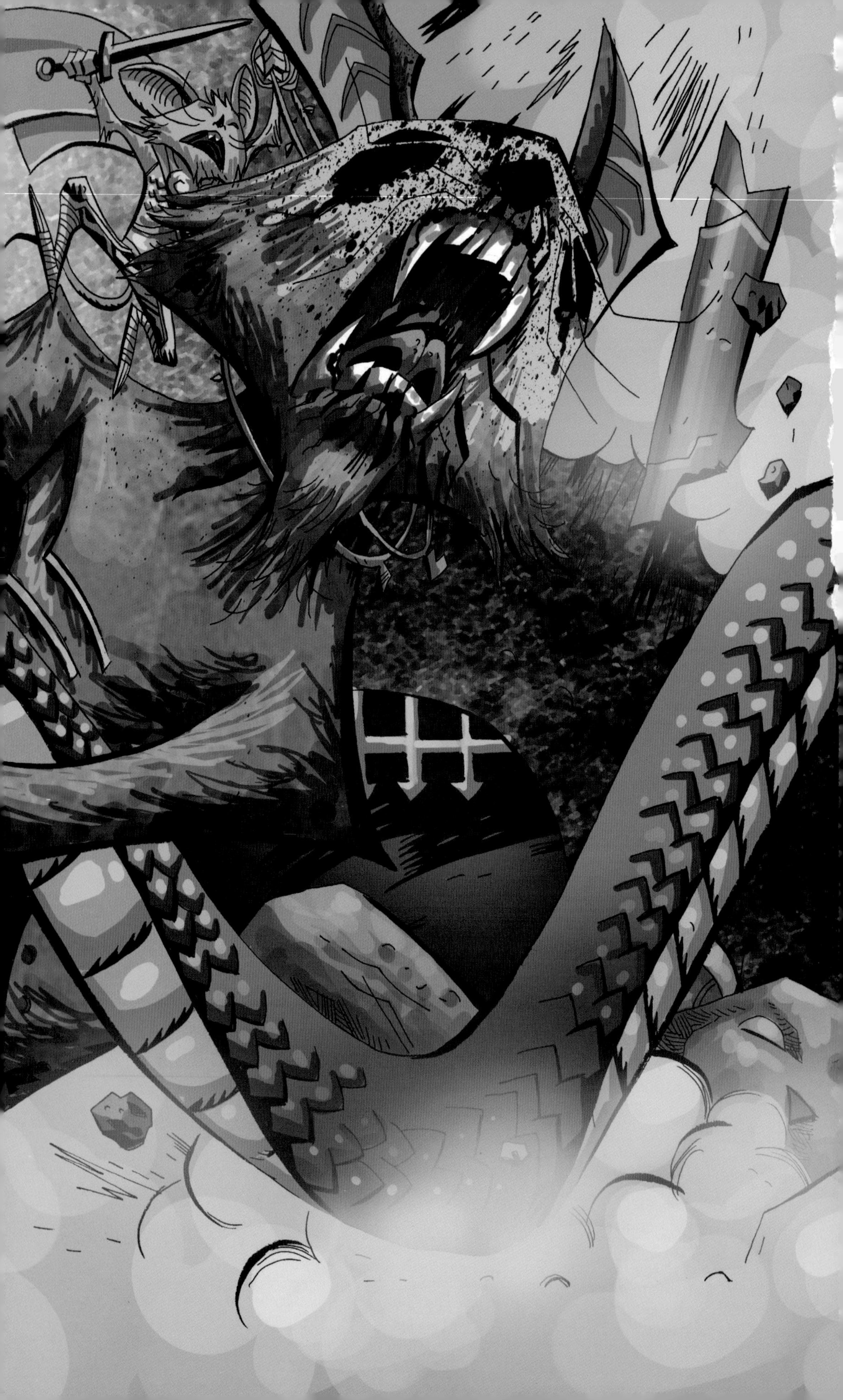

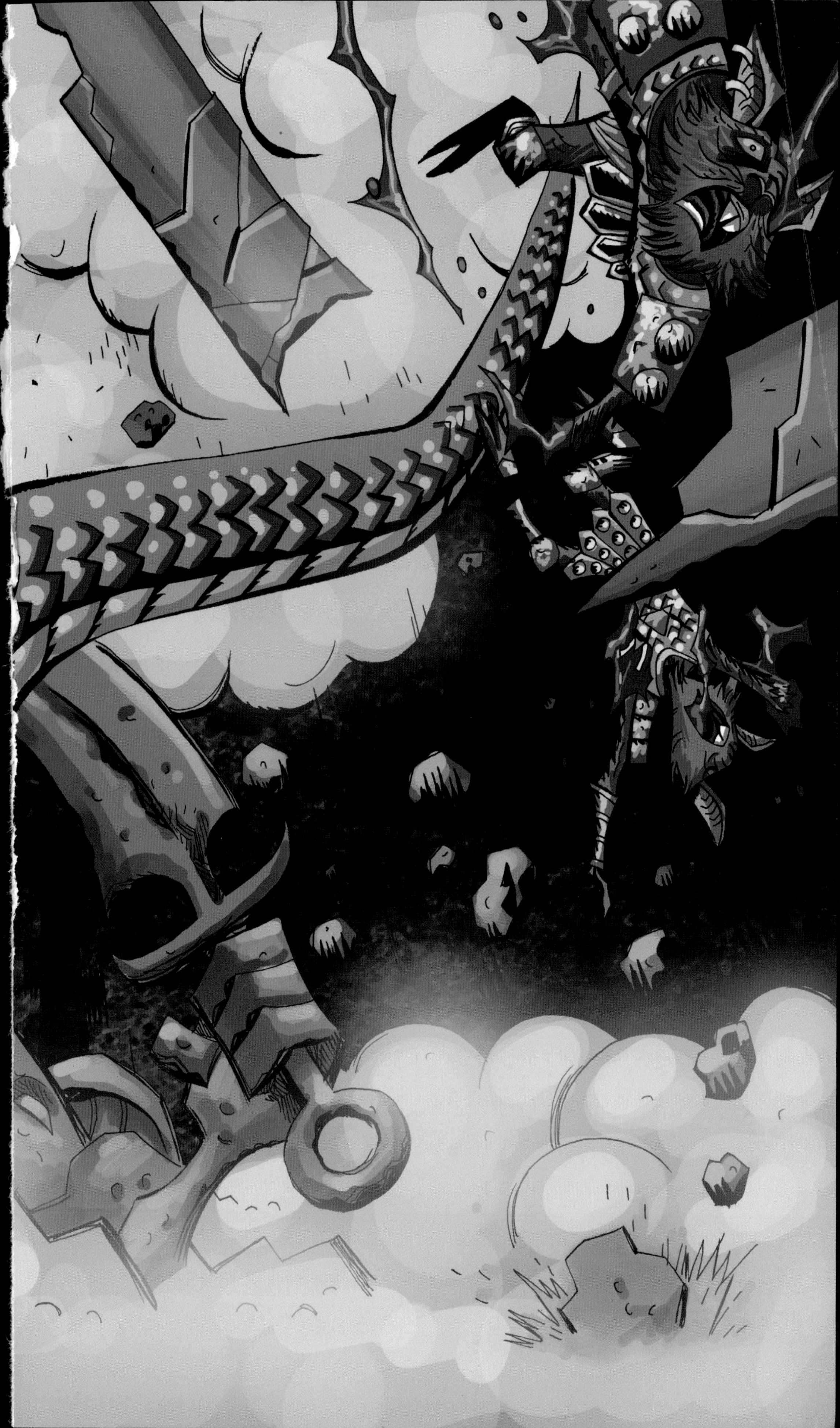

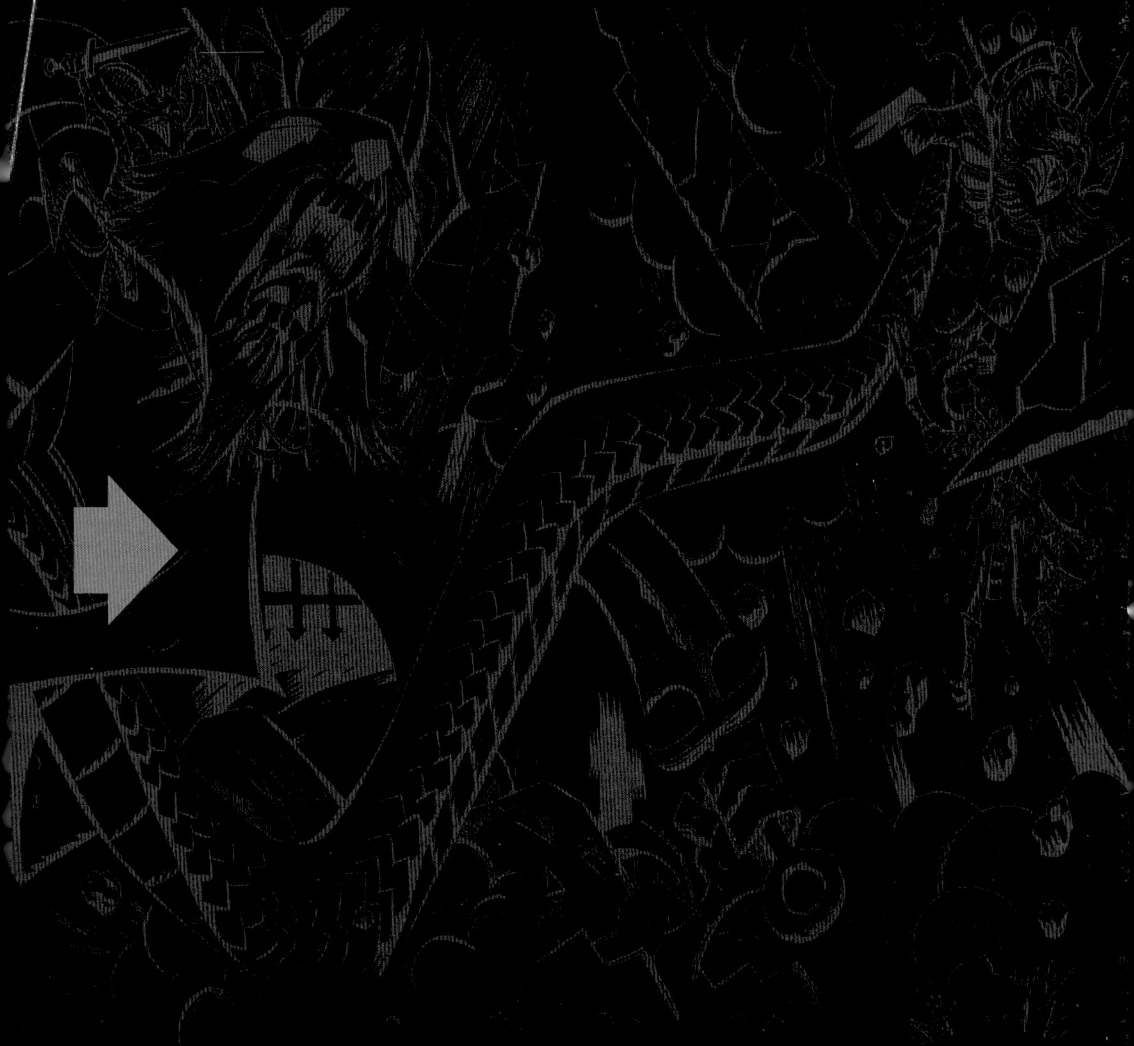

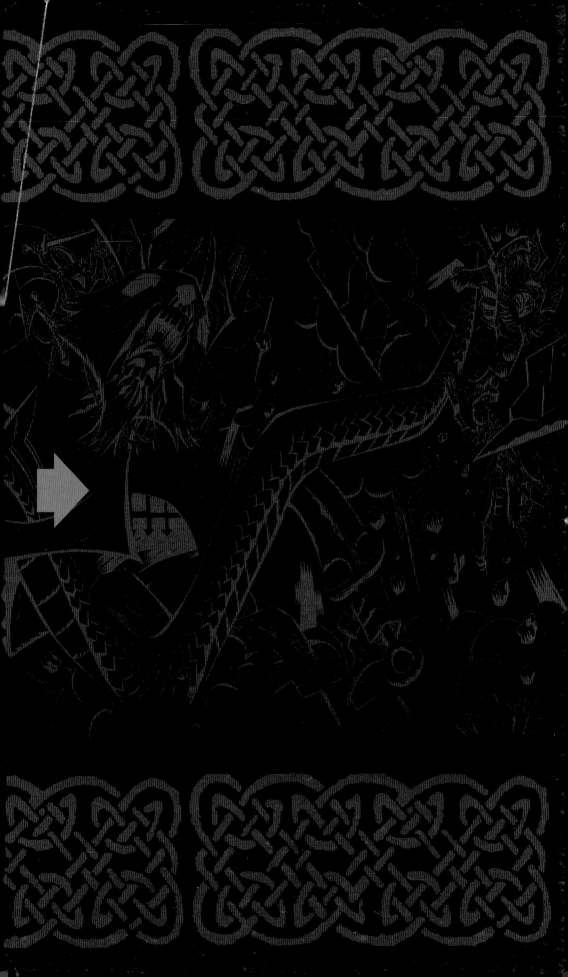

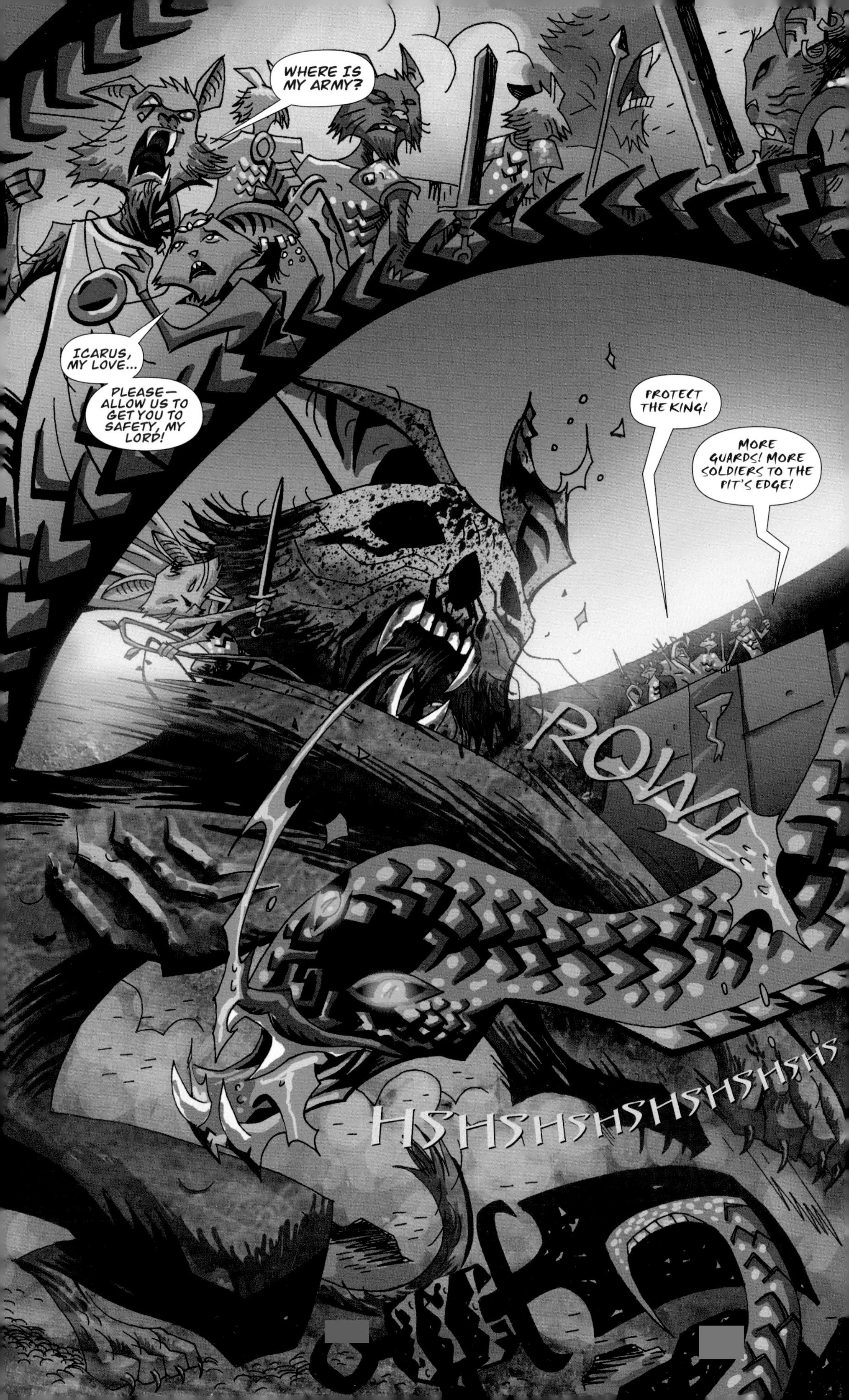
WHERE IS MY ARMY?
ICARUS, MY LOVE...
PLEASE— ALLOW US TO GET YOU TO SAFETY, MY LORD!
PROTECT THE KING!
MORE GUARDS! MORE SOLDIERS TO THE PIT'S EDGE!
ROWL
HSHSHSHSHSHSHSHSHS

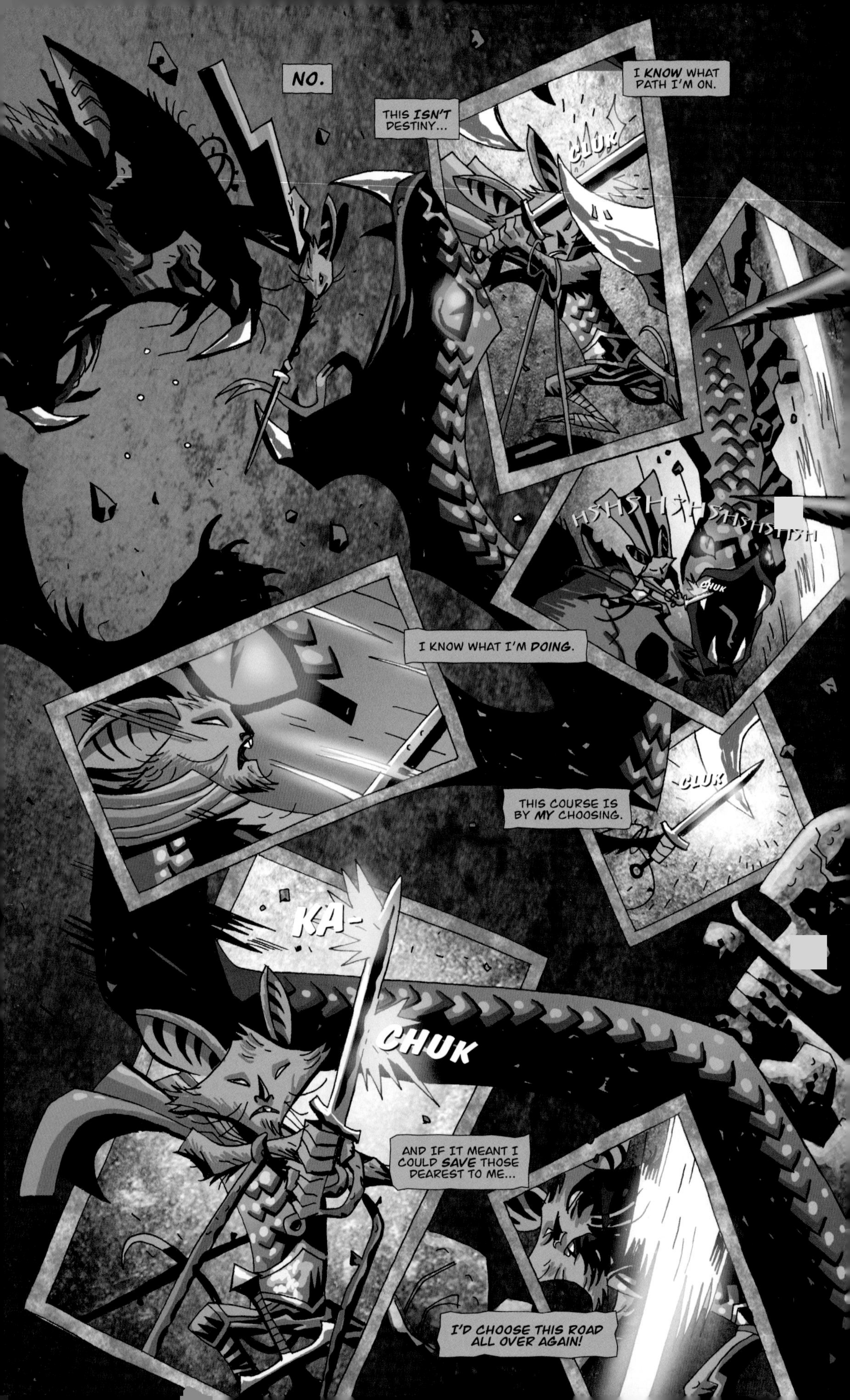
NO.
THIS *ISN'T* DESTINY...
I *KNOW* WHAT PATH I'M ON.
CLUK
CHUK
I KNOW WHAT I'M *DOING*.
CLUK
THIS COURSE IS BY *MY* CHOOSING.
KA-
CHUK
AND IF IT MEANT I COULD *SAVE* THOSE DEAREST TO ME...
I'D CHOOSE THIS ROAD ALL OVER AGAIN!

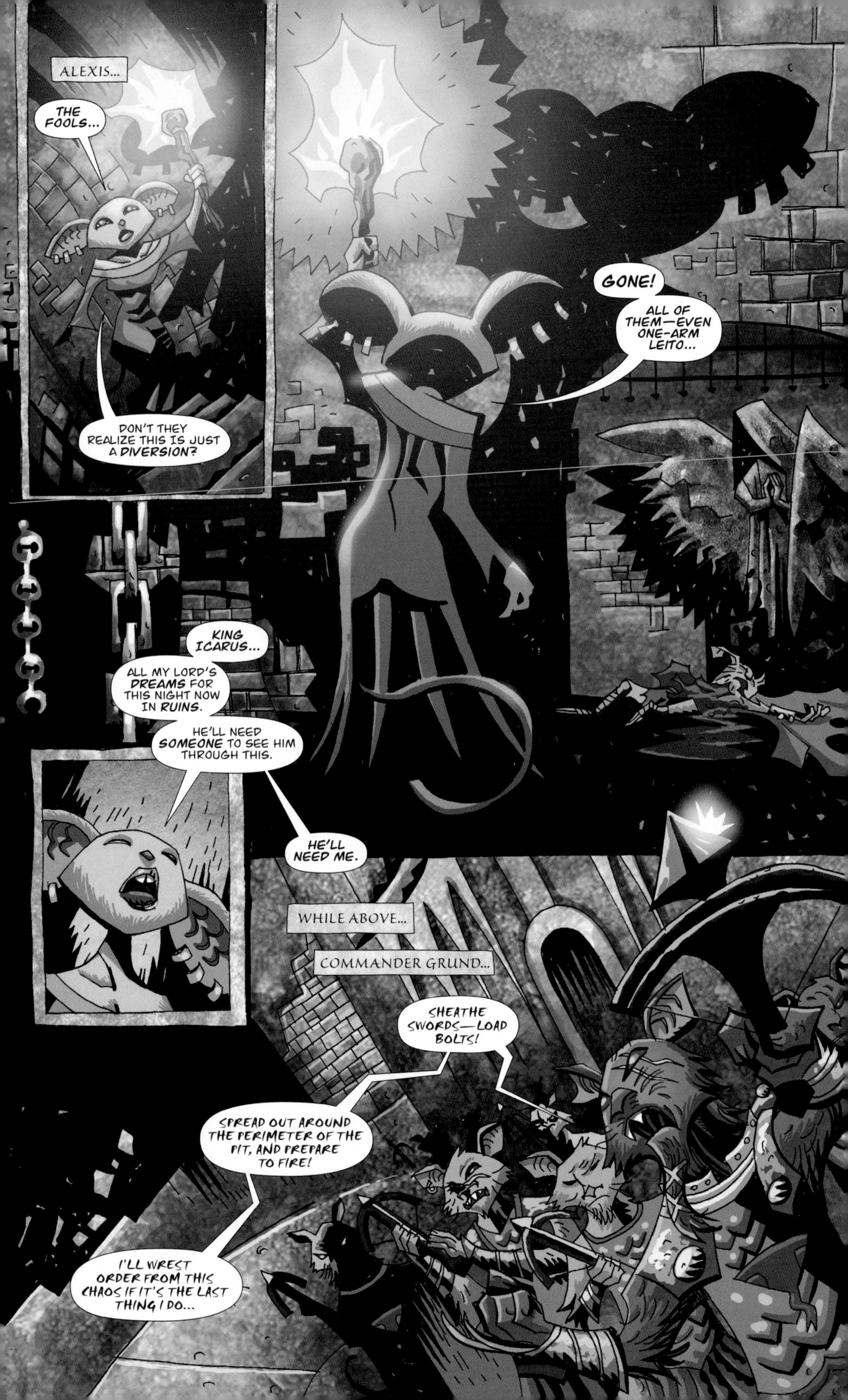
ALEXIS...
THE FOOLS...
DON'T THEY REALIZE THIS IS JUST A DIVERSION?
GONE!
ALL OF THEM—EVEN ONE-ARM LEITO...
KING ICARUS...
ALL MY LORD'S DREAMS FOR THIS NIGHT NOW IN RUINS.
HE'LL NEED SOMEONE TO SEE HIM THROUGH THIS.
HE'LL NEED ME.
WHILE ABOVE...
COMMANDER GRUND...
SHEATHE SWORDS—LOAD BOLTS!
SPREAD OUT AROUND THE PERIMETER OF THE PIT, AND PREPARE TO FIRE!
I'LL WREST ORDER FROM THIS CHAOS IF IT'S THE LAST THING I DO...

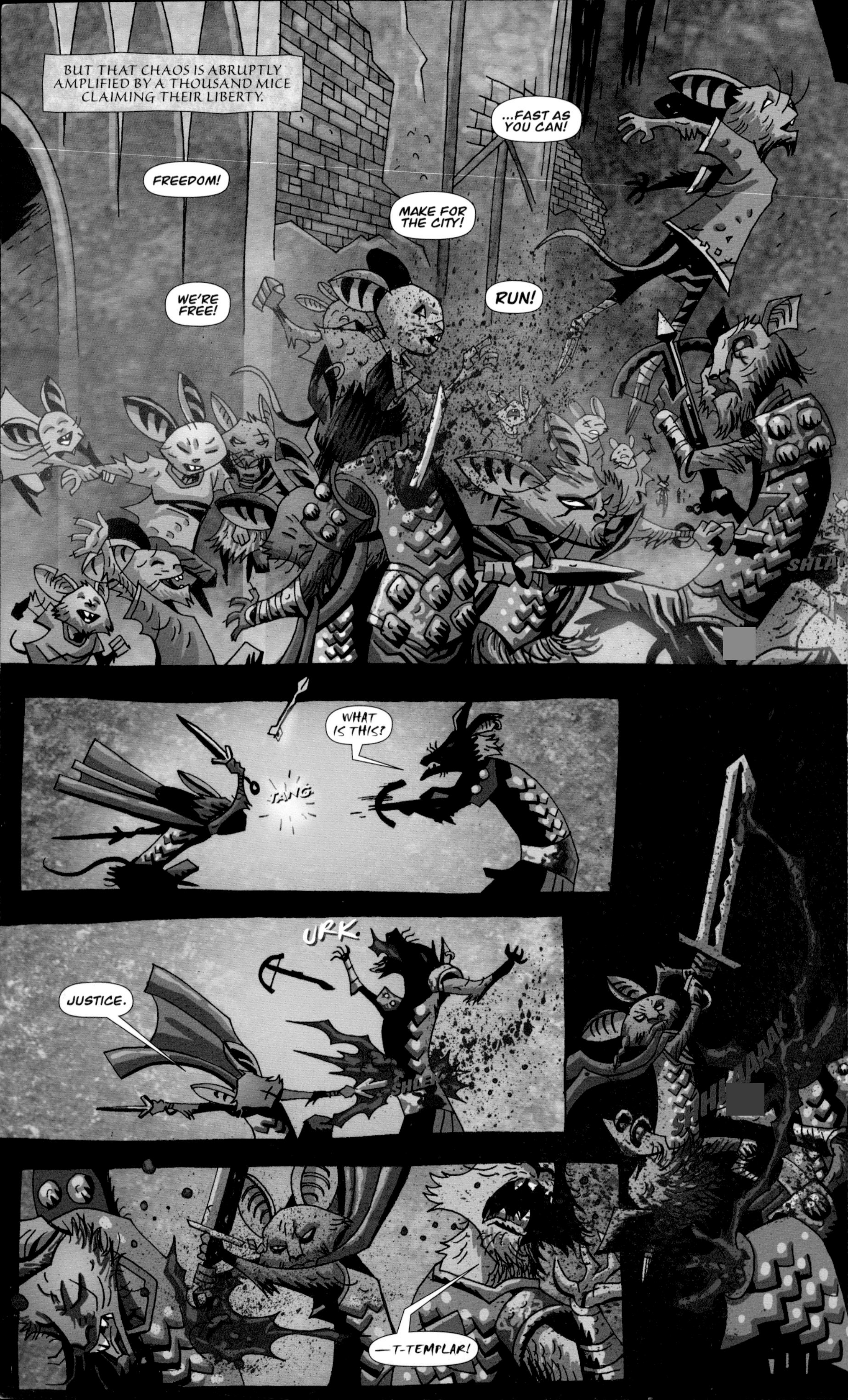
BUT THAT CHAOS IS ABRUPTLY AMPLIFIED BY A THOUSAND MICE CLAIMING THEIR LIBERTY.
...FAST AS YOU CAN!
FREEDOM!
MAKE FOR THE CITY!
WE'RE FREE!
RUN!
WHAT IS THIS?
TANG
URK.
JUSTICE.
—T-TEMPLAR!

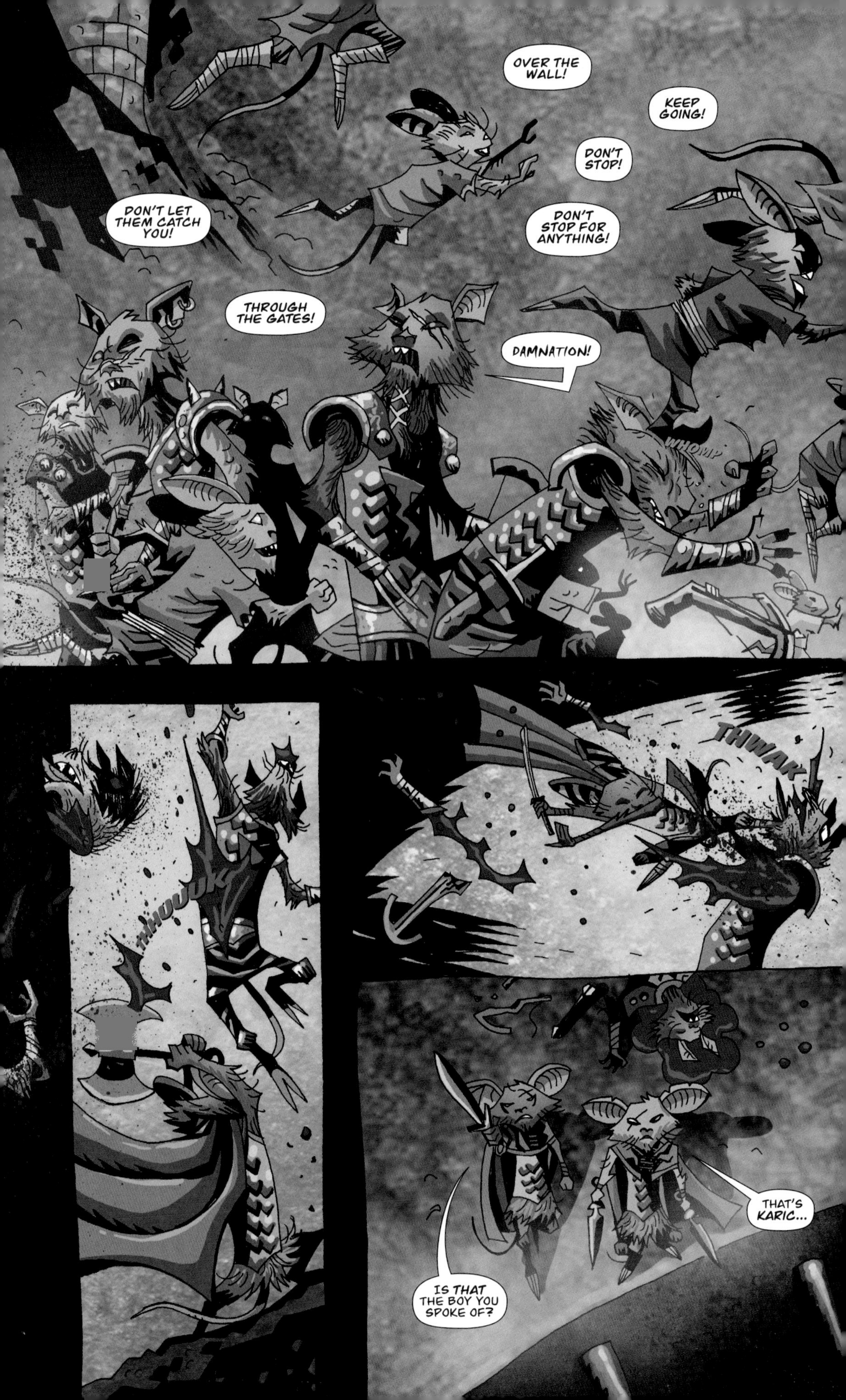
OVER THE WALL!
KEEP GOING!
DON'T STOP!
DON'T LET THEM CATCH YOU!
DON'T STOP FOR ANYTHING!
THROUGH THE GATES!
DAMNATION!
WHOMP
THHUUUK
THWAK
THAT'S KARIC...
IS THAT THE BOY YOU SPOKE OF?

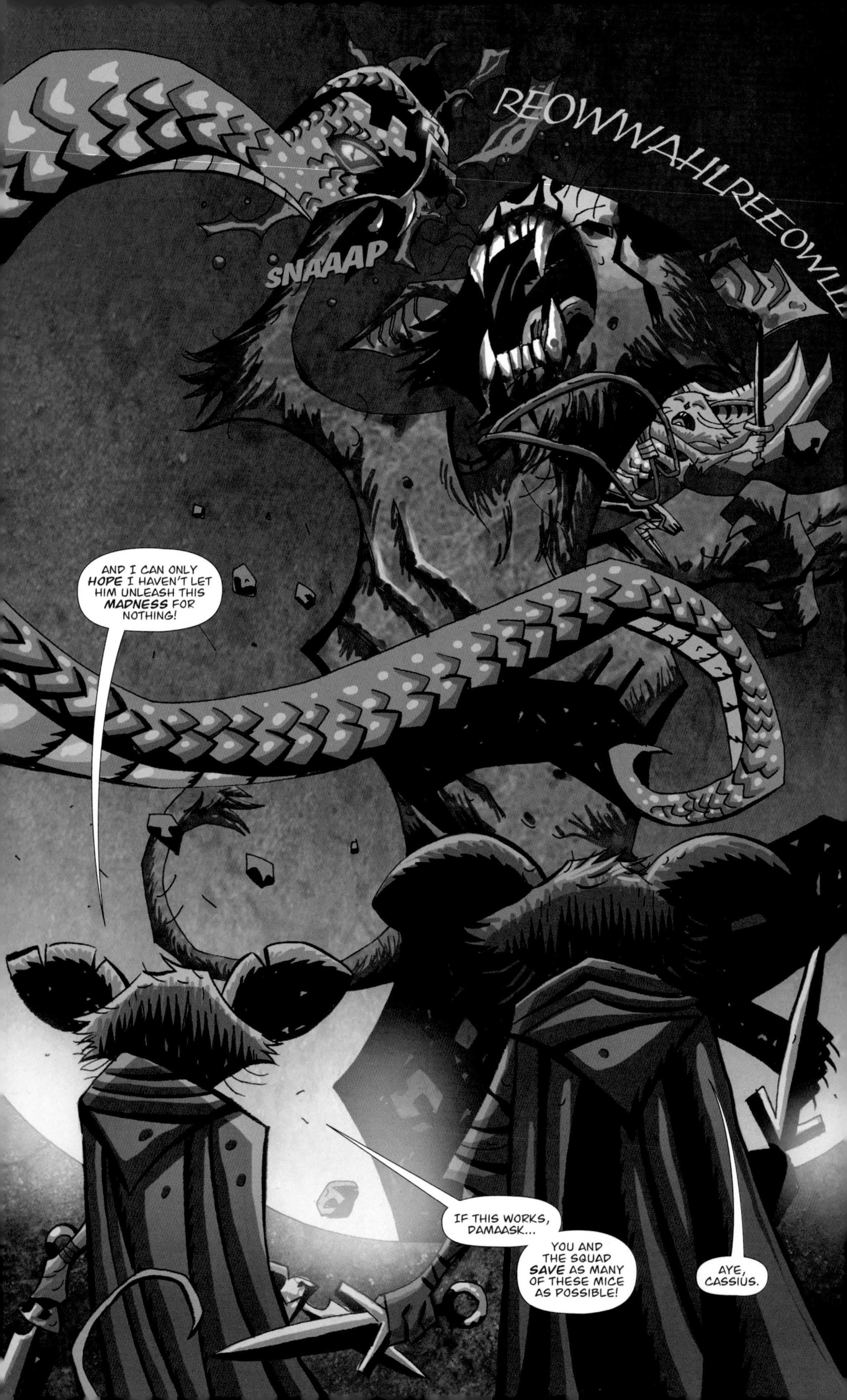

REOWWAHLREEOWLL
SNAAAP
AND I CAN ONLY HOPE I HAVEN'T LET HIM UNLEASH THIS MADNESS FOR NOTHING!
IF THIS WORKS, DAMAASK...
YOU AND THE SQUAD SAVE AS MANY OF THESE MICE AS POSSIBLE!
AYE, CASSIUS.

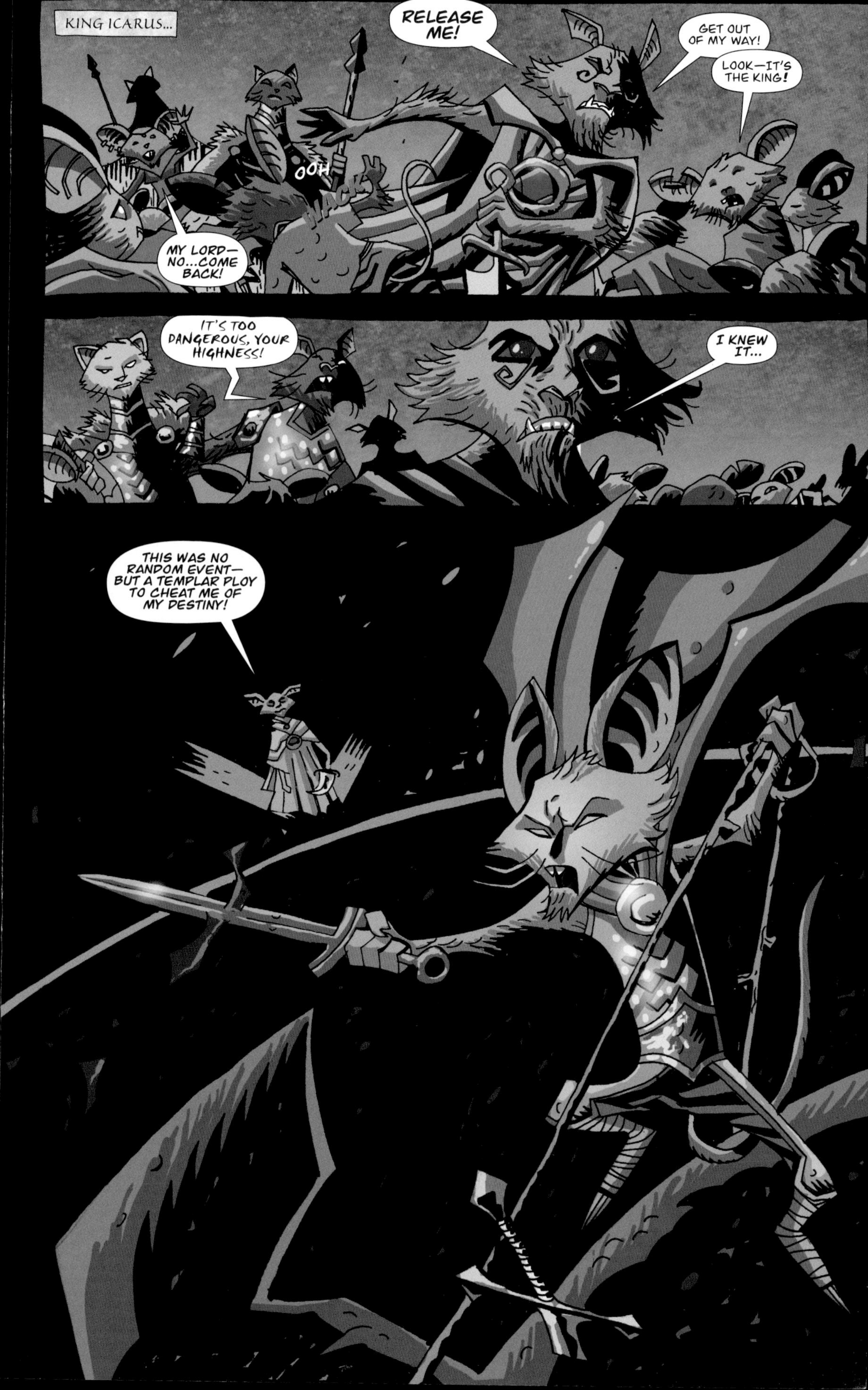

KING ICARUS...
RELEASE ME!
GET OUT OF MY WAY!
LOOK—IT'S THE KING!
OOH
MY LORD—NO...COME BACK!
IT'S TOO DANGEROUS, YOUR HIGHNESS!
I KNEW IT...
THIS WAS NO RANDOM EVENT—BUT A TEMPLAR PLOY TO CHEAT ME OF MY DESTINY!

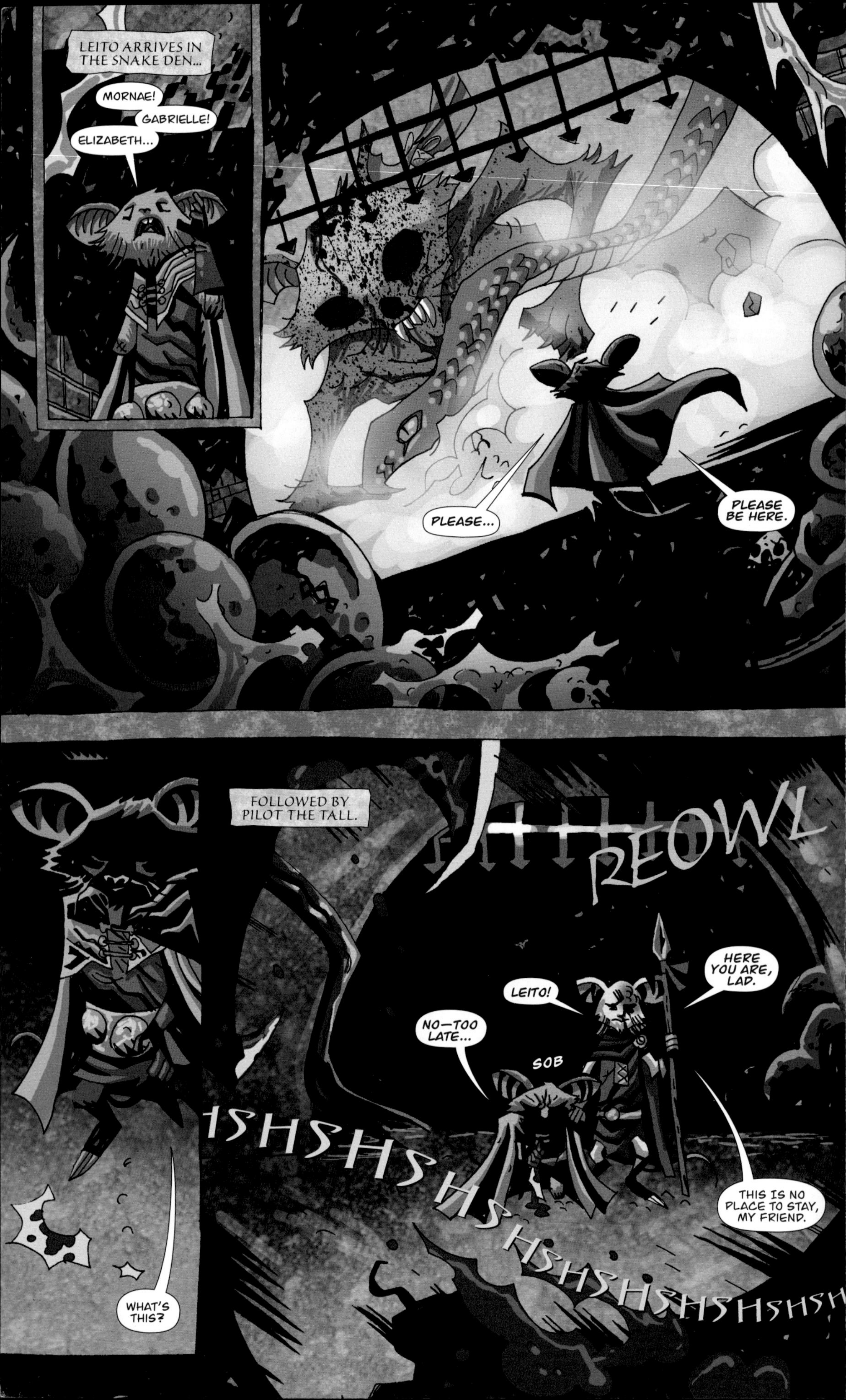
LEITO ARRIVES IN THE SNAKE DEN...
MORNAE!
GABRIELLE!
ELIZABETH...
PLEASE...
PLEASE BE HERE.
FOLLOWED BY PILOT THE TALL.
REOWL
WHAT'S THIS?
LEITO!
HERE YOU ARE, LAD.
NO—TOO LATE...
SOB
THIS IS NO PLACE TO STAY, MY FRIEND.
HSHSHSHSHSHSHSHSHSHSH

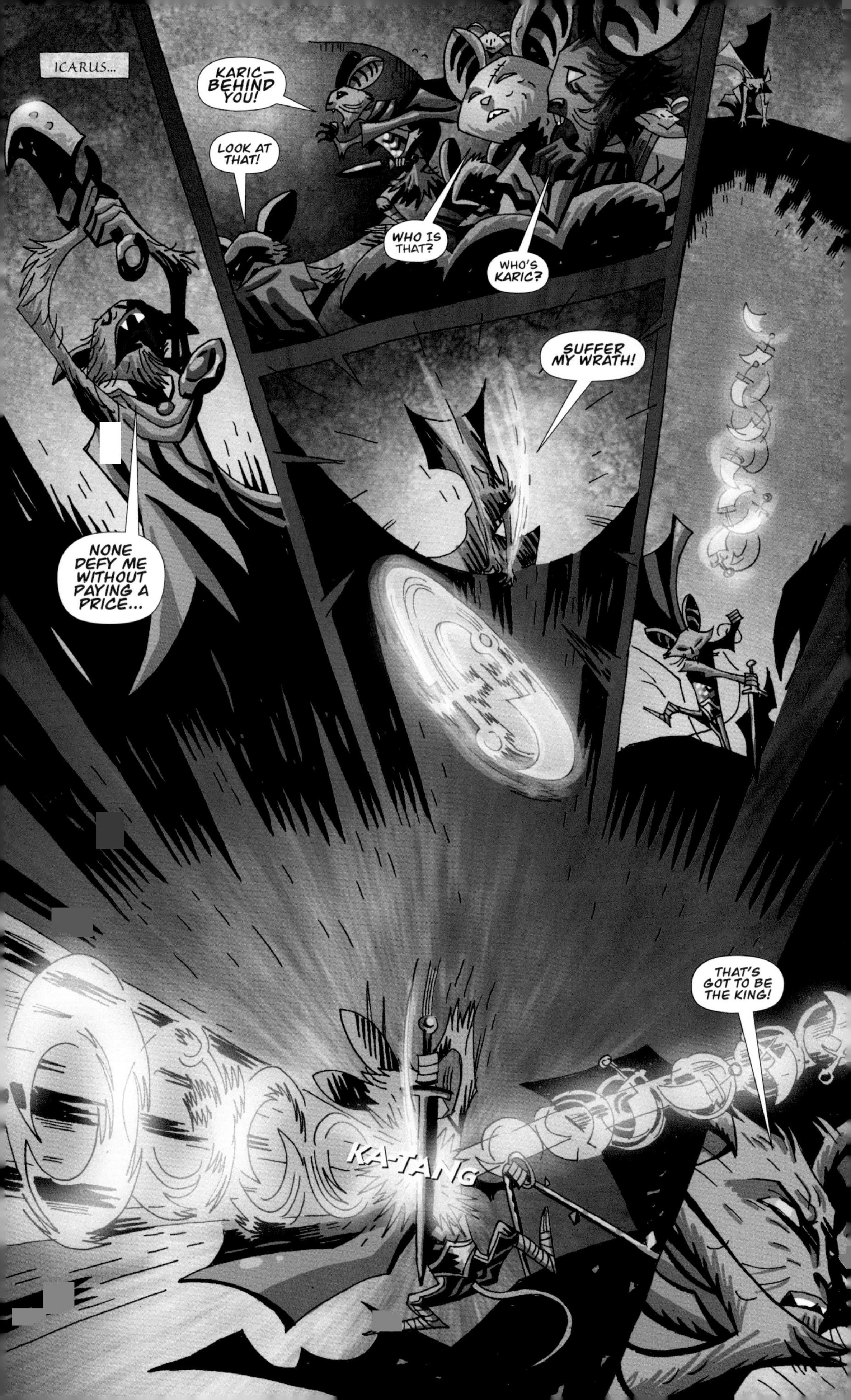
ICARUS...
KARIC—BEHIND YOU!
LOOK AT THAT!
WHO IS THAT?
WHO'S KARIC?
NONE DEFY ME WITHOUT PAYING A PRICE...
SUFFER MY WRATH!
THAT'S GOT TO BE THE KING!
KA-TANG

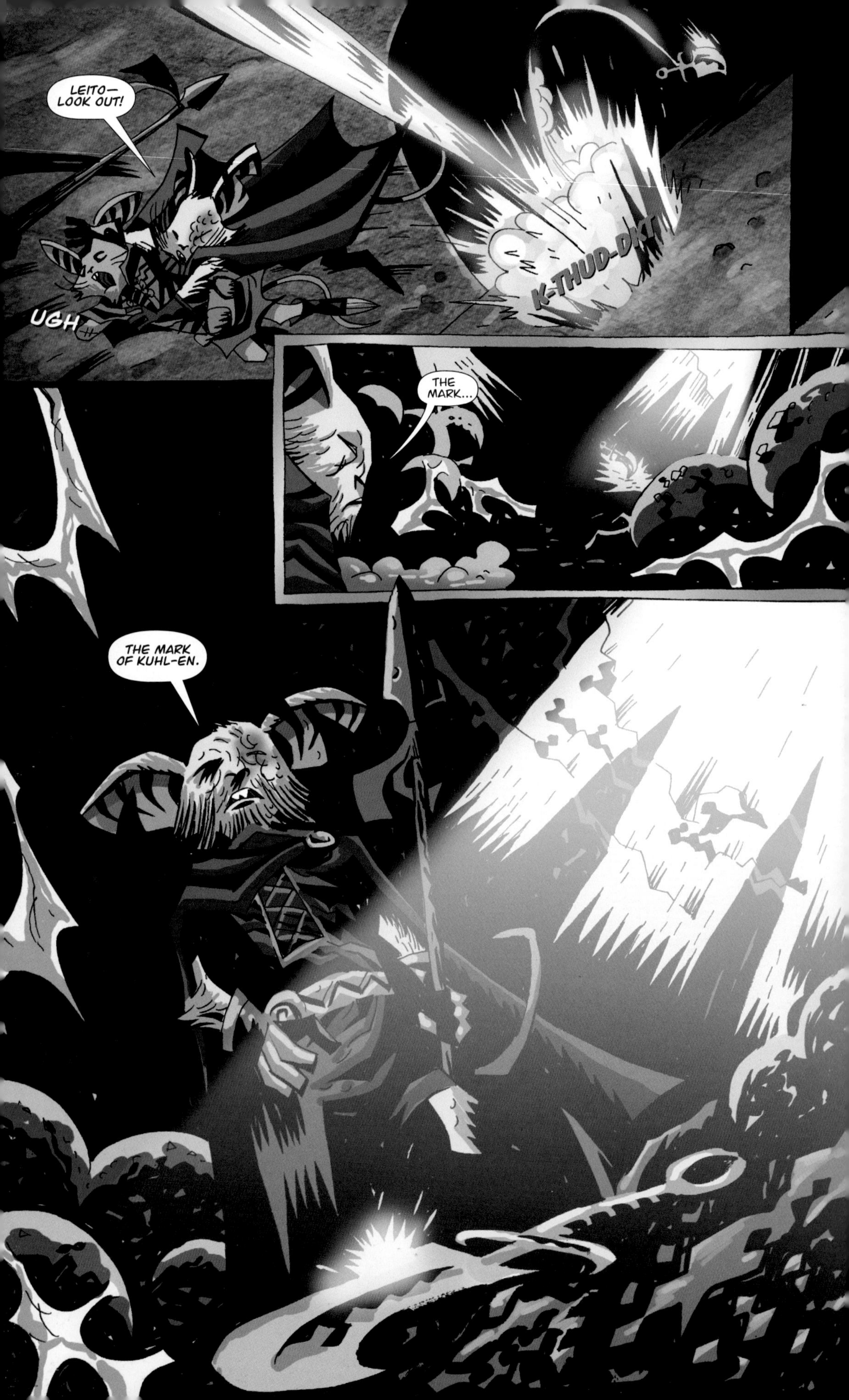
LEITO—
LOOK OUT!
UGH
K-THUD-DKT
THE MARK...
THE MARK
OF KUHL-EN.

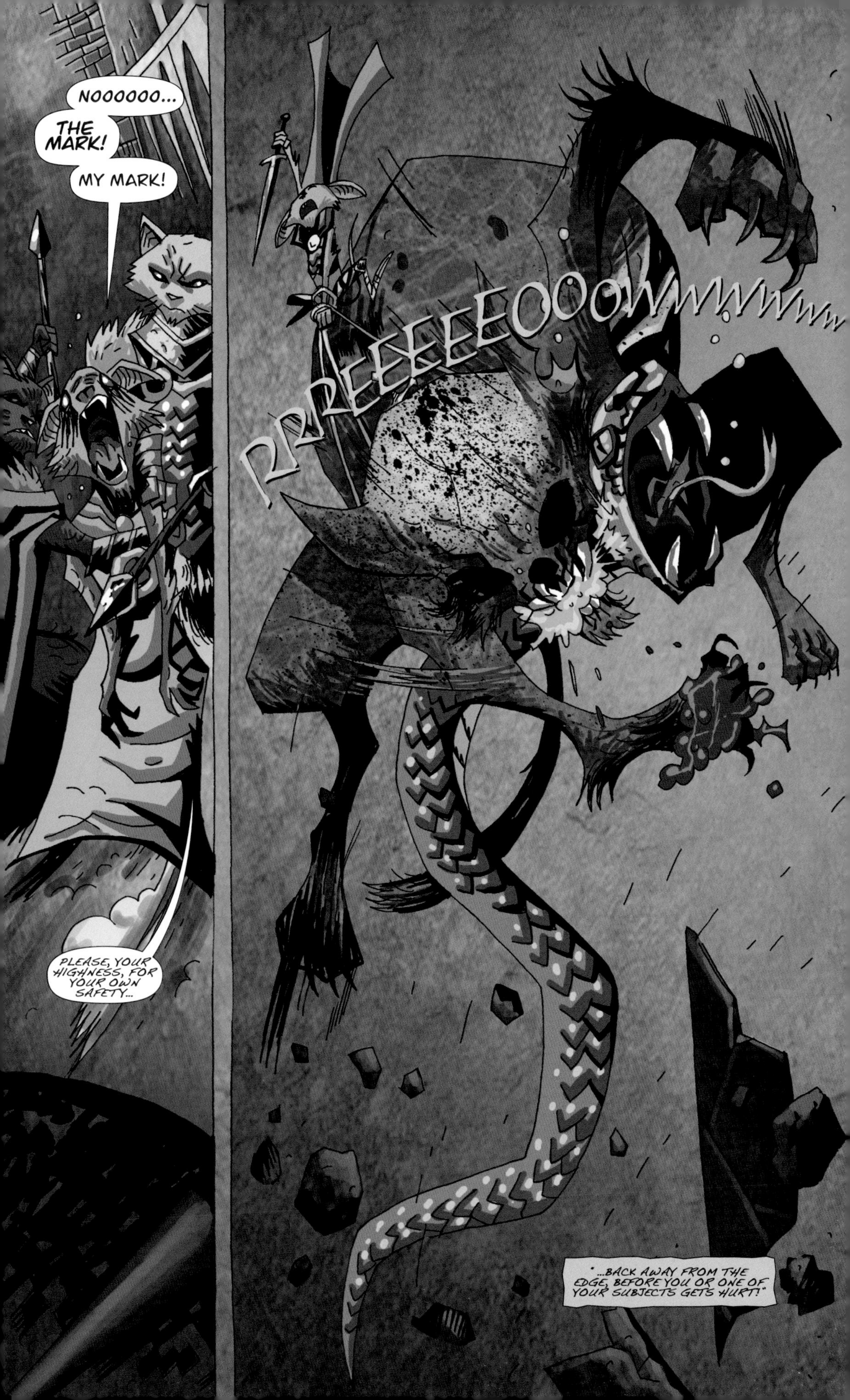
NOOOOOO...
THE MARK!
MY MARK!
PLEASE, YOUR HIGHNESS, FOR YOUR OWN SAFETY...
RRREEEEEEOOOOWWWWWW
"...BACK AWAY FROM THE EDGE, BEFORE YOU OR ONE OF YOUR SUBJECTS GETS HURT!"

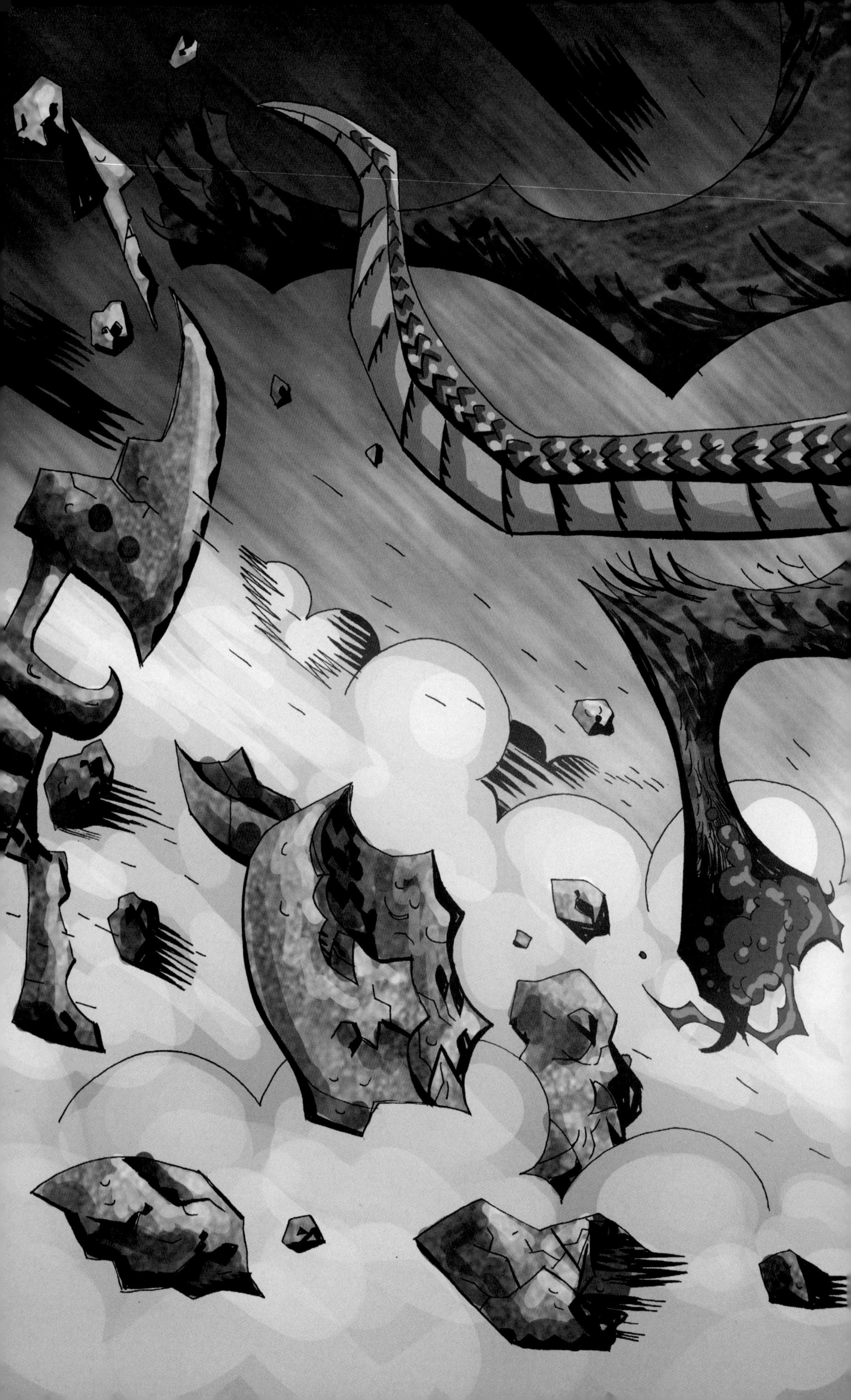

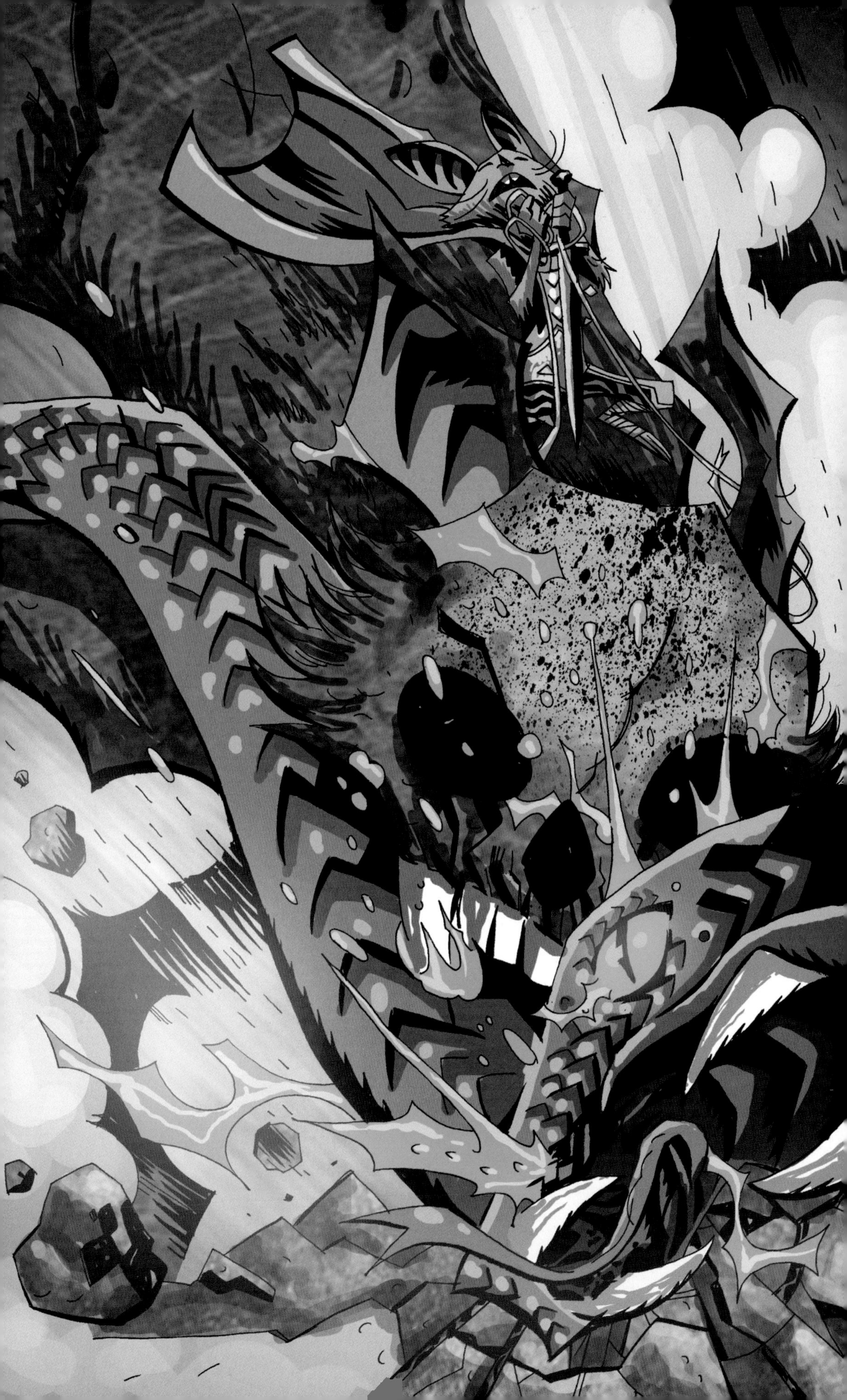

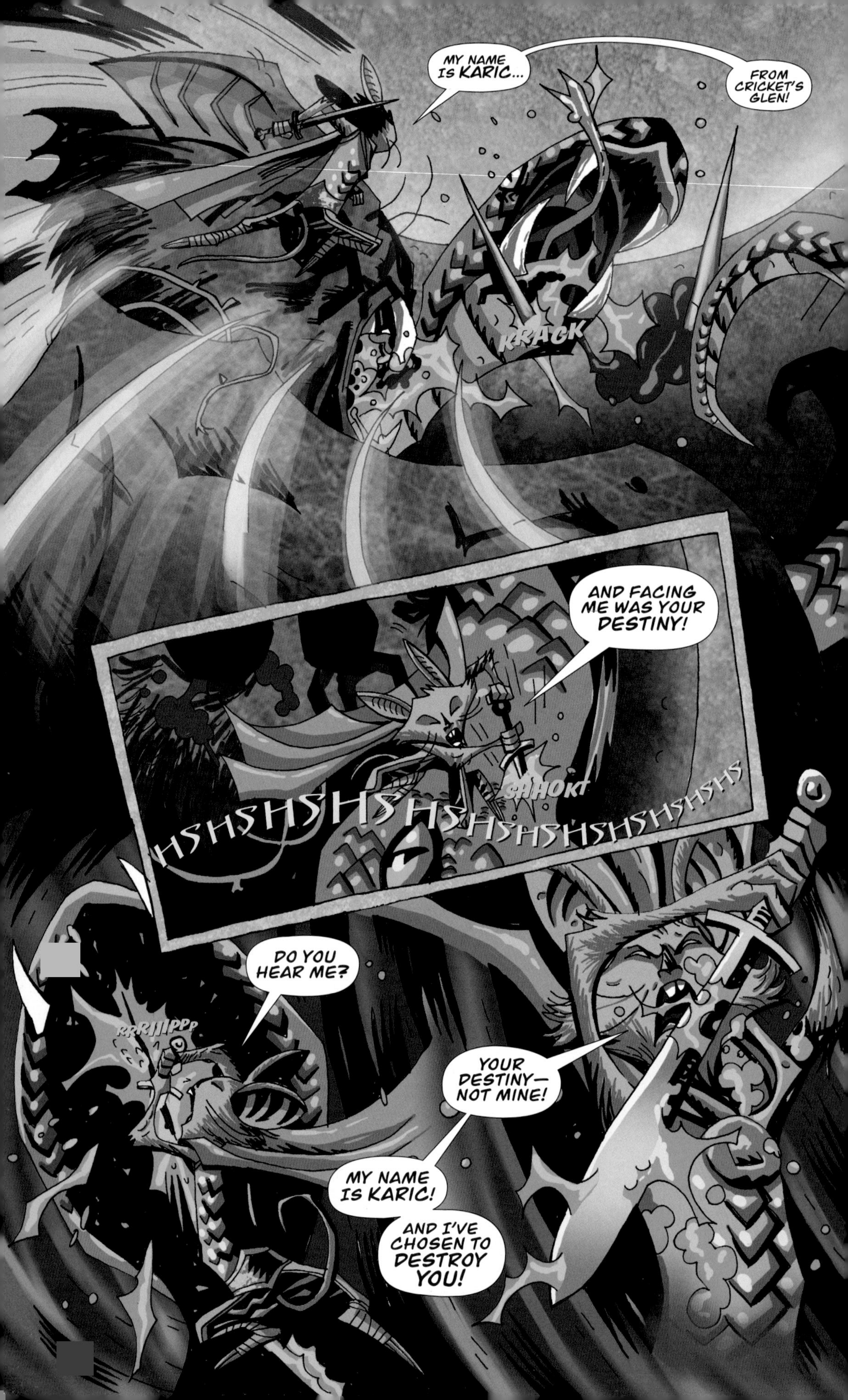

MY NAME IS KARIC...
FROM CRICKET'S GLEN!
KRACK
AND FACING ME WAS YOUR DESTINY!
SHHOK!
HSHSHSHSHSHSHSHSHSHSHSHSHS
DO YOU HEAR ME?
RRRIIIPPP
YOUR DESTINY— NOT MINE!
MY NAME IS KARIC!
AND I'VE CHOSEN TO DESTROY YOU!

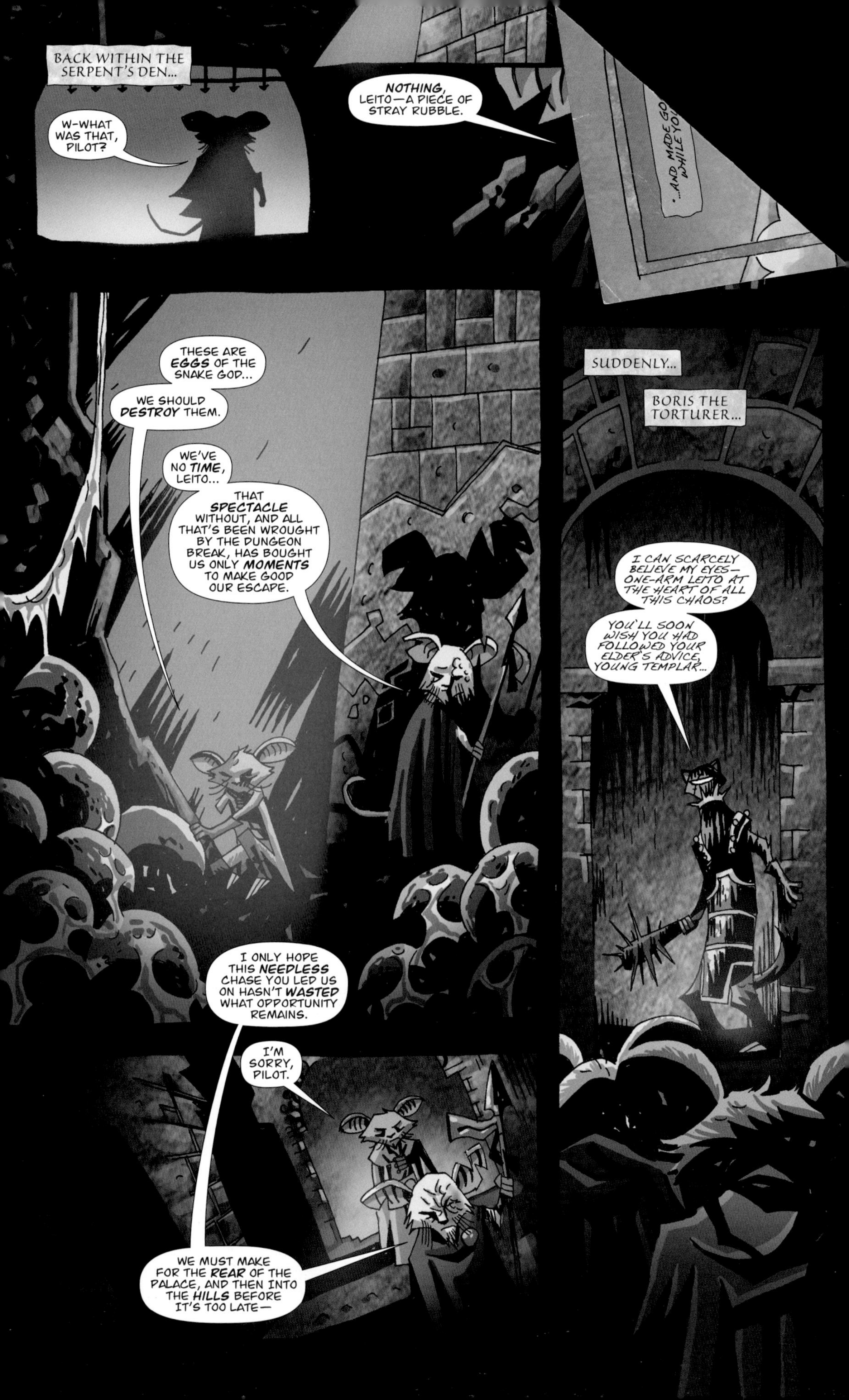
BACK WITHIN THE SERPENT'S DEN...
W-WHAT WAS THAT, PILOT?
NOTHING, LEITO—A PIECE OF STRAY RUBBLE.
THESE ARE EGGS OF THE SNAKE GOD...
WE SHOULD DESTROY THEM.
WE'VE NO TIME, LEITO...
THAT SPECTACLE WITHOUT, AND ALL THAT'S BEEN WROUGHT BY THE DUNGEON BREAK, HAS BOUGHT US ONLY MOMENTS TO MAKE GOOD OUR ESCAPE.
I ONLY HOPE THIS NEEDLESS CHASE YOU LED US ON HASN'T WASTED WHAT OPPORTUNITY REMAINS.
I'M SORRY, PILOT.
WE MUST MAKE FOR THE REAR OF THE PALACE, AND THEN INTO THE HILLS BEFORE IT'S TOO LATE—
SUDDENLY...
BORIS THE TORTURER...
I CAN SCARCELY BELIEVE MY EYES—ONE-ARM LEITO AT THE HEART OF ALL THIS CHAOS?
YOU'LL SOON WISH YOU HAD FOLLOWED YOUR ELDER'S ADVICE, YOUNG TEMPLAR...

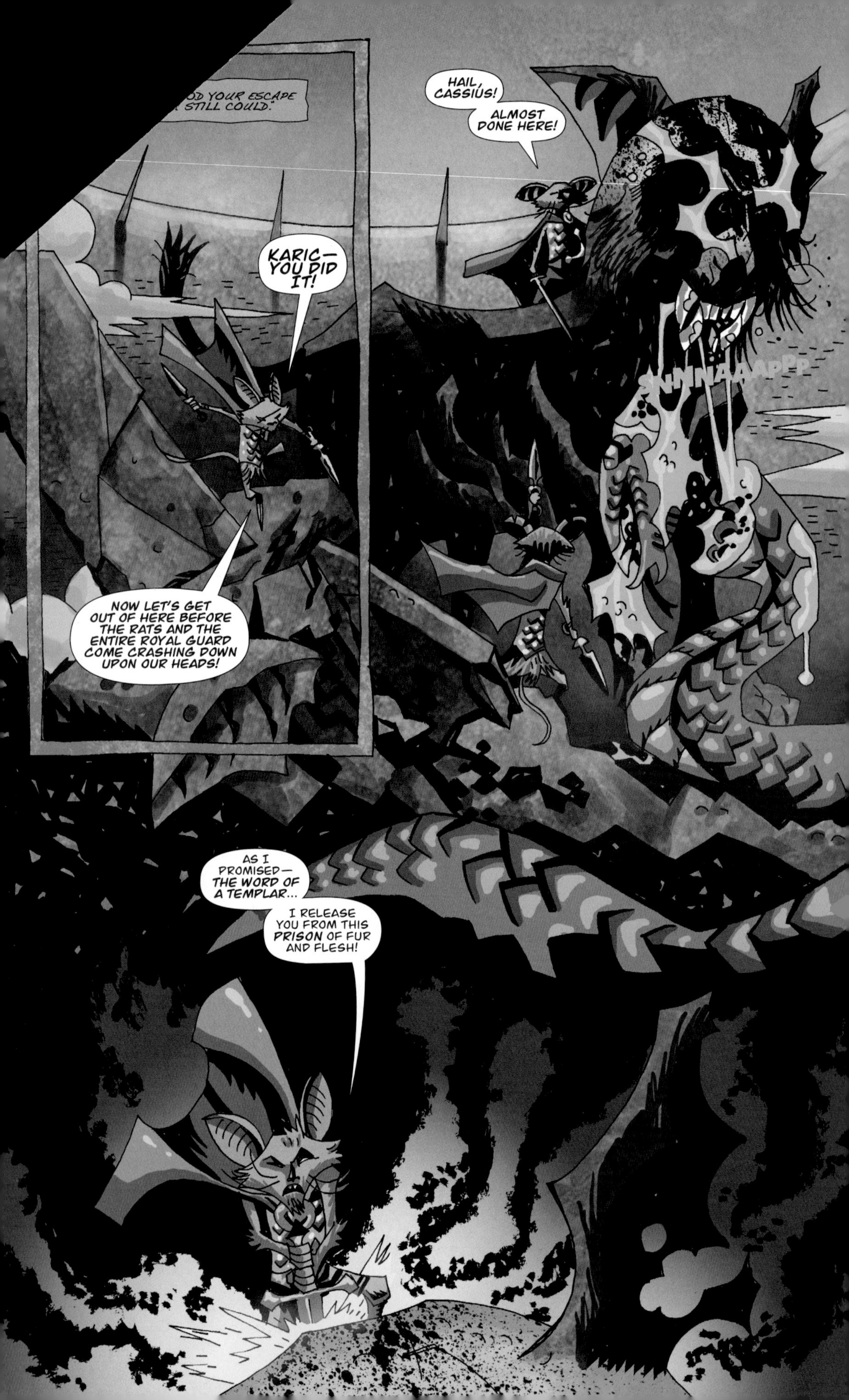
YOUR ESCAPE
STILL COULD."
HAIL, CASSIUS!
ALMOST DONE HERE!
KARIC— YOU DID IT!
NOW LET'S GET OUT OF HERE BEFORE THE RATS AND THE ENTIRE ROYAL GUARD COME CRASHING DOWN UPON OUR HEADS!
SNNNAAAPPP
AS I PROMISED— THE WORD OF A TEMPLAR...
I RELEASE YOU FROM THIS PRISON OF FUR AND FLESH!

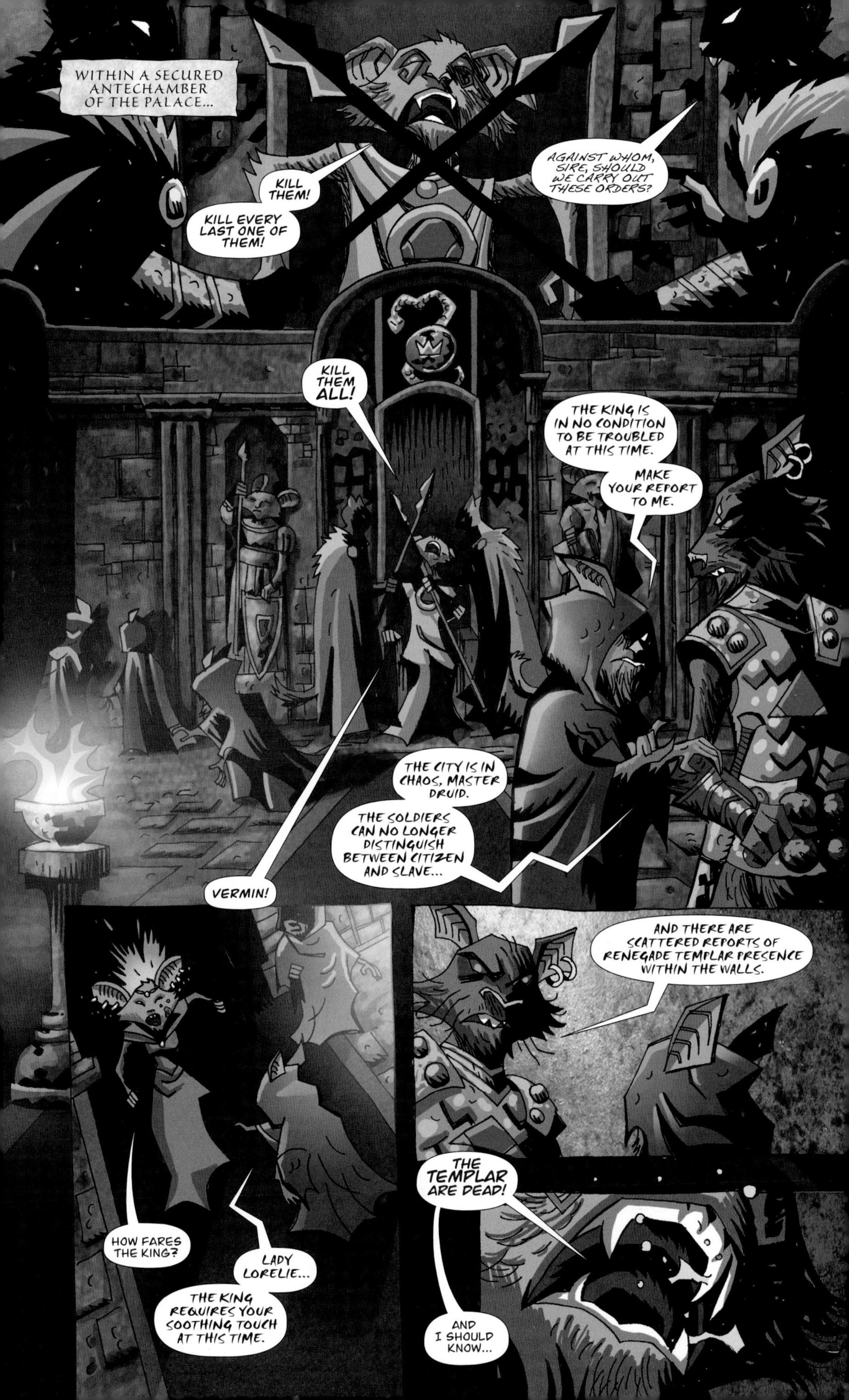
WITHIN A SECURED ANTECHAMBER OF THE PALACE...
KILL THEM!
KILL EVERY LAST ONE OF THEM!
AGAINST WHOM, SIRE, SHOULD WE CARRY OUT THESE ORDERS?
KILL THEM ALL!
THE KING IS IN NO CONDITION TO BE TROUBLED AT THIS TIME.
MAKE YOUR REPORT TO ME.
THE CITY IS IN CHAOS, MASTER DRUID.
THE SOLDIERS CAN NO LONGER DISTINGUISH BETWEEN CITIZEN AND SLAVE...
VERMIN!
AND THERE ARE SCATTERED REPORTS OF RENEGADE TEMPLAR PRESENCE WITHIN THE WALLS.
THE TEMPLAR ARE DEAD!
AND I SHOULD KNOW...
HOW FARES THE KING?
LADY LORELIE...
THE KING REQUIRES YOUR SOOTHING TOUCH AT THIS TIME.

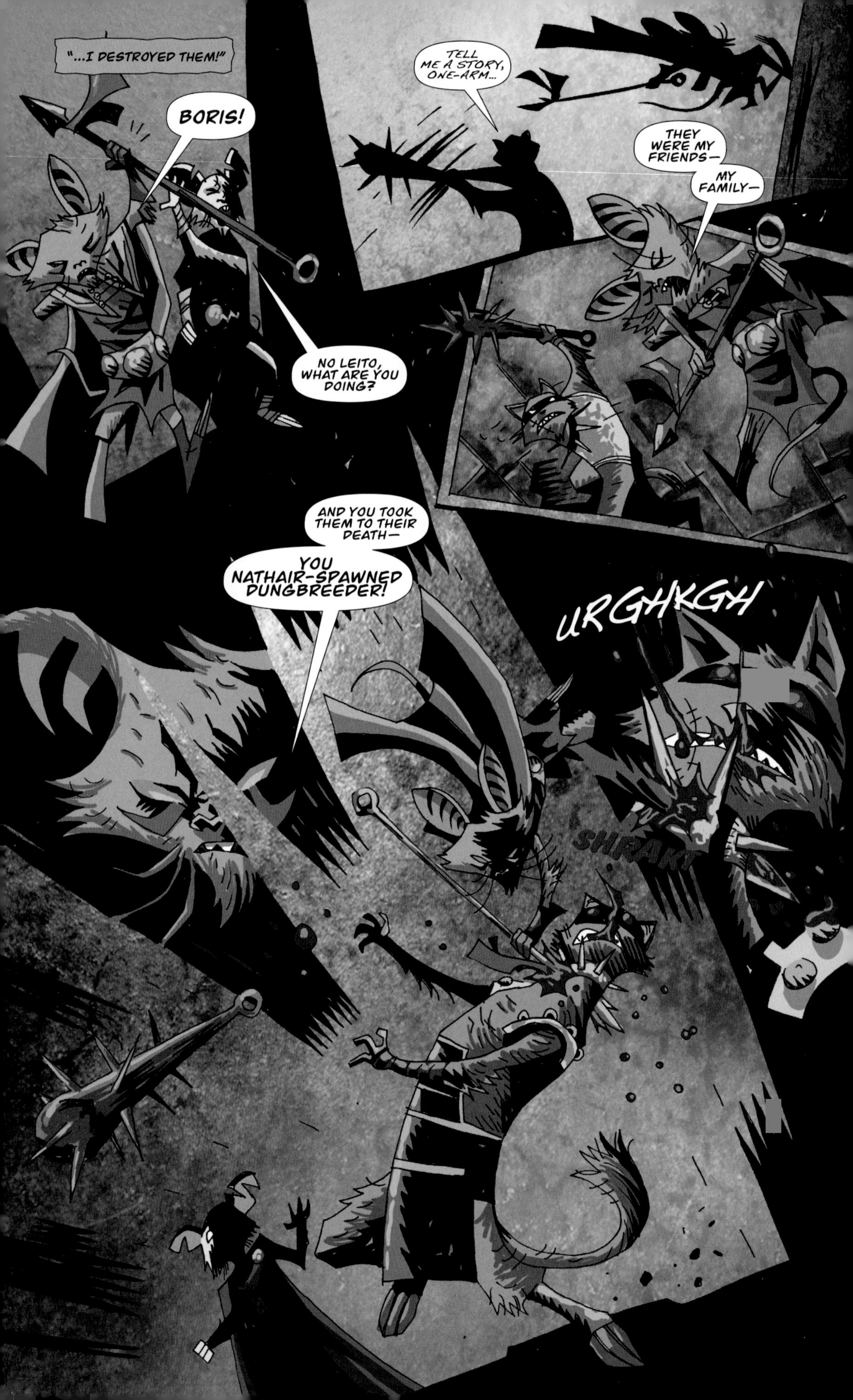
"...I DESTROYED THEM!"
BORIS!
NO LEITO, WHAT ARE YOU DOING?
TELL ME A STORY, ONE-ARM...
THEY WERE MY FRIENDS—
MY FAMILY—
AND YOU TOOK THEM TO THEIR DEATH—
YOU NATHAIR-SPAWNED DUNGBREEDER!
URGHKGH
SHRAK!

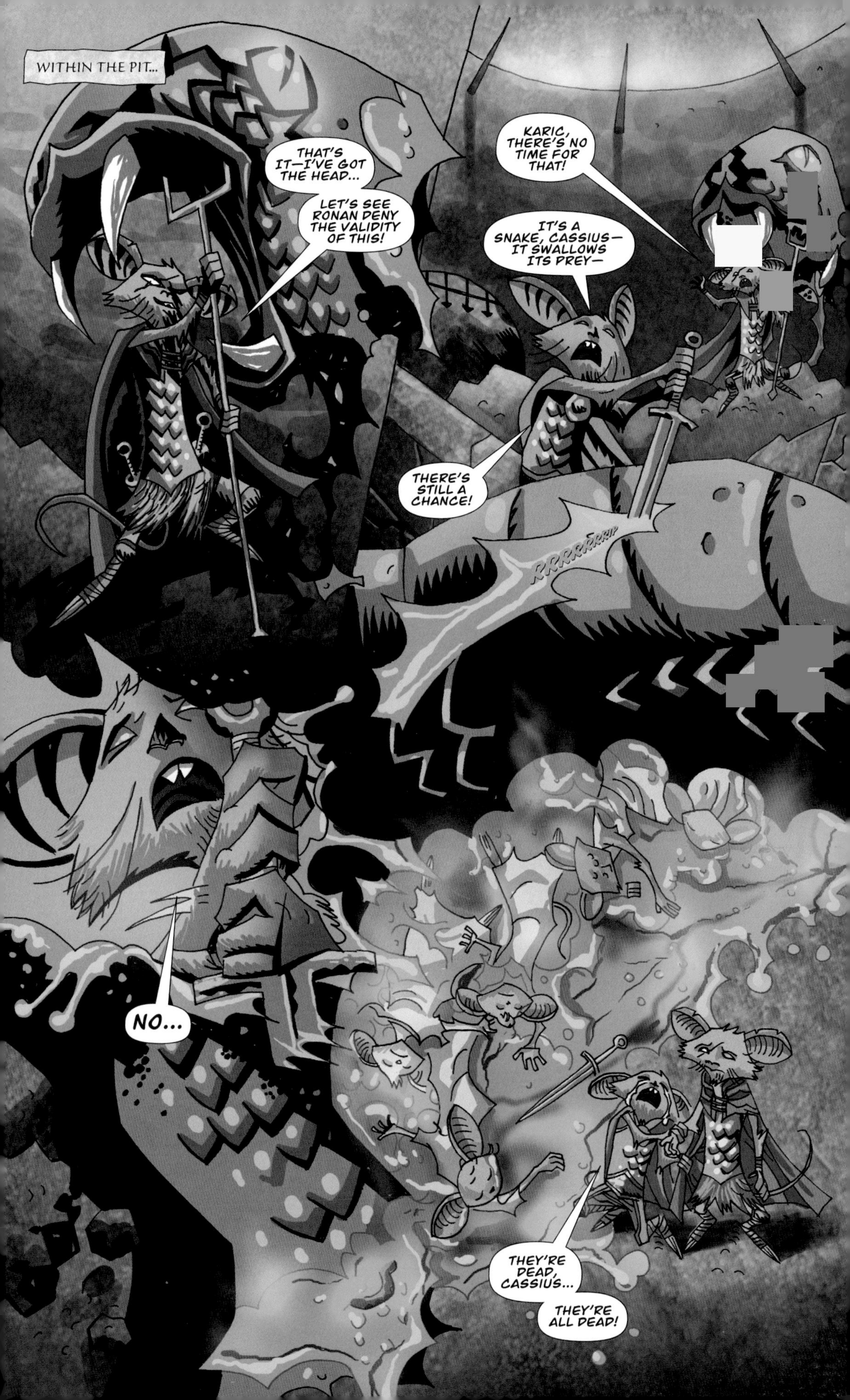
WITHIN THE PIT...
THAT'S IT—I'VE GOT THE HEAD...
LET'S SEE RONAN DENY THE VALIDITY OF THIS!
KARIC, THERE'S NO TIME FOR THAT!
IT'S A SNAKE, CASSIUS—IT SWALLOWS ITS PREY—
THERE'S STILL A CHANCE!
RRRRRRRRIP
NO...
THEY'RE DEAD, CASSIUS...
THEY'RE ALL DEAD!

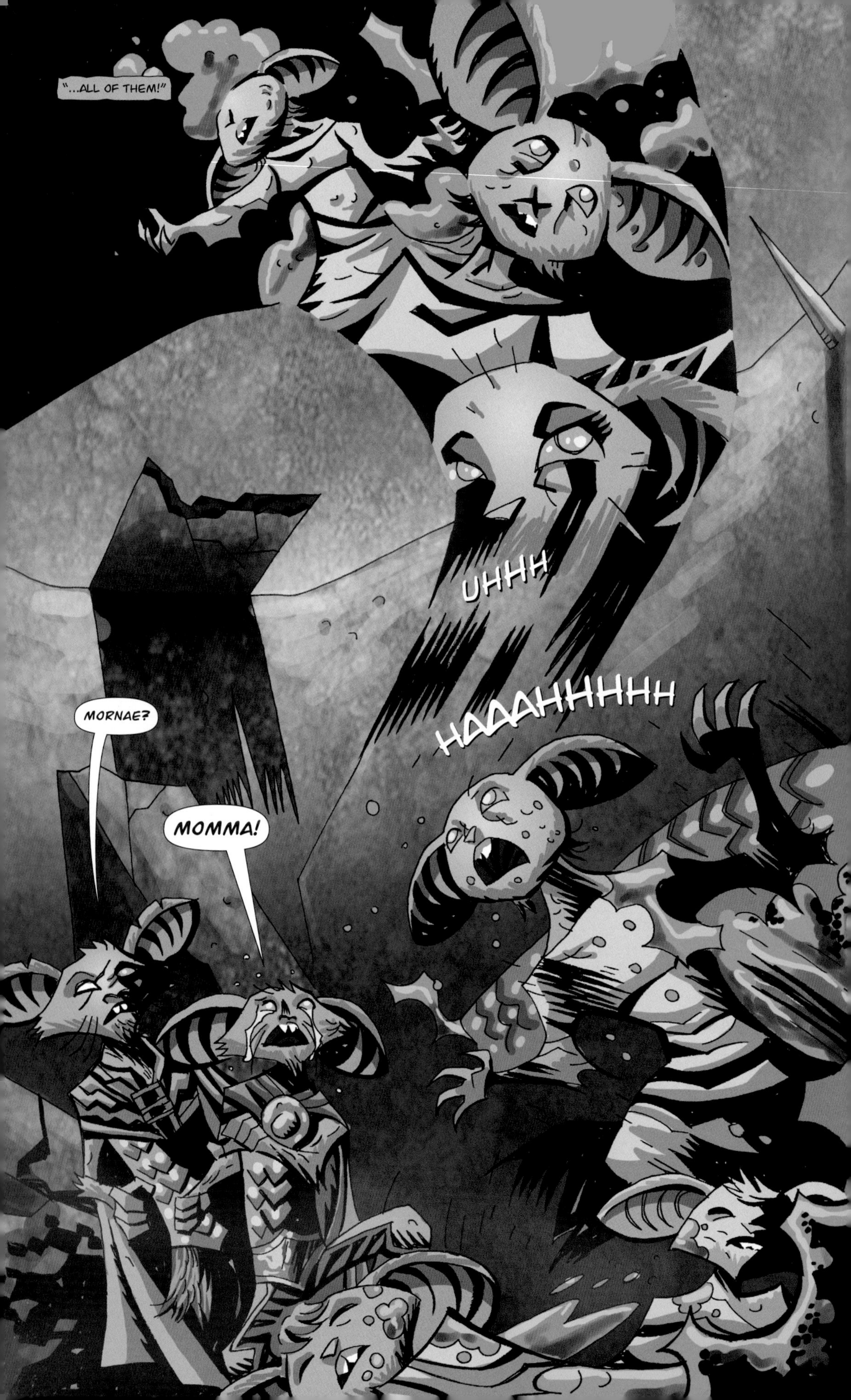
"...ALL OF THEM!"
UHHH
HAAAHHHHH
MORNAE?
MOMMA!

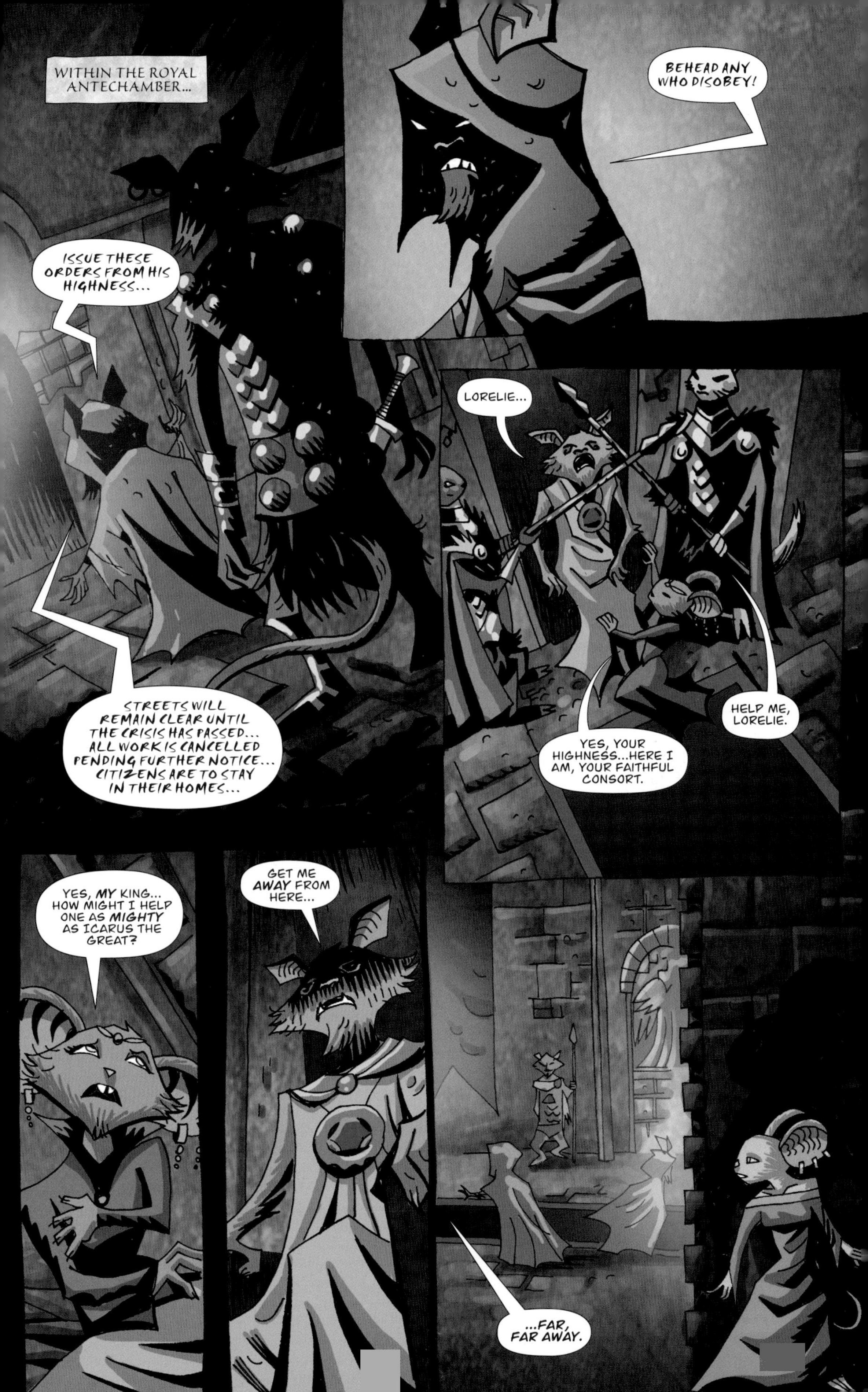
WITHIN THE ROYAL ANTECHAMBER...
ISSUE THESE ORDERS FROM HIS HIGHNESS...
BEHEAD ANY WHO DISOBEY!
STREETS WILL REMAIN CLEAR UNTIL THE CRISIS HAS PASSED... ALL WORK IS CANCELLED PENDING FURTHER NOTICE... CITIZENS ARE TO STAY IN THEIR HOMES...
LORELIE...
HELP ME, LORELIE.
YES, YOUR HIGHNESS...HERE I AM, YOUR FAITHFUL CONSORT.
YES, MY KING... HOW MIGHT I HELP ONE AS MIGHTY AS ICARUS THE GREAT?
GET ME AWAY FROM HERE...
...FAR, FAR AWAY.

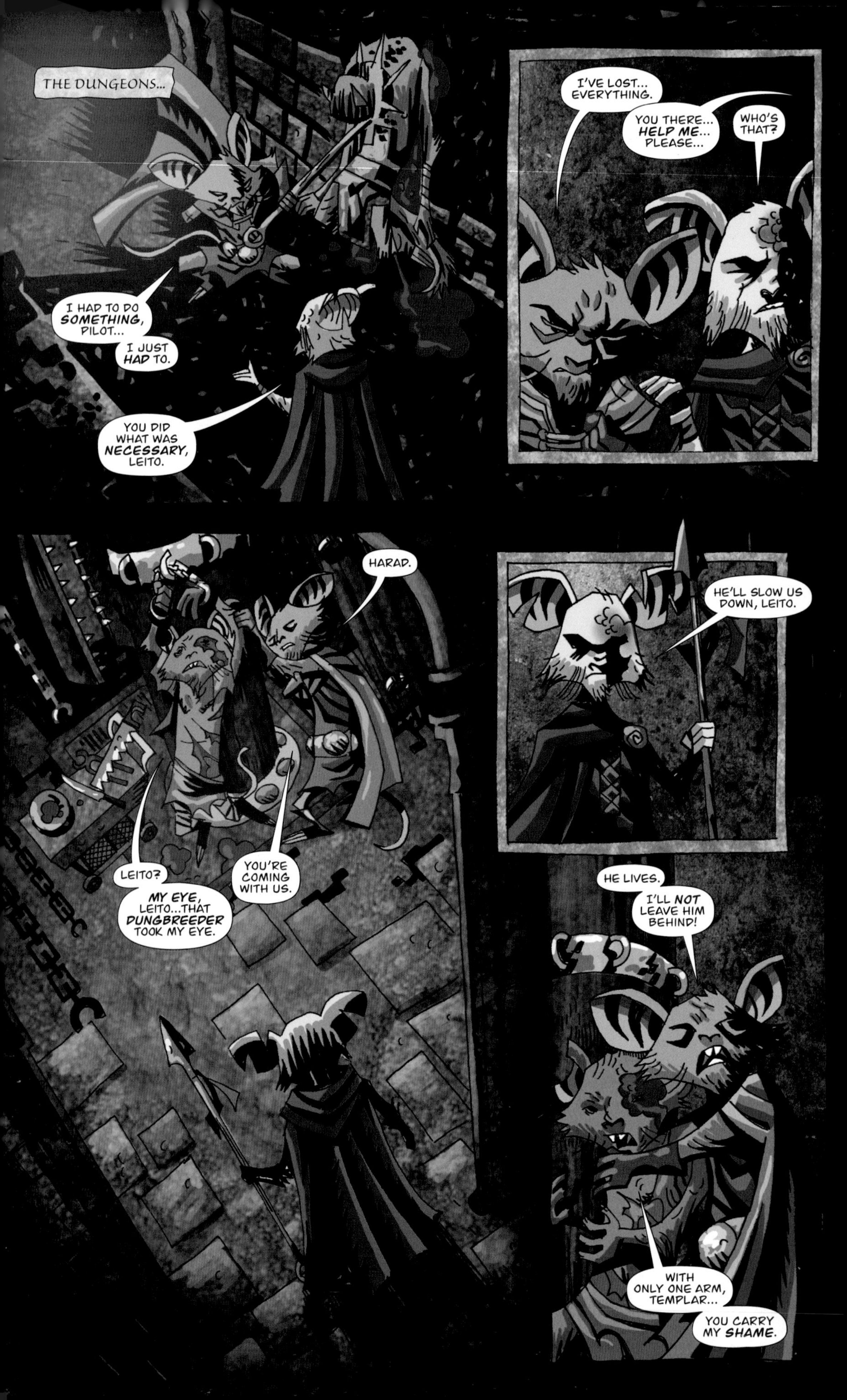
THE DUNGEONS...
I HAD TO DO SOMETHING, PILOT...
I JUST HAD TO.
YOU DID WHAT WAS NECESSARY, LEITO.
I'VE LOST... EVERYTHING.
YOU THERE... HELP ME... PLEASE...
WHO'S THAT?
HARAD.
LEITO?
MY EYE, LEITO...THAT DUNGBREEDER TOOK MY EYE.
YOU'RE COMING WITH US.
HE'LL SLOW US DOWN, LEITO.
HE LIVES.
I'LL NOT LEAVE HIM BEHIND!
WITH ONLY ONE ARM, TEMPLAR...
YOU CARRY MY SHAME.

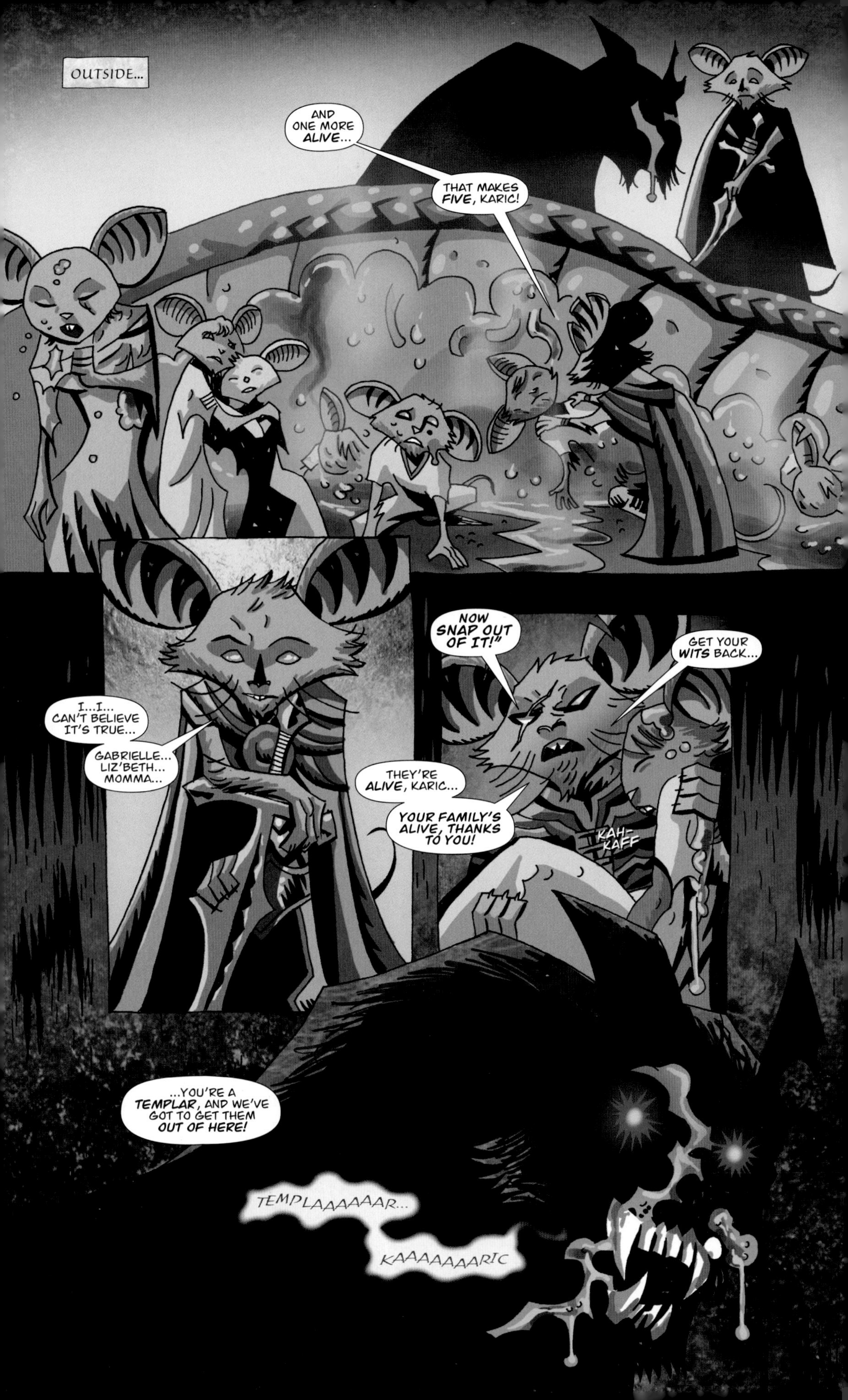
OUTSIDE...
AND ONE MORE ALIVE...
THAT MAKES FIVE, KARIC!
I...I... CAN'T BELIEVE IT'S TRUE...
GABRIELLE... LIZ'BETH... MOMMA...
NOW SNAP OUT OF IT!"
GET YOUR WITS BACK...
THEY'RE ALIVE, KARIC...
YOUR FAMILY'S ALIVE, THANKS TO YOU!
KAH-KAFF
...YOU'RE A TEMPLAR, AND WE'VE GOT TO GET THEM OUT OF HERE!
TEMPLAAAAAAR...
KAAAAAAARIC

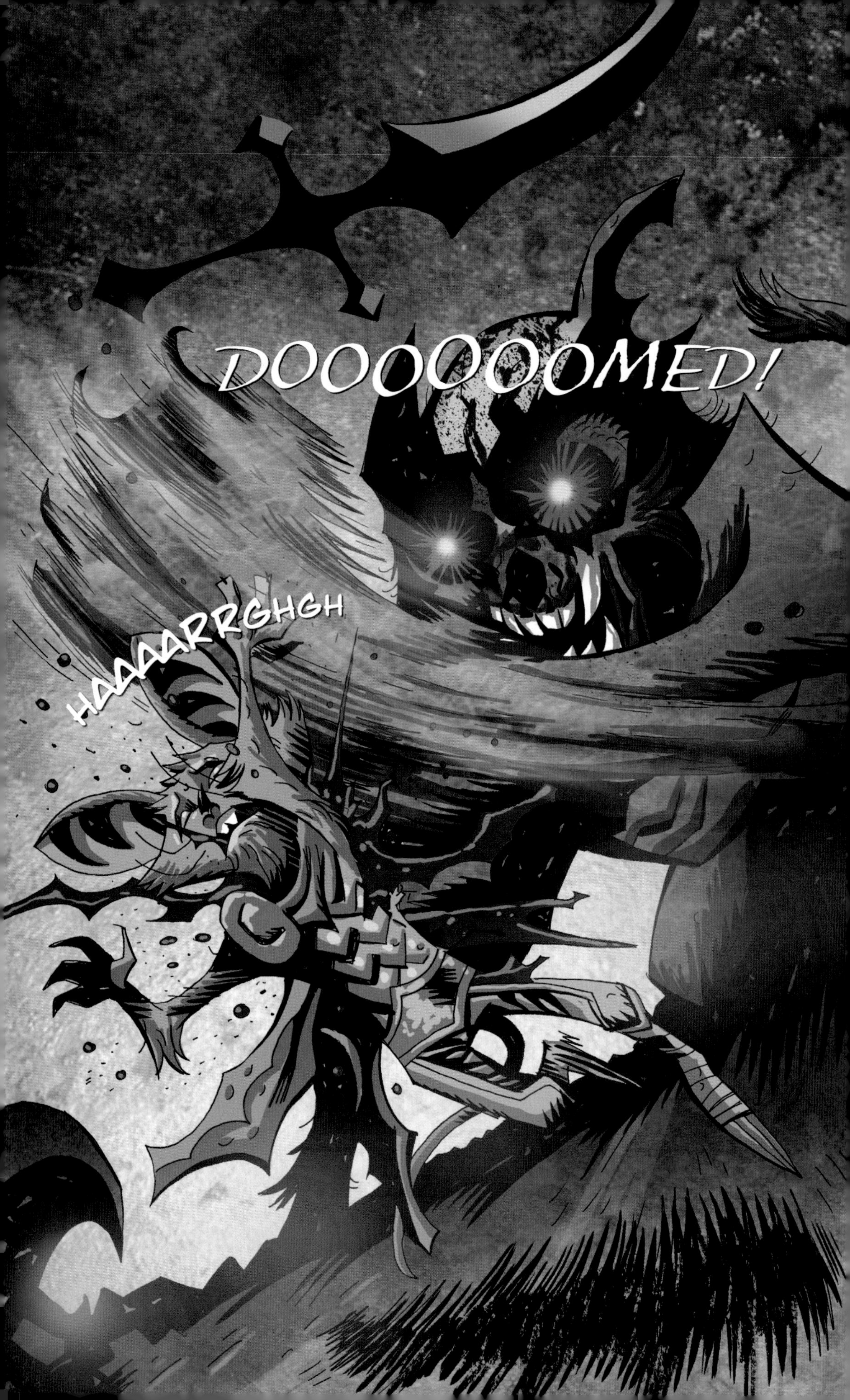
DOOOOOOMED!
HAAAARRGHGH

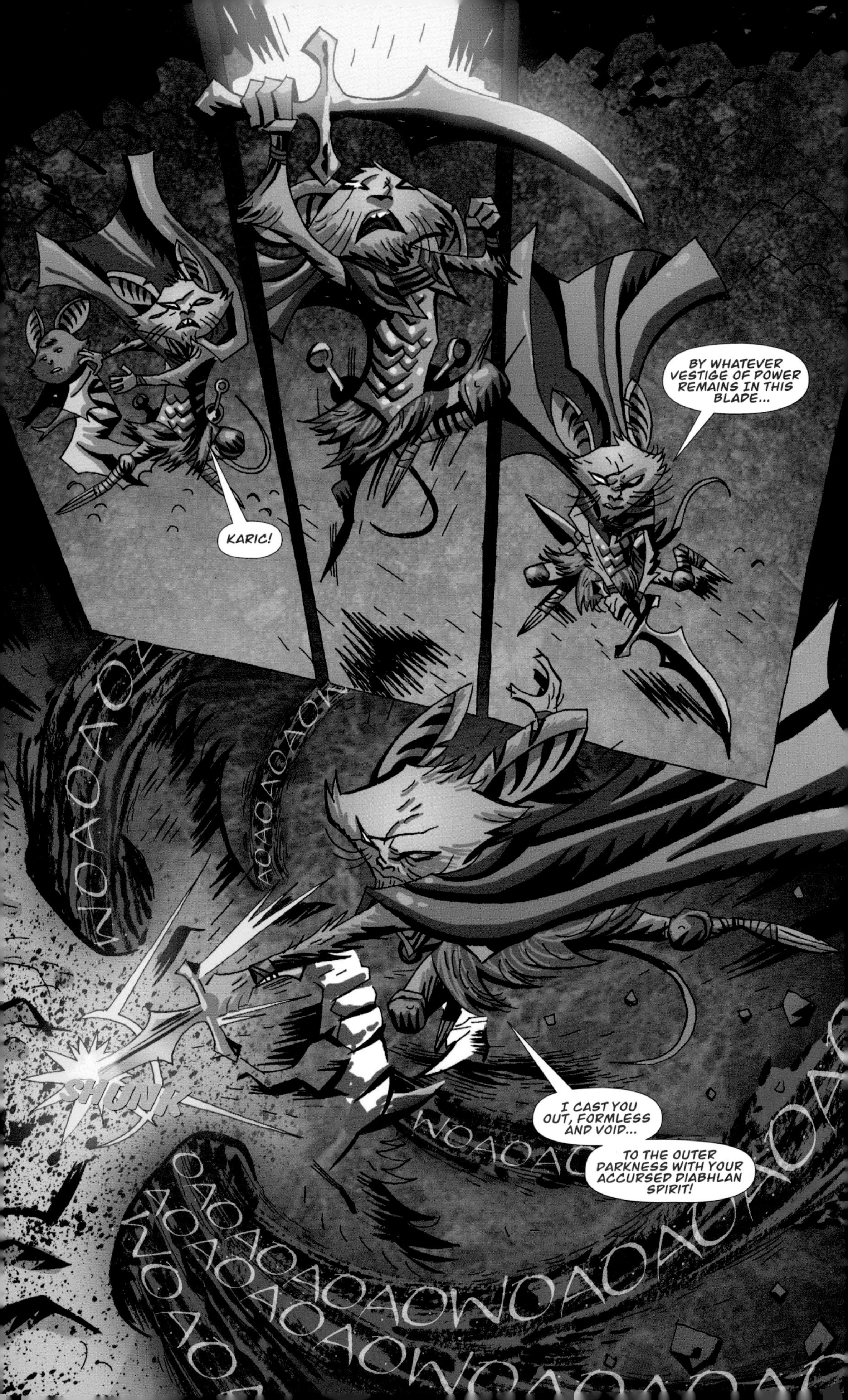
KARIC!
BY WHATEVER VESTIGE OF POWER REMAINS IN THIS BLADE...
SHUNK
I CAST YOU OUT, FORMLESS AND VOID...
TO THE OUTER DARKNESS WITH YOUR ACCURSED DIABHLAN SPIRIT!

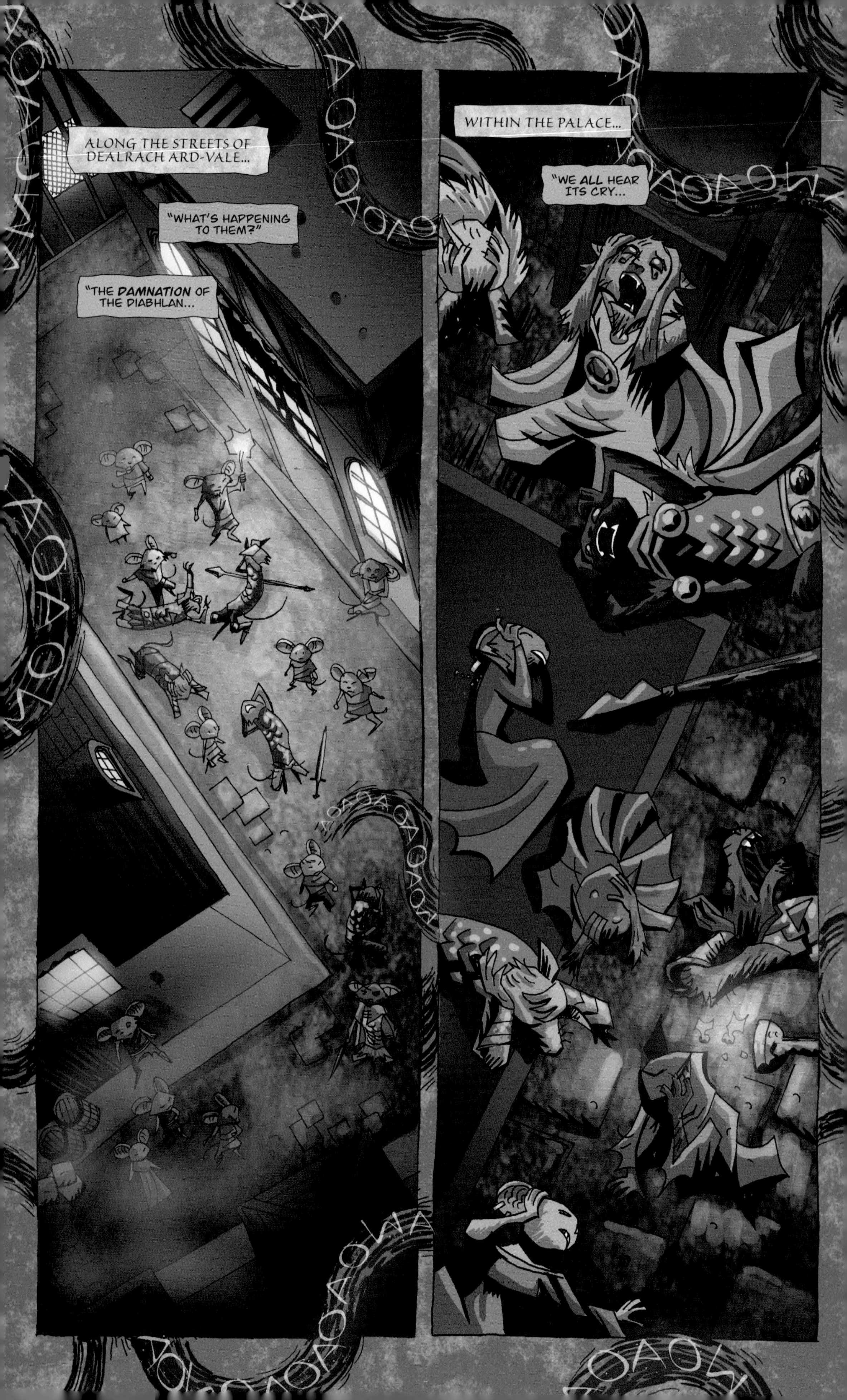
ALONG THE STREETS OF DEALRACH ARD-VALE...
"WHAT'S HAPPENING TO THEM?"
"THE DAMNATION OF THE DIABHLAN...
WITHIN THE PALACE...
"WE ALL HEAR ITS CRY...

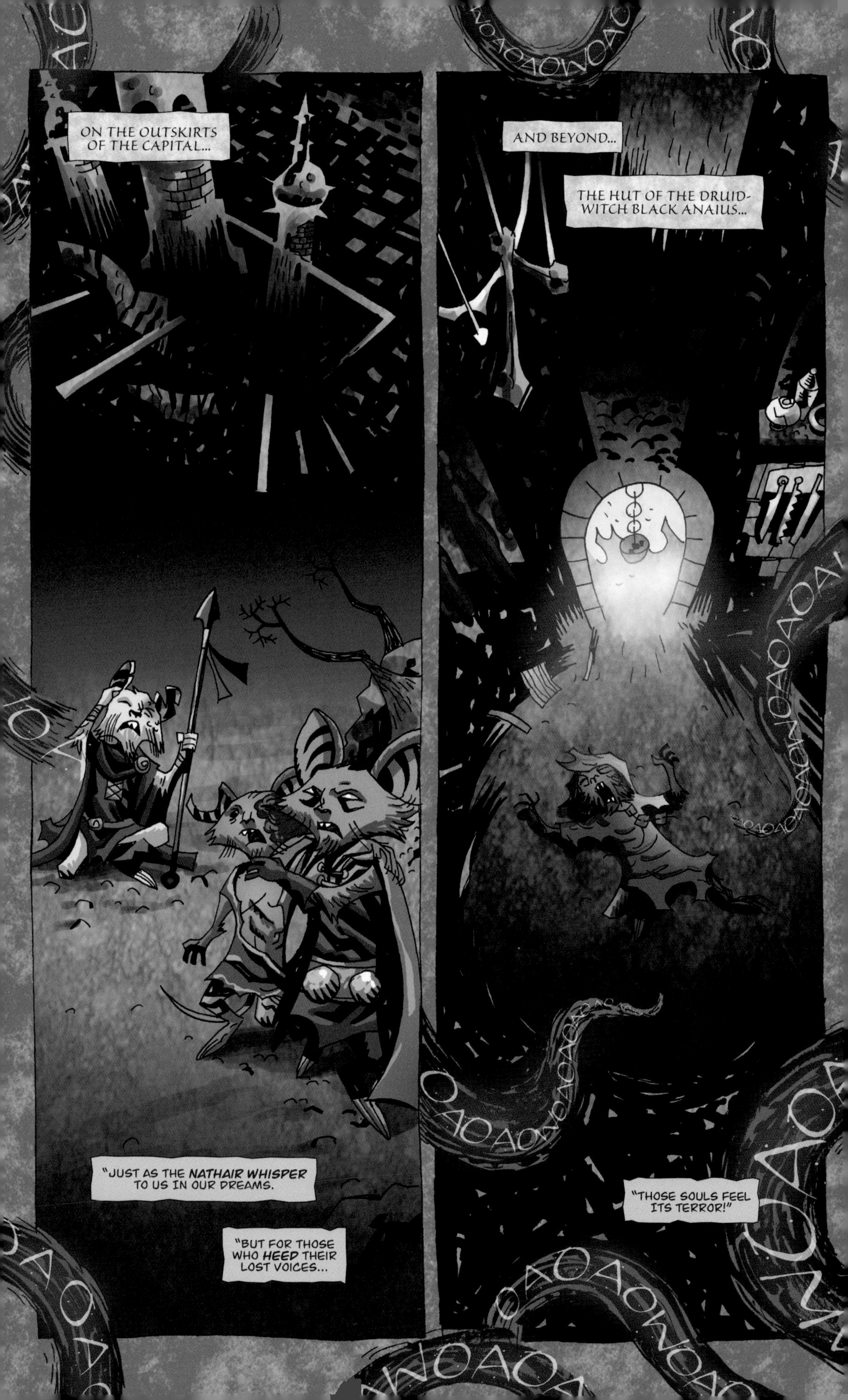
ON THE OUTSKIRTS OF THE CAPITAL...
"JUST AS THE NATHAIR WHISPER TO US IN OUR DREAMS.
"BUT FOR THOSE WHO HEED THEIR LOST VOICES...
AND BEYOND...
THE HUT OF THE DRUID-WITCH BLACK ANAIUS...
"THOSE SOULS FEEL ITS TERROR!"

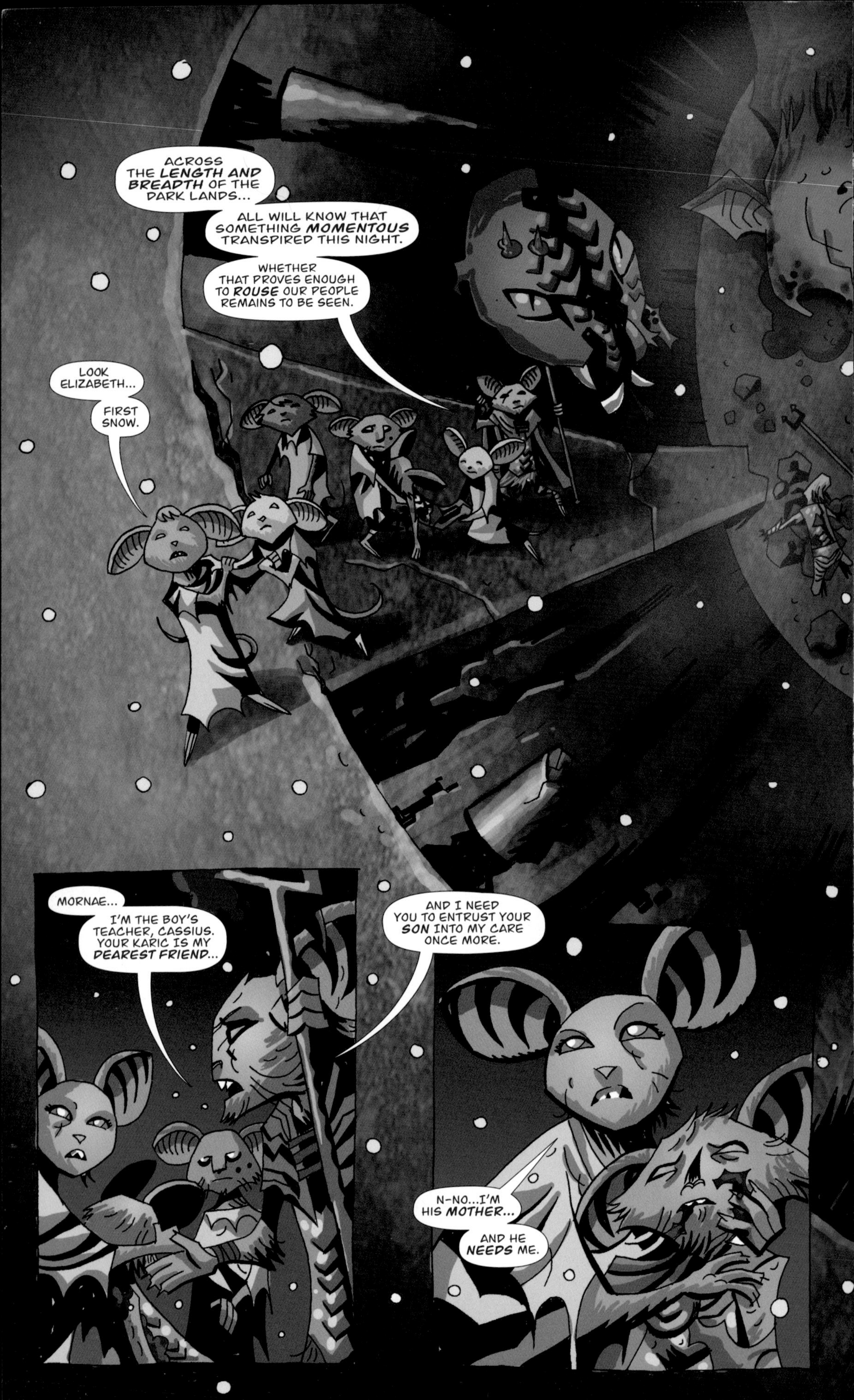
ACROSS THE LENGTH AND BREADTH OF THE DARK LANDS...
ALL WILL KNOW THAT SOMETHING MOMENTOUS TRANSPIRED THIS NIGHT.
WHETHER THAT PROVES ENOUGH TO ROUSE OUR PEOPLE REMAINS TO BE SEEN.
LOOK ELIZABETH...
FIRST SNOW.
MORNAE...
I'M THE BOY'S TEACHER, CASSIUS. YOUR KARIC IS MY DEAREST FRIEND...
AND I NEED YOU TO ENTRUST YOUR SON INTO MY CARE ONCE MORE.
N-NO...I'M HIS MOTHER...
AND HE NEEDS ME.

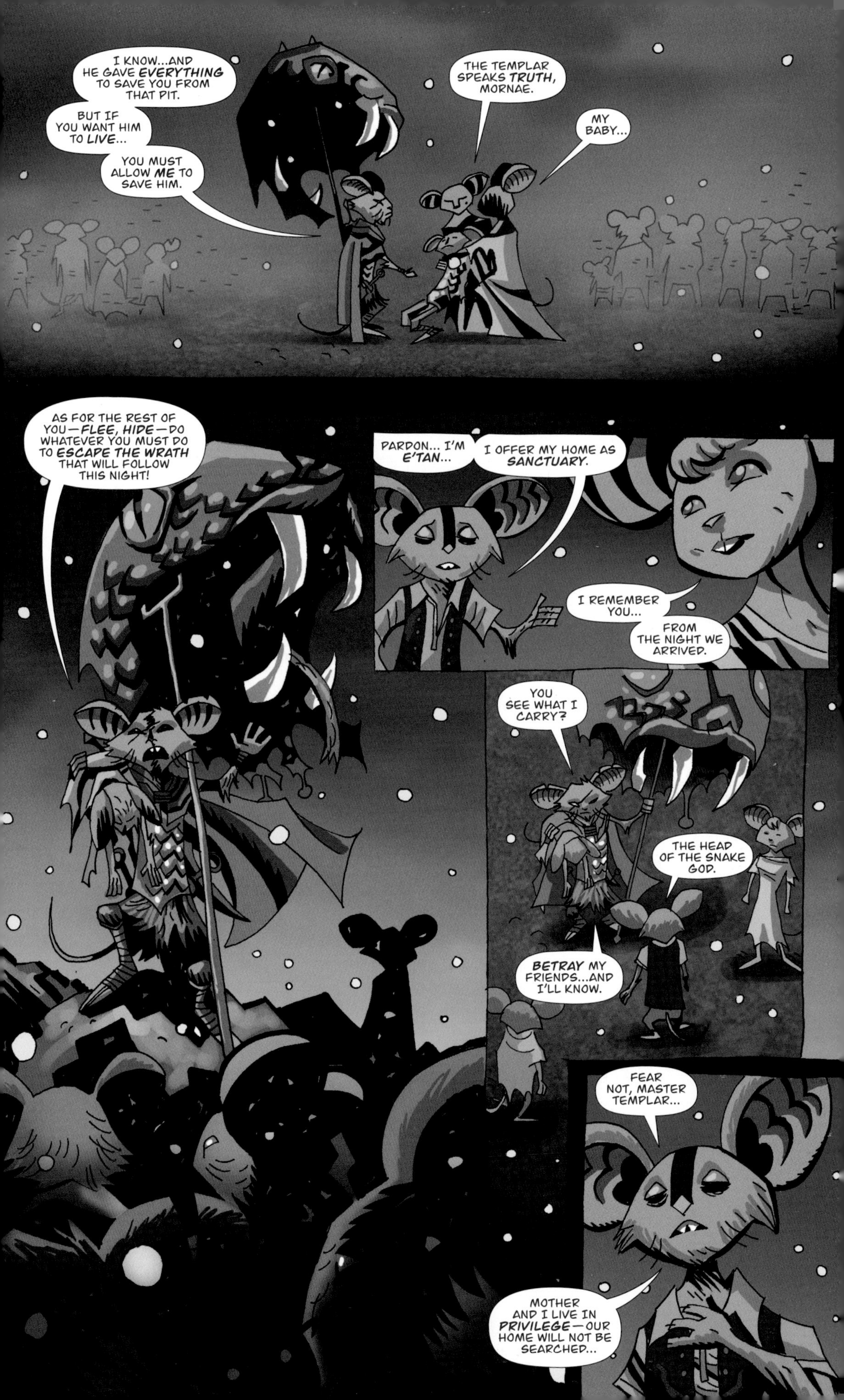

I KNOW...AND HE GAVE EVERYTHING TO SAVE YOU FROM THAT PIT.
BUT IF YOU WANT HIM TO LIVE...
YOU MUST ALLOW ME TO SAVE HIM.
THE TEMPLAR SPEAKS TRUTH, MORNAE.
MY BABY...
AS FOR THE REST OF YOU—FLEE, HIDE—DO WHATEVER YOU MUST DO TO ESCAPE THE WRATH THAT WILL FOLLOW THIS NIGHT!
PARDON... I'M E'TAN...
I OFFER MY HOME AS SANCTUARY.
I REMEMBER YOU...
FROM THE NIGHT WE ARRIVED.
YOU SEE WHAT I CARRY?
THE HEAD OF THE SNAKE GOD.
BETRAY MY FRIENDS...AND I'LL KNOW.
FEAR NOT, MASTER TEMPLAR...
MOTHER AND I LIVE IN PRIVILEGE—OUR HOME WILL NOT BE SEARCHED...

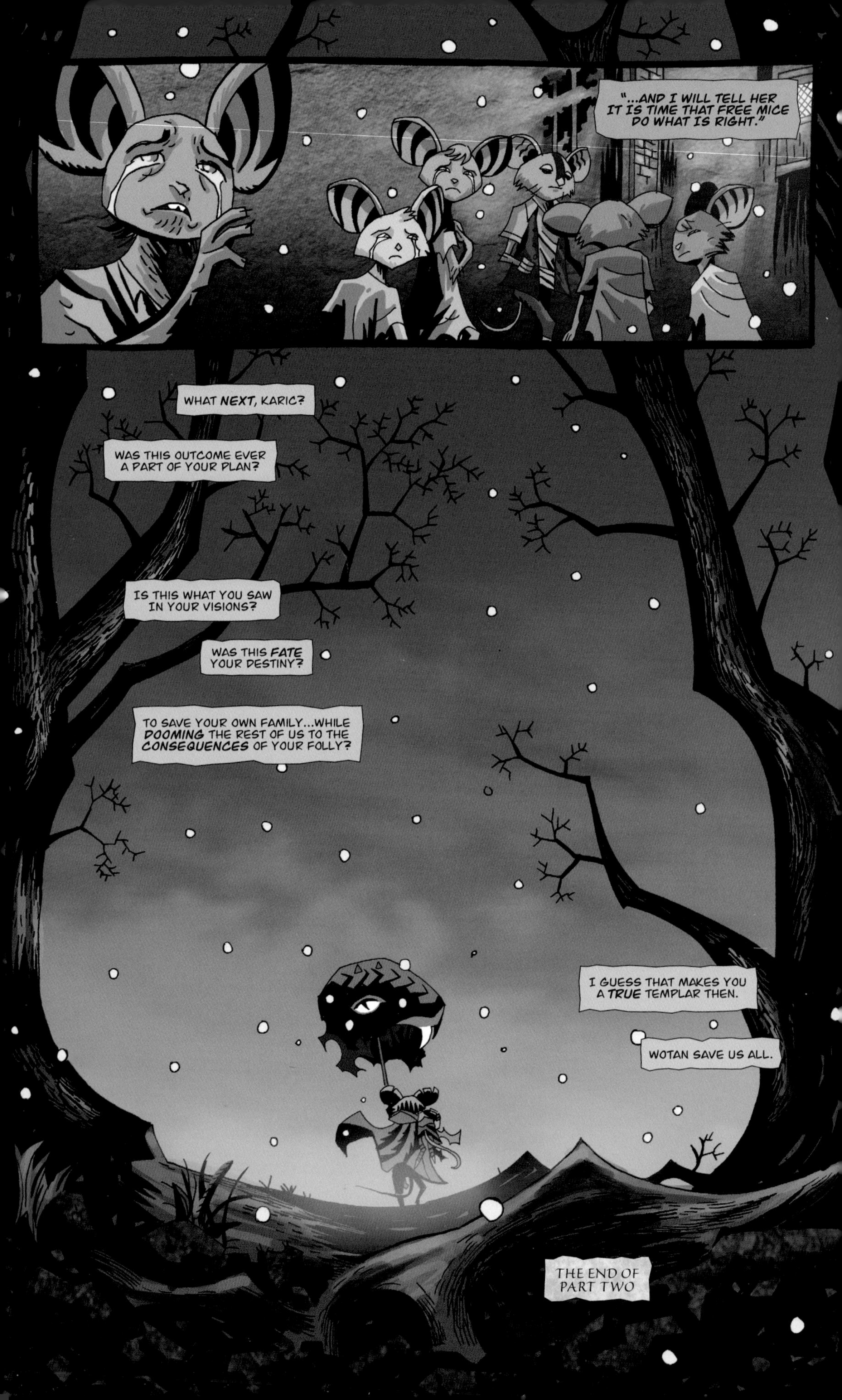
"...AND I WILL TELL HER IT IS TIME THAT FREE MICE DO WHAT IS RIGHT."
WHAT NEXT, KARIC?
WAS THIS OUTCOME EVER A PART OF YOUR PLAN?
IS THIS WHAT YOU SAW IN YOUR VISIONS?
WAS THIS FATE YOUR DESTINY?
TO SAVE YOUR OWN FAMILY...WHILE DOOMING THE REST OF US TO THE CONSEQUENCES OF YOUR FOLLY?
I GUESS THAT MAKES YOU A TRUE TEMPLAR THEN.
WOTAN SAVE US ALL.
THE END OF PART TWO

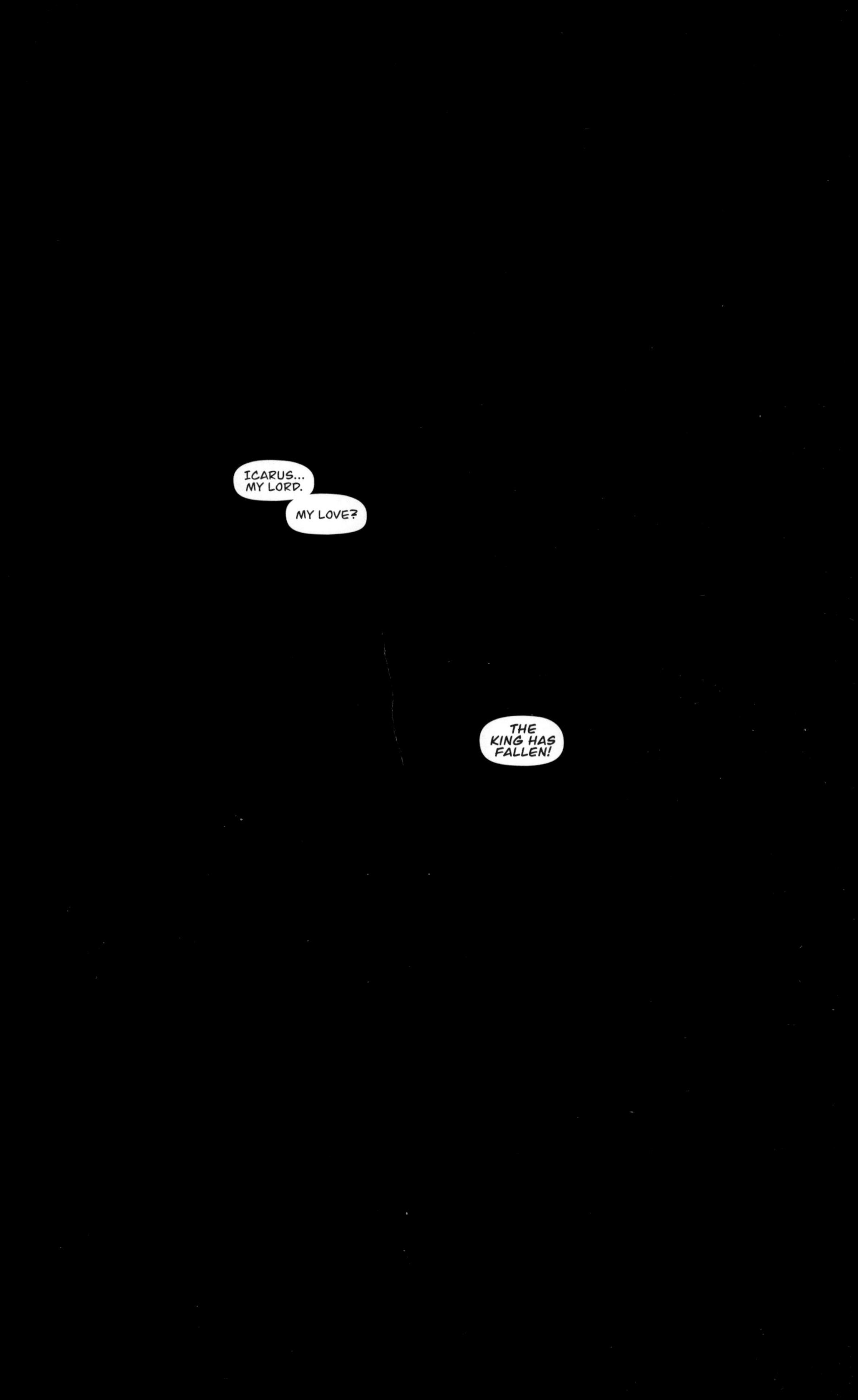
ICARUS... MY LORD.
MY LOVE?
THE KING HAS FALLEN!

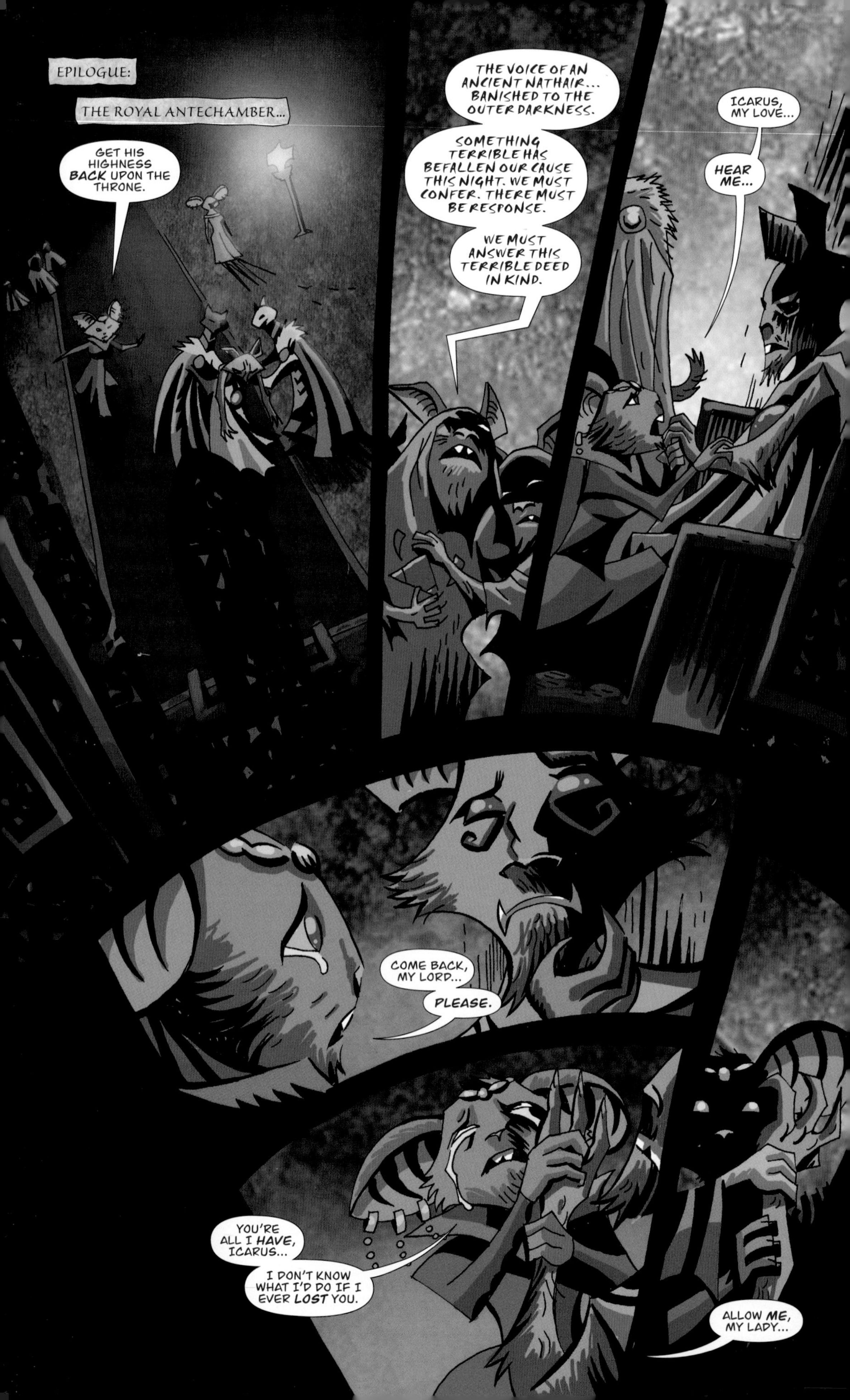
EPILOGUE:
THE ROYAL ANTECHAMBER...
GET HIS HIGHNESS BACK UPON THE THRONE.
THE VOICE OF AN ANCIENT NATHAIR... BANISHED TO THE OUTER DARKNESS.
SOMETHING TERRIBLE HAS BEFALLEN OUR CAUSE THIS NIGHT. WE MUST CONFER. THERE MUST BE RESPONSE.
WE MUST ANSWER THIS TERRIBLE DEED IN KIND.
ICARUS, MY LOVE...
HEAR ME...
COME BACK, MY LORD...
PLEASE.
YOU'RE ALL I HAVE, ICARUS...
I DON'T KNOW WHAT I'D DO IF I EVER LOST YOU.
ALLOW ME, MY LADY...

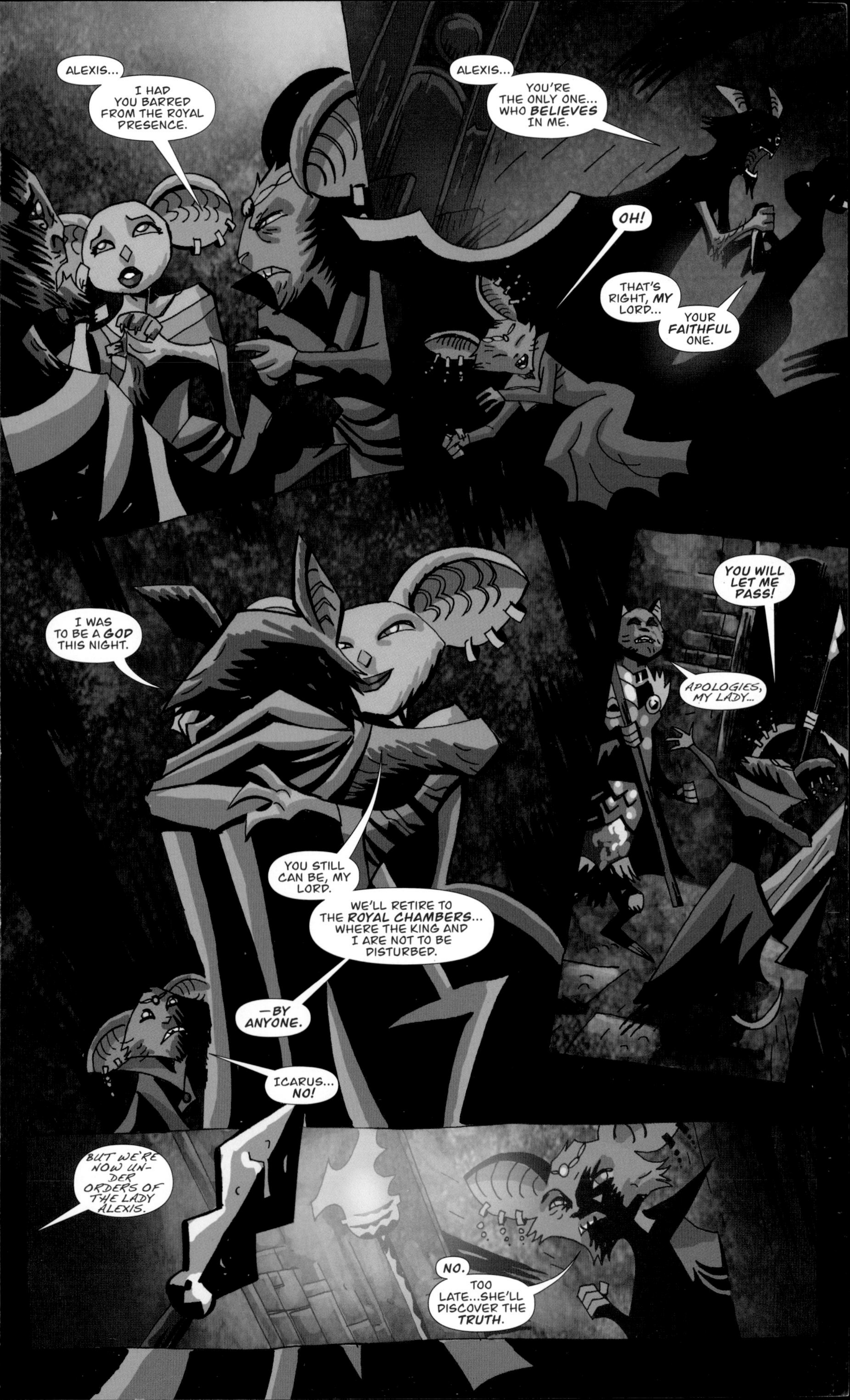
ALEXIS...
I HAD YOU BARRED FROM THE ROYAL PRESENCE.
ALEXIS...
YOU'RE THE ONLY ONE... WHO BELIEVES IN ME.
OH!
THAT'S RIGHT, MY LORD...
YOUR FAITHFUL ONE.
I WAS TO BE A GOD THIS NIGHT.
YOU STILL CAN BE, MY LORD.
WE'LL RETIRE TO THE ROYAL CHAMBERS... WHERE THE KING AND I ARE NOT TO BE DISTURBED.
—BY ANYONE.
YOU WILL LET ME PASS!
APOLOGIES, MY LADY...
ICARUS... NO!
BUT WE'RE NOW UNDER ORDERS OF THE LADY ALEXIS.
NO.
TOO LATE...SHE'LL DISCOVER THE TRUTH.

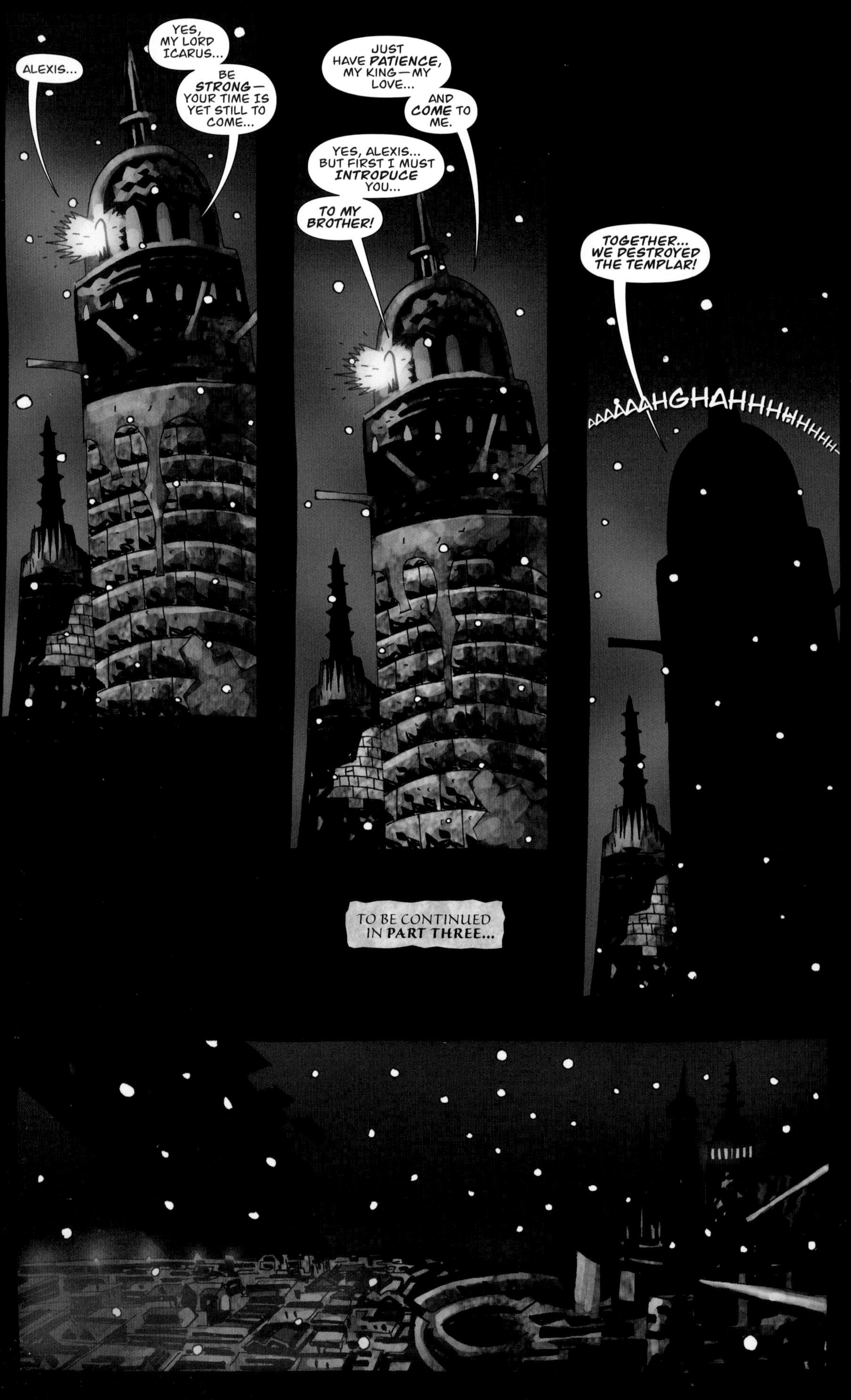
ALEXIS...
YES, MY LORD ICARUS...
BE STRONG—YOUR TIME IS YET STILL TO COME...
JUST HAVE PATIENCE, MY KING—MY LOVE...
AND COME TO ME.
YES, ALEXIS... BUT FIRST I MUST INTRODUCE YOU...
TO MY BROTHER!
TOGETHER... WE DESTROYED THE TEMPLAR!
AAAAAAHGHAHHHHHHHH-
TO BE CONTINUED IN PART THREE...

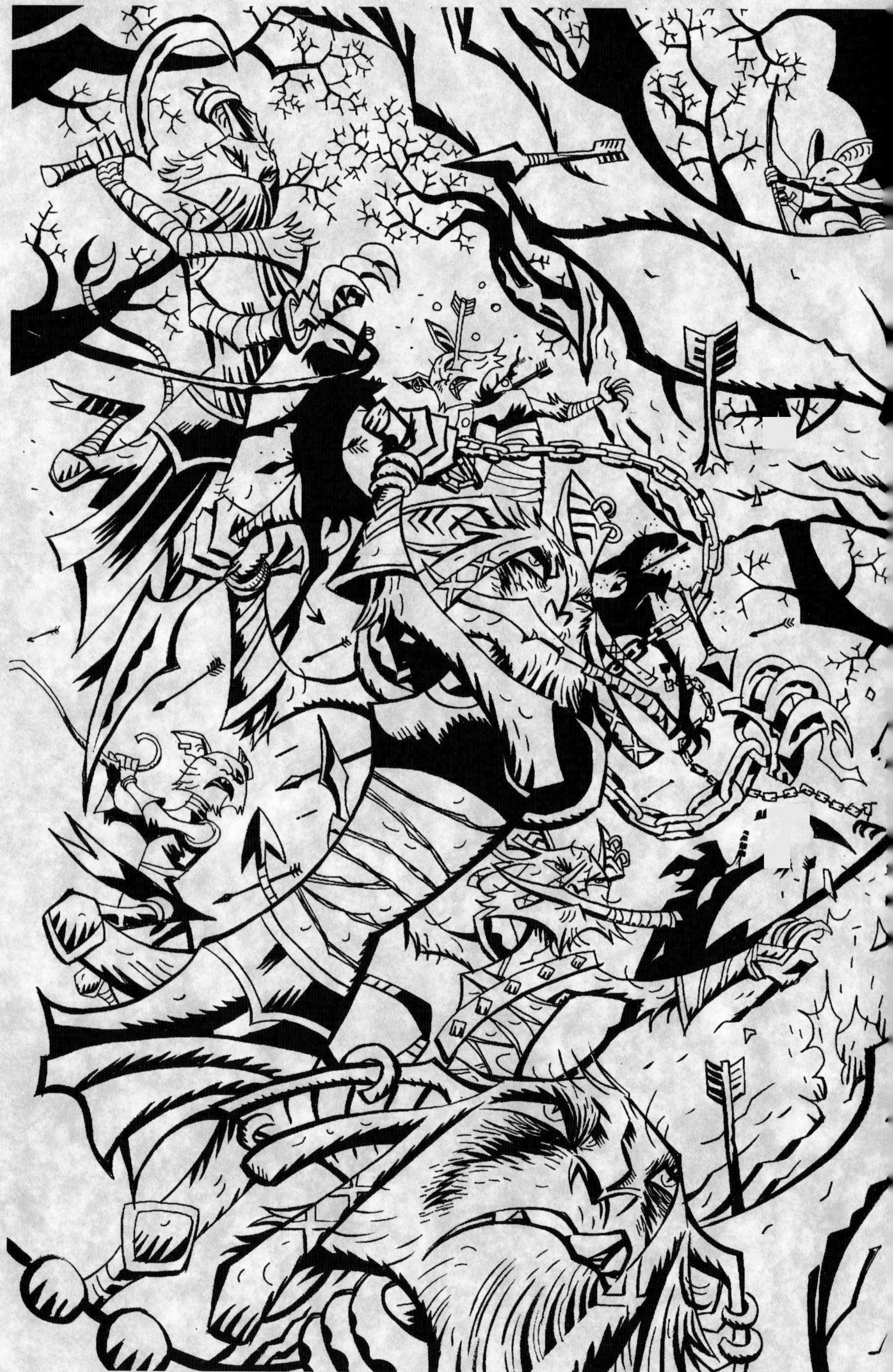

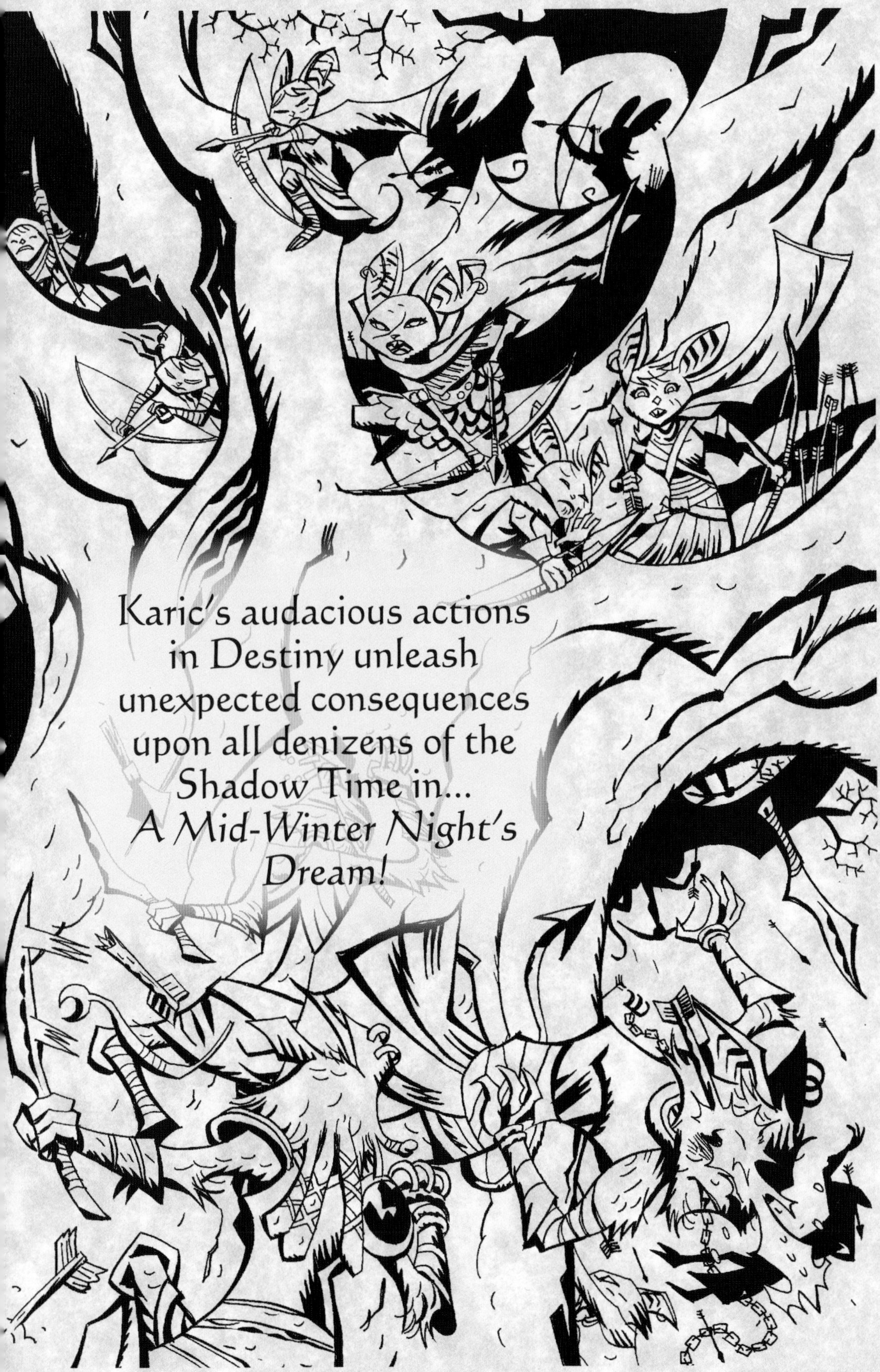
Karic's audacious actions in Destiny unleash unexpected consequences upon all denizens of the Shadow Time in...
A Mid-Winter Night's Dream!

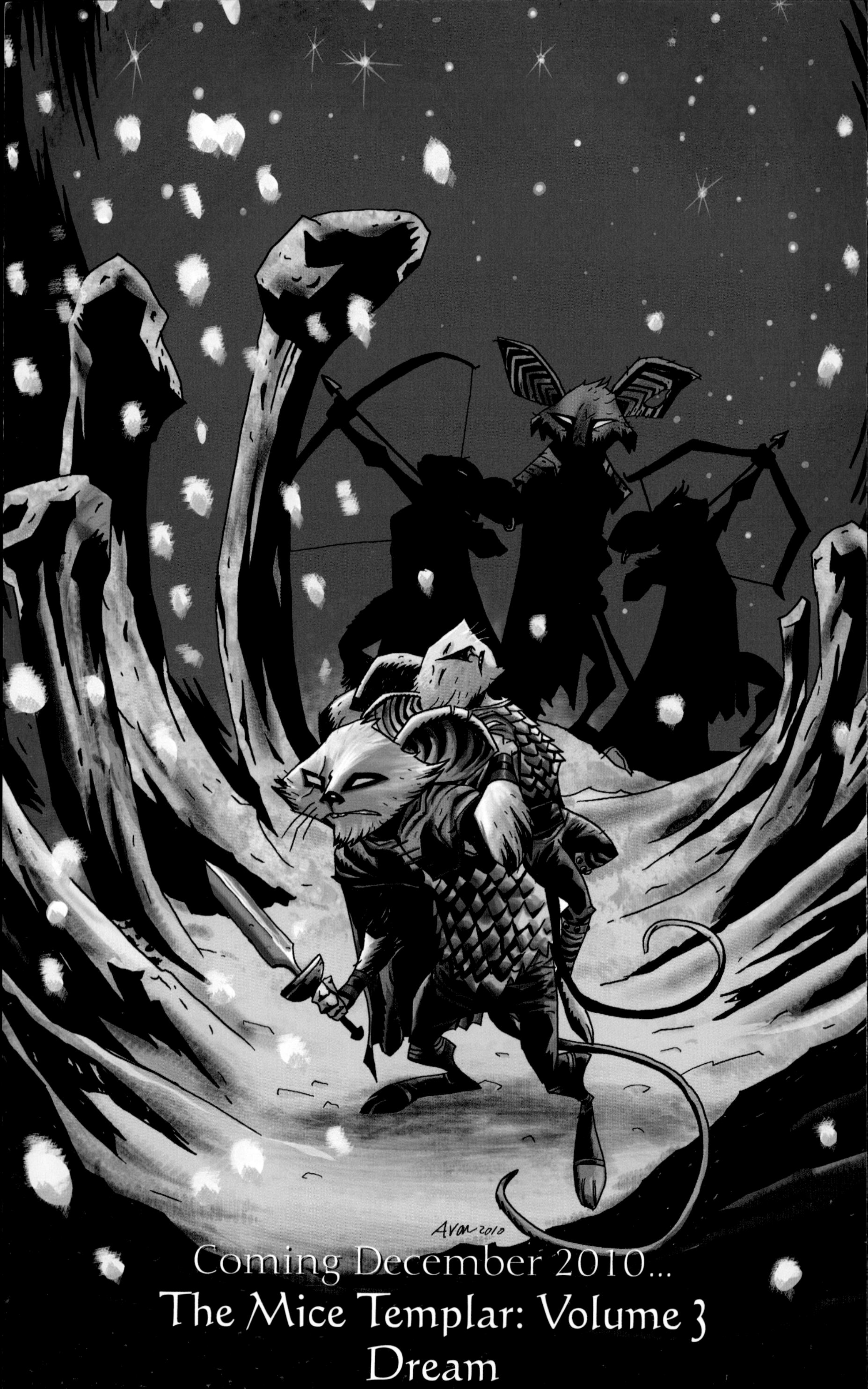
Coming December 2010...
The Mice Templar: Volume 3
Dream

Karic has accomplished his goal—the rescue of his family from captivity—but their freedom has come with a terrible price. Karic now lies comatose, his spirit lost to the realm of dreams, a nightmare portal to the Outer Darkness where dwell the ancient and accursed Nathair. Yet Cassius risks all for the young mouse who restored his faith, even death at the blade of his old rival Ronan. Meanwhile, in the capital, the druids unleash a new wave of tyranny in retaliation for Karic's audacious attack; political tension between rat and weasel is revealed; Lady Lorelie discovers a fearful truth she has long suspected. And One-Arm Leito passes the winter under the tutelage of fallen Templar, Pilot the Tall.

Thus continues an extraordinary adventure of magic and wonder, of faith and valor, and of one small mouse whose destiny may change the entire world. Created by Bryan J.L. Glass (*Magician Apprentice, Riftwar, Quixote*) & Michael Avon Oeming (*POWERS, Rapture, God Complex*).

Single issues available at all fine comic book retailers...and now available in electronic format from ComiXology.com

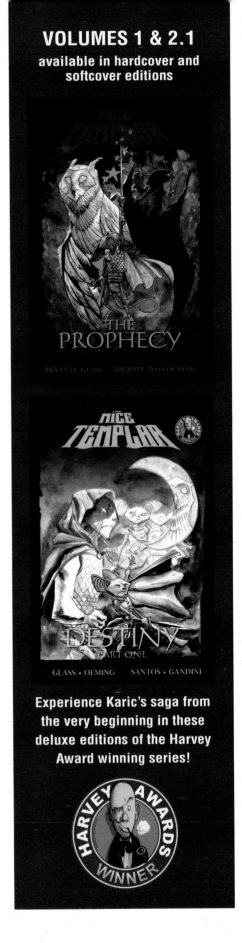

PASSING THE TORCH

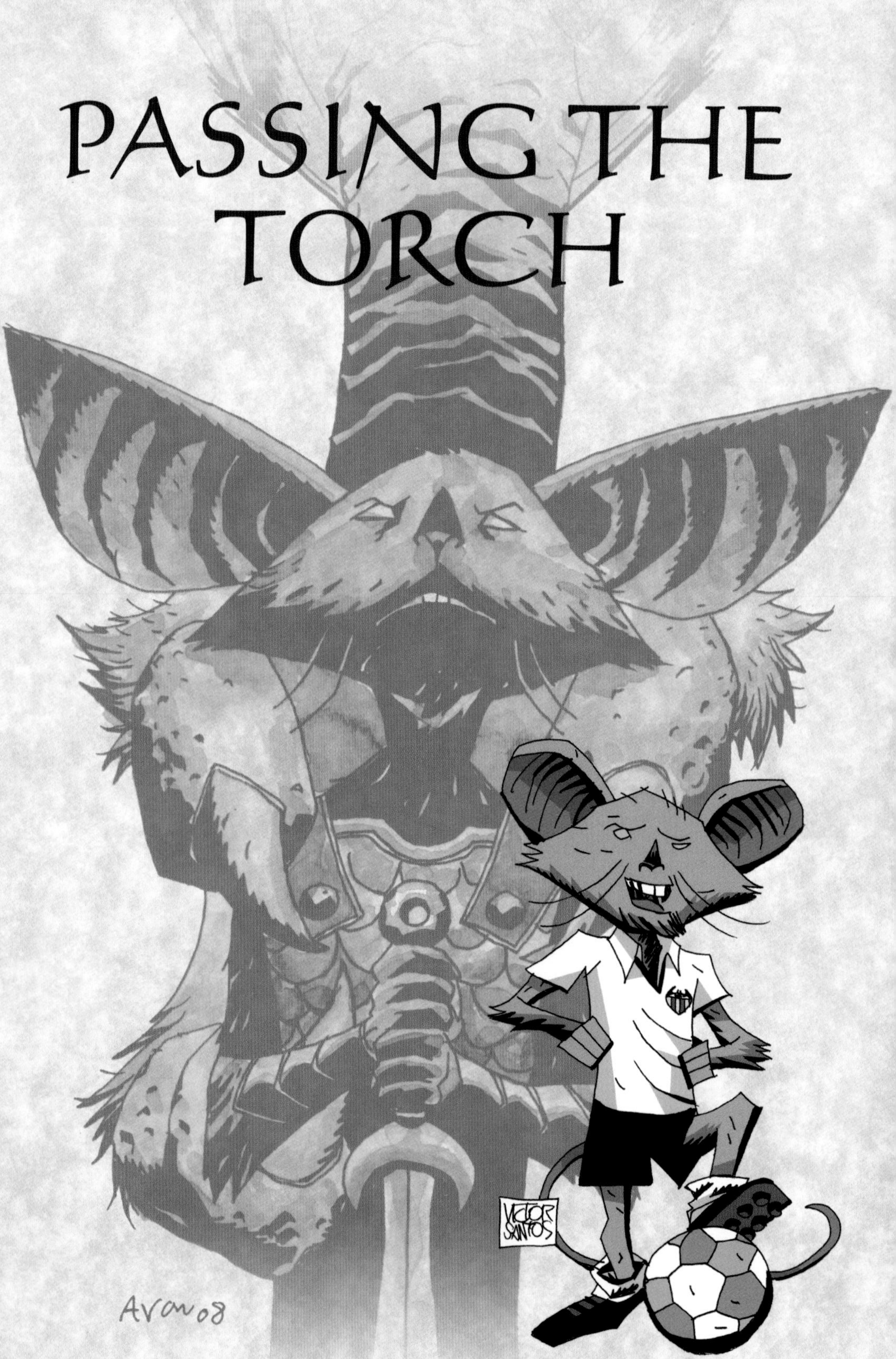

VICTOR SANTOS
Avon08

An Afterword
by Michael Avon Oeming

Wow, when did *Mice Templar* start? It's been over ten years since it was conceived for print, but it was three whopping years ago in 2007 when Issue One finally came out. It was a long-held dream of mine come true, brought to life by the writing of co-creator Bryan J.L. Glass. I had given Bryan a very short outline for six issues that became a sprawling epic of thirty-some issues. Together, we created something I hold proudly next to *Powers* as some of the best work I've ever done.

Sadly, however, executing this comic came at a very difficult time in my life. My entire paradigm shifted and life changed for me in big ways. This made the book perpetually late, and eventually, after struggling through those first six issues, I realized my participation had become a weight on the book that needed to be lifted. The idea that anyone else could possibly draw *Mice Templar* seemed impossible. It's not that we could not find another fine artist, but I draw the Templar in a very specific way—a "vibe" is all I can call it. Who could or would want to take on the series in my place, and yet leave the book feeling the same, as though only a subtle light had changed in the room? Enter Spanish artist Victor Santos.

Victor is an amazing artist and quite successful in Europe. At the time, he only had a few comics out here in the States: *Zombie* with Miles Gunter, and a few other things. We both have similar influences, from Mike Mignola to Bruce Timm. Luckily he was also a fan of the book. Even more lucky, I became friends with Victor during my many trips to Spain. We asked Victor and he was in. Victor has vigilantly carried the art torch for *Mice Templar* ever since, and, along with Bryan, Jim Glass, Veronica Gandini and everyone else working very, very hard on the series, has gotten the issues out on time every month since. We are a little more than halfway through the saga Bryan and I originally dreamed up, and now we have more dreamers with us to forge the future. Without Victor and Veronica (Vero, as we love to call her) this series would no longer be possible.

I enjoy being able to do what little *Mice Templar* work I have time for now: covers and occasional interior pages. But watching the story that Bryan and I crafted from this vantage point is wonderful. I get to be both co-creator and fan now.

Thank you, guys. ❧

Michael Avon Oeming
Seattle, WA

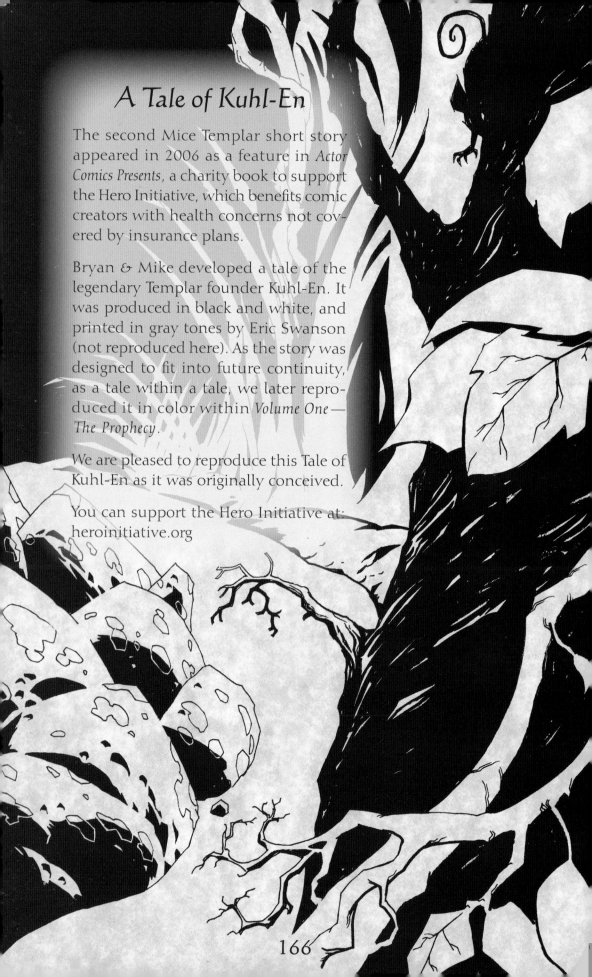

A Tale of Kuhl-En

The second Mice Templar short story appeared in 2006 as a feature in *Actor Comics Presents*, a charity book to support the Hero Initiative, which benefits comic creators with health concerns not covered by insurance plans.

Bryan & Mike developed a tale of the legendary Templar founder Kuhl-En. It was produced in black and white, and printed in gray tones by Eric Swanson (not reproduced here). As the story was designed to fit into future continuity, as a tale within a tale, we later reproduced it in color within *Volume One — The Prophecy*.

We are pleased to reproduce this Tale of Kuhl-En as it was originally conceived.

You can support the Hero Initiative at: heroinitiative.org

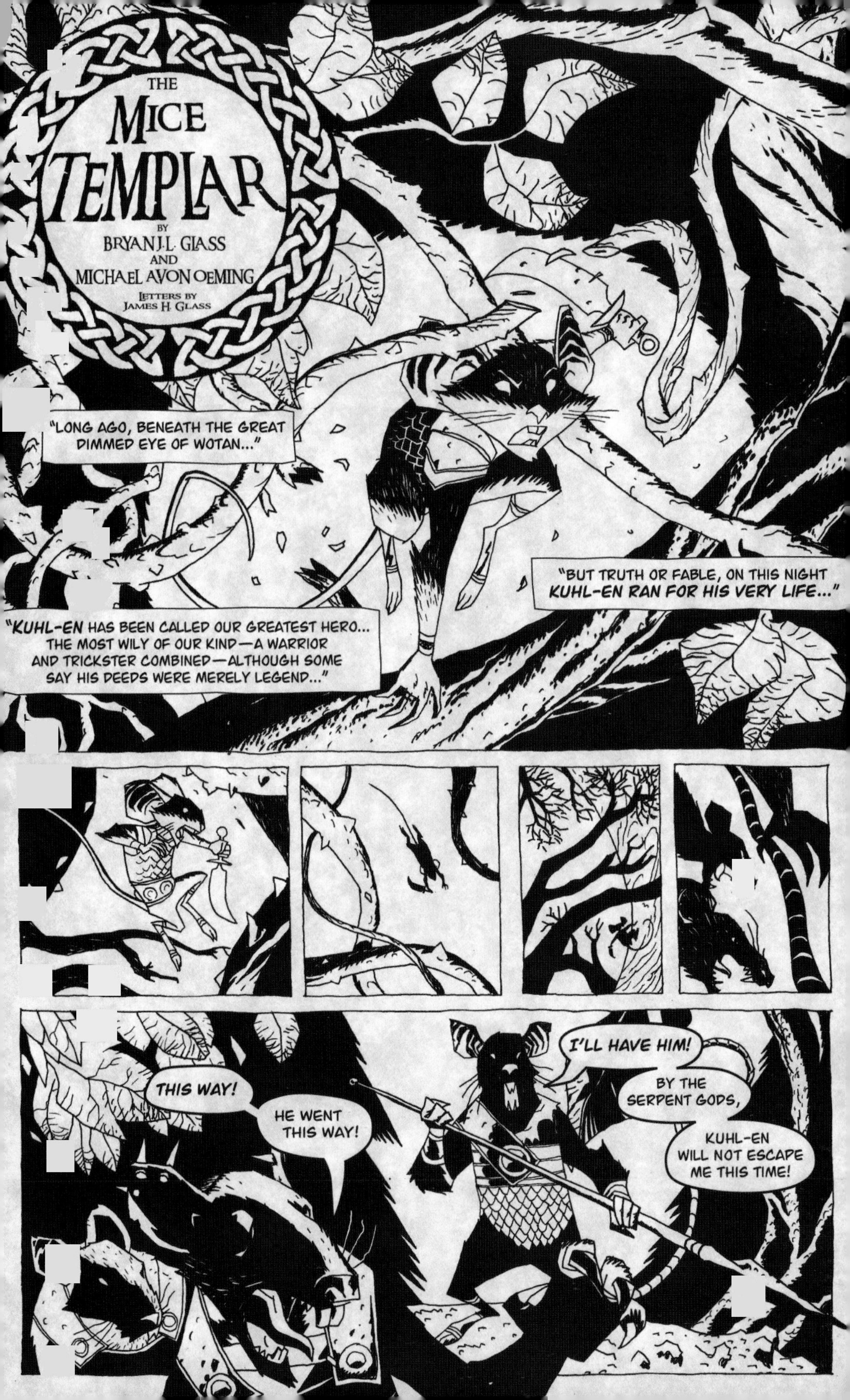
THE
MICE
TEMPLAR
BY
BRYAN J.L. GLASS
AND
MICHAEL AVON OEMING
LETTERS BY
JAMES H. GLASS
"LONG AGO, BENEATH THE GREAT DIMMED EYE OF WOTAN..."
"KUHL-EN HAS BEEN CALLED OUR GREATEST HERO... THE MOST WILY OF OUR KIND—A WARRIOR AND TRICKSTER COMBINED—ALTHOUGH SOME SAY HIS DEEDS WERE MERELY LEGEND..."
"BUT TRUTH OR FABLE, ON THIS NIGHT KUHL-EN RAN FOR HIS VERY LIFE..."
THIS WAY!
HE WENT THIS WAY!
I'LL HAVE HIM!
BY THE SERPENT GODS,
KUHL-EN WILL NOT ESCAPE ME THIS TIME!

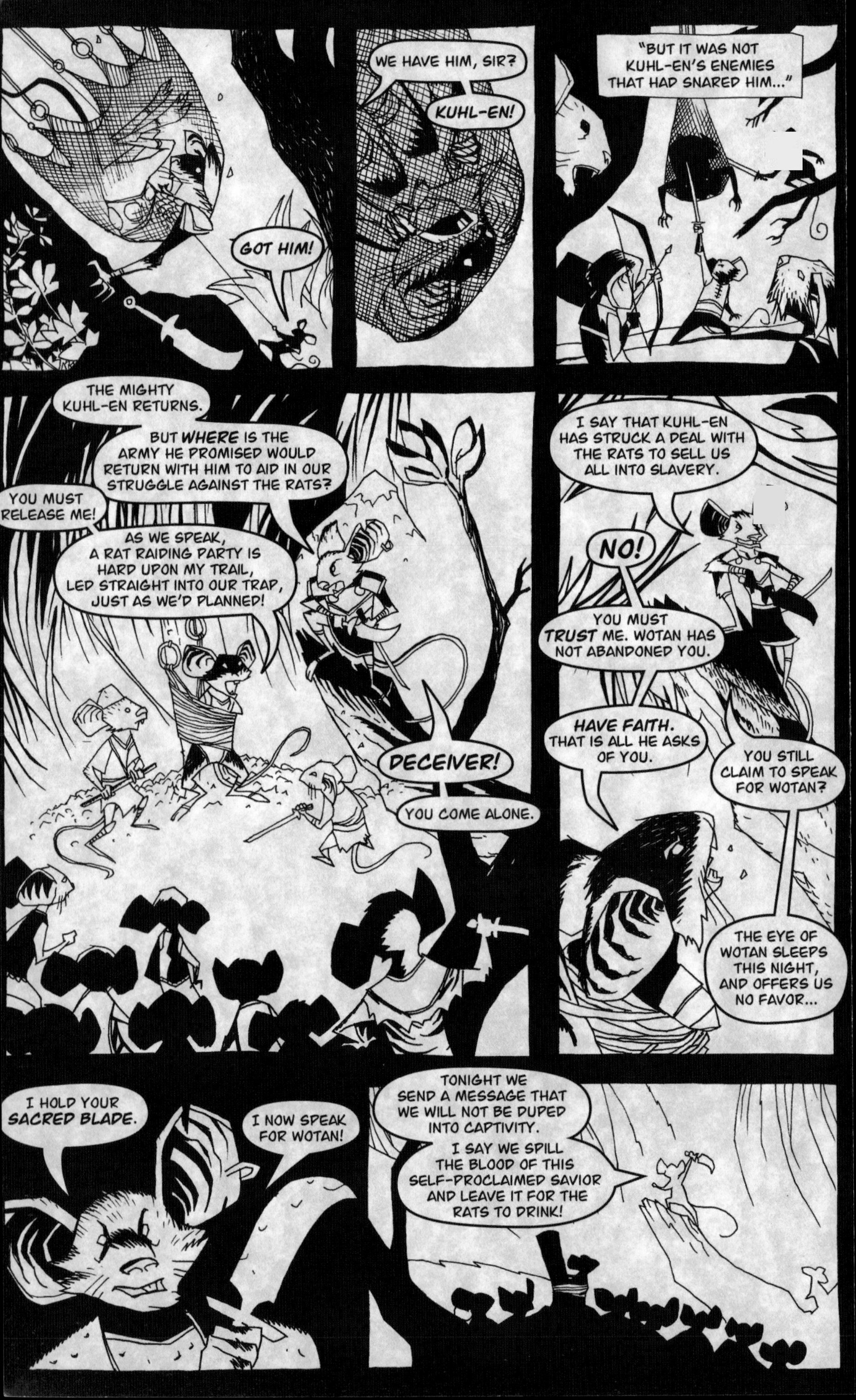
GOT HIM!
WE HAVE HIM, SIR?
KUHL-EN!
"BUT IT WAS NOT KUHL-EN'S ENEMIES THAT HAD SNARED HIM..."
THE MIGHTY KUHL-EN RETURNS.
BUT WHERE IS THE ARMY HE PROMISED WOULD RETURN WITH HIM TO AID IN OUR STRUGGLE AGAINST THE RATS?
YOU MUST RELEASE ME!
AS WE SPEAK, A RAT RAIDING PARTY IS HARD UPON MY TRAIL, LED STRAIGHT INTO OUR TRAP, JUST AS WE'D PLANNED!
DECEIVER!
YOU COME ALONE.
I SAY THAT KUHL-EN HAS STRUCK A DEAL WITH THE RATS TO SELL US ALL INTO SLAVERY.
NO!
YOU MUST TRUST ME. WOTAN HAS NOT ABANDONED YOU.
HAVE FAITH. THAT IS ALL HE ASKS OF YOU.
YOU STILL CLAIM TO SPEAK FOR WOTAN?
THE EYE OF WOTAN SLEEPS THIS NIGHT, AND OFFERS US NO FAVOR...
I HOLD YOUR SACRED BLADE.
I NOW SPEAK FOR WOTAN!
TONIGHT WE SEND A MESSAGE THAT WE WILL NOT BE DUPED INTO CAPTIVITY.
I SAY WE SPILL THE BLOOD OF THIS SELF-PROCLAIMED SAVIOR AND LEAVE IT FOR THE RATS TO DRINK!

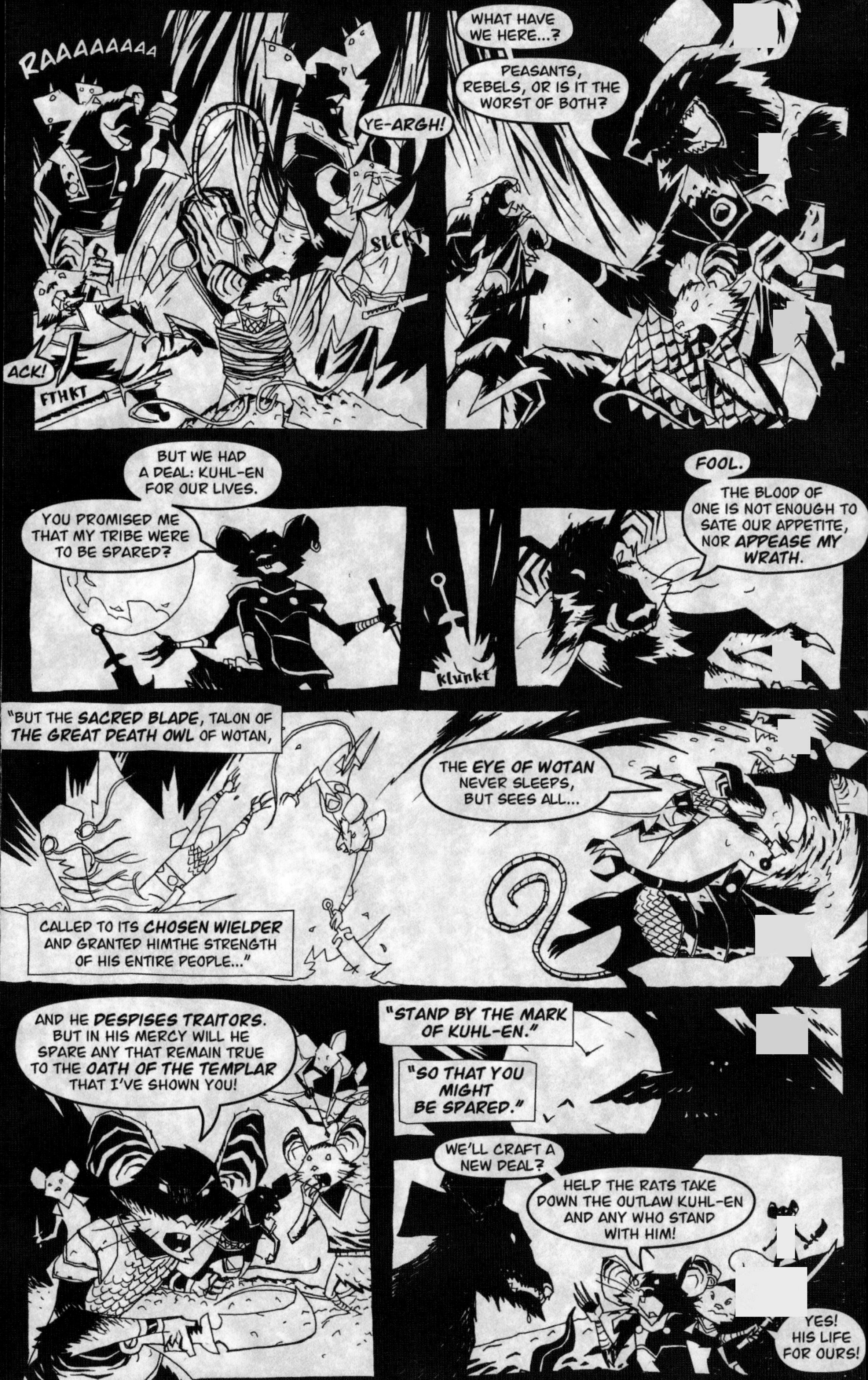
RAAAAAAAA
YE-ARGH!
SLCKT
ACK!
FTHKT
WHAT HAVE WE HERE...?
PEASANTS, REBELS, OR IS IT THE WORST OF BOTH?
BUT WE HAD A DEAL: KUHL-EN FOR OUR LIVES.
YOU PROMISED ME THAT MY TRIBE WERE TO BE SPARED?
KLUNKT
FOOL.
THE BLOOD OF ONE IS NOT ENOUGH TO SATE OUR APPETITE, NOR APPEASE MY WRATH.
"BUT THE SACRED BLADE, TALON OF THE GREAT DEATH OWL OF WOTAN,
CALLED TO ITS CHOSEN WIELDER AND GRANTED HIMTHE STRENGTH OF HIS ENTIRE PEOPLE..."
THE EYE OF WOTAN NEVER SLEEPS, BUT SEES ALL...
AND HE DESPISES TRAITORS. BUT IN HIS MERCY WILL HE SPARE ANY THAT REMAIN TRUE TO THE OATH OF THE TEMPLAR THAT I'VE SHOWN YOU!
"STAND BY THE MARK OF KUHL-EN."
"SO THAT YOU MIGHT BE SPARED."
WE'LL CRAFT A NEW DEAL?
HELP THE RATS TAKE DOWN THE OUTLAW KUHL-EN AND ANY WHO STAND WITH HIM!
YES! HIS LIFE FOR OURS!

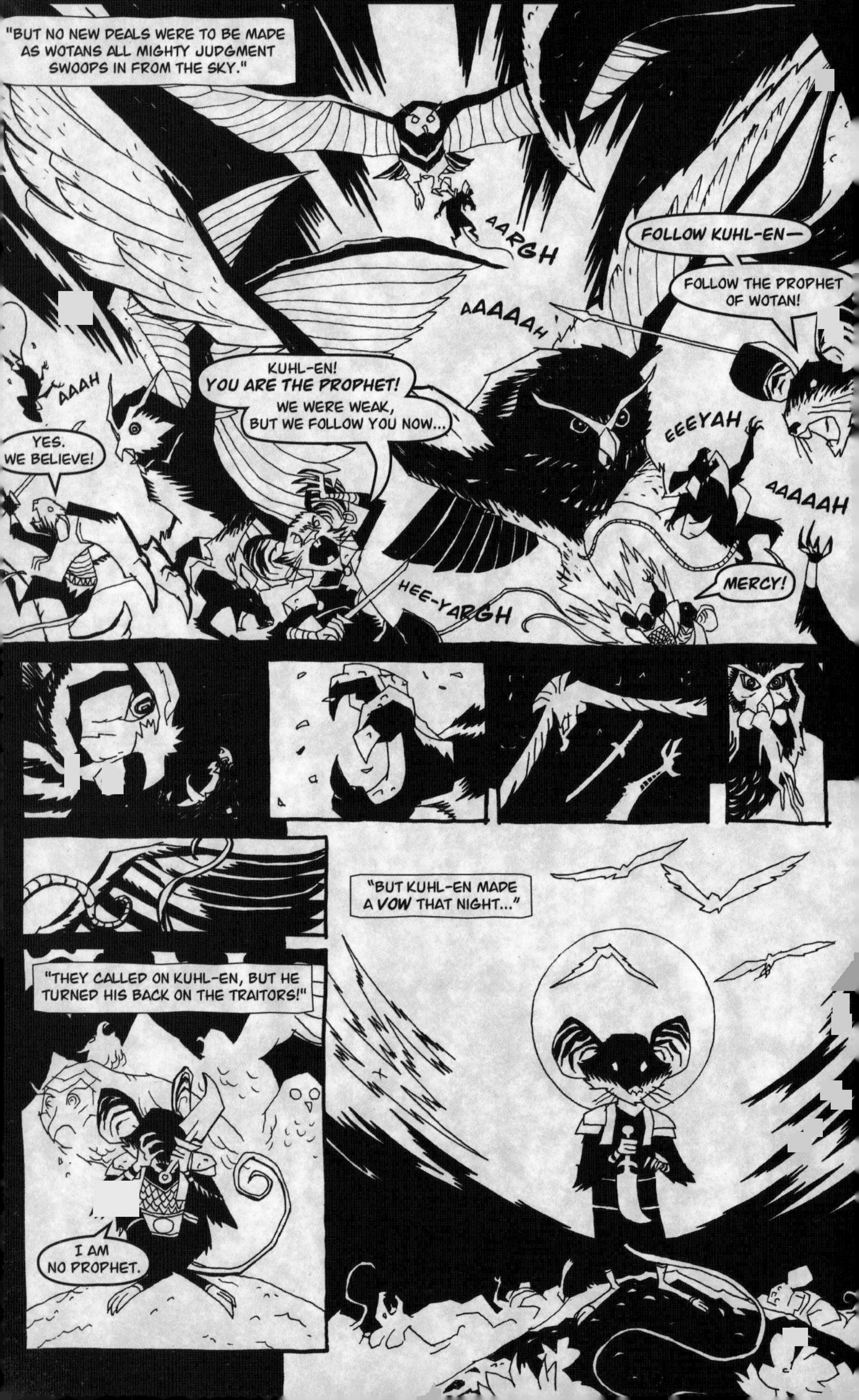
"BUT NO NEW DEALS WERE TO BE MADE AS WOTANS ALL MIGHTY JUDGMENT SWOOPS IN FROM THE SKY."
AARGH
FOLLOW KUHL-EN—
FOLLOW THE PROPHET OF WOTAN!
AAAAAH
AAAH
KUHL-EN! YOU ARE THE PROPHET! WE WERE WEAK, BUT WE FOLLOW YOU NOW...
YES. WE BELIEVE!
EEEYAH
AAAAAH
MERCY!
HEE-YARGH
"BUT KUHL-EN MADE A VOW THAT NIGHT..."
"THEY CALLED ON KUHL-EN, BUT HE TURNED HIS BACK ON THE TRAITORS!"
I AM NO PROPHET.

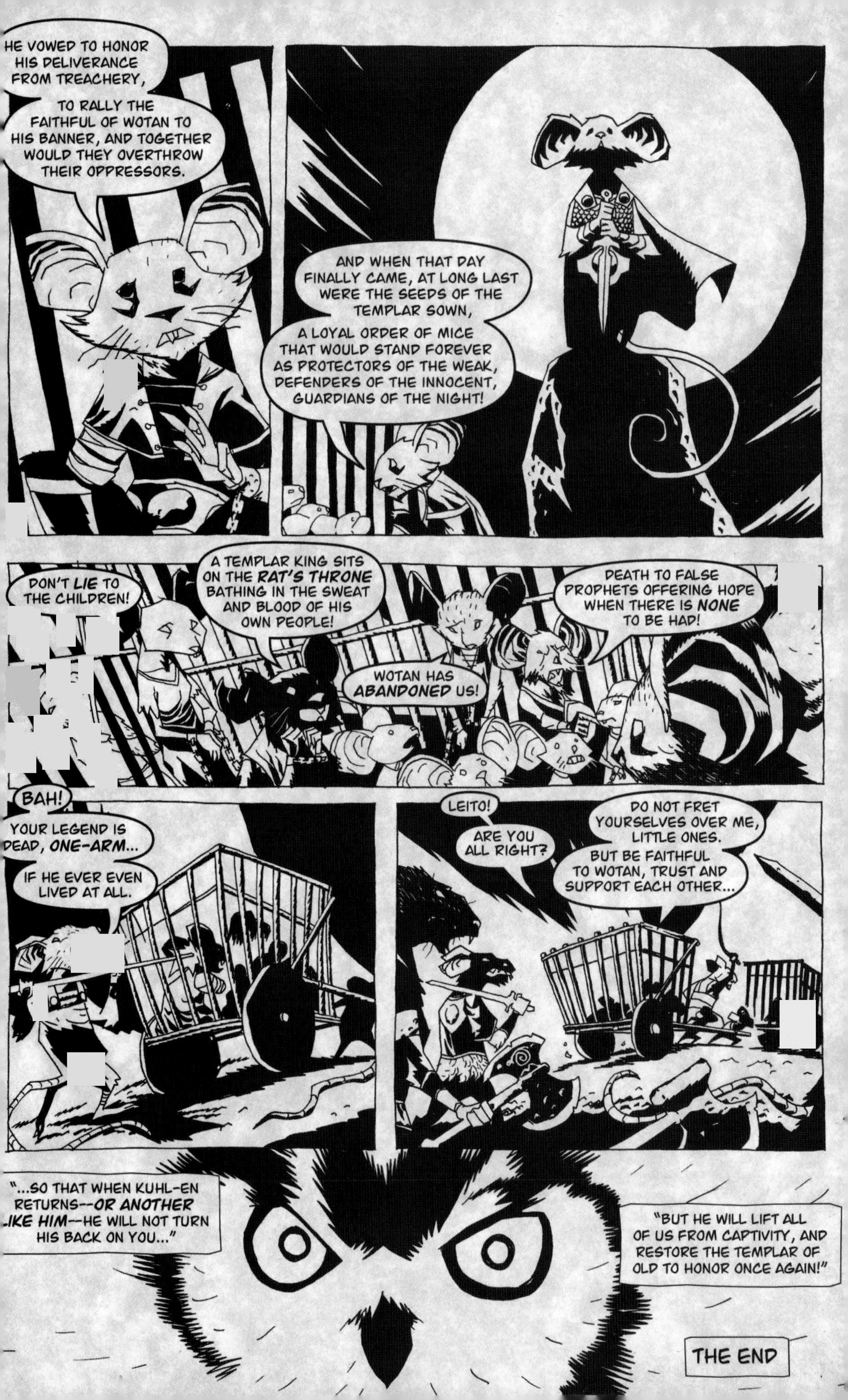
HE VOWED TO HONOR HIS DELIVERANCE FROM TREACHERY,
TO RALLY THE FAITHFUL OF WOTAN TO HIS BANNER, AND TOGETHER WOULD THEY OVERTHROW THEIR OPPRESSORS.
AND WHEN THAT DAY FINALLY CAME, AT LONG LAST WERE THE SEEDS OF THE TEMPLAR SOWN,
A LOYAL ORDER OF MICE THAT WOULD STAND FOREVER AS PROTECTORS OF THE WEAK, DEFENDERS OF THE INNOCENT, GUARDIANS OF THE NIGHT!
DON'T **LIE** TO THE CHILDREN!
A TEMPLAR KING SITS ON THE **RAT'S THRONE** BATHING IN THE SWEAT AND BLOOD OF HIS OWN PEOPLE!
WOTAN HAS **ABANDONED** US!
DEATH TO FALSE PROPHETS OFFERING HOPE WHEN THERE IS **NONE** TO BE HAD!
BAH!
YOUR LEGEND IS DEAD, **ONE-ARM**...
IF HE EVER EVEN LIVED AT ALL.
LEITO!
ARE YOU ALL RIGHT?
DO NOT FRET YOURSELVES OVER ME, LITTLE ONES.
BUT BE FAITHFUL TO WOTAN, TRUST AND SUPPORT EACH OTHER...
"...SO THAT WHEN KUHL-EN RETURNS--**OR ANOTHER LIKE HIM**--HE WILL NOT TURN HIS BACK ON YOU..."
"BUT HE WILL LIFT ALL OF US FROM CAPTIVITY, AND RESTORE THE TEMPLAR OF OLD TO HONOR ONCE AGAIN!"
THE END

A History of the Realm

Derived from scholarly analysis,
review and opinion of various and sundry
sacred texts, historic annals and
ancient writings

As compiled and translated by Bryan J.L. Glass
Visual interpretation by Anton Kromoff

THE FOUNDING OF
THE TEMPLAR

I: The First Hero

In the ancient, forgotten past, as the *Cycles of Chaos* began, mice lived under the full gaze of the two Great Eyes of Wotan, serving merely as prey for larger predators and scavenger hordes.

Following the division of the day into two distinct halves, the Bright Realm and Shadow Time, the *First Great Season* commenced, and Wotan blessed the mice with intelligence. He inspired the very first true hero of the mice, **Parthalon**, to lead his people into the *Dark Lands*, where they would learn cunning to escape their enemies. But in time, Parthalon's descendants scattered into disparate tribes, losing contact and kinship with one another, so that even fellow mice became enemies.

II: Sualtam

In the aftermath of the last Cycle—*the Nights of Shadow*,

when bats were cast down from the sky—the *Second Great Season* began with another mouse rising up to inspire his people: **Sualtam**. He encouraged his nomadic people to take an active part in discovering the role Wotan had for them in the world, but first they had to learn to live in harmony with each other; then they could extend that harmony outward to all other creatures. By doing so, he believed that mice could impact the Dark Lands for all seasons to come. But he was ultimately betrayed by the very mice he'd tried to save, mice who feared the future and were threatened by any change even to their sad way of life.

III: Rise of Kuhl-En

Following Sualtam's death, his son, the young mouse **Kuhl-En**, became a pariah of his people. Cast out alone into the wilderness to die, Kuhl-En journeyed to the **Kilmagenny Mountains**, climbed to the highest peak

overlooking the **Great Valley**, and dared Wotan to come personally and take him.

IV: Kuhl-En battles the Death Owl

In answer to Kuhl-En's challenge, a Great Death Owl came to claim Kuhl-En's life and carry his spirit back to Wotan, but the mouse fought back with a fury hitherto unseen in all the history of the Dark Lands. It is said that Kuhl-En battled the Death Owl for an entire cycle of Wotan's gaze (i.e., one month), and that during that span the mountain was wreathed in clouds both day and night, and the thunder and lightning were fierce enough to terrorize all creatures of the valley below.

Just as Kuhl-En could fight no more, he seemed to conquer his enemy. Yet as the mist around him parted, he saw that no less than six Death Owls had surrounded him all this time and could have claimed him at any point during the struggle. His strength and fury

spent, Kuhl-En then surrendered to his vanquished foe and submitted to what he assumed was his inevitable death. To his great surprise, however, his fearsome adversary broke off one of his own talons and presented it to Kuhl-En as a symbol of their struggle. The Owl spoke that Wotan had felt his pain, but that his father's vision, however noble in intent, was not the path of Wotan, for mercy alone, untempered by justice, led to anarchy. Sualtam's "peace" would have forever remained a false hope, never fulfilled, bringing only misery.

Kuhl-En was commissioned to return to his people with the true path of Wotan, the **Code of the Templar**, offering true justice tempered by genuine mercy, so that peace might one day be known by all creatures. Kuhl-En accepted the call on behalf of all his people and for the sake of future generations of mice, that they might no longer live in fear.

Kuhl-En fashioned the talon into a sword, one whose blade never dulled: a sacred blade that came to be known as the **Mark of Kuhl-En**. And when wielded by a true servant of Wotan, the bearer carried the authority to speak for Wotan, and gained the physical strength of his entire race, for his righteous deeds were truly being done for all.

V: The Templar

Kuhl-En descended from the mountain he now called the **Peak of Armagh**, and had many adventures as he sought to bring Wotan's **Templar Code** to the dispirited mice. He encountered numerous enemies from among the varied predators of the Dark Lands, as well as from amongst his own people. But as the seasons passed, their ranks were far surpassed by followers and supporters, whom he taught and trained.

In time, Kuhl-En took his twelve closest disciples to a vast field, for Wotan and all of the Dark Lands to bear witness, where he knighted them into what he now called the **Order of the Templar**. It is said that perched owls of all breeds encircled the field so that no predator would dare intrude upon the sacred ceremony.

Later, it was to the same field that Kuhl-En called the first gathering of the scattered mouse tribes assembled in peace, to now recognize each other as brothers. The field was named **Avalon** and was considered a sacred site where, throughout subsequent mouse history, the Templar would gather when their business was substantial enough that all the Dark Lands were symbolically summoned to bear witness.

VI: Mice and Rats

In time, the struggle for dominance of the Dark Lands came down to mice and rats: cousins by their very nature, together they came to epitomize the duality of all creatures. Rat culture tended

to embrace all that was base, loathsome, self-serving and ultimately destructive. Mice, on the other hand, when following the Templar Code, represented all that was noble and inspiring, self-sacrificial and to the benefit of the community and future generations. They were two sides divided by choice: converse reflections, and neither culture could live in harmony with the other. Thus Kuhl-En was ultimately forced to lead a mighty campaign to drive rats from the Great Valley.

The Templar campaign against the rats lasted generations, with many epic heroes made and lost on both sides.

In one adventure, a mighty rat general, *Titus*—the only rat to ever truly organize his race—stole the sacred blade, the Mark of Kuhl-En, and Kuhl-En found himself without Wotan's guidance for the first time since accepting his divine commission. During this time, Kuhl-En experienced his first encounter with the decep-

tion of bats, and as a result, he declared that no mouse was to seek their counsel ever again.

VII: The Readers of the Wheat

With his twelve closest followers, advisors and friends, Kuhl-En temporarily halted the campaign and embarked on a controversial pilgrimage, in order to discern the Will of Wotan. Rats held all the land surrounding the sacred Peak of Armagh, so Kuhl-En sought a new path to wisdom. He discovered a mighty **Ash Tree** at the center of a vast field of unruly wild wheat. The tree's hollowed husk was empty, for no creature of the Dark Lands would risk crossing such a vast, wide open field to get to it. Only Kuhl-En was bold enough to dare such an action, for only he had ever survived an encounter with the Great Death Owls of Wotan.

Within the ash tree, Kuhl-En and his company fasted, meditated and prayed.

It is said that a firefly of the dusk awakened Kuhl-En and guided him to the uppermost branches of the great tree and directed his vision out across the vast field of wild wheat wafting in the gentle winds. Only because his spirit was attuned, seeking the Will of Wotan, did he begin to discern messages in the shifting field, and Kuhl-En then realized that the winds, both gentle and fierce, were created by the mighty beating of owls' wings, and thus were the messages in the wheat sent by Wotan himself. He further realized that the Will of Wotan could actually be discerned from all around him, not merely by the Mark, so that he need never walk without guidance again.

The messages in the wheat conveyed to Kuhl-En that the burden of guiding his people was not his alone. His twelve disciples were chosen to become a sacred brotherhood within the Templar, to remain behind to discern the ongoing Will of Wotan on Kuhl-En's behalf.

And thus was established the **Readers of the Wheat**. As the seasons passed, the humble Readers considered themselves as merely priests conveying the message of Wotan to the people, but still the legend arose that the actual Readers were mystical beings whom the **Priests** merely represented. For the sake of their future security, the Readers deemed it wisdom to perpetuate the legend.

Kuhl-En later declared the firefly to be sacred, for they represented Wotan's Light in the darkness, and that any who were spiritually lost could find their way again by following their light.

VIII: Insects of the Dusk & Dawn

A band of renegade Templar, in defiance of Kuhl-En's having lost his blade, and rejecting the wisdom that came from the Readers of the Wheat, hacked the bulbs from the revered fireflies in order to physically light their way when Kuhl-En pursued them for their treachery. As morning approached, however, the insects of the dusk and dawn retaliated, devouring the desecrators to the bone. Horrified by what he witnessed, Kuhl-En nonetheless realized that the insects represented a potent force that could be harnessed in the current war. But the insects rejected his parley.

Toward the end of the great war, after Kuhl-En had recovered his sacred Mark and turned the tide of the battle against the rats, the survivors of a wounded and decimated rat raiding party stumbled into a mouse village. The mice took pity on the rats, offering them shelter and food, and binding their wounds. It seemed that peace between mouse and rat was possible. That is, until a mob of mice from a neighboring town rose up and demanded the rats be put to death. The kindly mice defended the rats, but all were soon put to the sword and their village to the torch.

Kuhl-En was en route at the behest of the village elders to witness for himself the peaceful coexistence they claimed was possible. Instead he found the results of his own people's treachery. Filled by a fury he'd not experienced since the day he climbed the sacred peak and battled the Great Death Owl, Kuhl-En pursued the perpetrators back to their own town, and then out into the wild, day and night for forty days. With all of them nearing exhaustion, he realized that they would escape him.

Kuhl-En pleaded with the insects of the dawn to stop them. They would not, despite Kuhl-En's descriptions of their vilest deeds. In anger, Kuhl-En drew upon the power of the Mark to bind the insects to his will, calling them to become a living wall between the worlds of night and day. As a result, the rebellious Templar did not escape again into the dawn of a new day, but were instead devoured. Then the order spread, binding the hive mind of all insects to

Kuhl-En's command, cursing their kind to become eternal guardians between the worlds, and Kuhl-En discovered he could not undo that which he had wrought in his fury. The barrier remained, and evil creatures of the Dark Lands soon learned they could not easily escape the justice of the Templar. Thereafter, it was said that Kuhl-En feared his own power and gained an even greater respect for the responsibility of his call.

These insects became known as the Guardians of the Dusk and Dawn, drawn to conscious thought, to devour it, flesh to bone, to silence the voice of condemnation that only they hear ringing in their minds. And thus all creatures found themselves bound by the consequences of Kuhl-En's rage.

It was still possible, however, to thwart the barriers, by passing deep under water or ground, where the transition of day into night holds no sway. But only the highest Templar leaders possessed such knowledge to pass between worlds: that by bearing a representative Mark of Kuhl-En, and invoking the shame of its curse over the Guardians, it was possible for small parties of up to thirteen in number, symbolic of Kuhl-En and his twelve Disciples, to cross unhindered.

In later generations, many Templar tried lifting the curse, but no power of will, word, or deed, nor even the Mark itself, was ever strong enough to break the bond forged by the original *Curse of Kuhl-En*.

IX: The Forty-Season Council

Kuhl-En called a *Great Council* of the Priest Readers and all who carried Templar authority. It had been forty seasons before (i.e., ten years) that Kuhl-En had first gathered the disparate mouse tribes and united them, an act that had launched the first great campaign against rats and which they had only recently won.

In the aftermath of declaring his curse upon the insects and burdened by conscience, Kuhl-En established the tradition of the Forty-Season Council to regularly and officially evaluate the performance of the Templar with regard to their Sacred Calling. He truly believed that the Templar needed to earn the continued Blessing of Wotan by means of their conduct. Thus, every forty seasons, the elders would gather to assess the past, the present, and future of the Order. Few mice ever lived to experience three such Forty-Season Councils in their lifetime.

X: The Passing of Kuhl-En

History records that Kuhl-En ultimately lived the lifespan of ten mice, and that his offspring married into all families so that every mouse now living carries his blood in their veins. At the end of his days, Kuhl-En was not slain, nor even snatched away by the Great Death Owl. It is said that he knew when his time had come, and that once again he climbed up the *Peak of Armagh*, and submitted his spirit unto Wotan. ☙

Myth, Legend & The Mice Templar

BY ROD HANNAH

QUEEN MAEVE

The goddesses of ancient and medieval cultures have represented, among other aspects, the female empowered with the facets of war. Possessing superhuman qualities, these powerful deities have inspired storytellers to give women the often rare opportunity to compete with their male counterparts. Today, those goddesses most remembered for their association with their abilities on the battlefield include the likes of Artemis, the Greek goddess of the hunt, and Athena, goddess of wisdom and war. Lesser known are the Irish triune goddesses called the Morrigan, the Norse goddess Freya, and the magical Valkyries. While these warrior goddesses share similar appointments, in Irish mythology there is one who stands above the others and whose very name has served as the inspiration for *The Mice Templar's* Maeven Archers.

Queen Maeve is the paragon of the strong-willed and independent woman who refuses to sit idle without sword or voice. Her Gaelic name, Medb, is cognate with mead and likely connected to her role as sovereignty goddess and the royal inauguration ritual in which the king symbolically shares a drink with the goddess as part of a sacred marriage. The effect she typically had on men, causing them to lose two-thirds of their strength, might be seen metaphorically as intoxication with her beauty. She had a voracious sexual appetite, taking whatever man she pleased and offering them the gift of her "friendly thighs." In this way she brewed a host of rival suitors, many of whom were of royal blood and vied for her affections.

However, Maeve's powers extended far beyond the superficial realms of divine beauty. She had aspects in common with territory and fertility goddesses, she could run faster than a horse, and was both a warrior queen and commander of armies. Over time, her legend was rewoven by medieval Irish clerics in an effort to historicize her, resulting in her role in the epic *Ulster Cycle*.

Yet Maeve alone is not the only precedent for the Maeven of the *Mice Templar* series. Tales of women warriors have graced both myth and history through the ages.

"My men have become women, and my women men." - Xerxes
The Histories of Herodotus
Book VIII: Urania

Immortalized by Herodotus, the aptly named Artemisia I of Caria, named for Artemis, is an historical example of a warrior woman. Artemisia came to power over Halicarnassus when her husband, a vassal of Xerxes, died. Persia, which ruled Ionia at the time, fared poorly against the Greeks during the Battle of Salamis in 480 BC. Artemisia personally commanded five ships for Xerxes, and her prowess against an enemy trireme earned her Xerxes' admiration. However, some facts of the story are far less romantic: Artemisia had accidentally sunk a little known ally trireme in an effort to evade capture, but by good fortune this fact failed to find Xerxes' ears!

While there are many examples of warrior women in myth, there are far fewer historical instances of female warriors among a nearly exclusively male dominion. Names such as Queen Boudica and Jeanne d'Arc have survived though history to give us a glimpse of remarkable women wielding the tools of death. In Greek myth, the Arcadian princess Atalanta joins the hunt for the Calydonian Boar. Despite the objections of the men at her participation, she is the first among them to draw blood from the boar with her spear.

Amazons and Shieldmaidens

The women of ancient Sparta offer one of the few examples of a culture where women were not only trained in athletics, better nourished and more independent than the women of the rival Greek city-states, but they were also responsible for defending their husbands' property from invaders. Artemis was the patron goddess of Sparta, and with her bow and arrow has come to symbolize the popular perception of the Spartan warrior woman.

The most well-known and also the most mysterious warrior women of myth and legend

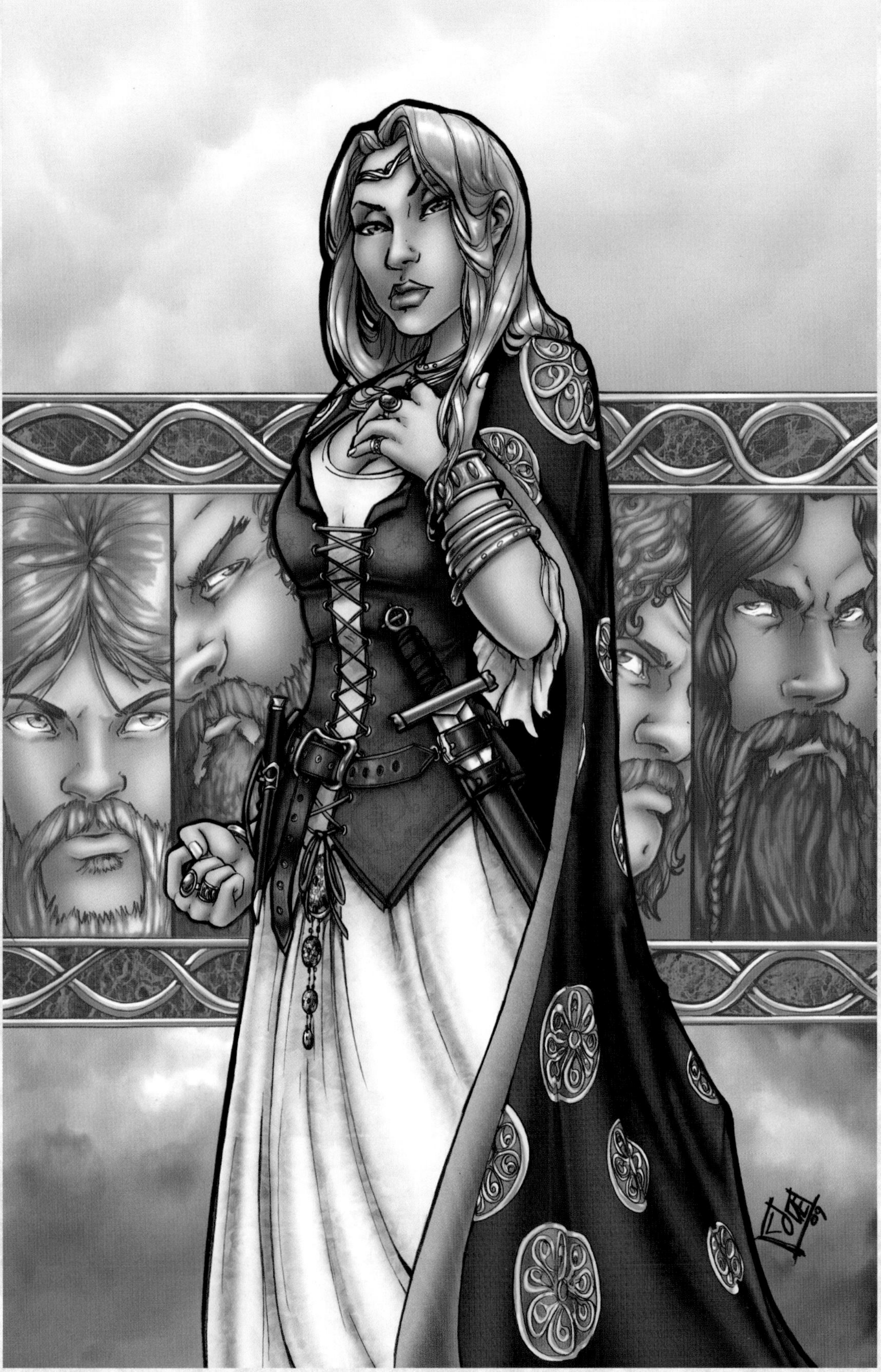

Queen Medb
by Comfort Love
UniquesComic.com

are the Amazons. The historians Plutarch and Herodotus of ancient Greece were divided on whether the Amazons ever actually existed. These women "from the fierce and untamed northlands" were feared by the Greeks. Thought to inhabit the Black Sea region north of Anatolia, the Amazons threatened Attica and the city of Athens. Raised from birth to be warriors, legend has it that the right breast of each woman was seared during adolescence, enhancing their use of a bow and contributing to the fierce reputation and extreme pragmatism of these warriors. Even so, they were not invincible. During the Twelve Labors of Hercules, the Greek hero not only defeated the Amazon queen Hippolyta, taking her divine girdle, but effectively dispersed her tribe.

Freydis, daughter of Erik the Red, accompanied her brother Leif Erikson on his expedition to Vinland. While pregnant, she insisted on accompanying the men against the natives. Caught while alone, she warded off an attack, bare-breasted and with sword in hand. Freydis later returned to Vinland on her own expedition, having her men murder her allies so as not to share the spoils, and personally killing the five women in the group to protect her dark secret upon her return to Greenland.

The reality is that women did indeed travel with the men on the high seas, and, according to the Byzantine victors at the battle of Kiev, armed female warriors were found among the dead Viking attackers. Three hundred female soldiers fought in the legendary Battle of Brâvalla, three of whom are heroes of the tale. These shieldmaidens, as they are known in myth and folklore, were those women in Scandinavian and Germanic society who were free of family obligation and had chosen a warrior's life.

The most common story of the warrior woman across cultures is that of an atypical individual disguising herself as a man in order to live by the sword. The Hervarar saga tells of a woman named Hervor who grew up a slave, but disguised herself as a man and took the name Hjorvard so that she could live a warrior's life. Her granddaughter shared her name and was a shieldmaiden of the Goths, and commander of a fort facing the Hun invasion. J.R.R. Tolkien drew from Norse culture and mythology when shaping his world of Middle-Earth, in which Eowyn, niece of King Theoden, became a shieldmaiden of Rohan, facing an Orcish horde and defying the Lord of the Nazgûl.

The Maeven

Established during the Third Great Season of the world's history, the Maeven emerged as a sister order of the Templar. During this Golden Age of peace, the Maeven were granted the blessing of the Templar and permitted to function independently. However, following the division of the Templar during the civil war fought on the Fields of Ruin, Ronan and Lochloraine established a training camp for the outcast mice, overseeing the training of new generations of Templar and Maeven side by side.

Like the Amazonian archers of Artemis, and the liberties and athleticism of the women of Sparta, the Maeven archers are the female counterparts of the Templar Knights in *The Mice Templar*. Lochloraine, leader and mentor of the Maeven, shares a parallel with the legendary Pictish warrior woman Scathach from the *Ulster Cycle*, who taught martial arts at her residence Dun Scaith (Fort of Shadows). Although she teaches the hero Cuchulain, Maeve's enemy, many feats of arms at her school, she is not wholly unique. Scathach's rival, Aife —yet another free-willed

warrior woman—challenges Cuchulain to a duel.

Unlike the Templar, the Maeven rely far more on nimble light weight armor, stealth, and long range attack. Young are trained to perfection in the use of the bow and arrow, yet the temperament of wisdom that a warrior needs to truly become a master can only be learned through the trial of battle itself. This separates Lochloraine from young protégés such as Aquila, whose zeal has yet to be tempered by the burden of leadership. In this way, Lochloraine is the epitome of that which the Maeven Archer aspires to be. She is the equal of her male counterparts, loyal to Wotan and yet governed by her own will. Queen Maeve, with her red cloak and, by some accounts, flaming spear, is not only the inspiration for the Maeven in name, but the amalgamation of the warrior woman's very spirit. ✺

Sources:

James MacKillop, A Dictionary of Celtic Mythology, Oxford University Press, 1998
ISBN 0-19-280120-1

Scott Littleton, ed., Mythology: The Illustrated Anthology of World Myth and Storytelling, Duncan Baird, 2002
ISBN 1-904292-01-1

Jessica Amanda Salmonson, The Encyclopedia of Amazons, Paragon House, 1991
ISBN1-55778-420-5

The Eighth Book of Histories, Called Urania
www.bostonleadershipbuilders.com/herodotus/book08.htm

Shieldmaiden
http://en.wikipedia.org/wiki/Shieldmaiden

THE FATES

Like much of Greek myth, the Fates are credited with various origins, owing to the sundry storytellers who have spun their tales over the centuries. Some claim they are the daughters of Zeus and the Titaness Themis, whereas others say they are primordial beings who preceded the Olympians. Whatever the case, their role finds parallels in the ancient mythologies of many cultures, in which they serve as analogy for the eternal human questions of destiny versus free will.

Most commonly depicted as three female deities, the Fates, also known as the Moirae, are traditionally regarded as the agents of destiny. Their dominion is the fate of all mortals, symbolized by the thread of life.

The Moirae were three sisters, Clotho, Lachesis and Atropos, who could be portrayed as remorseless old hags or as beautiful young maidens. Even the gods held them in reverence for their all-seeing wisdom. In Aeschylus' *Prometheus Bound*, the titular Titan reveals that even Zeus must bow to the Fates and the Furies. No one is above their power or influence.

These sometimes malevolent seers are perhaps the best known of the triune goddesses in the Western world and are most closely paralleled with the Norns of Norse mythology. In either tradition, the prophetesses share the duty of appearing before a newborn and laying down its future. It is this aspect that generates one of the most interesting questions prompted by their very concept: Do we humble mortals merely follow a script for our lives, or can we in fact write our own?

Bradán Feasa and the Calling of the Fish Gods.

The question of free will versus pre-ordained destiny underscores the first story arc of *The Mice Templar* and beyond. Swallowed by Bradán Feasa, the Salmon of Knowledge, Karic receives the first of several visions of what lies ahead on his journey. When Karic encounters the Fish gods in the cavern under the lake, the three divine fish, like the Fates, ordain the would-be hero with his calling. There, for the first time, Karic is given a vision that far exceeds his own childhood aspirations of greatness:

"Lord Wotan is above all gods… and he declares you Liberator of the Dark Lands. As Kuhl-En of old… so will you now be."

Such prophecies prove useful tools for the politically motivated, who filter the meaning to their own dark ends. Pilot was able to lead Karic astray even as Wotan sent the young mouse dreams and visions of his ancestor, the legendary Kuhl-En who united his people and brought peace and order to the lands. Kuhl-En, now disregarded and even discredited by many as the stuff of mere legend filled with supernatural impossibilities, was left as a matter of faith for Karic to maintain against Pilot's cynicism and manipulation.

Karic's belief in the prophecy gains strength, however, when he faces the ant hordes of The Many in the Barren Lands. He recalls the voices of the Fish gods, who had bestowed upon him a pouch containing "all the waters of the world," and here Karic unleashes from it a mighty torrent that sweeps away the enemy. This miracle not only affirms Karic's belief that "the gods are never wrong," but it reveals the youngster to Pilot as a genuine opportunity for his own redemption and rise to power. He takes

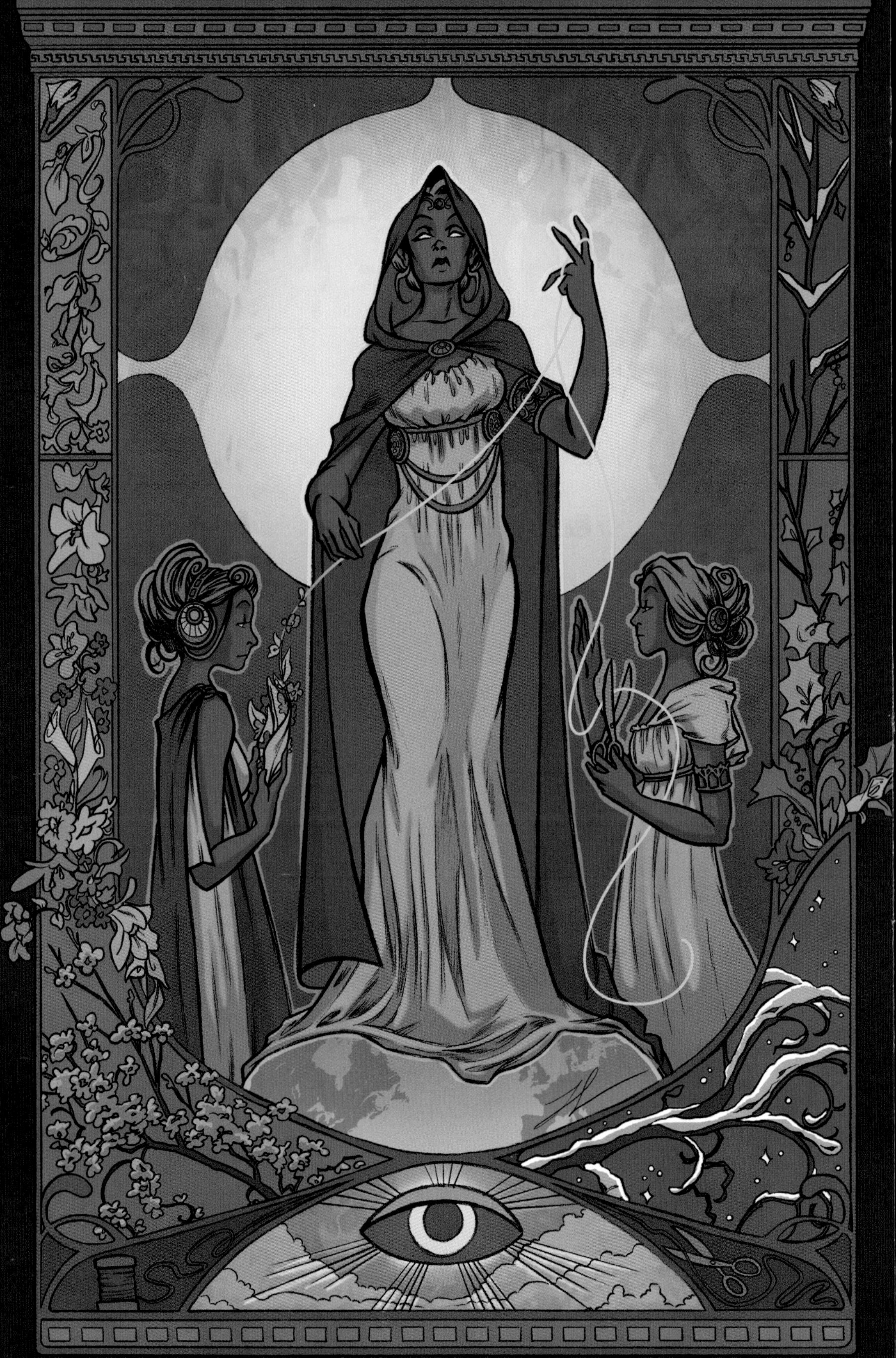

The Fates

Karic to Black Anaius, the druid-witch of Kildre Hill, who offers Pilot confirmation of Karic's ordained fate as the chosen one. But for Pilot, the prophecy is merely another thing to be twisted and manipulated, just as Karic is to him little more than a puppet of his own agenda.

Of Prophecy...

Karic's fate hangs in the balance, nothing but a playing piece to those vying for power. Once Black Anaius is alerted to Karic's calling, the druid-witch warns Donas the Nathair of the coming prophecy:

"Wotan stirs from his slumber... another pawn has been chosen at last... and a weak vessel is he, my lord..."

Having seized power during the Templar civil war, King Icarus now rules in the mouse capital of Dealrach Ard-Vale, collaborating with both rats and weasels, old enemies of mice, for reasons known only to himself. Encouraged by the dark and perversely attained prophecies of the Rat Druids, Icarus has come to believe his fate can be nothing less than apotheosis. After all, he is the bearer of the ancient symbol of sovereignty, known as the Mark of Kuhl-En. This sword, fashioned from the talon of the Great Death Owl of legend, grants Icarus the unquestioned and incontrovertible right to rule, and fuels his egomania. Surely he is destined for divinity himself!

Yet not all prophecies are truths, as Karic discovers. Caught between the feud of Pilot and Cassius, Karic is impaled whilst trying to aid his false mentor. As Karic's life teeters on the precipice, Wotan himself appears to Karic in a vision. He takes the shape of the Great Owl with whom the legendary Kuhl-En fought atop the mountain peak of Armagh, and shows Karic the division that has fallen upon the race of

Mice. When Karic sees his captive family, Wotan offers to save them but asks what Karic will offer in exchange. The small mouse simply and without hesitation responds: "Everything." In this scene, Karic once again faces the destiny that others would lay out for him, but this time it is his choice alone.

...And Destiny

Karic recovers from his wound, only to learn that Pilot had been manipulating the prophecy for his own selfish ends. It is at this point that Karic succumbs to his doubts as he realizes the lies of Pilot and now questions his own self-belief. High Priest Micah, leader of the Templar Priests, had also once received a prophecy from Wotan "that a deceiver shall bring forth a truth which he himself does not truly believe." Witnessing this very thing taking place before him in the Great Ash Tree, Micah realizes the hope that Karic can bring to his people. Acting upon his own judgment, Micah determines to play his part in the fate of the humble mouse by knighting him.

This moment is significant to the question of destiny versus free will as Karic is given a choice, not only to trust in his faith, but to take responsibility for himself. Micah offers Karic the path of the Templar and the fate declared for him by Wotan. At last, the prophecy of the Fish gods becomes

destiny as Karic chooses of his free will to accept and follow the guidance of Wotan. In so doing, Karic pledges to fight, pulling himself out of the blackness of death, taking stock, at last, of the realities of his divided world, and accepting his responsibility to his family and his people.

The ceremony brings with it another vision which culminates in the miraculous appearance of the Great Death Owl. The voice of Wotan breaks its long silence to the Templar and reveals to them that Karic is his chosen vessel.

In Euripides' tale of Alcestis, Apollo tricks the Fates and saves King Admetus from death. But the prophecies of the Fates cannot be circumvented without a price of equal measure. Queen Alcestis offers her life as an exchange. Apollo is unable to stop Death from taking her, and while he divines the arrival of Heracles who will rescue her from the Underworld, she must first die in her husband's place.

Destiny is often viewed as an immutable sequence of events, preordained by something outside of oneself, yet it can also occur as the result of the willingness of the hero to undertake the necessary choices to make their own way. Karic refuses to be the symbol of anyone but Wotan himself and in essence has, at last, chosen his own fate. ✆

Sources:

Scott Littleton, ed., *Mythology: The Illustrated Anthology of World Myth and Storytelling*, Duncan Baird, 2002
SBN 1-904292-01-1

Ellen Snodgrass, *Greek Classics*, Wiley Publishing Inc, 1998
ISBN 0-8220-0566-2

Petra Press, *Great Heroes of Mythology*, Metro Books, 1997
ISBN 1-56799-433-4

SAMHAIN

The Gaelic festival of Samhain is the origin of many of the customs we associate today with Halloween and All Saints' Day, yet it is a far older tradition, having existed in various forms since the time of the ancient Celts. All Saints' Day was introduced by Pope Boniface IV in the seventh century A.D. to supplant pagan rituals of the dead. Nevertheless, some of these customs found their way into Christian traditions as they were assimilated into Celtic culture, such as the warding off of evil spirits by means of specially carved turnips and pumpkins, used like gargoyles to protect the front door of the family home. The journey from door to door while guising as ghouls and ghosts has developed into an annual tradition in the United States. The enduring popularity of Halloween says much for the influence of this ancient Celtic festival.

Samhain (pronounced *sow-win*) is the Modern Irish spelling for *Samain*, which in Old Irish means "summer's end." It is still celebrated by the Irish and Scottish descendants of the Celtic peoples, marking the first day of the Celtic calendar, similar to the ancient Gauls, who believed a period of dark preceded a period of light, reflecting the transition of winter to summer.

While the seasonal timing of Samhain coincides with the final harvest of the year, the traditions have varied and evolved over the centuries from one Celtic nation to another. But the festival has universally heralded the onset of the darker half of the year, and, as with most harvest festivals, is characterized by celebrations to honor the gods and seek their blessings. Sitting darkly among the most ancient traditions of the Celts are divine fertility rites as well as Roman and Greek reports of human sacrifice.

The Hill of Tara

On October 31st bonfires are lit on the hills of Tlachtga and Tara, initiating a festival of historical and mythological importance. The flames inspire the imaginations of those who observe the Samhain festival in the tradition of their ancestors. In those distant times, the bones of slaughtered cattle were cast upon the flames, giving the origin of the word bonfire: *bone fire*. Family hearths were lit with a flame carried from this blaze to each house, bonding the community and symbolizing the start of a new year.

The night of Samhain is a key date in Irish mythology. Ireland's *Cath Maige Tuireadh* of the Ulster Cycle sees several stories beginning on the night of the Samhain feast. Fertility rites commemorated the Dagda's ritual copulation with the female Irish deity, the Morrigan. The location at the hill of Tara is equally significant. It not only plays a key role in Samhain rituals today, but the hill of Tara is thought to be the site of ancient kingship rituals, where the would-be king shared a cup of ale with the warrior goddess Medb (Queen Maeve), symbolizing his divine right to rule through marriage.

Human Sacrifice!

Sacrifices were made by the Gauls to the god Dis Pater, who rep-

resented death and the cold of winter. Sacrificial victims were drowned in vats for the god Teutates, while Taranis was appeased by the immolation of victims in wooden cages. Today, the symbols of the bonfire with ancient sacrifice can easily blur with witch burnings and the occult, along with the ancient druids and their grisly auguries, divined from the entrails of their victims. These associations began with the writings of Greek and Roman authors who painted a brutal, if propagandist, picture of the ancient Celts and in particular, their elite class, the druids.

Traditionally, Samhain is a time for assuaging evil spirits and communing with lost loved ones. While Samhain has been observed for centuries in Ireland, it derives from similar festivals of the early Celtic peoples that coincided with this important time of year. According to the writings of Diodorus and Strabo, human beings were offered to propitiate the Celtic gods. The sacrifices were placed within giant wicker man cages and set ablaze.

"They devote to death a human being and stab him with a dagger in the region above the diaphragm, and when he has fallen they foretell the future from his fall, and from the convulsions of his limbs and, moreover, from the spurting of the blood, placing their trust in some ancient and long continued observation of these practices."
Diodorus,
Bibliotheca Historica

It is from this dark world that the pagan elements of *The Mice Templar*'s rat druids are drawn. The Celtic druids believed the worlds of the living and the dead were at their closest during the festival of Samhain. For the mouse city of Dealrach Ard-Vale, the festival is the perfect time for the rat druids to invoke the darker spirits of their otherworld

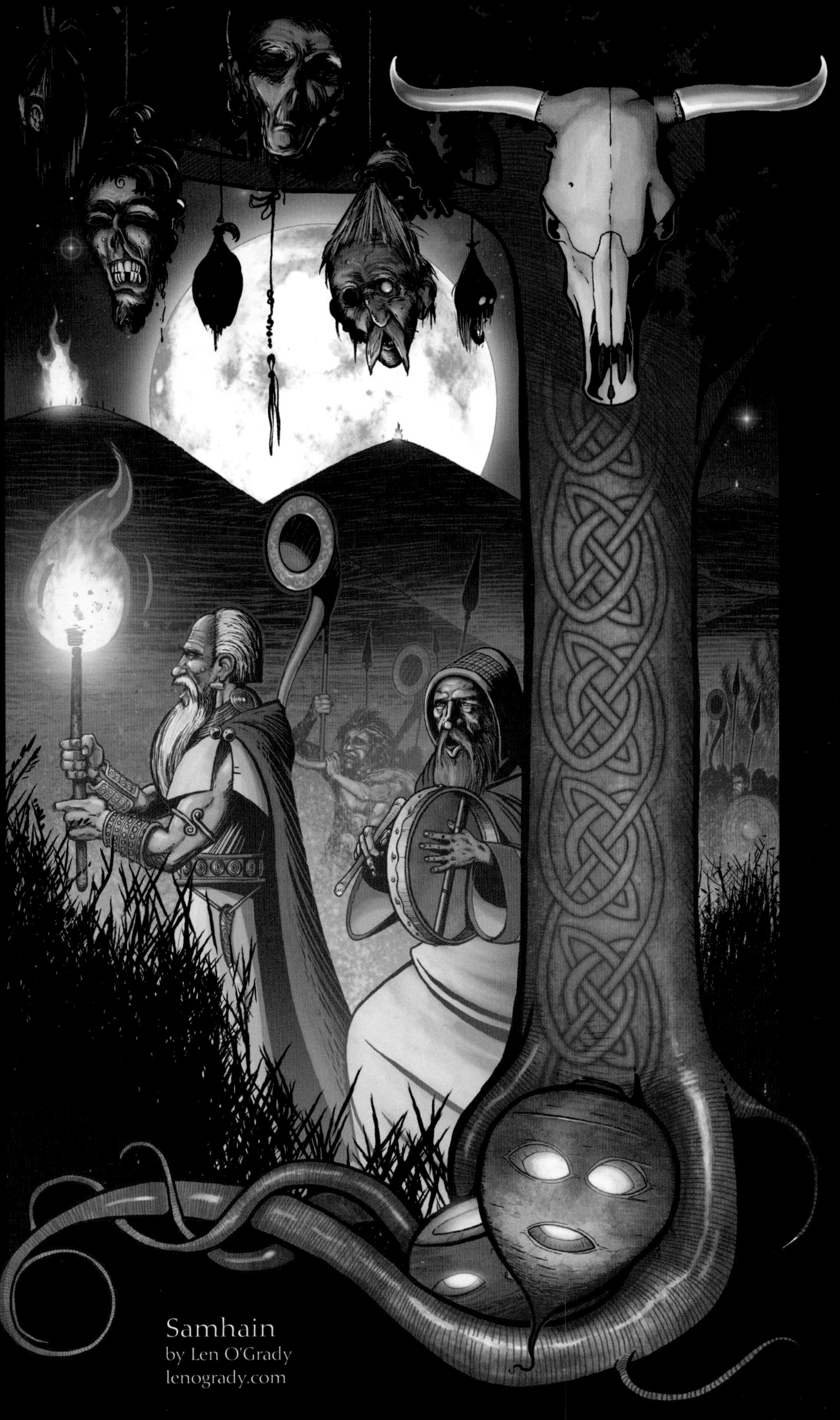
Samhain
by Len O'Grady
lenogrady.com

The Rat Druids

The rats felt spurned by the god Wotan, who had chosen the mice as his emissaries. In their jealousy, the rat druids drew upon the ritual magic from the Lost Days in an attempt to rival Templar power. The conflict resulted in the systematic eradication of their species at the hands of the mice. Besieged within the *Efrafan Forest*, the desperate rats turned to cannibalism and ritual sacrifice, unleashing Diabhul spirits from the Otherworld against the Templar priests. The terrible war ended in a crushing defeat for the rats, leaving the ground upon which they fought blighted with evil. The *Haunted Wood* suggests a proximity to the Otherworld where the dead can manifest in ghostly form and torment the living.

The oppression of the rats and the forbidden Death Magic of their druids loosely parallels the Roman and even some of the later Christian conquests of the Celtic peoples, wherein gods, festivals and holy places were assimilated, with Dis Pater being linked with Pluto and Teutates with Mars. As with any violently oppressed culture, the desire to usurp the mice simmered and seethed in the hearts of the rats. The rats were left with an unyielding animosity that could only be satisfied by the mass extermination of the mice.

The opportunity for revenge came when division among the mice led to the mouse king Icarus aligning himself with the rats and weasels in order to maintain his tyrannical rule over mouse culture. Swayed by the influence of the newly enfranchised rat druids, Icarus allowed the persecution and enslavement of mice from beyond the city walls. The rats dug a great pit in which they placed a snake god whom they propitiated by offerings of mice prisoners. The clandestine influence of the druids grew, in part, thanks to their support of the king and fostering his narcissistic belief that he was destined for godhood. Through their dark arts they promised apotheosis by ritual sacrifice at the annual festival of Samhain...

The Truth about Druids

Books and movies such as *The Wicker Man* have instilled a horrific perception of the rituals of ancient pagans. However, archaeological investigation has produced little evidence of human sacrifice among the Celts.

In their pre-Christian heyday, the druids comprised an entire caste of Celtic society whose superior learning frequently placed them as scholars, advisors, officials and religious leaders. Over time, however, they were gradually denigrated into soothsayers, wizards and witches, and their pantheon diminished into lesser fairies and demons. Druidic teachings were passed down exclusively by oral tradition, in order to keep their knowledge from falling into the wrong hands. Unfortunately, this restriction has left historians with little information from the Celts themselves.

It is important to distinguish the Samhain of the Middle Ages from the mysterious practices and legends associated with primeval Celtic myth and traditions. Halloween and All Saints' Day are almost wholly rituals of the dead, whereas to the Celtic world, Samhain is equally concerned with the harvest and fertility. Samhain and many of its customs and aesthetics have been adopted by modern day spiritualists, neo-pagans, neo-druids and wiccans. For them, it was and continues to be a time of merriment, celebration and promise for the new year.

Sources:

James MacKillop, *A Dictionary of Celtic Mythology*, Oxford University Press, 1998
ISBN 0-19-280120-1

Peter Berresford Ellis, *A Brief History of the Druids*, Running Press, 2002
ISBN 978-0-7867-0987-8

Rick Branch, *Samhain: History of Halloween*
www.watchman.org/occult/samhain.htm

The Geography of Strabo, Book IV, Chapter 4.
http:// penelope.uchicago.edu/Thayer/E/
Roman/Texts/Strabo/4D*.html

Scott Littleton, ed., *Mythology: The Illustrated Anthology of World Myth and Storytelling*, Duncan Baird, 2002
ISBN 1-904292-01-1

FALL OF THE KNIGHTS TEMPLAR

On November 22, 1307, Pope Clement V issued the papal bull *Pastoralis Praeeminentiae*, ordering the mass arrest of all Templar knights throughout Europe. Within five years, the Pope had completely dissolved that era's most powerful Western military order and burned them at the stake. The upheaval that these events inflicted upon medieval society, for whom the Templar had once been a positive force, leaves a dark chapter in medieval history. If this sounds akin to the persecution of the Jedi Knights of the *Star Wars* prequel trilogy, that's because it is. These historical events have become legend, forever capturing the imaginations of historians and storytellers alike.

The Rise

The Seal of the Knights Templar is simple and symbolic: two knights share a horse, each sporting a shield emblazoned with the Red Cross, hearkening to their humble Christian beginnings. Yet as a Christian charity with support from the Roman Catholic Church, the order soon rose above its impoverished origins and developed a monastic financial system that laid the foundation for banking throughout the entire Western world

The avowed role of the Templar was to serve the papacy and see to the protection of pilgrims who risked their lives traveling to the poorly defended Holy Lands that had been captured in the First Crusade. The Order grew rapidly, and with the support of the Church, members were granted tax exemption and freedom of movement through all borders, answerable only to the Pope. Such independence and growing power would prove an obvious challenge in the struggle for political dominance between European monarchs and the papacy. The elite ranks of the Order of the Temple were estimated to be between 15,000-20,000 members, although as few as ten percent of their number are believed to have been actual knights.

While not all Knights Templar were warriors, those who did enter the battlefield comprised the most disciplined units of the Crusades, with an advanced infrastructure of supply and support on the battlefield. Forbidden from retreating in battle unless grossly outnumbered, they earned a fierce and courageous reputation among their foes and allies alike.

The Templar built fortifications and churches across Europe and the Holy Land and bought up countless farms and vineyards, thereby establishing and securing their military and financial power. Pilgrims traveling to the Holy Lands could now deposit their valuables with a Templar house in exchange for a letter of credit. This allowed them to travel without risk of robbery, and then safely withdraw their funds upon reaching their destination. Soon, this system was appropriated by wealthy nobles, who entrusted their fortunes to the Templar, thereby propelling the Order into a position of ever-increasing financial influence. Thus the role of the Templar evolved from protecting pilgrims physically to protecting the vast stores of wealth now being entrusted to them, and monarchs and rival orders alike found their success hard to ignore.

The Betrayal

The most powerful contemporaries of the Knights Templar were the Teutonic Knights and the Knights Hospitaller. The Teutonic Knights founded Prussia, their own monastic state within the Germanic kingdoms,

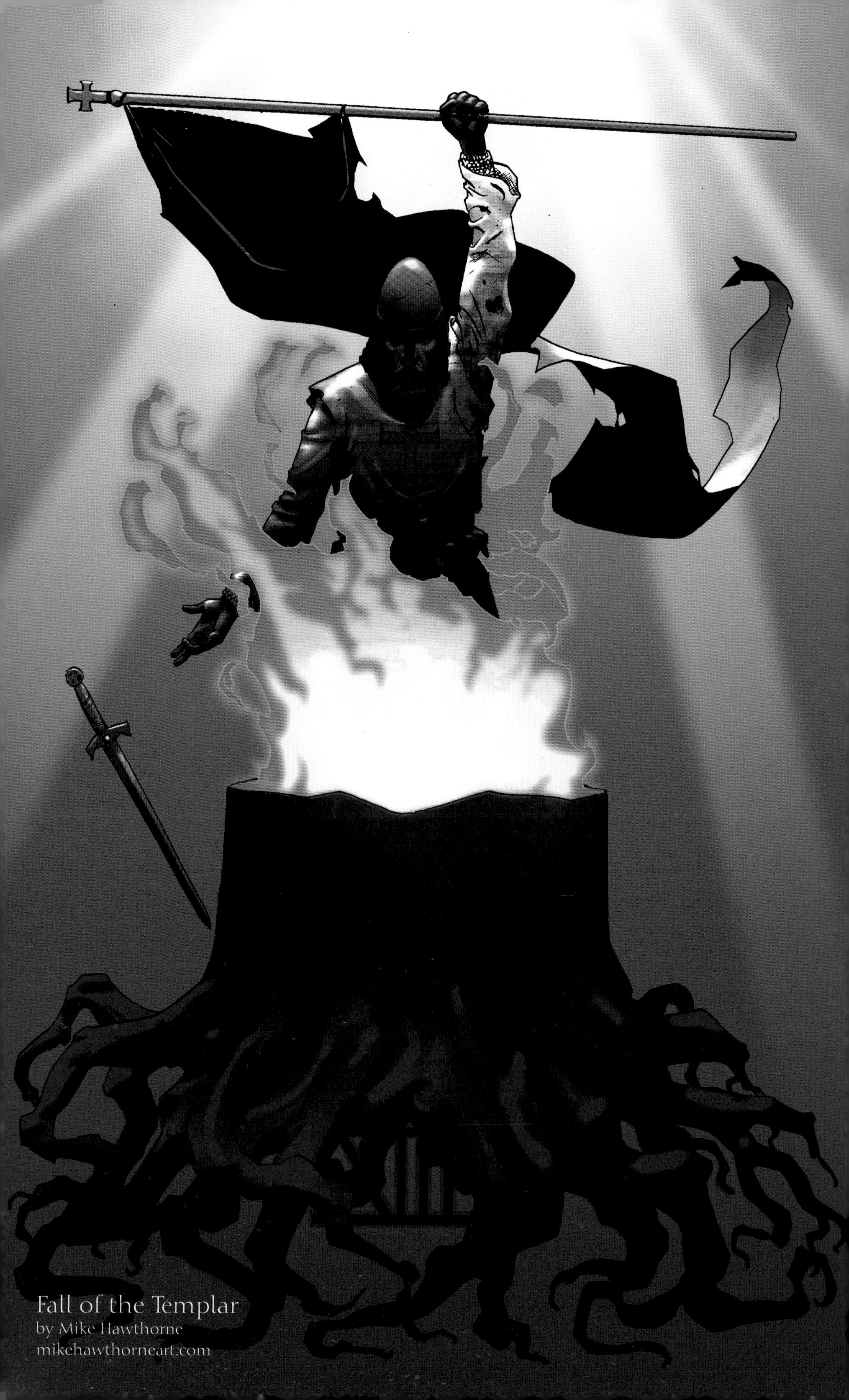
Fall of the Templar
by Mike Hawthorne
mikehawthorneart.com

and possessed their own standing army. This set up a dangerous precedent which King Philip IV of France feared the already powerful Templar would follow.

On Friday, October 13, 1307 AD, King Philip ordered the mass arrest of the Templar, accusing them of various crimes from heresy to financial corruption. In truth, Philip was himself heavily in debt to the Templar and needed loans to help fund his war with the English. Philip raised levies on French clergy and arrested many Jews, seizing their assets in an effort to continue the prosecution of his expansionist monarchy. Pope Clement V had met with Templar Grand Master Jacques de Molay the previous year in an unsuccessful effort to merge the order with the Knights Hospitaller. De Molay seems to have convinced Clement that the rumors concerning the Templar were false. However, when Clement wrote to the king requesting assistance, Philip responded by trumping up the rumors, using them as justification to destroy the power of the Templar and escape his debt. The following month, Clement —threatened by King Philip— bowed to pressure and made a universal order against the Templar. The Christian monarchs of Europe were instructed to arrest the Templar, seize their assets and, at their discretion, subject them to torture. However, despite the Pope's calling for papal hearings for each Templar, an unhappy Philip soon blocked the formality of these trials in 1310. Forced confessions were now all that was needed to have the Templar burned at the stake.

Clement furthermore issued papal bulls at the Council of Vienna in 1312, removing the support of the papacy and formally dissolving the Order of the Knights Templar.
"...it is not without bitterness and sadness of heart that we abolish the aforesaid Order of the Temple, and its constitution, habit and name, by an irrevocable and perpetually valid decree; and we subject it to perpetual prohibition with the approval of the Holy Council, strictly forbidding anyone to presume to enter the said Order in the future, or to receive or wear its habit, or to act as a Templar." *Vox in excelso*, Pope Clement V, 1312

In defiance, De Molay retracted his forced confession and insisted that he be bound at the stake so that he faced the Notre Dame Cathedral with his hands together in prayer. Pope Clement died the following month and King Philip met his death in a hunting accident at the end of the same year.

The Parallels

The Star Wars mythology draws upon the Papal betrayal and special order against the Templar in Emperor Palpatine's Order 66. This pre-programmed command, once activated by Palpatine, turned his clone army on their Jedi commanders and began his great Jedi purge in earnest. Philip IV's initial order to arrest the French Templar fell on Friday 13th, giving rise to the contentious claim that the superstitions associated with that day stem from this historical event. The connection has been further popularized in Dan Brown's novel *The Da Vinci Code*, yet many scholars agree the superstition did in fact exist before its very modern invention in the early 20th century.

It is easy to understand why modern fiction has been inspired by the romantic tragedy inherent in the fall of the Templar, who, at least in their humble beginnings, were a noble and just order who tasked themselves with the protection of the weak, only to be betrayed by the Church that they served. Although it was in fact King Philip IV who pressured and then threatened Clement to support his edict against the Templar, it was the Pope himself who endorsed the sweeping betrayal of the Order across Europe. By means of the notorious Inquisition, thousands of Templar were forced to make false confessions, which were then used to legitimize their violent eradication.
It may not be the best comparison to associate the Inquisitors with Star Wars' Clone troopers, loyal enforcers of the Emperor's will; after all, it was Philip who was the driving manipulative force behind the Pope. Regardless, one could argue that the two most prominent historical figures behind the fall of the Templar inspired the singular evil of Emperor Palpatine.

The Madness of King Icarus

In the Mice Templar, it is King Icarus who takes the role similar to that of Pope Clement V, with the power to order and dissolve the Templar. However, Icarus—the former pacifist leader turned tyrant—not only allows but endorses the persecution of the Templar, perceiving them as a threat to the institution of his own power and absolute authority. Icarus' belief in his destined godhood reflects King Philip IV's belief in the spiritual authority of the monarch, versus the papal supremacy claimed by Pope Clement V's more resolute predecessors. At the same time, this madness of King Icarus has become an exploitable weakness for his inquisitorial rat druids.

For two hundred years, the Knights Templar were the greatest fighting force among the crusaders in the Holy Lands. While Philip IV is primarily responsible for their demise, it may have been inevitable. After losing the Holy Lands to an increasingly organized and fanatical opponent, the Templar fell from favor with the public, losing a large body of their support. With their dissolution, the religious military orders were given a violent warning should they ever entertain the prospect of a breakaway state or challenge a monarch's power. In parallel, the Mice Templar, divided by civil war, were exploited by their perceived corruption and removed as a threat to Icarus' hubris. It seems the Mice Templar, just like their real world counterparts, earned themselves far too many enemies, finally succumbing from within.

Sources:

Malcolm Barber, *The Trial of the Templars*, Cambridge University Press 2003. ISBN 0521457270

George Smart, *The Knights Templar Chronology*, Bloomington: Authorhouse 2005. ISBN 1418498890

Piers Paul Read, *The Templars: The Dramatic History of the Knights Templar, the Most Powerful Military Order of the Crusades*, Macmillan 2000. ISBN 0312266588

Nathaniel Lachenmeyer, *13: The Story of the World's Most Popular Superstition*, Running Press; illustrated edition 2004. ISBN 1568583060

The History of the Knights Templar http://en.wikipedia.org/wiki/History_of_the_Knights_Templar

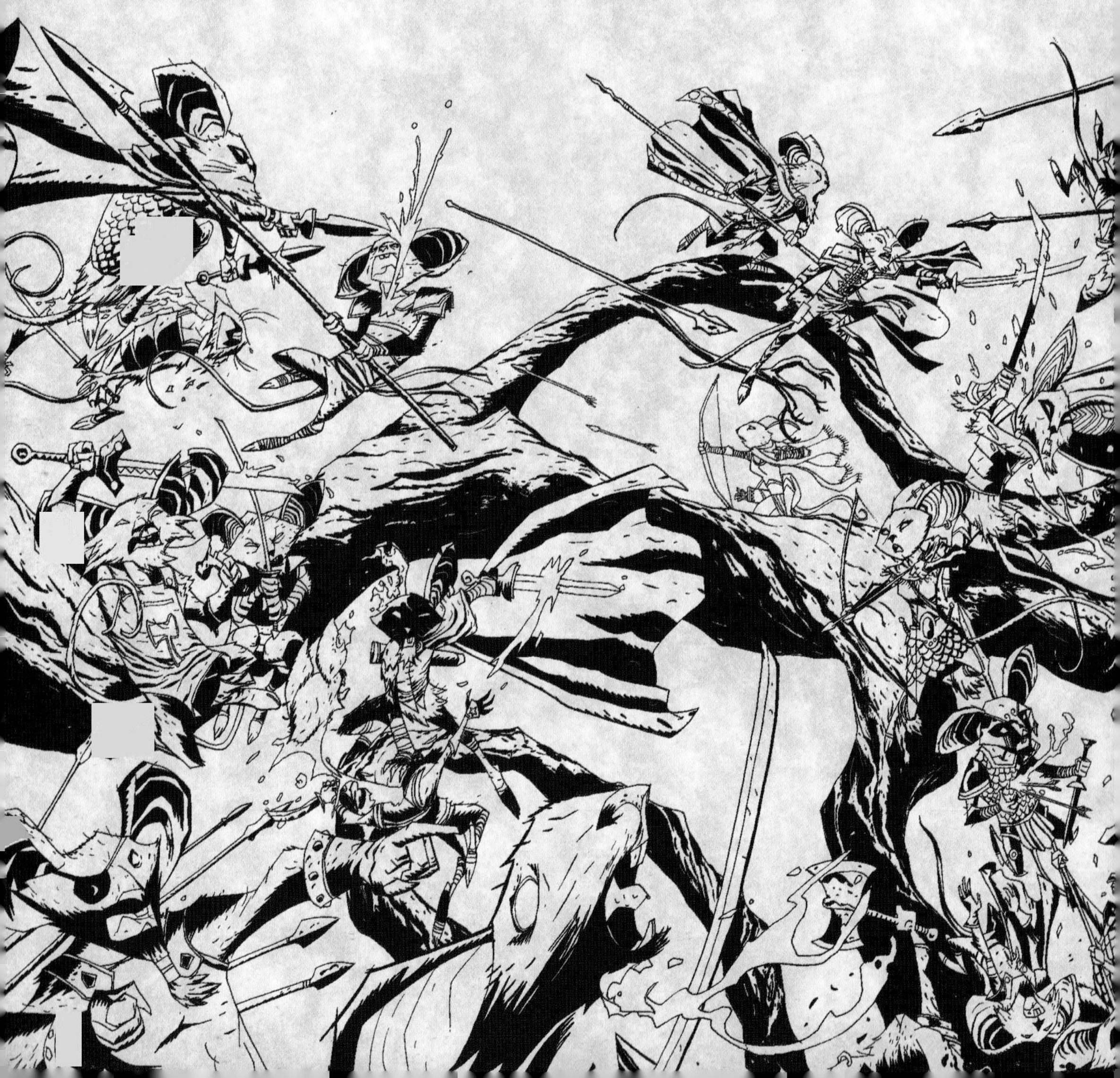

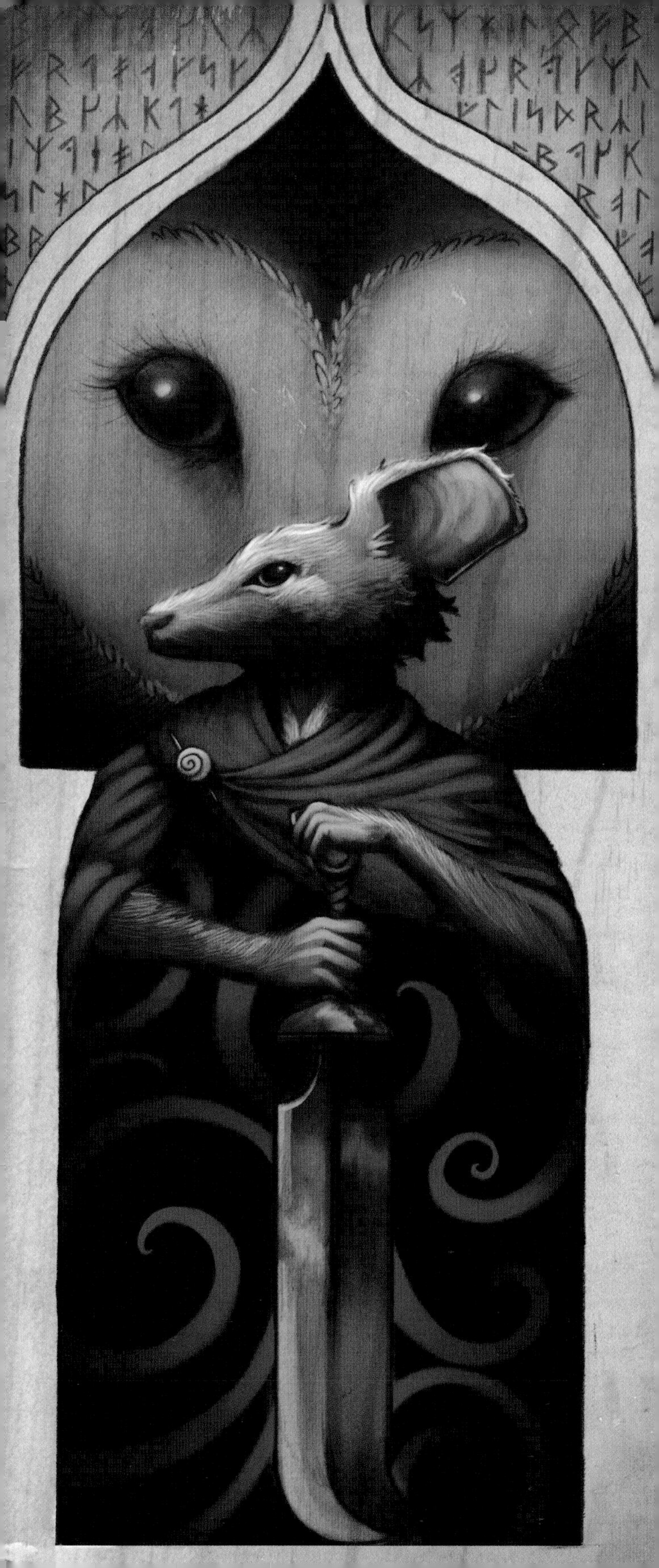

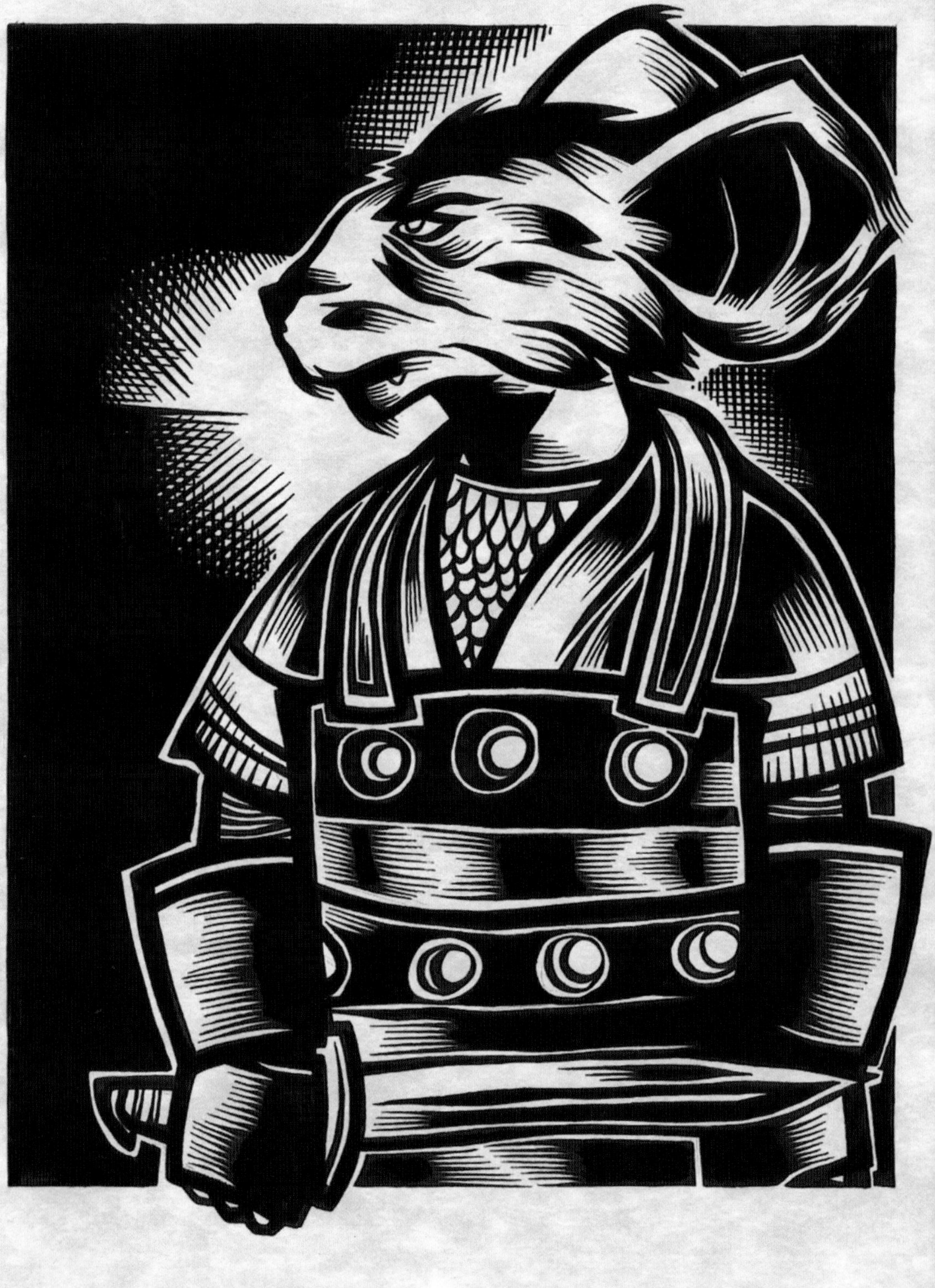

Warrior of the Templar by Brian Quinn

bcqillustrator.blogspot.com

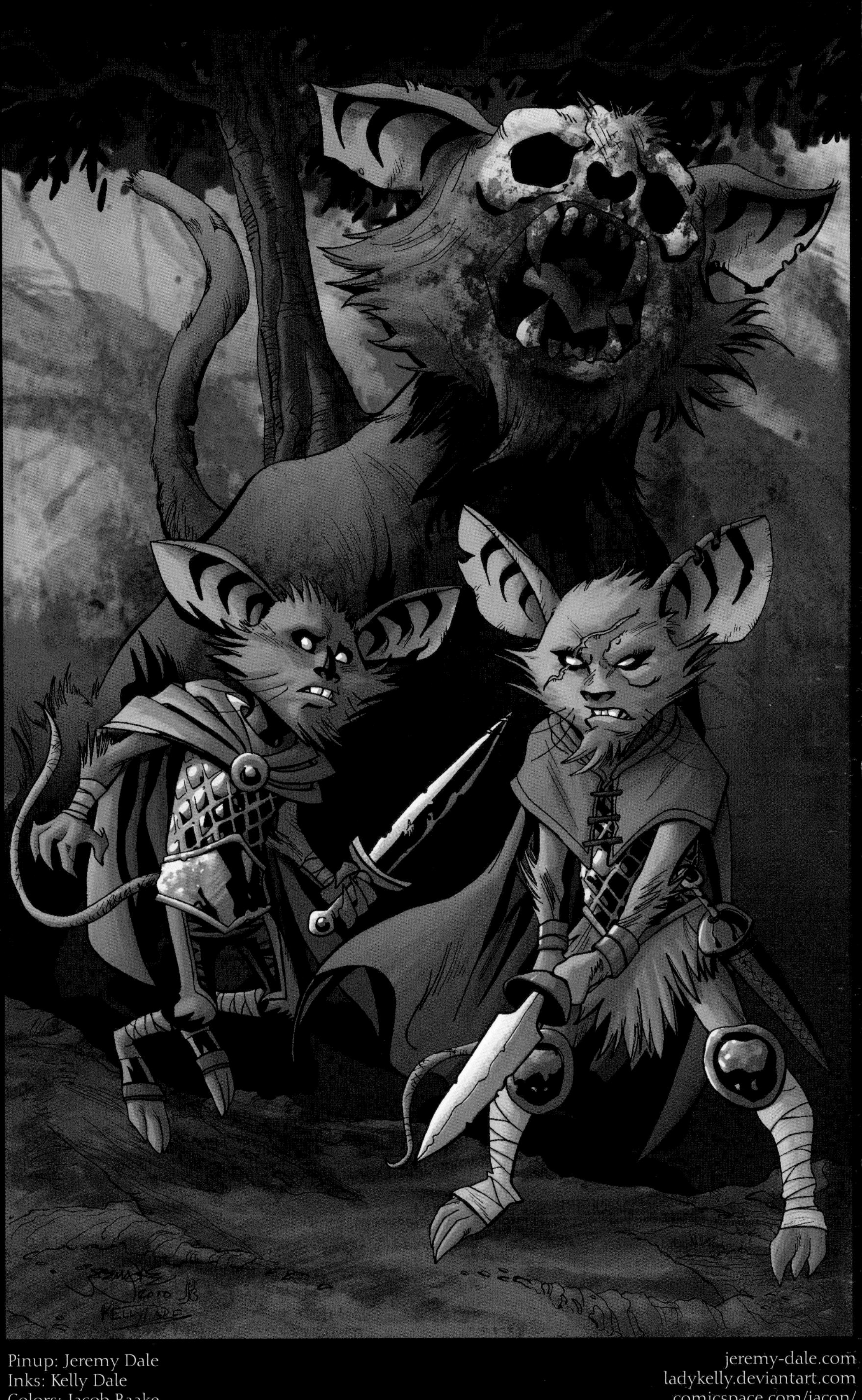

Pinup: Jeremy Dale
Inks: Kelly Dale
Colors: Jacob Baake

jeremy-dale.com
ladykelly.deviantart.com
comicspace.com/jacon/

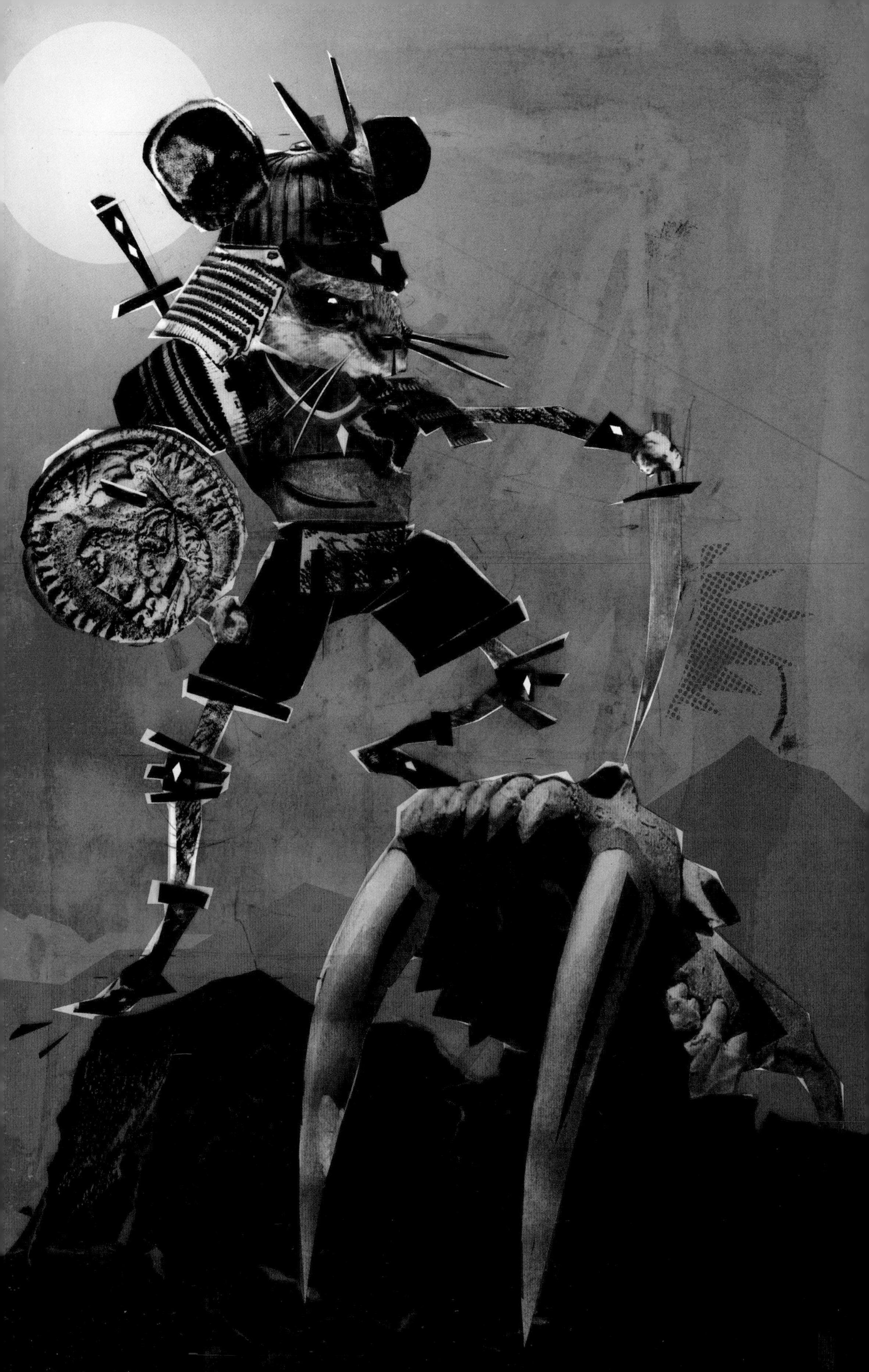

Kody Chamberlain kodychamberlain.com

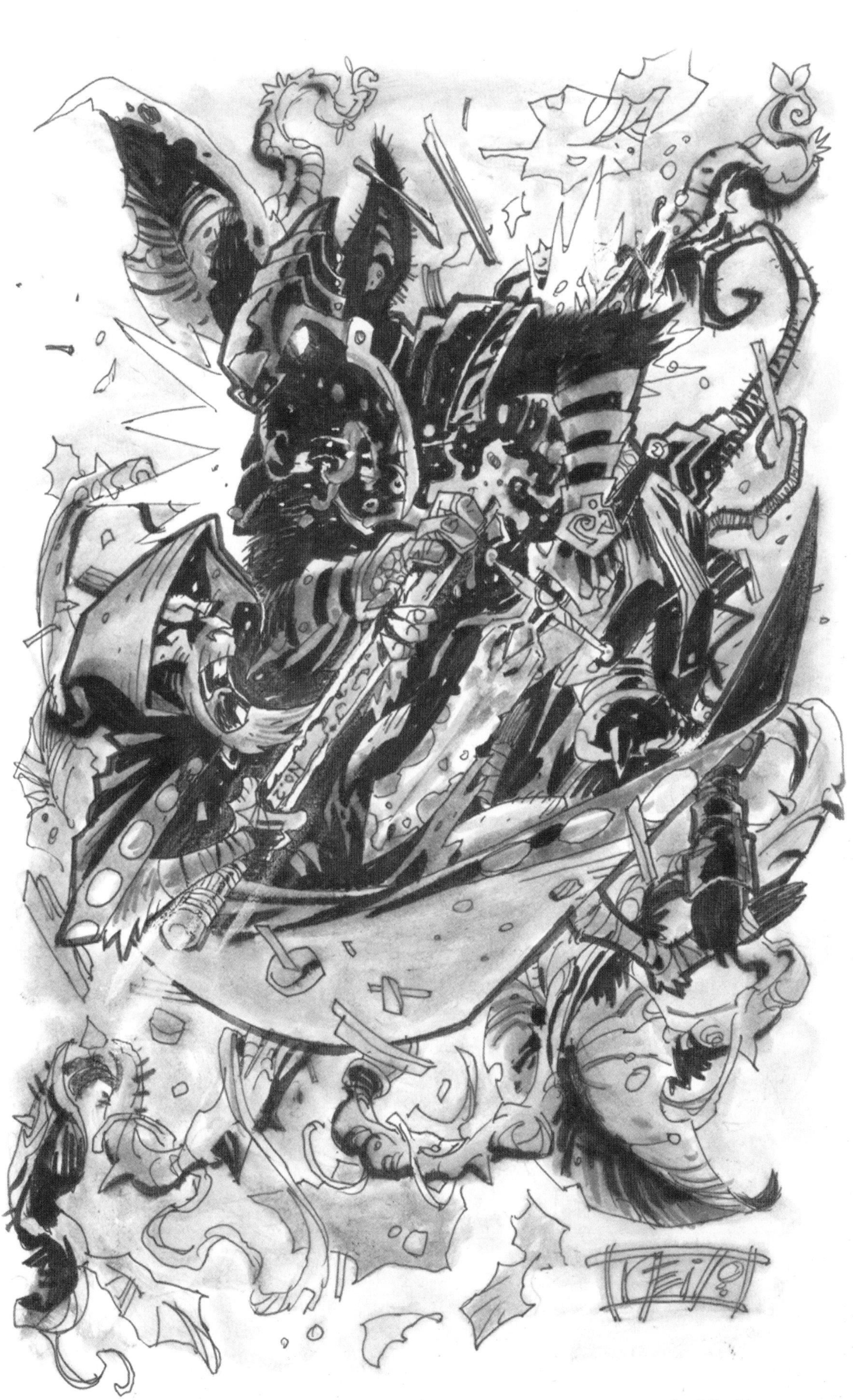

Pilot by Neil Vokes

vokesfolks.blogspot.com

MY TRIBUTE

Artist **Michael Golden** is a comic industry legend.
On the right is his cover for *The Mice Templar: Destiny #9*.
For me, Mr. Golden's participation has been a dream come true.

My discovery of comic adventures began in the late 1970s. My imagination was captured by many titles of the era, yet none more fervently than the Marvel Comics series *The Micronauts*, based upon the classic Hasbro toy line. On a monthly basis, the stirring adventure unfolded, conveyed by the masterful writing of Bill Mantlo and stunning artistry of Michael Golden. Issue after issue, Michael's artwork drew in the unwary and transported them to another world. I was enamored with the art style, as was much of the comic industry and fandom, and soon the interiors and cover artwork of Mr. Golden became collection-worthy...

Batman in *Detective Comics*, *The Micronauts*, *ROM Spaceknight*, *Avengers*, *Doctor Strange*, *Howard the Duck*, *The 'Nam*, *G.I. Joe*, *Jackie Chan Adventures*, *Bucky O'Hare*...and a multitude of others.

A vast number of professionals working in the comic industry today cite the artwork of Michael Golden as one of their primary inspirations.

Shortly after *The Mice Templar* debuted as a series in August '07, I was astounded to discover that Mr. Golden was already a fan. Not long after, I was privileged to call him friend. Thus was set in motion the cover you see here, and the fulfillment of a young man's imaginative dream: that one day his favorite artist would craft a cover for his very own professional comic series.

Enjoy! ✆

Bryan J.L. Glass
June 2010

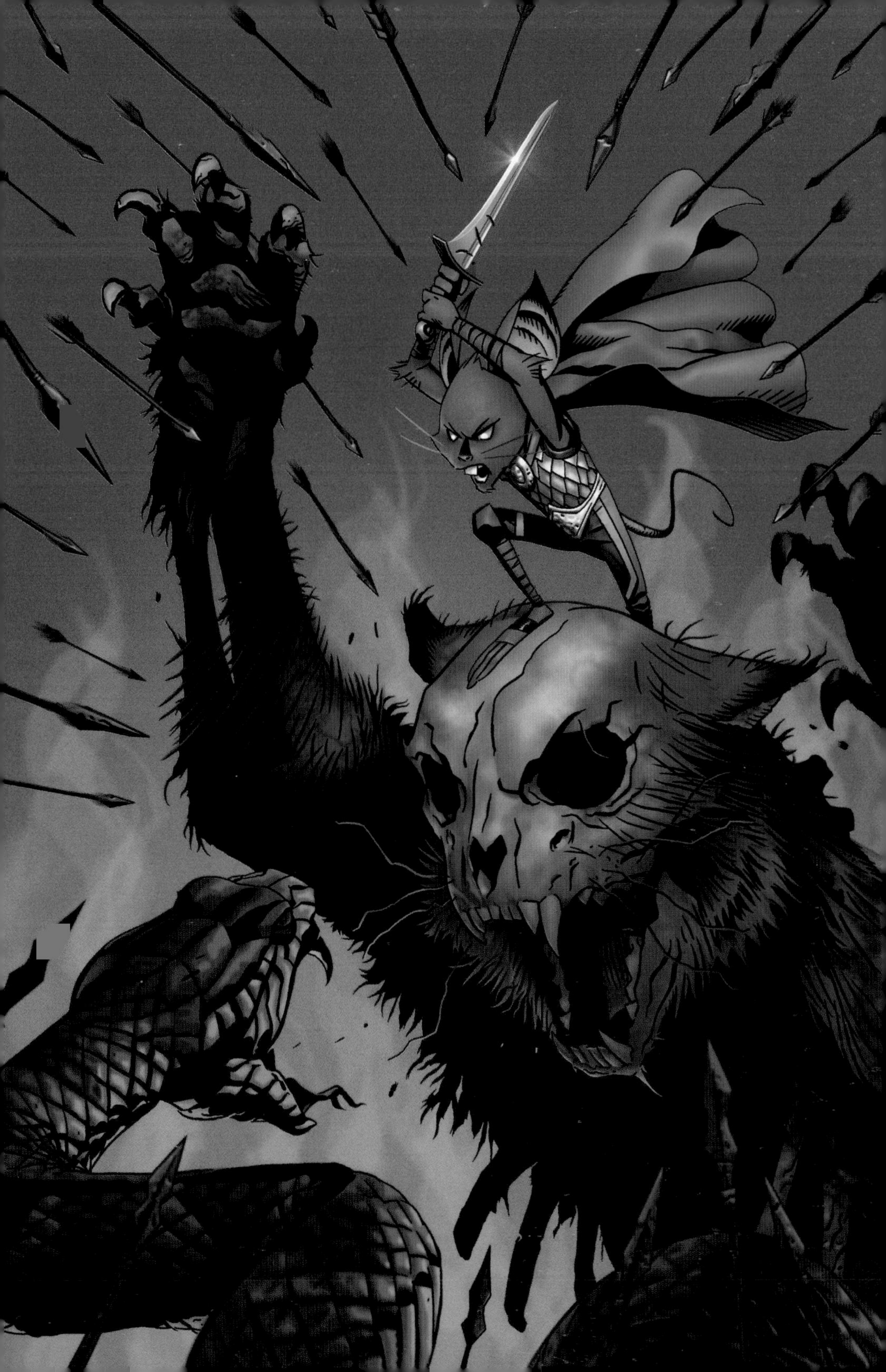

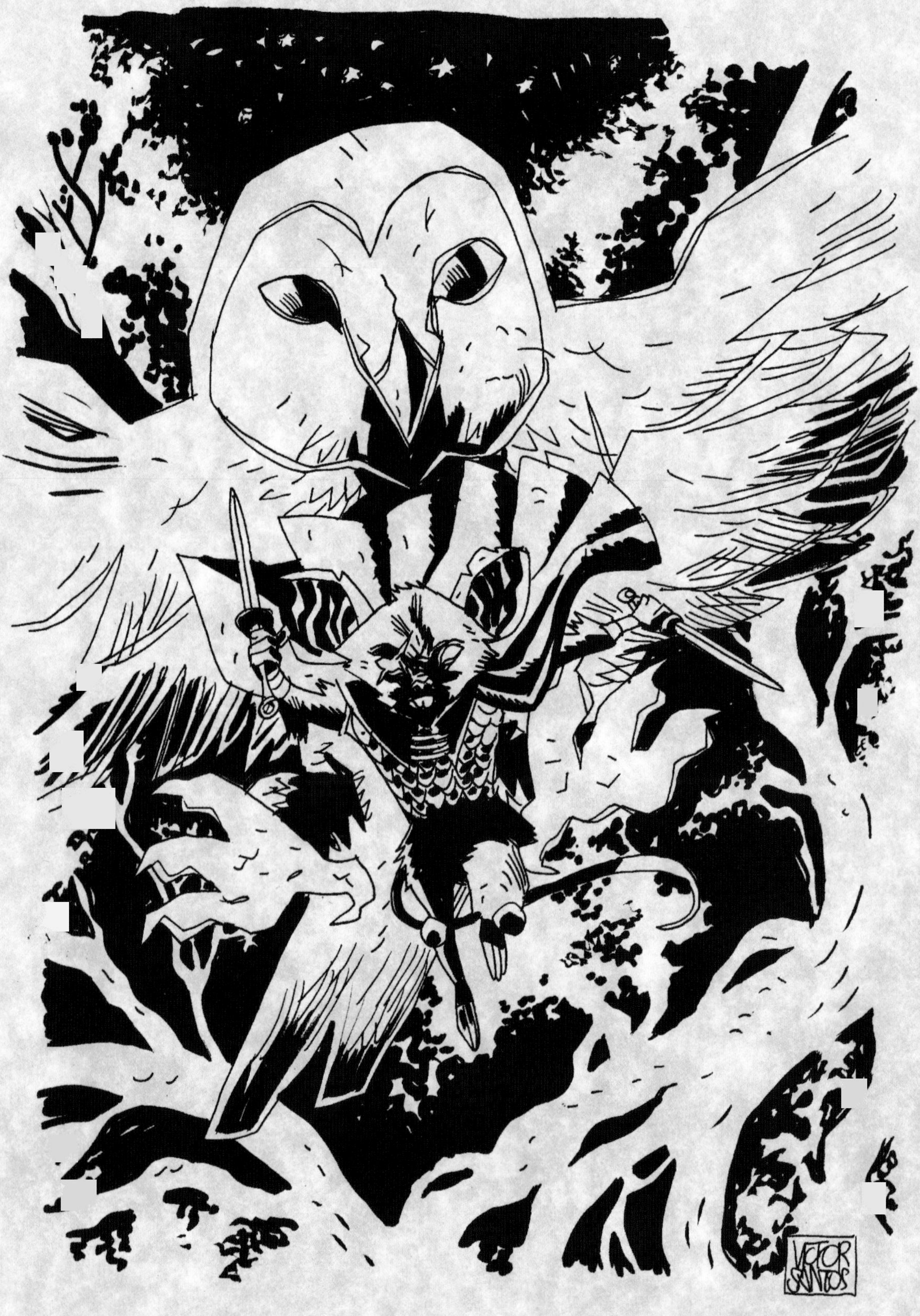
VICTOR SANTOS

CREDITS & ACKNOWLEDGMENTS

THE MICE TEMPLAR
Created by Michael Avon Oeming & Bryan J.L. Glass

PRODUCTION TEAM
Victor Santos • Veronica Gandini • James H. Glass • Judy Glass • Harry Lee

FOREWORD
Ed Brubaker • edbrubaker.com
Illustration: Josh Finney • josh-finney.deviantart.com/

MAP OF THE DARK LANDS
Brian Quinn • bcqillustrator.blogspot.com

A HISTORY OF THE REALM
Bryan J.L. Glass & Anton Kromoff • facebook.com/Conanton

MYTH, LEGENDS & THE MICE TEMPLAR
Rod Hannah • rodhannah.com
    Queen Madb: Comfort Love • UniquesComic.com
    The Fates: Lora Innes • thedreamercomic.com
    Samhain: Len O'Grady • lenogrady.com
    Fall of the Templar: Mike Hawthorne • mikehawthorneart.com

PIN-UP ILLUSTRATIONS
Tim Durning • timdurning.com
Brian Quinn • bcqillustrator.blogspot.com
Neil Volkes • vokesfolks.blogspot.com
Kody Chamberlain • kodychamberlain.com
Jeremy Dale • jeremy-dale.com
Kelly Dale • ladykelly.deviantart.com
Jacob Baaks • comicspace.com/jacom/
Michael Golden • evainkpublishing.com

WEBMASTER
Tim Daniel • hiddenrobot.com

SPECIAL THANKS
Allen Hui • Joe Keatinge • M. Sean McManus
• Marc Nathan • Dr. Phil Ryken • Will Swyer •
Dr. Michael Ward

Image Comics: Branwyn Bigglestone,
Drew Gill, Betsy Gomez, Monica Howard,
Tyler Shainline, Eric Stephenson

For as long as he can remember, Bryan has told stories. Expressing himself in a variety of media, all of his efforts inevitably returned him to the craft of storytelling. While originally pursuing a career in filmmaking, his first work in the comics industry was providing a photo-cover to Bill Willingham's *The Elementals* in 1983. That led to shooting another photo-cover for Matt Wagner's *Mage*, followed by a series of interior photos for Eliot R. Brown's *Punisher Armory* for Marvel Comics.

Exchanging his pursuit of film in the early '90s for the pursuit of writing, Bryan collaborated with his good friend Mike Oeming and created the indie comic series *Spandex Tights*, a humorous take on the superhero genre. When Mike's career soon took him away to work at the "Big Two," Bryan continued his series with artists P. Sky Owens, Bob Dix, Paul Bonanno and G.W. Fisher. Later, Bryan collaborated again with Mike Oeming on their dark humored sci-fi series *Ship of Fools*.

Mike's success on *POWERS* enabled him to reunite with Bryan again for the prose novel *Quixote*, for which he provided hundreds of spot illustrations. Their collaborations continued with *86 Voltz: The Dead Girl*, the comic adaptation of the Raymond E. Feist fantasy classic *Magician Apprentice*, and *The Mice Templar*.

Bryan won the 2009 Harvey Award for "Best New Talent" for his work on *The Mice Templar* (which had been nominated in four categories).

Outside of his comic work, Bryan founded the touring theatre troupe *mere*Breath Drama (mereBreathDrama.blogspot.com), alongside John J. McGready and Elliot Silver, where he served as producer, writer, director, and sometimes actor, in the original stage productions *Asylum*, *Perfect Justice*, *Edifice*, *Skit*, *The Eschaton*, and *The Inner Room*. Here is where he met Judy Hummel, his amazing wife—as well as his first and best editor.

Bryan appeared as the face of Eastern State Penitentiary's annual event, *Terror Behind the Walls*, as featured on the Travel Channel's *America's Scariest Halloween Attractions*. He also achieved anonymous notoriety in 1997 as the infamous "Area 51 Caller" on the *Coast-to-Coast A.M.* radio program—a call that can now be heard on the Tool album *Lateralus:* "Faaip de Oiad."

Bryan's three primary interests are books, movies, and music. J.R.R. Tolkien's *The Lord of the Rings*, Richard Adams's *Watership Down*, Stephen King's *The Shining*, Dan Simmons's *Hyperion*, and F. Paul Wilson's *The Keep* were all major influences in his work. *Casblanca* and *The Fisher King* are his favorite films. The film scores of John Williams, Jerry Goldsmith, Hans Zimmer, and Howard Shore typically accompany him as he writes. And he sings along to Kerry Livgren in each of his musical incarnations: Kansas, A.D., solo, and his original band Proto-Kaw.

Bryan is currently developing several new comic series in multiple genres, and will release *Thor: First Thunder* from Marvel Comics in Fall 2010. ◎

micetemplar@gmail.com
bryanjlglass.blogspot.com

Bryan with his father Harry on Bryan's wedding day,

Mike began his comics career at the age of 14, breaking in as an inker. From inker to penciling/inking to writing, Mike has spread his creative wings in both indie and mainstream comics. Growing up in a small town, Mike found tutelage under Neil Vokes and Adam Hughes, while corresponding with *Nexus* creators Steve Rude and Mike Baron. Dedicated to his craft, Mike was eventually kicked out of high school for skipping class—to stay home and draw—and from his teens into his twenties, he languished in the indie field.

His first big break was as an inker on *Daredevil*, and shortly after as penciler/inker on DC's version of *Judge Dredd*, then *Foot Soldiers* at Dark Horse Comics. During the mid-'90s comics crash, Mike moved back into indie comics, starting on his path of creator-owned comics with *Ship of Fools*, co-created with Bryan J.L. Glass. While drawing *Ship of Fools*, Mike continued with other paying work, such as inking Neil Vokes on *Ninjack* and drawing *Bulletproof Monk*, which later became a John Woo film. Business was slow, so when Mike's first child was born, he got a "real job" working as a security guard—where he drew on the job, of course. This was when Mike experimented with a new, simpler style of drawing, and began developing several projects, including *The Mice Templar*, *Hammer of the Gods*, *Quixote*, and what would become *POWERS* with Brian Michael Bendis, whom Mike had met several years earlier.

POWERS became the dream project Mike and Brian had worked so hard for—a creator-owned project they could live on. *POWERS* has been nominated for a Harvey Award and won an Eisner Award, and Mike himself was nominated for an Eisner for his work on the book. With *POWERS* ongoing, Mike has since tackled several other projects, including *Hammer of the Gods*, *Bastard Samurai*, *Bluntman and Chronic*, *Parliament of Justice*, *Hellboy*, *Catwoman*, *86 Voltz: The Dead Girl*, *The Goon*, *Quixote*, *Blood River*, *Six*, *What If?*, *Magician Apprentice* (with Bryan J.L. Glass) *The Cross Bronx*, *The Darkness*, *The Spirit* and *Red Sonja*. His writing stint on the final run of the original *Thor* as well as on *Thor: Blood Oath* has been widely acclaimed. *Beta Ray Bill* and *Ares* are amongst his other Marvel Comics writing credits.

Currently he is busy with *POWERS*, *The Mice Templar*, *God Complex* and the upcoming *Rapture* trade paperback collection with creator Taki Soma...even as you read this. ❧

michaeloeming.com

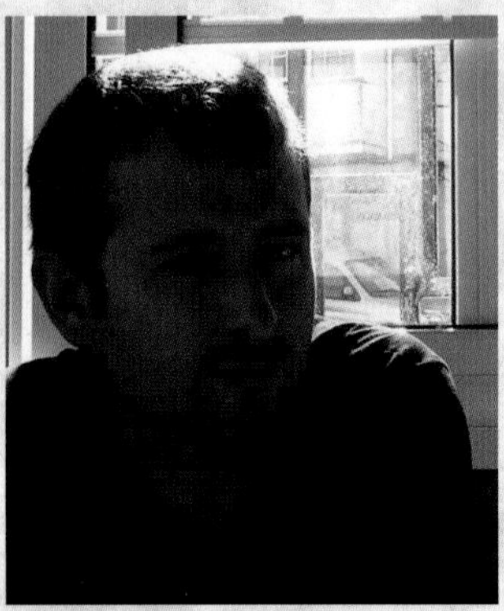

VICTOR SANTOS

Born in Valencia in 1977, Victor has written and illustrated a variety of comics in Spain and France, including *Los Reyes Elfos*, *Pulp Heroes* and *Young Ronins*. In recent years he has begun his American adventures with *Demon Cleaner* and *Zombee*, written by Miles Gunter, and *Filthy Rich*, written by Brian Azzarello, one of the first titles of DC Vertigo's new crime line. He lives in Bilbao, Spain.

victorsantoscomics.blogspot.com.

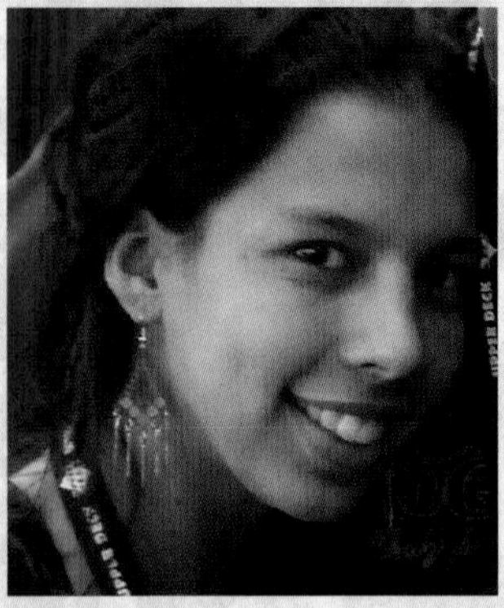

VERONICA GANDINI

A native of Buenos Aires, Argentina, Vero first started coloring when her boyfriend, Leo Freites, a penciller, inker and sculptor, asked her to try coloring one of his drawings. She had been studying architecture for two years by then, but loved this experience of coloring so much that she changed her major to Graphic Design. In 2005, she and Freites self-published *Ñorairo*, their first comic, in Argentina. She subsequently worked for Ape Entertainment, Atlantis Studios, Silent Devil Productions and BOOM! Studios on several comic series and graphic albums. Following her work on Image's *The Mice Templar*, she is now also working for Marvel Comics. Vero loves her work and looks forward to continuing to meet more amazing people like everyone she has had the pleasure of working with so far, including those on the *Mice Templar* team.

verogandini.blogspot.com.

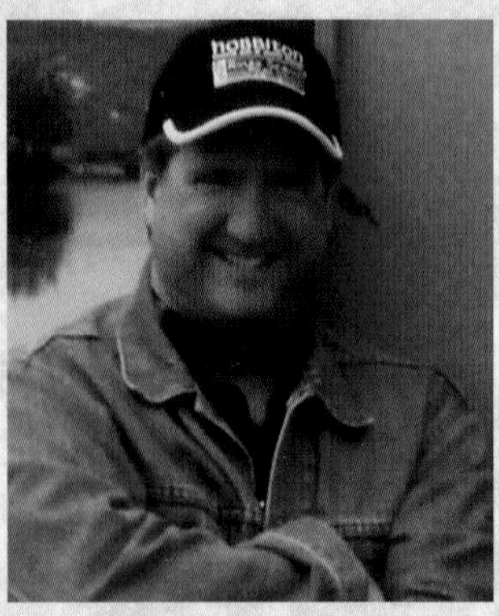

JAMES H. GLASS

Despite his relationship to the author, there is absolutely no nepotism whatsoever responsible for securing Jim's distinguished position as *The Mice Templar* letterer. He has crafted a distinct voice for each race represented through his discerning use of font styles. Jim shares his love of great stories—fantasy, sci-fi, and sweeping historic narrative—with his brother Bryan, and is proud to be associated with the outstanding creative team responsible for this book.

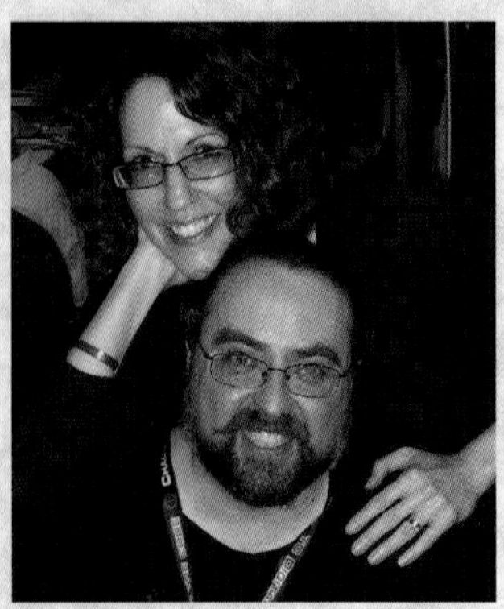

JUDY GLASS

Judy has always loved good stories, and from an early age aspired to write her own. While that hasn't yet materialized formally, she has nevertheless had a lifelong enjoyment and profound appreciation for the craft of writing and the art of a well-turned phrase, and has tended to gravitate to jobs and other venues that enable her to use these skills. As luck would have it, she met and married Bryan Glass, who has no lack of stories to tell and who proved a quick study on a few grammatical basics to better communicate the brilliant creative universes in his mind. When not exercising her editing skills, Judy enjoys yoga and Pilates, as well as healthy but yummy cooking. Judy is privileged to be part of the team producing *The Mice Templar*.

ROD HANNAH

Born in the UK and raised in New Zealand, Rod now writes articles for UK-based animation magazine *Cereal:Geek* from his home in Maryland, U.S.A. He has written his own comic, *Sovena Red*, and is the co-creator of the *Star Wars* parody webcomic Blue Milk Special (bluemilkspecial.com) with his illustrator wife Leanne Hannah. In between working on new writing projects, including children's books, Rod holds down a day job in marketing and design to pay the bills, supporting his hobby and first love of storytelling.
rodhannah.com

HARRY LEE

Crossing the snow-covered passages of the Alps is no small feat in any weather. But Harry Lee, with the aide of his personally trained pack of pacaderms, will go to any lengths to wrestle himself some genuine Italian pasta and sausage… Rome or bust!

TIM DANIEL

Born in Philly, raised in Northern California, Tim discovered comics at about the time Jean Grey was sacrificing herself on a hidden moon base and saving humanity. In the process, she saved Tim too, opening the door to a lifelong love affair with comics. After earning a BA in English from Southern Oregon University in 1997, Tim fell in love with Erin, now his wife of 11 years, had a daughter (Elle), and has since gotten older but has never grown up. Tim has written for Image Comics' *Popgun Anthology* Vol. 2, the *POWERS Encyclopedia*, and his design work can be seen on covers of books such as *Sky Pirates of Neo Terra, Existence 2.0, Forgetless, God Complex, Shuddertown* and more!
hiddenrobot.com

BY BRYAN J.L. GLASS

The Mice Templar
    The Prophecy
Magician Apprentice
    Volumes 1 & 2
Riftwar
    Comic adaptation of the
    Raymond E. Feist novel

86 Volts: The Dead Girl
Quixote: A Novel
Ship of Fools
    Dante's Compass
    Death & Taxes

BY MICHAEL AVON OEMING

Powers
    Who Killed Retro Girl
    Roleplay
    Little Deaths
    Supergroup
    Anarchy
    Sellouts
    Forever
    Legends
    Psychotic
    Cosmic
    Secret Identity
    The 25 Coolest Dead Superheroes
    of All Time
    Definitive Hardcover Collection
    Volumes 1-3
Rapture
The Mice Templar
    The Prophecy
Spider-Man/Red Sonja
Highlander Volume 1
Red Sonja: She-Devil with a Sword
    Volumes 1-5
Omega Flight: Alpha to Omega

Magician Apprentice
Volume 1 Comic Adaptation
The Cross Bronx
Thor: Blood Oath
Ares: God of War
Blood River
Wings of Anansi
Stormbreaker: The Saga of Beta Ray Bill
Doctor Cyborg
86 Voltz: The Dead Girl
Quixote: A Novel
Avengers: Disassembled—Thor
SIX
Parliament of Justice
Bastard Samurai
Hammer of the Gods
    Mortal Enemy
    Hammer Hits China
    Back From the Dead
Bluntman & Chronic
Bulletproof Monk
Ship of Fools
    Dante's Compass
    Death & Taxes
The Foot Soldiers

BY VICTOR SANTOS

SPAIN

Los Reyes Elfos (The Elf Kings)
   El Señor de Alfheim
   (The Lord of Alfheim)
   La Emperatriz del Hielo
   (The Empress of the Ice)
   La Espada de los Inocentes
   (The Sword of the Innocents)
   Hasta los Dioses mueren
   (Until Gods Die)
   La Doncella y los Lobos
   (The Maiden and the Wolves)
   Historias de Faerie
   (Tales from Faerie) Vol. 1-3
   Glirenn, Reina de los Elfos Negros
   (Glirenn, Queen of the Dark Elfs)
Pulp Heroes
   Pulp Heroes
   Bushido
Faeric Gangs
Protector
Lone in Heaven
Aventuras en el Mundo Jung
(Adventures in Jung World)
Al mejor postor y otros relatos

violentos (To the highest gigger and
other violent tales)
Black Kaiser
La Sangre de las Valkirias
(The Blood of the Valkyries)
Silhouette

FRANCE

Young Ronins
   Rentrée des classes
   (The beginning of the class)
   Lóffensive Osaki
   (Osaki attacks)

USA

Witch & Wizard:
   Battle for Shadowland
Zombee
Demon Cleaner
Filthy Rich

BY VERONICA GANDINI

Fiction Clemons
Minions of Ka
Toy Story: Mysterious Stranger
Finding Nemo: Reef Rescue
Warhammer 40k:
   Defenders of Ultramar
   Fire and Honor
Black Widow & the Marvel Girls
Realm of Kings: Son of Hulk
X-Men Vs. Agents of Atlas
Uncanny X-Men: First Class

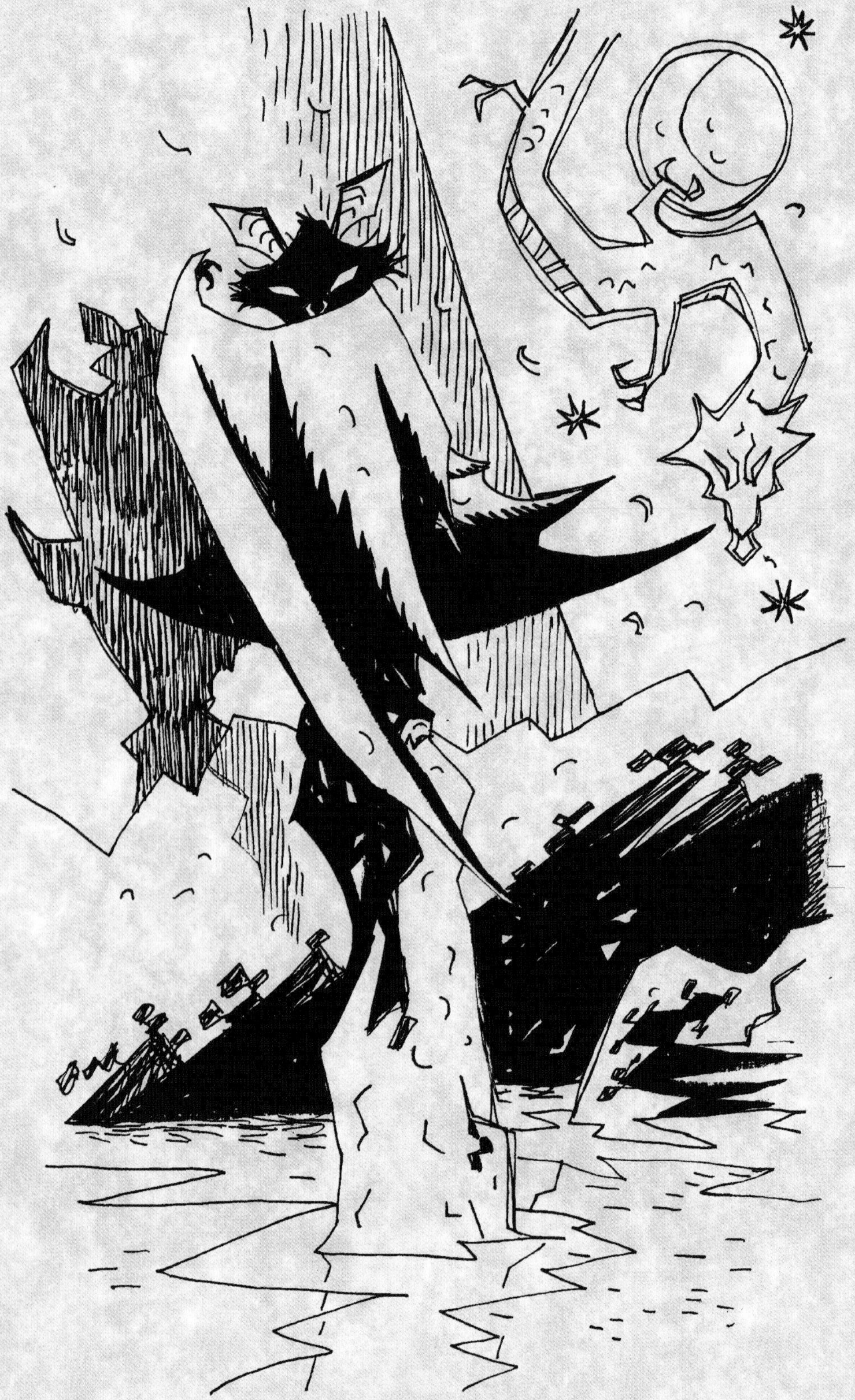